# ADVENTURING
## IN
# FLORIDA

# THE SIERRA CLUB ADVENTURE TRAVEL GUIDES

# ADVENTURING IN FLORIDA

*Includes the Georgia Sea Islands
and the Okefenokee Swamp*

ALLEN DE HART

Sierra Club Books
San Francisco

The Sierra Club, founded in 1892 by John Muir, has devoted itself to the study and protection of the earth's scenic and ecological resources—mountains, wetlands, woodlands, wild shores and rivers, deserts and plains. The publishing program of the Sierra Club offers books to the public as a nonprofit educational service in the hope that they may enlarge the public's understanding of the Club's basic concerns. The point of view expressed in each book, however, does not necessarily represent that of the Club. The Sierra Club has some sixty chapters coast to coast, in Canada, Hawaii, and Alaska. For information about how you may participate in its programs to preserve wilderness and the quality of life, please address inquiries to Sierra Club, 730 Polk Street, San Francisco, CA 94109.

LIBRARY OF CONGRESS CATALOGING IN PUBLICATION DATA

De Hart, Allen.
    Adventuring in Florida / by Allen de Hart.
       p.  cm.
    Includes bibliographical references and index.
    ISBN 0-87156-373-8
    1. Outdoor recreation—Florida—Guide-books. 2. Outdoor recreation—Georgia—Guide-books. 3. Florida—Description and travel—1991- —Guide-books. 4. Georgia—Description and travel—1991- —Guide-books. I. Title.
GV191.42.F6D4 1991
790'.09759—dc20                                 91-12430
                                                           CIP

PRODUCTION BY Robin Rockey
COVER DESIGN BY Bonnie Smetts
BOOK DESIGN BY Susan Colen, Park Press
MAPS BY Ronna Nelson

PRINTED IN THE UNITED STATES OF AMERICA ON ACID-FREE, RECYCLED PAPER, CONTAINING A MINIMUM OF 50% RECOVERED WASTE PAPER, OF WHICH AT LEAST 10% OF THE FIBER CONTENT IS POST-CONSUMER WASTE

10 9 8 7 6 5 4 3 2 1

# CONTENTS

# PREFACE

Florida, the nation's *Pascua de Flores*, is a tropical continuum of "the Feast of Flowers": scarlet hibiscus, silky lavender lupine, and royal poinciana. A sunny utopia with matchless beaches, it is 300 miles closer to the equator at its southern tip than New Orleans, and 1,000 miles closer than the French Riviera. It is also the only state from which we can leave planet Earth for an infinite frontier.

All who have not been to this promised land of sabal palms, mosquitoes, Mickey Mouse, alligators, and sweet bay honey dream or plan to go there. We all claim Florida as our state, much as we do Alaska, whether we live there or not. But we all sense and describe it differently. Spanish explorers saw "bear fattened on crabs and turtle eggs" where Miami Beach's famous Fountainebleau Hilton now stands, and faced "the claws of wild beasts" in the Saint Johns hinterland. John and William Bartram wrote about botany and "incense-bearing trees" in the 1760s; Charles Dodge wrote that Florida was "green isles under a genial winter sun" in 1894; and William T. Cash wrote a serious and classic four-volume history of the state in 1938. But no one has made us more aware of the significance of the Everglades, "grassy water," than conservationist Marjory Stoneman Douglas with her immortal *The Everglades: River of Grass* in 1947. Thousands of writers, among them novelist Ernest Hemingway, poet Sidney Lanier, and Okeechobee Cracker humorist Lawrence E. Will have sensed and described those "special Floridas." We continue to write about the diversity, that "irresistibly playful spirit" and the "shadows" explored by journalist Kathryn Kilgore.

I am one of those who dreamed of going to Florida. My first trip was in 1930. I was four, and my older brother, Moir, took me there with his reading of the January edition of *National Geographic*. I do not remember the details of that snowy night in Patrick County, Virginia, but I remember some of the autochrome pictures. Huge alligators were packed together: "six thousand of them," my brother read. "One of them could eat a little boy like you in one bite." He brought the magazine closer to my face. There were pictures of green turtles as big as wheelbarrows, and "wings of fire" flamingoes that my brother said walked on stilts. None of these creatures was in my Gabriel Sons and Company *Animals to Color.*

Two years later my first grade teacher had a long row of what must have been every edition of *National Geographic,* early ones that I had never seen. She required all of her students to look at the pictures while she explained them. I looked again at the alligator picture in John La Gorce's "Florida: The Fountain of Youth." The picture seemed less threatening now, certainly no more so than the etching I had seen in the big family Bible about Korah and his friends when "the earth opened her mouth and swallowed them up, and their houses." I particularly liked the magazine picture of swimming underwater with the fish, and the outdoor class-room in Saint Petersburg. I remember asking the teacher how far away was Florida. After all, there was a photograph of a bicyclist heading there with his suitcase lashed to the handle-bars. From those and other vivid and unforgettable pictures of George Shiras's "fruitful expeditions," I set a childhood goal of seeing the Land of Flowers. Someday I would go to Florida.

That someday came 30 years later when I was a National Science Foundation graduate teacher at Florida State Univer-sity. With my wife, Flora, I visited county after county and during one summer made a leisurely adventure of the entire coastline, collecting shells, hiking trails, and listening to stories of local culture. We heard firsthand tales from early settlers who remembered "the old Florida" of Herbert K. Job and A. W. Dimock, writers for *Outing* and *Harper's* maga-zines, and of Frank Chapman of *The Century* magazine in the first decade of the 1900s. Natives and snowbirds alike agreed that Florida was the best place to live and visit in the nation. During my residency and visits, every expedition brought new adventures in the state's natural areas. Each foot trail and canoe trail, each fishing trip from island to island, each feature point from Lakewood to Fort Jefferson brought the world of John La Gorce and George Shiras closer to my first dreams of the original Florida. From those hundreds of expeditions developed the inspirational building blocks for *Adventuring in Florida.*

# ACKNOWLEDGMENTS

Without the assistance of university professors and librarians, government specialists, rangers, guides, and friends, *Adventuring in Florida* would not have been possible. From the beginning of the project, Mary Ann Twyford, senior trail planner of Florida's Division of Recreation and Parks, was a lead contact and information source. She reported on new recreational areas, changes, and government regulations and referred me to a wide range of resource personnel outside government offices. For the book's second edition, Mary Anne Koos, trail planner, was the chief source of information. From the Florida Game and Fresh Water Fish Commission, Lt. Stan Kirkland, public information specialist, was my chief resource assistant. Patricia Evans, of the Bureau of Economic Analysis, and Roland S. Lawrence, economic development specialist, were helpful in the Department of Commerce. Other assistance came from Loretta Peterson of the Bureau of Wildlife Research and Barry Inman of the Department of Transportation. W. W. Green, Jr., forestry operations administrator at Blackwater State Forest, provided research information. Research on the De Soto Trail was provided by Richard F. Hite, National Park Service. The following district rangers helped with information about the national forests: Keith Lawrence of Osceola; Jerry Clutts (Lake George) and Mitchell H. Cohen (Seminole) of Ocala; and Bob Riser (Apalachicola), Larry Ford (Wakulla), and Steve Sherwood and Mason Miller (trail coordinators), all of Apalachicola. Florida State University Professors Edward A. Fernald, Department of Geography and director of the Institute of Science and Public Affairs, and William Tanner, Department of Geology, were of special counsel. University of Florida Professor Larry Harris was my chief source of information and encouragement at the Department of Forestry.

I would like to express particular appreciation to those who endured trips in rainy, hot, uncomfortable, and dangerous weather conditions; swamped canoes; bug bites; and fatigue. They, and others who helped with information, directions, shuttle service, accommodations, and other hospitalities are Bob Atwater, Robert Baker, Stuart Boyd, Roscoe Chandler, John and Marsha Chess, John Coleman, Nancy Craft, Mellisa Denarro, Greg Frederick, Rusty Hamilton, Joe and Betty King, Steve and Lynn King, Tony Kleatus, Angel Lauredro, Armando Manuel, Carlin and Louella Morton, Dennis Parrish, Marvin Pettili, Kimberly Richardson, Todd Shearon, Renee Spriggs, Parker Taylor, Ray and Barbara Warden, Scott Wereston, James and Peggy Wicker, Jennifer Woodruff, and Kevin Zoltek. I am grateful also to my friend and neighbor Jeannette Lord, who volunteered time to assist in proofreading the manuscript and master galleys.

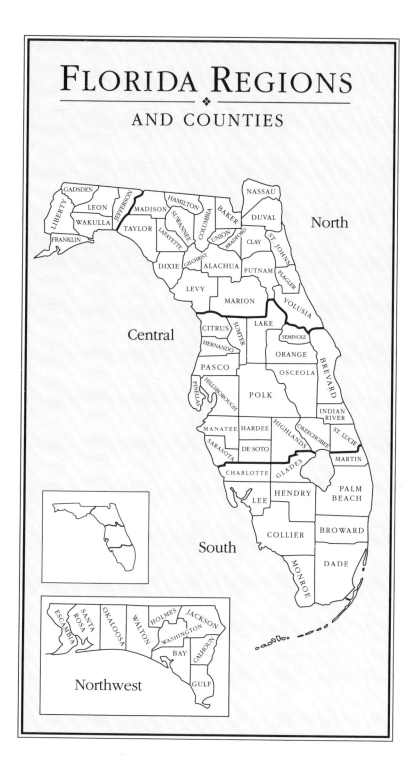

# FLORIDA REGIONS

## AND COUNTIES

# 1

# INTRODUCTION

Florida, the Sunshine State, is a land of many natural areas. *Adventuring in Florida* invites you to locate, explore, and appreciate what the state and federal governments and citizens with private property have preserved and protected for future generations: a magnificent gift of more than 21 million acres of forests, lakes, marshes, and beaches.

You may wonder where these natural sanctuaries are located, particularly if you have seen the vehicular traffic on US Highway 1 from Georgia to Key West, on Interstate 95 from Georgia to Miami, on Interstate 275 through Tampa and Saint Petersburg, or on the intersecting mazes near Orlando and at the Miami International Airport. But, though you may have to use the busy highways and pass through metropolitan areas to arrive at them, natural areas do exist.

This book will lead you on many journeys that will remind you of those who have adventured before you: extinct or modern tribes of American Indians; European explorers with charters for territorial acquisition; conquistadors searching for gold and silver; missionaries and religious zealots; sea-wise pirates, smugglers, and ship scavengers; Carolina plantation owners looking for escaped slaves; Caribbean slave kidnappers; white Crackers from Georgia with pioneer cowhands and homesteading farmers; Oriental and Italian railroad workers; Greek sponge harvesters; timber barons; commercial fishermen; snowbelt settlers; visiting naturalists like William Bartram and John Muir; scrupulous and unscrupulous entrepreneurs buying millions of acres of scrub and marsh; industrial and cultural leaders; tin-can campers; and political

1

refugees from the Caribbean and from Central and South America.

Whatever your adventurous goals, Florida will reward you. You will be tempted to leave the natural areas to explore art museums, zoos, alligator farms, seaquariums, citrus orchards, theme and amusement parks, Spaceport USA, and Florida's incredible major attraction, the phantasmagoric Walt Disney World. As many Floridians will tell you, even if you spend only one month or one winter with the state's natural and cultural attractions, you may find Xanadu. On your next visit you may come with a moving van.

You have remarkable choices. You can find solitude on Florida's forty-five hundred islands, such as Saint Vincent, Cayo Costa, or the Dry Tortugas, accessible only by boat or seaplane; canoe to mangrove hammocks in the sequestered Everglades or in eerie open and subterranean waters of the Aucilla River; backpack or ride horseback through a forest of soughing longleaf pines; or bicycle on back roads bordered with wildflowers in Jefferson, Madison, and Hamilton counties. Indian guides can take you on swamp buggies or airboats into the water prairies of Big Cypress Swamp; cowhands can take you across the state on the Cracker Trail; or naturalists can guide you into wildlife habitat in the 96,000-acre Babcock Wilderness Area, or to North America's only living coral reef park in Key Biscayne. Wherever you go you will find wildlife—in some locations an enormous variety of species—and see tropical plants.

Along the way to the natural areas are some historic towns where you may learn about the cultures and peoples and meet some of the adventurous local citizens: Examples are Arcadia, Palatka, Baker, Eastpoint, and Everglades City. At Cedar Key you can meet Harriet Smith, affectionately called "the bird lady," a naturalist who knows about all the birds on the islands and every trail in the nearby hammocks. An adventure into the famous Fisheating Creek area would not be complete without meeting explorer Tom Gaskins and seeing his incomparable collection of cypress sculpture, or meeting Carl Forrester, who knows better than anyone else the secret dark delta passageways of the silent Choctawhatchee River. If you wish to hike sections or all of the Florida Trail, ask a trail officer such as Wiley Dykes Sr., who knows all about the trail's condition. Dreamy, ethereal Lake Lochloosa has monster bass under the lily pads; if you go there, go with Danny and Betty Thurmond of Orange Springs, who know the secrets of a successful catch. These people and thousands of others like them will make your adventures complete.

Florida advertises itself as "The Sunshine State," a peninsula "coast to coast to coast," and "One Florida Many Faces." To see its many faces, call for a copy of *Florida Visitors Guide* (904-487-1462) before you plan your adventures. Take excursions to state and national parks, forests, and preserves; warm, clear springs; beaches; rivers and canals; swamps, estuaries, and marshes; lakes; savannahs and hammocks; and islands and reefs. This book will also describe the nearby and historic Georgia Sea Islands and the enchanting Okefenokee Swamp, "the land of the trembling earth." The time you spend at each of these natural areas may be less than a week or more than a month. The maps should enable you to locate general routes.

The remainder of this chapter introduces Florida's human and natural environment, while Chapter 2 gives basic information for planning a trip and indicates what adventurous activities will be considered. Beginning with Chapter 3, the remaining chapters describe twenty-four adventures in Florida and two in southeastern Georgia. To give you a sense of orientation, each chapter has a map of the major highways that provide access to the point(s) of entry. In some events, you can use the map and the narrative for a reverse journey. Adventure descriptions cover the conditions of highways and back roads, the remote and hazardous places, and the outdoor activities to be experienced. At the end of each description is a listing of county names, average temperatures, property supervision, chambers of commerce, and services and amenities. The counties are listed in order of the adventure route.

Appendices include a list of endangered and threatened animal and plant species, lakes and forests, navigational charts and scuba diving areas, state government and citizens' groups, foreign consular offices, a glossary, and a bibliography.

If you follow my routes, you will notice that I have left out some details. I did this because of page limitations for the book, but it may be to your advantage as you will find more surprises. Included are select places of the original, natural Florida, where I have traveled or led expeditions, usually more than once. The description for each adventure indicates a base camp or campground at the beginning and end of the trip where food is available. I have made no effort to rank campground facilities, other than to indicate "full service" when electric and water hookups, sewage service, and, frequently, laundry service are available. Costs of campgrounds, motels, and restaurants are not listed because of likely price changes. Although I have included excursions to some isolated ecosystems, I intend to help protect those wild areas and hope that you will do the same. Where possible, I have avoided all heavy traffic routes and metropolitan areas. Facts on these journeys are perpetually changing, and important information may have been inadvertently omitted. Your response and corrections to me or the publisher will be appreciated.

In your travels you will find—as I have—that Florida is more than moonvines, oranges, beaches, custard apple, catfish—and, of course, alligator. Florida is multifarious; its place in the sun is your place too.

### THE HUMAN FLORIDA

The rapid increase in Florida's population is phenomenal; housing developments smother whole counties. Towering white condominiums line long sections of sunny seashore on both the Atlantic and the Gulf sides of the peninsula. Large chunks of real estate are for sale or resale in a continuing land-sale frenzy reminiscent of the 1920s. Signs along State Highway 82 between Fort Myers and Immokalee and Interstate 75 north of Naples offer thousands of acres. At Lehigh Acres developers have planned into the twenty-first century with vast subdivisions. Similar vacant streets stretch for miles between Cape Coral and Punta Gorda, and at the west edge of Big Cypress Swamp the unnamed and unnumbered roads of the Golden Gate development pierce to the horizon and into a panther habitat north of the Fakahatchee Strand. The population is expanding so much that residents are finding that the Florida being built is crowding out the Florida they came for. (According to the 1990 census, the state's population was 12,937,926.) A delicate environment is being strained; the southern region's Lake Okeechobee hovers on the brink of ecological death. In 1989 Governor Bob Martinez proposed directing state road dollars to urban road development to prevent further hemorrhaging into the countryside.

But the days of Hamilton Disston, who purchased 4 million acres for 25 cents an acre in 1881, are over. Large tracts are becoming increasingly rare and are available only at a great premium. Once small, quiet agricultural towns such as McCloud and Kissimmee, neighbors to Orlando and Tohopekaliga and East Tohopekaliga lakes, now advertise themselves as "resort areas" on huge billboards; toll expressways channel tourists to theme parks; and shopping malls are replacing orange groves and ranches. Older citrus groves in the center of the state have been cleared for urban development, while new groves are being planted in the more poorly drained acreage near Lake Okeechobee. By the year 2000, state officials predict, the east coast from Jacksonville to Miami, the west coast from Crystal River to Naples, and central Florida from Tampa to Daytona Beach will be completely urbanized. Increased urbanization in other localities of the rich fruit and vegetable farms is likely to change Florida's number-one national ranking for citrus, sugar cane, tomato, and ornamental foliage production and number-two ranking for honey and strawberries.

In 1940, Florida ranked twenty-seventh in population in the United States and last in the twelve southeastern states. It moved up to twentieth in the nation in 1950, tenth in 1960 (a 76 percent increase), seventh in 1980, and fourth (with more than 12 million inhabitants) in 1990. The state Bureau of Economic and Business Research reports that one thousand new adult residents (the majority retirees) immigrate to Florida daily. Among the state's sixty-seven counties, population density is highest in Pinellas County (Spanish for "Point of Pines"), the Saint Petersburg megalopolis with more than three thousand residents per square mile. Next are Broward and Dade counties (the Miami area) and Duval County (the Jacksonville area). The lowest density is in Liberty County, which includes the Apalachicola National Forest and has about six persons per square mile, followed by Lafayette County, which adjoins the west bank of the Suwannee River. Glades, Dixie, and Franklin counties also have low densities.

Florida's senior population is increasing. The median age of citizens had risen to the age of thirty-five in the mid-1980s; in some counties such as Pasco (Tampa area), it is now over fifty, and Charlotte County (Punta Gorda area) has the highest median age at fifty-seven. In addition to permanent residents, part-time residents (called "snow birds") and more than 38 million annual tourists populate the state. Printed materials in foreign languages now cater to increasing numbers of foreign tourists, mainly from Europe, South America, Canada, and Japan—particularly in Miami and at public attractions such as Everglades National Park.

The first human inhabitants in Florida were Indians who migrated from the north, probably between 10,000 and 8000 B.C. About 1000 B.C. they developed from hunters, fishers, and food gatherers, to horticultural food producers. Mounds of shells on the banks of major rivers and at lake edges are evidence of their early settlements. By the time the Spanish explorers arrived in the sixteenth century, an estimated one hundred thousand Indians from six major groups with many subgroups populated the peninsula. The largest tribes were the Timucuan (with forty thousand) in the north-northeast, probably from Tampa Bay to Cumberland Bay; the Apalachee (with twenty-five thousand) in the northwest Panhandle area; and the Calusa (also spelled Caloosa; with twenty thousand) in the southwest and south, from Port Charlotte to the Keys and central to Lake Okeechobee. Others were the Tequesta, Mayaimis, and Viscanos (from whose name came Biscayne) in the southeast, and the Matecumbes on the Florida Keys. The Tocobaga Indians lived around Tampa Bay, and the Ais and Jeaga lived in the region from Cape Canaveral to the Saint Lucie River.

Most of what is known about the Indians is from the writings of the early French, Spanish, and English explorers and missionaries, and from the findings of twentieth-century archeologists. The Indians made a variety of mounds, some habitat, some ceremonial, and others burial. Kitchen middens were mainly of shell and animal bones. Thousands of these mounds were once on the banks of the rivers and lakes, along harbors, and on islands, but many have been lost because early white settlers used them for house foundations or fill materials for road construction. Among the major excavations are Big Mound City near Canal Point and Chosen Mounds near Belle Glade, both excavated in 1933–1934 by the Smithsonian Institution. Other mounds are in Saint Petersburg, Sarasota, Melbourne, Ormond Beach, Sanibel Island, and Fort Walton Beach, and at Pineland on Pine Island. At Pineland, private homes rest on the mound summits. 

None of the aboriginal tribes live in Florida today; all disappeared after 2 centuries of fighting the Spanish and English, dying from European communicable diseases, or being captured as slaves and sent to Spanish Cuba or elsewhere. Between 1702 and 1708 Englishman Col. James Moore, from the Carolinas, with the help of Indians he had armed, razed all the thirty or more Spanish missions among the Timucuan and Apalachee tribes. Indians who did not voluntarily follow were forced to go with Colonel Moore to the Carolinas. By 1763 all the southern Indians had been taken as slaves to Cuba by the Spanish. During this time other tribes were entering Florida from Alabama, Georgia, and South Carolina to escape white settlers. Among them were the Creek, Chiaha, Oconee, Sawokli, Hitchiti, and Eufaula. From these groups the word *Seminole* developed. The Creek Indians called the Oconee "Esta Semoli," meaning runaways, or those who prefer to live alone.

But the Indians' retreat to Florida did not bring them permanent security. In the First Seminole War (1817–1818) Gen. Andrew Jackson invaded Florida and wiped out whole settlements. In the Second Seminole War (1835–1842) the federal government enforced the Congressional Removal Law of 1830 to ship all the eastern Indians to the Arkansas Territory. Micanopy, the Seminole head chief, was old, war-weary, and ready for peace, but the war produced two younger Indian resistance leaders: Osceola, who was captured and later died in an army garrison in Charleston, South Carolina, and his successor, Coacoochee, who finally surrendered. Although 3,824 Seminoles were shipped across the Mississippi River in 1842, it took the Third Seminole War (1855–1858) to catch another Indian resistance leader, Billy Bowlegs, and his followers. In 1859 another seventy Indians surrendered, but approximately two hundred to three hundred continued to hide in the saw grass and hammocks of The Everglades and Big Cypress Swamp. The white settlers of Florida, tired of the pursuit, abandoned further efforts to locate the Indians, and the federal government ceased forcing them to emigrate.

Today the descendants live in southern Florida reservations or communities where they fish, farm, and have small businesses. The majority, called Mikasukis (Miccosukee), speak the Hitchiti language. A Seminole paper war developed in the late 1980s when the U.S. government granted a $46 million trust fund to reimburse them for lands seized in 1823. Based on a 1906 population figure, the funds would be split evenly between the 10,000 individual Oklahoma Seminoles and the 1,750 Florida Seminoles. Both groups claimed all the

*Seminole Indians at Cypress Hollow.*
PHOTO BY Florida Dept. of Commerce.

money; the U.S. Congress or the courts may have to settle the bitter bout. Once hounded like wild animals to be killed or captured in Big Cypress Swamp saw grass, the Seminole guides now charge deer hunters $1,000 to $2,000 for a single deer-kill in the same saw grass of their sovereign Big Cypress Reservation.

Official credit goes to a Spanish explorer of noble birth, Juan Ponce de León, for the discovery of Florida in 1513, though there is evidence of prior discovery by Europeans. An Alberto Cantino map of 1502 shows the Florida coast and may reflect the reports Englishmen John and Sebastian Cabot made of their Atlantic coast voyages in 1497 and 1498. Ponce de León was not a stranger to the new world; in 1493 he had accompanied Christopher Columbus on his second voyage, and in 1509 his army had captured Puerto Rico, where he was governor for 2 years. In early March of 1513 he set out from Puerto Rico with three ships to search for the land of Bimini, a small island in the Bahama chain, east of present-day Miami

Beach. (If he was searching for a Fountain of Youth it was not a primary mission.) Ponce de León missed Bimini, where the king of Spain had promised him a new governorship, and instead landed on the Florida coast between Saint Augustine and the Saint Johns River sometime in early April. According to his patent, he took possession there in the name of the Spanish king, calling the land Florida, meaning "Feast of Flowers," because the calendar date was Easter Sunday. After exploring farther north, he turned southward, stopped at a few places along the coast, passed through and explored the Keys, and sailed at least as far as Charlotte Harbor in the Gulf. By September he had returned to Puerto Rico, and in 1514 he returned to Spain. With a colony of Spaniards in 1521 he attempted a settlement on the Gulf coast. Facing hostile Calusa Indians, he was wounded by a poison arrow; he died in Cuba, June 1521, at the age of sixty-one, and was buried in Puerto Rico.

Wishing to reward Pánfilo de Narváez for his service in the conquest of Cuba, Charles V of Spain granted a patent for Narváez to settle Florida. Narváez left Spain in June 1527 with six hundred colonists, but his ill-fated expedition suffered desertion in Santo Domingo and shipwreck in Trinidad. With his remaining four hundred men he arrived at Tampa Bay in April 1528 and marched inland in search of gold among the Apalachee Indians of the Florida Panhandle. Severe overland hardships, starvation, and ship loss followed, with only eighty survivors washing ashore in a storm on the Texas coast. Four of the survivors, given up for dead, wandered through Mexico for 8 years and reached Mexico City in June 1536 to tell their heroic story.

In March 1539, wealthy and young Hernando de Soto began his overland explorations from Tampa Bay. His army entourage of knights and choice fortune hunters was the most aristocratic group yet brought to the New World. With 550 armed men, 200 horses, and a few Catholic priests, he explored north to Lake City and west to Tallahassee in Florida, journeyed through Georgia and South Carolina, crossed north of the Smoky Mountains in North Carolina into Tennessee (according to some chronicles), returned to Georgia, and went west across the Mississippi River, probably to what is now Arkansas and Texas. On the way, at Mavilla by the Alabama River, de Soto was wounded in a major fight with the Indians; he lost nearly 100 men. On the return in May 1542, de Soto died of a fever and was buried near the mouth of the Arkansas River. About 300 men and 40 horses survived the approximately 3,500-mile expedition and arrived in September 1543 at Tampico, Mexico. Not all the survivors returned to Spain; some remained in Mexico, and others went to Peru. They and the Spanish government considered the 4-year expedition a failure because no gold or state-level societies had been found.

Following this expedition, Spanish interest in searching for gold and other precious metals in North America declined. But in Spanish America, the viceroy of Mexico, Luis de Velasco, pushed for the settlement of Florida, gold or not. He named Tristán de Luna y Arellano, a Spanish nobleman, to head an expedition that left Mexico City in 1559. The expedition failed, mainly because of too many questionable characters and unproductive workers among the five hundred soldiers and one thousand civilians. Also, two tropical storms diminished the expedition's ships, horses, and food. With starvation and dissension among the colonists, the strong leader Angel de Villafane replaced de Luna in 1561. Plans were to hold Pensacola and set up at Santa Elena on the Atlantic coast. Failing to accomplish this, de Villafane returned to Spain.

While the Spanish government was deliberating on whether to abandon Florida, the French sponsored an expedition to the Saint Johns River in April 1562 led by Huguenot Jean Ribault and with a fleet of 3 ships and 150 colonists. That expedition met with friendly Indians, but the mission had to be aborted because of mutiny among the colonists and a fire that destroyed the food supply. A few desperate men started back to France without any navigational equipment on a small boat they had constructed and miraculously made it nearly halfway across the Atlantic. By chance an English ship discovered them and returned them to France. Ribault returned to Europe, but France chose another explorer to replace him, René Goulaine de Laudonnière. He arrived at the Saint Johns River in June 1564 with 3 ships, 300 men, and 4 women. Again the Timucuan Indians were friendly. Laudonnière named his settlement Fort Caroline, but as with Ribault, a mutiny and dissension among the colonists followed. While the Frenchmen were waiting for a favorable wind to return to France in the summer of 1565, Ribault arrived with a sizable reinforcement of troops and a government order to replace Laudonnière.

Meanwhile, the Spanish government was aware of this threat to its claim of territory and sent Pedro Menéndez de Avilés to remove the French and protect the claim. Menéndez left Spain in June 1565 with a patent from Phillip II and an armada of 19 ships with horses, cattle, hogs, sheep, and 1,504 colonists, including slaves, militia men, and artisans. A storm near the Canary Islands scattered the fleet; because of the urgency to confront the French, Menéndez proceeded with 5 ships and a military force of 700. He reached the Saint Augustine area September 8, 1565, not knowing that Ribault had arrived at Fort Caroline only 11 days earlier. Menéndez officially declared Saint Augustine Spanish territory and opened a celebration with a Catholic Mass. Even the friendly Indians were invited to the ceremony and feast that followed. From September 20 to November 26, Menéndez crushed French colonial plans. After destroying Fort Caroline, he massacred 245 French Protestants at an inlet which was named Mantanzas, meaning "Place of Slaughter." The tiny Saint Augustine settlement was not threatened for the next 20 years; then, in June 1586, the huge 42-ship fleet of Englishman Sir Francis Drake arrived, sacked the village, and destroyed the fruit trees and vegetable crops. After Drake left, approximately 300 settlers who had fled to the forest returned and rebuilt their community.

During the seventeenth century, Spanish colonization spread across northern Florida. A major objective was to Christianize the Indians, and by 1675 there were thirty-six Franciscan missions, some of which were north on the Atlantic coast or on the Georgia Sea Islands. By 1612 the bishop of Cuba had created the Santa Elena province that covered all the territory of the Florida peninsula, Georgia, and South Carolina. Not only did the missions serve a frontier religious function, they also imposed Spanish cultural, economic, and political control on the Indians. A high point came in 1674 when Bishop Don Gabriel Vara Calderón visited each mission and reported more than thirteen thousand Indian converts. But the Indians rebelled against the physical work, some of which was slavery, and against cultural change, such as when Bishop Calderón requested the bare-breasted Indian Christian women to cover themselves with Spanish moss. Even the friendly Timucuan and Apalachee Indian chiefs joined other chiefs to murder ranchers and priests.

Spain also had to contend with increased British colonization on the south Atlantic and with the French, whose Robert Cavalier Sieur de La Salle made a claim to the lower Mississippi River Valley in 1682. Furthermore, English and French pirates attacked and stole from the Spanish, a practice of which the Spanish could not claim innocence.

The history of Florida, and Saint Augustine in particular, might have been different if not for the Spanish construction of the Castillo de San Marcos. The fort, begun in October 1672 and completed after 15 years, had 12-foot-thick walls of coquina stone from Anastasia Island. As an example of its importance, it protected the settlers under British siege in 1702 and 1704. In the 1704 attack, Governor James Moore of Carolina destroyed the Spanish missions and kept the fifteen hundred inhabitants of Castillo de San Marcos captive for 2 months, but he could not penetrate. And in 1740, when Gen. James Oglethorpe of Georgia invaded Saint Augustine with 7 warships and sixteen hundred men, the outnumbered Spanish settlers retreated to their fort. Rain, dysentery, and tropical storms forced General Oglethorpe to retreat. He tried again in 1742, but again failed, and the siege was lifted.

By 1763 Spanish Florida contained a garrison at Saint Marks and a settlement in Pensacola on the Gulf as well as Saint Augustine on the Atlantic. In the Seven Years' War between Spain and England, beginning in 1783, the British captured Havana. At the end of the war Spain agreed to give Florida to England as ransom for Havana, but in 1783 England returned Florida to Spain in exchange for the Bahamas and Gibraltar. When the century ended, the Spanish agreed in the Treaty of San Ildefonso to relinquish their claim on northwest Florida. By the end of the American Revolution, the British and the Spanish had lost the chance ever to reclaim their interests in Florida. In 1821 the United States acquired Florida, and in 1822 Congress provided for a governor and President James Monroe signed a thirteen-member legislature into law. The infant legislature was to meet in alternative years at Saint Augustine and Pensacola, with the first meeting at Pensacola, but it was agreed in 1824 that an Indian village, the more centrally located Tallahassee, would be the capital.

In early meetings the council discussed inland transportation—canals, roads, and railroads—already raising questions of growth, development, and protection of the natural environment. At least twenty railroad corporations were chartered between 1830 and 1860, the first to operate being the Leon Railway Company (to become the Tallahassee Railroad Company), which transported cotton bales and passengers from Tallahassee to Saint Marks in 1836. In 1860 the first east-west railway was completed between Cedar Key on the Gulf and Fernandina on the Atlantic. To connect Pensacola and Saint Augustine via Tallahassee, the first long public road was begun in 1824. The Bellamy Road (constructed by John Bellamy, because the state government thought it would save money by hiring a private contractor rather than the U.S. Army Corps of Engineers) followed an old Indian trail, rough with stumps, patched with corduroy logs, and hardly wider than a wagon. This was a period when the population had doubled, there were signs of a land boom to come, and new settlers were frustrated because land grants could not be cleared from earlier title rights without long delays.

Florida became the twenty-seventh state in 1845, with William D. Moseley, a Jefferson County farmer, as first governor. In 1861 it followed South Carolina and Mississippi in seceding from the Union. Floridians expected the secession because 84 percent of its convention delegates owned slaves or held slaves in trust, and most farmers had roots in the adjoining slave states. When Florida delegates went to Montgomery, Alabama, to help form the Confederate States of America (CSA), they and the Texas delegation were the only representatives not native born. During the Civil War Florida presented fifteen thousand volunteers to the CSA, a third of whom died. The state was too young to contribute much to the main economy, but it did contribute valuable salt, pork, and beef; cattle baron Jacob Summerlin supplied the Confederate Army with an estimated twenty-five thousand head of cattle between 1861 and 1863. The state also contributed fish; in 1864 alone the Confederacy requested 20 million pounds.

Governor William D. Bloxham, elected in 1880, tried to be optimistic about the state's economy, but Florida was deeply in debt and needed cash. Without cash, prosperity, with better roads and education and with increased population, was not possible. The state's choice asset was its public lands, but the court had declared that the land could be sold only for cash. The solution to the state's economic crisis came from Hamilton Disston of Philadelphia, who was persuaded to buy 4 million acres of land for 25 cents an acre by fishing friend Henry Sanford of Saint John and Governor Bloxham. Many homesteaders criticized the governor for the sale, but the cash got the state out of debt and cleared state land titles.

Disston, at the age of thirty-seven, became the nation's largest landowner. Later, near Orlando, he resold some of the land for $4 and $5 an acre. For 10 years he worked toward a grand plan to dredge rivers and connect lakes, build railroads, create sugarcane plantations, and develop huge settlements.

Then came a depression, the panic of 1893, and his empire crumbled. Meanwhile, H. B. Plant was working to develop western Florida; he completed a railroad from Waycross, Georgia, to Jacksonville in 1881. By the end of the century, his Plant Investment Company owned one third of the 1,665 miles of railroad in the state, including a railroad to Tampa, and his Gulf and Caribbean steamers serviced his famous hotels from Tampa to Fort Myers. Henry M. Flagler, dubbed "the Magician of Florida," was also a railroad and luxury hotel entrepreneur. He amassed his fortune in the Standard Oil Company and fell in love with Florida on his first visit to Jacksonville in 1878. His railroad went to Palatka and then to Daytona. In April 1896 the first rails reached Miami, and by 1912 his "Overseas Railroad" was servicing Key West.

The century ended with the Spanish-American War in 1898. Ammunition, supply lines, and nearly 200,000 soldiers moved on the rails and steamers to military camps set up in Tampa, Jacksonville, Miami, and other cities. The greatest fear of Floridians, that Cuba might be annexed as an economically competing state, was negated when Congress passed a law to prevent such annexation. When the war ended, thousands of soldiers went back north as potential promoters of the Sunshine State.

In the beginning of the twentieth century Florida's charismatic reformer, Governor Napoleon Bonaparte Broward, rode a wave of popularity similar to that for the nation's outdoorsman and reformer then-President Theodore Roosevelt. Each of the two launched a series of policies to increase the power of government to protect the individual citizen. Roosevelt's policy on setting aside national forests (194 million acres) included the Ocala and the Choctawhatchee (now Eglin Air Force Base) in Florida in 1908. Broward advocated policies for the conservation of fish, oysters, wildlife, and forests (though he didn't go as far as to stop dredging in the Everglades); consolidation of state universities; and better public transportation. His successors, Albert W. Gilchrist and Park Trammell, continued to emphasize his policies. In 1910 Governor Gilchrist wrote a feature for the *Chicago Examiner*, "Florida the Marvelous," to praise the state's natural beauty, and Trammell proposed in 1912 an experimental station in the Everglades to study its soils.

In the same year, farmer John Collins was experimenting with fruit trees on a barrier sandbar and mangrove island across Biscayne Bay from Miami. With the help and financing of Carl Fisher, an Indianapolis millionaire who had moved to Miami in 1910, Collins began dredging the bay's silt in 1915 to create what has become Miami Beach. Fisher made it a manicured paradise with exotic plants and birds, elite sports facilities, and ornate hotels such as the Flamingo.

During World Wars I and II, Florida was the site of armed service training camps, shipbuilding, and food processing. When the wars ended, thousands of military personnel returned home to promote tourism in the state. Between the wars Florida had had the face of Janus, a face of contrasts. The first decade was a happy, hedonistic one of revolutionary expansion of public paved roads, increased tourism and population, and overextended railroads. Millionaires sold dry and wet lots, built flimsy and grand hotels, and gambled in the stock market and on dog racing. Rum running, alien smuggling, and clear cutting virgin forests also brought fast money. In spite of inflation, construction of the Tamiami Trail Highway through the Everglades was completed by 1928. But by 1925, the financial face had begun to turn. A September 1926 hurricane killed 243 people and affected 17,784 families, and in September 1928 another hurricane drowned as many as 2,000 people near Lake Okeechobee. In October of the following year the stock market crashed and the Great Depression began. Before it was over both rural and urban Florida would suffer financially.

But a few years later a nongovernmental act in central Florida changed the image and economic future of the state forever. Later considered the founder and leader of the modern tourist industry, Richard Downing Pope, who had moved to Florida in 1908 from Des Moines, Iowa, opened

Cypress Gardens in 1936. He charged each visitor 25 cents to see his botanical garden, the state's first major tourist attraction. For 3 decades the flamboyant leader promoted Florida around the world. He added to his original inexpensive 16 acres of swampland and eventually owned 223 acres, worth a fortune, visited by nearly a million tourists each year. The gardens became a backdrop for the natural resources of the lakes area, where extravagant exhibitions and underwater movies were promoted. Great Depression or not, Pope had set an example for other lucrative theme parks to follow.

Following World War II, Florida's rapid population growth transformed the economy and challenged the state legislature for more and better public services, such as improved public education. Governor Spessard L. Holland first pressed for improvement in education in 1944, and in 1947, under Governor Millard Caldwell, lawmakers began to show serious concern. Funding of new schools, improved teaching conditions, and higher educational standards resulted, and in 1947 the legislature adopted the concept of expanding higher education that would lead to Florida's highly successful community college system. Public health, stronger sources of state revenue (Florida does not tax income), and protecting the environment were other concerns. In response to the latter, $2 million was appropriated in 1947 to purchase additional private land for Everglades National Park, which was dedicated in December of that year.

During the 1950s the state advanced in highway construction. A major showpiece was the north-south 265-mile Florida Turnpike (the Sunshine State Parkway) through the heart of the state, begun in 1955 and completed in 1964. (By the 1990s Florida had 1,500 miles of interstate and more than 100,000 miles of other highways, roads, and streets.) As state and county roads cut through the backcountry of ranches and farms, highway accidents and human deaths from roaming livestock increased. Highly opposed by ranchers, a legislative act begun in 1949 ended a frontier character of open ranges for livestock in 1952 by requiring that all cattle be fenced.

With the arrival of the space age in the 1960s at Cape Canaveral (launching site of the first manned suborbital flight by Alan B. Shepherd in 1961 and the first circling of the Earth—three times—by Lt. Col. John H. Glenn, Jr., in February 1962) and the Walt Disney World theme park at Orlando in October 1971, tourist traffic soared and even more highways became necessary. Each time large segments of new roads were constructed, more canals were opened, more sprawling subdivisions were constructed, and more Floridians became concerned about the use of their natural resources, the subject of the remainder of this chapter.

## THE NATURAL ENVIRONMENT

Section 7, Article II, of the Florida constitution states that "it shall be the policy of the state to conserve and protect its natural resources and scenic beauty." This policy becomes increasingly important with rapid development and with the public's abuse and misuse of the state's valuable natural resources. To help support this policy, entrusted to the Department of Natural Resources, you can call toll free the Resources Alert Program, (800) 342-1821 (24 hours a day), when you know of law violations and environmental abuse; you will not be required to give your name.

In Florida's first 100 years, some argue, such a policy was greatly ignored for economic or political reasons. But the state's population growth since the 1950s has made it necessary to fully honor the policy now. As you travel across the state, you will notice that Floridians are more committed than ever to safeguarding their priceless heritage. There are local, state, and federal programs to acquire endangered lands and water (Save Our Coast, Save Our Rivers, Save Our Everglades); to conserve and properly manage marine resources; to protect the quality of the air, water, and soil; and to protect endangered and threatened species of wildlife and wild plants (Save the Manatee and Save the Florida Panther). In addition to government programs, private citizens groups are working to conserve and protect the natural Florida: the Florida Audubon Society, Corkscrew Swamp Sanctuary, The Conservancy, Inc., Archbold Biological Station, The Nature Conservancy, and Southwest Florida Land Preservation Trust are examples.

A desire to drain the swamps and overflow lands for farming, livestock ranches, and home sites was common to the frontier spirit of the settlers. Among the chief areas drained were the Saint Johns and Kissimmee river basins and the Everglades proper, an enormous wet area south of Lake Okeechobee and spreading out east-west for up to 50 miles and south-southwest for 100 miles to the Gulf of Mexico. As early as 1850, the state showed interest in claiming these wet areas by passing legislation to control them, with the Internal Improvement Fund administering them. But it became apparent during the next 50 years that the state could not depend on private efforts to accomplish its costly drainage program. In 1905, under Governor Broward, comprehensive drainage laws were enacted and a Board of Drainage Commissioners appointed. From then until the present, significant controversy has surrounded the issue of the public's best interest, particularly regarding the aquiferous Everglades, which has evoked national concern. Issues for the Everglades concerned the building of multiple canals from Lake Okeechobee to the east coast (an elevation drop of about 8 feet); two major highways: US 41 (the Tamiami Trail) and state road 84 (Alligator Alley/Everglades Parkway/I-75); the freshwater supply for millions of residents on the southeast coast; water to irrigate thousands of farming acres; and water to retain the natural flow through what is now Everglades National Park.

One of the most controversial canals (which has damaged the Oklawaha River irreparably) has been the Cross-Florida Barge Canal, authorized in 1942 to connect Jacksonville and the Atlantic Ocean on the east coast to the Gulf of Mexico, near Crystal Bay. Construction began in 1964, protests began in 1969, and plans were thrown around as a political football thereafter until President Richard Nixon ordered construction of the half-completed canal to cease in 1971. Congress finally deauthorized the expensive project in 1986. In another environmental victory, South Florida Jetport plans in the Everglades were abandoned in 1969.

Floridians began to become more aware and take more action to control and protect their natural resources by the middle of the twentieth century; in the 1970s, under Governor Reubin O. Askew, a landmark effort began an unprecedented decade of action to protect natural resources. The Water Resources Act of 1972 extended the principles of drainage and water control, providing the Department of Natural Resources with the responsibility to manage, conserve, protect, and control the state's waters. A major protection clause stipulated that the Council on Environmental Quality make a final decision on federal projects that may affect the environment. Other acts passed in 1972 were the Environmental Land and Water Management Act, the State Comprehensive Planning Act, and the Land Conservation Act. In the late 1970s and into the 1980s, additional legislation created the Safe Drinking Water Act, the Hazardous Waste Management Act, the Water Quality Assurance Act, and the Wetlands Protection Act.

The state implemented another decision in 1974 that protected the 870-square-mile Green Swamp area with controlled alterations. The high-elevation water pressure of Green Swamp, significant because it supplies 70 percent of the state's water, prevents salt water from the Atlantic and Gulf from entering the web of caverns that are part of the Floridian Aquifer. The source of five rivers—Hillsborough, Kissimmee, Oklawaha, Peace, and Withlacoochee—Green Swamp is composed of lakes, rivers, forests, and sandhills bounded by the cities of Brooksville, Chermont, Haines City, Lakeland, and Zephyrhills. Also in 1974 the National Park Service purchased the 570,000-acre Big Cypress National Preserve (40 percent of Big Cypress Swamp). It adjoins Everglades National Park and provides a freshwater supply crucial to the park's future. The Department of Natural Resources spent $200 million to acquire twenty-two fragile, endangered marshes, beaches, and estuaries (a total of 362,200 acres). The DNR also added 24 new state parks to its list of 63. (In 1990 Florida had 150 state parks, historic sites, and other environmentally protected properties.)

By the early 1980s the state was giving attention to restoring the ecosystem of the Kissimmee–Okeechobee–Everglades Watershed, and in 1983 Governor Robert Graham announced a combined effort in the Save Our Everglades program with the Department of Environmental Regulation, the Florida Game and Fresh Water Fish Commission, the Department of Natural Resources, the Department of Community Affairs, and the South Florida Water Management District. Another restorative project was to return the Kissimmee River to its natural route. By 1994, the U.S. Army Corps of Engineers had so far filled 22 miles of the Kissimmee Canal for a return of water to the natural river channel. (See page 197.) Governor Graham also spearheaded Save Our Coast, a $200 million bond program to purchase and preserve ecologically sensitive coastal lands, primarily beaches. Endangered properties would be selected jointly by the state's Interagency Management and Outdoor Recreation Advisory committees and administered by the Division of Recreation and Parks. State government also moved to protect the shoreline from pollution, and in 1989 Governor Bob Martinez led efforts to ban offshore oil drilling and the dumping of waste at sea near the state's beaches. In 1990 President George Bush supported Governor Martinez and Congress in a moratorium on oil drilling, and all of Florida's U.S. Senate and House members voted for the 1990 Clean Air Act.

Floridians are seriously concerned not only about how their state government responds to their needs for environmental protection, but also about how national policy affects them. In December 1988 an editorial in the *Miami Herald* claimed that President Bush's environmental concern was "cloudy." Interior Secretary Manuel Lujan had a "troubling resemblance" to his predecessors, James Watt and Donald P. Hodel with their heavy-handed policies, the editorial declared. Within 9 months, President Bush pushed for "no net loss" of wetlands, which resulted in a veto from the U.S. Environmental Protection Agency for a Lake Forest development west of Sanford that would destroy a section of wetlands. Under strict orders from President Bush, the EPA appeared tough. But a few weeks later (almost a year after the editorial appeared) Secretary Lujan, under pressure from the oil industry, objected to the "no net loss" policy.

In 1994 the state legislature passed, and Governor Lawton Chiles signed, the Florida Everglades Forever Act, that provides a "broad, long-term restoration effort." In 1989 Congress enacted the Everglades National Park Expansion Act and by 1994 the park had added 49,553 acres of the authorized 107,600 acres in northeast Shark River Slough and east Everglades. In March of 1994 President Clinton signed the Everglades National Park Protection and Expansion Act Amendment for flood mitigation. There is also continuing progress in restoring the water quality of Lake Okeechobee, authorized by the state's Surface Water Improvement and Management (SWIM) plan, and in protecting Big Cypress Swamp through state and federal government land acquisition acts.

To acquaint you briefly with Florida's natural environment, the remainder of this chapter reviews beaches, coastlines, and islands; climate and weather; forests and plants; geology; hydrology; and wildlife.

### *Beaches, Coastlines, and Islands*

State Department of Commerce surveys report annually that among the top ten activities most enjoyed by visitors, number one is to visit the sandy beaches to enjoy the scenic beauty, sunning, swimming, surfing, and fishing. The entire eastern shore from Georgia to Miami has sandy beaches, some exceptionally wide (Daytona), some historic (Saint Augustine), and some preserved (Cape Canaveral National Seashore). On the Gulf side, sandy beaches are from Marco Island north to Honeymoon Island and Crystal Beach, and from Saint George Island west to Pensacola. Except for Alaska, Florida has the longest coastline of any state, 8,426 miles, includi. ç islands, bays, inlets, and estuaries. In addition, Florida has 23,753 miles of shoreline along rivers and streams, 96 miles along mangrove stands, and 438 miles along marshes—all of which give the aquatic adventurer extraordinary space to explore. There are twenty-five state beach parks and a number of city and county parks, such as Howard County and Venice Municipal. The state's Save Our Coast objective is to continue purchasing natural beach property for recreation in harmony with preservation. Some of the preserved national seashores are Cape Canaveral (26 miles) and the Gulf Islands (50 miles).

Shorelines are frequently changing, depending on types of sand, wave and wind action, and sea-level fluctuations. High-energy shorelines have natural sand dunes, banks of sand made possible only by dune-building grasses. One is the sea oat (*Uniola paniculata*), so important to dune protection that Florida law prohibits picking, breaking, or trampling the plant. All Florida beaches are open to the public between the average high-tide line and the water—in the wet sand area. A few counties or cities—for example, Amelia Island, Saint Augustine, and Daytona Beach—allow regulated automobile traffic on the beaches. The Daytona Beach sand is exceptionally hard packed—hard enough that auto racer Sir Malcolm Campbell set a speed record of 276.8 miles per hour there in 1935. The beach, hardly a course for fair competition for turtles and terns, has not been used as a speedway since 1959. Florida's territorial boundaries also include thousands of island beaches, again second in number only to Alaska. The islands are predominantly from Biscayne Bay to Pensacola Bay; others are in inlets, harbors, lakes, and rivers. At least forty-five hundred islands cover 10 or more acres.

### Climate and Weather

Warmed by the breezes from the Gulf of Mexico and the Atlantic Gulf Stream, Florida's mild, balmy winters are magnetic to visitors from cold climates. Winter is also the driest period of the year, with summer and early fall (June through October) being the rainy season. Sea breezes mitigate the summer heat. Summer thunderstorms are most frequent in a belt from Tampa to Daytona Beach, but Tallahassee, Pensacola, Apalachicola, Jacksonville, and West Palm Beach also get heavy rainfall. Lightning is most frequent in and near Ocala, the Bradenton-Tampa area, and Panama City, and on the east coast between Saint Augustine and Daytona Beach. Tornado occurrences average thirty annually, and hurricanes are most likely near Pensacola, Naples, the Keys, and the Miami area from the Everglades to West Palm Beach. The Florida peninsula experiences more hurricanes than any other state, usually between June and November, with an apex in September. Floridians are accustomed to weather disasters, but most were not prepared for Hurricane Andrew, which ravaged South Miami/Homestead/Florida City on August 24, 1992. (See Chapter 6.) Tropical storms can also be severely damaging. When tropical storm Gordon passed through south Florida twice between November 14 and 16, 1994, it left the Everglades with its highest water level in fifty years. Rainfall, up to 80 inches annually, is greatest in the Panhandle from Alabama east to Tallahassee, and in an area on the east coast between Lake Okeechobee and Miami. November and April usually have the least rainfall. Snow, which is rare, has been measured as far south as Lake Alfred, and frost, the bane of citrus and vegetable farms, has reached all the way to the Everglades.

The most sunshine is in November, February, and April, with Key West having the maximum percentage of sunshine: 75 percent or more. The hottest months are June, July, and August, which are normally between 85 and 95 degrees Fahrenheit. Winter months usually average between 45 and 70 degrees in the northern half of the state and 70 to 80 degrees in the southern half. Springtime has the lowest relative humidity (65 to 70 percent). For long-distance backpacking, canoeing, birding, exploring, and camping trips, wintertime is the most desirable.

### *Forests and Plants*

Florida has some 3,500 vascular plants, of which at least 315 are native trees. Some exotic trees, such as the Australian pine and the Brazilian pepper, smother the native plants in central and south Florida. Another tree, melaleuca (also called the punk tree, or bottlebrush), proliferates and is a great nuisance to underground pipelines. It blooms in all seasons in the southern half of the state and supplies an estimated one third of Florida's allergy pollen. Vegetation first appeared in north (including the Panhandle) and central Florida, and later in south Florida, millions of years ago. The least forested areas are the Everglades and the southern section of the Kissimmee River basin. Otherwise the state is forested moderately to heavily with hardwood and with longleaf and slash pines. The primary section of loblolly and shortleaf pines is in the Ocala National Forest and north to Tallahassee. Segments of oak-gum-cypress and oak-hickory forest are scattered from Okaloosa County in the Panhandle southeast to Lee County near Big Cypress Swamp.

On your Florida adventures you will notice hundreds of species of wildflowers, including the lantana. It blooms in all sections of the state in spring, summer, and fall, with mixed colors of cream, yellow, pink, orange, and red. Another colorful wildflower is the pine lily, found blooming in the summer and fall throughout the state. Among the wild orchids, none is more striking than the rare epiphytic spider orchid (*Brasia caudata*) that blooms in the winter, spring, and summer in a few hammocks of the Everglades. Throughout the state are the aromatic and evergreen bayberry (wax myrtle) and the sweet bay with its white flowers that smell clean and refreshing. Other fragrant plants are the black titi and the snowbell, which bloom in the spring, both found in north Florida. The state flower, sweet orange (*Citrus sinensis*), also fragrant, blooms in the spring and is found in central and south Florida. Ferns are prominent throughout the state; among them are the mosquito, chain, Boston, bracken, cinnamon, royal, resurrection, and climbing. Palms, with at least one hundred species, are more prominent here than in any other state in the nation. The most frequently seen are the cabbage palmetto (*Sabal palmetto*) and the saw palmetto (*Serenoa repens*). Classic and tropical in design, the royal palm is found sparingly near Fort Myers and in the Fakahatchee Strand. Among other tall palms is the coconut palm, usually found in south Florida. Its future is threatened by a disease called lethal yellowing. Botanists fear this disease may spread to other palm varieties.

Twelve of Florida's counties are more than 80 percent forest, led by Liberty County with 96.3 percent forested. Forests occupy about 50 percent of the entire state, covering about 75 percent of the northwest, 70 percent of the northeast, and 25 percent of the central region. As one might expect, timber harvesting is a major commercial business, with 56 percent of it pulpwood. (If you are interested in learning about Florida's eighty-one national champion trees, contact the American Forestry Association, 1319 Eighteenth Street, NW, Washington, DC 20036, [202] 467-5810.) A 1989 report from the U.S. Department of Agriculture indicated that Florida and California would lead the nation in plant-life extinction during the 1990s. Overseeing these plants is the Florida Endangered Plant Advisory Council. (For the council's most recent endangered list, see *Appendix*.) Another 280 species are threatened.

### Geology

Florida's landmass is part of the Floridian Plateau, a large projection, mainly submerged, that separates the Atlantic Ocean from the Gulf of Mexico. The plateau is geologically linked to the Caribbean Islands. Between 500 and 230 million years ago, in the Paleozoic era, Florida was an arc of volcanic mountains. Erosion from these ancient mountains caused the formation of thousands of feet of limestone. As the limestone layers arched, Florida rose above sea level. Marshes and lagoons began to form about 20 million years ago in the

Tertiary period. One million years ago, animals including mastodons and large reptiles, became plentiful. As the most recent ice age retreated in North America, the contemporary shape of Florida appeared.

The soils of north Florida are largely gravel and coarse sand, with sandy clay and clay in the western Panhandle. About equal sections of clayey sand, medium to fine sand and silt, and shelly sand and clay are in the north and central areas, except in the Big Bend area, where there are limestone and shell beds. South Florida is almost all limestone and peat.

Florida is mineral rich. Titanium and zircon are found in the northeast. Phosphate mines, the most productive in the nation, dot the central part of the state. In Florida's upper half is underground karst terrain composed of soluble limestone and dolomite rock types. Characteristic here are hundreds of caves, sinkholes, sinkhole lakes, springs, solution valleys, and prairies.

The entire Gulf coastline has a low ocean floor of 10 fathoms (60 feet) or less from 3 miles out near Panama City to 40 miles out near Cedar Key and Cape Sable. On the east coast the low area runs north from West Palm Beach, widening as it approaches Georgia. Immediately off the coast near Miami the ocean floor drops from 100 to 1,000 fathoms, making this the closest area to the continental shelf. If Florida's sea level were to drop 10 fathoms, the state would be nearly 40 percent larger than it is today; if the sea level were to rise 6.66 fathoms, half the state would be submerged. An increase in global temperature of 4 degrees Fahrenheit would melt enough polar ice to raise the sea level 10 to 15 feet by the twenty-second century. All of Florida south of Okeechobee and all the major cities except for Orlando, Gainesville, and Tallahassee would be inundated.

### Hydrology

No other natural resource is as important to the future of Florida as its fresh water. Florida has an average 150 billion gallons of daily rainfall (110 billion of which plant life uses in evapotranspiration). An additional source of water is river inflow from Georgia and Alabama. Some of the state's fresh water is stored in lakes and streams, but most is in underground water reservoirs, or aquifers. Each aquifer has rock layers containing many connected spaces. The water may be anywhere from a few feet underground to a depth of 3,500 feet in central Florida. The artesian Floridian Aquifer (called Florida's rain barrel) underlies the entire state, and five surficial and intermediate aquifers overlie it, including the nonartesian Sand and Gravel Aquifer in the extreme west of the Panhandle and the Biscayne Aquifer in the southeast. Critical to the welfare of Florida's large population is the underground water table whose pressure prevents saline intrusion from the Gulf and the Atlantic.

Of thirty-four major rivers in Florida, all except seven tributaries flow to the east or west coast. The Saint Johns River is the only major one to also flow north. Four of the rivers flow from origins in Georgia and six from Alabama. Largest in terms of flow are the Apalachicola, Suwannee, Chatowhitchee, and Escombia: longest are the Saint Johns (273 miles), Suwannee (177 miles), Kissimmee (134 miles), and Saint Marys (107 miles). Many of Florida's seventeen hundred streams and rivers have low water quality because of pollution and are in need of restoration.

Also among Florida's freshwater assets are its seventy-eight hundred lakes, the two largest of which are Lake Okeechobee (681 square miles) and Lake George (73 square miles). Osceola, Orange, Lake, and Polk counties have the most lakes. Located in the center of the state, these four counties are generally known as the Land of the Lakes. Florida is also known for the 325 clear, mineralized warm springs (usually between 70 and 75 degrees Fahrenheit) that dot the northern and western parts of the state. Every day 8 billion gallons of water surge from them. Spring Creek, a submarine spring in Wakulla County, discharges 1.3 billion gallons daily and is the state's most powerful. It is one of 16 submarine springs below sea level in the Gulf or the Atlantic Ocean. Open to the public are 50 springs, including Crystal River, Silver Springs, Rainbow Springs, Alapaha Rise, Saint Marks, Ginnie, and Wakulla, described elsewhere in this book. Surprisingly, considerable solids and minerals have perculated through the limestone into the clear water that you see. Silver Springs, for example, carries 210,000 tons of solids annually to the Oklawaha River. Some of the Indian tribes believed the springs to be of medicinal and youth-retaining value, a belief accepted by early Spanish explorers. By the early twentieth century, Floridians had commercialized a number of springs. To illustrate, Suwannee Springs near Live Oak advertised the water as "infallible mineral water to heal malaria, liver disease and kidney troubles." In addition to the many underwater spring caverns, nearly three hundred dry caverns are known; Florida Caverns, a state park at Marianna, is open to the public. These caverns are described in more detail in Chapter 4.

The largest area of surface water in Florida is the wetlands, which includes cypress ponds, strands and prairies, river swamps and flood plains, freshwater marshes, wet prairies, salt marshes, and mangrove swamps. Water is present most of the year in cypress ponds found throughout the state; cypress dominates the pond interior. Cypress strands are diffuse stream areas, such as the Fakahatchee Strand and dwarf cypress in Big Cypress Swamp. Prairies differ from cypress ponds and strands more in degree than in type; in Big Cypress Swamp, you will see prairies between cypress ponds and strands. Apalachicola and the Choctawhatchee are river swamps; in them plant productivity is high and activated floodplains usually have good wildlife habitat. On the Gulf Coast and lower Saint Johns River are hydric hammocks, home to red cedar and cabbage palm. Freshwater marshes are abundant in Florida; the best example is in the Everglades, where saw grass is prominent. Similar to freshwater marshes but dry for a longer period of time are wet prairies. Tropical mangrove swamps (an estimated 470,000 acres) are found principally in southern Florida, but may be seen as far north on the Gulf as Cedar Key. Called walking trees, they are significant because they create the nursery area for fishes, crustaceans, and shellfish. They also protect uplands from storm winds and floods; some waterfowl use them for rookeries. The salt marshes (also called tidal marshes) are coastal wetlands rich in marine life. Formed on low-energy shorelines, Big Bend, between Apalachee Bay and Cedar Key, is a fine example.

Whatever the water sources and their flow, Floridians currently use about 45 percent of the supply for agricultural irrigation and allied purposes, 40 percent for services, and 13 percent for manufacturing.

### *Wildlife*

Florida wildlife is likely to be a primary interest on your adventures into the natural areas. Birds, fishes, mammals, and reptiles are abundant. The state's geography, climate, and diversity of habitat accommodate a range of species not seen elsewhere in the nation. Herpetofauna, for example, has 125 native species and 25 introduced species of reptiles and amphibians, the most discussed being the American alligator (*Alligator mississippiensis*), designated the state reptile by the state legislature in 1987.

The alligator's range is from the Great Dismal Swamp of Virginia–North Carolina, with its coastal climate, to the Rio Grande in Texas (except in southern Arkansas and extreme southeastern Oklahoma). The reptile is found statewide in Louisiana and Florida. Its ancestry is estimated to extend back 150 million years, but the most recent evolution is from *Alligato olseni* about 2 million years ago. The alligator is one of three groups of crocodilians in the world. (The true crocodile group has thirteen species, one of which is the Florida crocodile [*Crocodylus acutus*]. With about 350 Florida crocodiles in existence, the species is protected by law in the Crocodile Lake National Wildlife Refuge in Florida Bay.) Alligators have broad, rounded snouts and are cold-blooded, elongated reptiles that live in freshwater marshes, swamps, and bayous. When sunning to increase their body heat, they appear lazy and sleepy; when walking they are clumsy. But they swim powerfully, bellow loudly during mating season, fight other alligators fiercely on territory claims, and roll over in the water rapidly when drowning prey. They have webbed feet, tough black hides and scutes on their backs (in contrast to crocodiles, which have greenish skin). The alligator's belly is cream yellow and soft. One of the two sets of eyelids is transparent and can be closed so that the animal can see under water, and flaps cover the nostrils and small ears when it swims. Because it has a complex circulatory system with a four-chambered heart (in contrast to two chambers in most other reptiles), an alligator can hold its breath and easily stay submerged for 45 minutes. Its low metabolic rate enables it to go without food for weeks, but normally it eats weekly, nourishing itself with turtles, snakes, raccoons, fish, otters, wading birds, and dogs. An alligator will attack deer, other alligators, and humans. It swallows rocks, pebbles, and hard pieces of wood to aid the digestive process in its gizzards. The powerful jaw muscles can easily crush a large turtle in one bite; as Sumter County's professional nuisance alligator trapper Jimmy Douglas says, an alligator could "crush my fiberglass boat like it was paper."

Alligators breed as early as mid-February in south Florida and as late as May farther north. The female, without the help of the male, builds a conical mound of saw grass and cattails above the water level for her nest. In June, she lays thirty to sixty eggs, which hatch in September. Dampness in the mound provides 90 percent humidity, and the sex of the newborn depends on the temperature under which it is incubated—above 91 degrees Fahrenheit all are male; below 85 degrees all are female; the middle range yields a balance of the sexes. Upon hearing the hatched 6-inch-long babies lightly squealing, the mother, if necessary, will tenderly carry them to the water in her mouth. A 20-year-old male alligator is usually about 11 or 12 feet long, and the female is about 8

*Alligator, Everglades National Park.* PHOTO BY Allen de Hart.

or 9 feet. (In 1956 a 17.5-foot alligator was killed at Apopka, Florida.)

Alligator hide hunting became a profitable commercial business by 1860 and remained so until 1960 when Florida recognized that its alligator population was endangered. In 1961 a state law made hunting illegal except for licensed hunters of nuisance alligators that endangered humans. Poaching followed, but the law became stronger when Congress enacted the federal Endangered Species Act in 1973. By 1988 the alligator population had reached about 1 million. As a result, the reptile lost its endangered status, and in September of that year the state permitted 230 hunters (each under tight hunting restrictions) to harvest up to fifteen 'gators each. Public interest was high for a number of reasons, one for the sport itself, another that alligators had intruded upon residential areas in recent years.

Two other animals of public interest in Florida are the endangered West Indian manatee (*Trichechus manatus*), also known as the Florida manatee, and the Florida panther (*Felis*

*concolor coryi*), also endangered. The state legislature designated the manatee the state salt-freshwater mammal in 1975.
Efforts continue to protect it from its chief enemy, motorboat
propellors. The ancestry of the warm-blooded manatee, a
distant cousin to the elephant, can be traced to plant-eating
mammals 60 million years ago. A manatee can weigh around
1,000 pounds, grow 15 feet long, and live up to 50 years. Its
front legs are flippers, and its flat tail propels it. Manatees can
stay submerged for about 10 minutes before surfacing to
breathe and must stay in water at least 65 degrees Fahrenheit;
otherwise, they are subject to colds, pneumonia, and death.
In the winter months, they congregate in warm springs and in
the thermal discharge from power plants. They are harmless
to all animals, including man, and peacefully munch on
aquatic plants 7 hours per day. Devoted mothers, females bear
young only once every 3 to 5 years. Although the state first
protected them by law in 1893, not until 1978 did the Florida
Manatee Sanctuary Act make the entire state a refuge for them.
Only an estimated one thousand are in existence today. Kings
Bay of Crystal River is one of Florida's major manatee sanctuaries. For information, call Manatee Hotline, (800) 342-2762.

In 1982 the state legislature designated the Florida panther
the official state animal. Today it is near extinction, with some
thirty-five to forty-five remaining in Big Cypress National
Preserve and Everglades National Park, where they roam over
as much as 150 to 200 square miles in a month. The graceful,
agile, shy cat prowls mainly at night, usually alone, to reaffirm
its territory and search for food. A healthy male feeds on about
one deer every 10 days, or an equal diet value of ten raccoons.
While raising young, a female needs a deer every 3 days for
her energy supply. Other prey are wild hogs, rabbits, cotton
rats, birds, snakes, and armadillos. If a panther has more to eat
at one time than it needs, it stores its prey covered with leaves
for a later meal. Panthers avoid dogs, and no documented
reports have been made of attacks on humans.

Mature males normally weigh between 100 and 145
pounds and are nearly 7 feet long, including the long tail. The

female weighs less, 65 to 100 pounds, and is shorter than the male. Similar to other cougar subspecies, Florida panthers are tawny brown, with white flecks on their shoulders and necks. Mating occurs every other year from November through March, and healthy females bear one to four spotted kittens, each weighing about one pound at birth. Kittens stay with the mother up to 2 years for food and protection from males, which may kill them. The normal life span of the panther is between 10 and 15 years.

Considered to be among the most endangered mammals in the world, the Florida panther is legally protected by a number of state programs. But that protection may have come too late. As recently as 1958 the panther was feared and hunted as a game animal, and not until 1973 was it listed under the federal Endangered Species Act. By 1986, the state had created the Florida Panther Interagency Committee, consisting of the U.S. Fish and Wildlife Service, the National Park Service, the Florida Game and Fresh Water Fish Commission, and the Florida Department of Natural Resources. As one of their scientific research efforts in 1981 the committee began fitting panthers with lightweight radiotelemetry receiving collars to aid in studying the animals' range and behavior. The survival of the Florida panther depends both on its natural mortality and on human intrusion on its habitat. Among the natural threats are inbreeding, infrequency of breeding, loss of kittens to predators, disease, infections and parasites (distemper, anemia, pseudorabies), and health of male sperm (up to 90 percent may be abnormal or defective). Humans threaten the animals by destroying habitat contiguous with roads and highways, increasing population, hunting illegally, hunting and killing the panther's food supply, and spreading exotic plants such as the impenetrable melaleuca.

Sensitive to these and other human threats, the state is now taking action to save the panther. Among other things, it is constructing twenty-three wildlife crossings under 100-foot elevated bridges on I-75 (Alligator Alley), which allows wildlife to move under the interstate. Additionally, thirteen

I-75 bridges that cross water have been widened to allow wildlife to pass on dry land. Other efforts have been to create the Florida Panther National Wildlife Refuge north of I-75 in 1989, to increase outbreeding, to reintroduce the animal to other protected areas, and to reduce the thousands of registered off-road vehicles that destroy and pollute the natural environment of Big Cypress National Preserve.

In addition to the natural and human threats to the Florida panther's survival, crossbreeding with descendants of the South American pumas now threatens the species' genetic purity. Seven of the hybrid pumas, believed to be Florida panthers, were released in southeastern Everglades National Park between 1957 and 1967. Since then, research by the Florida Game and Fresh Water Fish Commission has revealed that the pure Florida panther has a cowlick on its back and a kinked tail; the puma hybrid has a smooth back and a straight tail. Although crossbreeding could alter the panther's endangered species status, the commission and the U.S. Fish and Wildlife Service have decided not to make an effort to keep the families separate. One speculation is that a mixture of the hybrid puma and the panther might increase the chance of survival for the Florida panther without changing its name.

For information on the status of the Florida panther, contact the Florida Panther Interagency Committee, Office of Information, 6209 South Meredian Street, Tallahassee, FL 32399, (904) 488-3831. Ask for a free subscription of *Coryi*, the committee's official newsletter. Or call Florida Wildlife Federation, (904) 656-7113, or Save the Florida Panther, (800) 5-FLA-CAT. If you see an injured or dead panther, call Resource Alert, (800) 432-2046 (in Florida only).

At least 200 species of natural freshwater fish compete with 50 exotic species in south Florida. Some of the most common are the Florida largemouth black bass (*Micropterus salmoides*), the state's freshwater fish and the largest bass species in the world; black crappie (also called speckled perch); bream (bluegill); catfish (three species); chain pickerel (pike, jackfish); shellcracker (redear); stumpknocker; and warmouth. Among the prominent saltwater fish are barracuda, bluefish, dolphin, grunt, grouper, ladyfish, mackerel, marlin, redfish, mullet, sailfish (the state's saltwater fish), shark, sheephead, snapper, pompano, snook, tarpon, tuna, sea trout, and warhoo. Florida is also known for its shellfish, which include blue crab, clams (quahogs), Florida conch, Florida lobster, oysters, scallops, shrimp, and stone crabs. (See *Fishing*, Chapter 2.)

You will see birds almost everywhere you go in Florida. With more than 450 species, the state has about half of all bird species in the nation. Only two other states, Texas and California, have similar bird populations. The climate and environment favor the production of both native and migratory species. Among the species you will see or hear year-round are the state bird, the mockingbird (*Minus polyglottos*, designated by the state legislature in 1927), common and boat-tailed grackle, anhinga, red-tailed and red-shouldered hawks, turkey vulture, northern bobwhite, common moorhen, killdeer, mourning dove, red-bellied and downy woodpeckers, blue jay, American crow, barred and eastern screech owls, Carolina wren, European starling, northern cardinal, white-eyed vireo, rufous-sided towhee, and red-winged blackbird, as well as a wide range of warblers and sparrows, egrets, herons, and ibis. Mainly coastal are the brown pelican, laughing gull, royal tern, black skimmer, and willet. More specific locations of birds, fishes, and mammals are mentioned in the chapters ahead. (For a listing of Florida's endangered and threatened animals, see *Appendix*.)

# 2

## BEFORE YOU LEAVE

### PLANNING YOUR TRIP

#### *When and How to Go*

Most visitors travel in Florida during the last 2 weeks of December and throughout most of March, June, July, and August. Because most people come chiefly to visit family and friends or to vacation (usually at the beach and major theme parks), you may find these months as uncrowded in the wild as any other time. If you are making campground or motel reservations during these periods, however, plan early. February, April, and May have less tourism; September has the least of all months. Winter rates for accommodations are usually higher, particularly in south Florida and the Keys. In the forest and around lakes and rivers, the colder the temperature the fewer problems you will have with mosquitoes and humidity, particularly in the Everglades and Big Cypress Swamp. Also consider that the winter season is the dry season.

If you are arriving by train, consult Amtrak, which runs two trains, *Silver Meteor* and *Silver Star,* from New York to Miami. Station stops are in Deerfield Beach, De Land, Delray Beach, Fort Lauderdale, Hollywood, Jacksonville, Kissimmee, Lakeland, Ocala, Okeechobee, Orlando, Palatka, Sanford, Sebring, Tampa (Saint Petersburg, Sarasota, Clearwater, and Bradenton are served by bus from Tampa), Waldo, West Palm Beach, Wildwood, Winter Haven, and Winter Park. Call (800) USA-RAIL or contact Amtrak Station, 8303 NW 37th Street,

Miami, FL 33147, (305) 835-1225. In Canada, call (800) 4AM-TRAK. Ask for a travel guide and advanced reservations. Statewide bus service is by Greyhound, and reservations are not required. Airlines travel to one hundred cities in the state, but the following cities have international terminals: Fort Lauderdale, Jacksonville, Miami, Orlando, St. Petersburg, Tampa, and West Palm Beach. Check your local airport or the 1-800 numbers for major airlines that service Florida. If you are flying from a foreign country, contact a U.S. Travel and Tourism Office or a U.S. Embassy for information about visas and visitor services, or contact the Bureau of International Tourism (107 W. Gaines St., 410-D Collins Bldg., Tallahassee, FL 32399, [904] 488-7598). In London, there is a Florida office at 18/24 Westbourne Grove, London, England W2 5RH, (071)-727-1661. For information on sea transportation, contact a travel agency or call the Division of Tourism in Florida, (904) 487-1462. Request the brochure *Florida Travel Tips* for information on safety precautions.

### *How Much Your Adventure Will Cost*

One of Florida's appeals is its affordability: Accommodations and meals are low cost, and budget-priced facilities are widespread. Car rental rates are frequently lower than in most other states. A *Mobil Travel Guide, Bantam's Florida, Fodor's Florida,* and *Frommer's Florida,* which list lodging and restaurant costs, are updated yearly. You will find campground fees expensive at some resort-type locations, but others are easily affordable. Fees range between $10 and $30 per night. Some of the state parks, generally inexpensive, may charge as much as commercial campgrounds. Allow for fees to visit historic sites, and keep reserve funds for emergencies. Finally, keep in mind that the children may beg to go to Disney World or Silver Springs; will you be able to say no? Plan your budget accordingly.

Some useful agencies to contact in the state capital are (*all area code 904*): Florida Attractions Association, 222-2885;

Division of Tourism, Visitor Inquiry, 487-1462; Historic Sites, 487-2335; National Forests, 942-9300; State Forests, 488-6611; State Parks, 488-9872; and Florida Wildlife, 488-1960. (See *Appendix D,* Government Agencies and Citizens' Groups, p. 408, for the names of more agencies and organizations, and the *Information* section at the end of each chapter.)

### Accommodations

Seven percent of Florida's millions of annual visitors stay in a public or commercial campground. Accommodations at the six hundred campgrounds vary. Suggested sources of information are the free *Florida Camping Directory* (Florida Campground Association, 1638 North Plaza Drive, Tallahassee, FL 32308, [904] 656-8878) and *Woodall's Campground Directory* (Florida) and *Woodall's Tenting Directory,* available at your local bookstore. Other sources are available from the Division of Tourism (126 Van Buren Street, Tallahassee, FL 32301, [904] 487-1462) and the chambers of commerce listed at the end of each adventure. National and state forests and parks also have free lists of accommodations and costs. I have listed their addresses throughout. The Florida Hotel and Motel Association's 108-page accommodations directory is available upon written request (Florida Hotel and Motel Association, 200 W. College Ave., Tallahassee, FL 32301; [904] 224-2888, or 800-VISIT-FL); there is a $2 mailing fee in U.S., $4 outside U.S. If you are a motel patron, purchase the *Mobil Travel Guide* at your bookstore, or contact the Florida Hotel/Motel Association (P.O. Box 1529, Tallahassee, FL 32302, [904] 224-2888). Bed-and-breakfast lodgings and restaurants on or near adventure routes are also listed. Suggested guidebooks for bed-and-breakfast accommodations are *Guide to Small and Historic Lodgings of Florida,* by Herbert R. Hiller (Pineapple Press, Sarasota), and *The Official Bed and Breakfast Guide,* by Featherston Ostler (National Bed and Breakfast Association, P.O. Box 332, Norwalk, CT 06852).

### *What to Take*

It is difficult to suggest all the equipment for all the potential trips covered in this book or for expeditions you might want to take other than those described here. Choose your equipment based on factors such as time of season, the number in your party, whether you will be traveling with children, your physical condition, your preference for RV or primitive camping, and how long you plan to be traveling.

Shorts, short-sleeve shirts, and tennis shoes are standard in spring, summer, and early fall, unless you are in the backcountry, where long trousers and long-sleeve shirts will protect you from saw grass, saw palmettoes, briars, and insects. A hat and a bandana will protect you from insects and sunburn. Light hiking or walking boots are recommended for long trails, though sturdy tennis shoes are frequently used on trails where wading is necessary. Florida is often sunny, but it can also be rainy in spring and summer, so take rain gear on all long trips. Short trips may also require rain gear because of sudden storms or thunderstorms. If you will be canoeing or fishing in open bays, rivers, and estuaries, bring strong hooded rain gear to protect yourself from the wind. From mid-December to mid-March in the Panhandle and north and central Florida the weather can be temporarily cold, even below freezing, and hypothermia is possible, so bring a sweater, a mackinaw jacket, flannel shirts, and windproof jackets. A woodman's cap or watch cap can be useful against the wind in the daytime and serve as a head warmer in your tent at nighttime. Cold weather is normally of short duration. You would also do well to always pack an extra change of dry clothes for an emergency.

Generally, for a day hike you should take a day pack, food, a water bottle or canteen, a first-aid kit with antivenom materials and pharmaceutical syrup of ipecac, a compass, any necessary medication, insect repellent, a map, notepaper and pencils, trash bags, and a camera. Also pack a flashlight with extra batteries, waterproof matches, extra food, and a space blanket in case an emergency requires you to be out over-night. For a long hiking, canoeing, or camping trip, take all of the above, plus a backpack, a tent with insect-proof screen, a sleeping bag, lightweight cooking and eating utensils, a propane stove and fuel, a water purifier, sunscreen, and citronella candles. Lightweight binoculars are optional. Food should be nonperishable, except for fresh fruit, raw veg-etables, and bread. Powdered and dried foods are available at grocery stores, and dehydrated and freeze-dried foods at sports stores. A good guideline is to buy light in weight and heavy in energy. Foreign visitors may find it more practical to purchase supplies after they arrive in the United States. Florida is famous for its fishing in all seasons, so pack fishing gear and do not forget to acquire or renew your license. It is best to leave family pets at home with friends or at a kennel.

### Maps and Guidebooks

In addition to the general location maps in this book, you will need a current Florida highway map, available free at all interstate visitor centers, most commercial travel and tourist centers, chambers of commerce, and the state Department of Transportation (Haydon Burns Building, 605 Suwannee Street, Tallahassee, FL 32399, [904] 488-3111). Automotive service stations also have highway maps, usually for a small fee. I recommend that you purchase the *Florida Atlas and Gazet-teer,* which has detailed, multicolored highway maps and a location listing guide to the state's wildlife areas, historic sites, parks, forests, beaches, springs, canoe routes, fishing areas, campgrounds, and more. If you cannot find it at bookstores, contact the DeLorme Mapping Company (P.O. Box 298, Freeport, ME 04032, [207] 865-4171). County maps provide additional detail; they are available for a nominal fee from county courthouses, local chambers of commerce, and the state Department of Transportation. City maps are available at bookstores and city newsstands in the state for a small charge. Some chambers of commerce provide them free. If you plan to explore a remote wilderness area, bring a topographic map and a compass. Topographics, the most detailed of all maps, are usually available at city blueprint stores or at outdoor sports centers in the state. Otherwise, order from Branch of Distribution (USGS, Box 25286, Federal Center, Denver, CO 80225). Because you must pay in advance, write first for a free Florida Map Index and order form (expect 2 to 4 weeks for delivery). Special maps of the national and state forests, parks, and wildlife areas are available from the addresses listed under *Information* in the adventure chapters. Specific guidebooks will assist you in some of your adventures, as on the Florida Trail or the state canoe trails. Addresses for these books are listed where the subject is covered or in the *Appendix*.

**HIGHWAYS AND BACK ROADS.** Three interstates enter Florida: I-95 and I-75 from Georgia and I-10 from Alabama. Seven US routes from Georgia and four from Alabama and several state and county roads also channel into the peninsula. Within the state are eight other interstates and nine toll roads, including the longest, the 318.6-mile Florida Turnpike from Wildwood to Homestead. Federal highway signs are color coded for easy recognition (for example, US 41 is orange, US 98 black, US 19 red, US 192 green, US 17 yellow, and US 92 blue). State primary road signs (abbreviated SR) are white, almost square, with black numbers and a partial outline of state boundaries. (State maps and some commercial maps show the signs in a circle.) Occasionally a state road will have a spur with the same number but with a letter suffix, such as A, B, or C, and sometimes it will become a county road (abbreviated CR) at a county line. County road signs have yellow writing on a dark blue pentagon. Some roads follow historic routes of Indians, explorers, or cattle drivers. Examples are the 332-mile De Soto Trail from Bradenton north on US 41, 301, 441, 90, and 319 to the Georgia line north of Tallahassee; the Cracker Trail on SR 64 and 66, US 98 and 441, and CR 68 from Tampa Bay to Fort Pierce (described in Chapter 5); and the Buccaneer Trail on A1A from Fernandina Beach to Daytona Beach (described in Chapter 3).

In the national forests, the road sign (abbreviated FR for forest road) may be a small rectangular brown sign with two or three digits. Some roads in the state forests, such as Blackwater, may not be marked at all, but forest maps show assigned numbers. Because most back roads are sandy, it is easy to get stuck in ditches or pull-offs. Avoid parking in front of gates or cattle-crossing routes. Other backcountry roads, public or private, may be impassable in wet weather unless you have a jeep or four-wheel-drive vehicle.

### Health and Safety

An ideal trip is challenging, exciting, educational, and pleasurable, but it must also be safe. Regardless of how experienced or familiar you are with a location and activity, an accident can happen. If this is your first trip and you are going with a group, make sure that all know the safety rules for water sports, backcountry backpacking, and rescue. Park and forest officials, who usually must arrange for rescues, recommend that you do not go alone. If you do, leave your itinerary with them and with your relatives. If you are taking children, you may wish to call ahead to inform yourself about safety precautions for them. If you are a beginner, you might wish to read *Emergency Survival Handbook,* by the American Outdoor Safety League, and *Wilderness Survival,* by Bernard Shanks.

On all of your adventures take a first-aid kit, and if possible, have someone in your party who can administer cardiopulmonary resuscitation (CPR) and treat hypothermia. Florida's winter weather, except in the south region, is cold enough to cause hypothermia, a condition resulting from a lowered body temperature. A tragic example is the death of four Army Rangers in swampy water at Eglin Air Force Base January 15, 1995. Sweaty or wet clothes commonly cause the condition, which the victim often is not able to detect. Symptoms are uncontrollable shivering; vague, incoherent speech; frequent stumbling; and drowsiness. Immediate treatment is to dry and warm the victim. Also be sure to carry pure drinking water; use other water only if it has been designated uncontaminated by park or forest officials or local health departments. Purify all water with a filter, or boil the water for at least five minutes. Iodine crystals may help against some pollutants, but they will not prevent giardiasis.

If you become lost, use the universal distress signal of any three sounds or sights: light flashes, yells, whistles, or smoke signals. Do not panic, but stay on the trail or in one place. Make a fire and prepare to stay warm and conserve energy, food, and water. Climb a tree if doing so will help you understand your map and compass reading. During thunderstorms, stay away from trees, power lines, open boats, and the beach, and do not cross streams or marshes. If you are in the backcountry during the hurricane season, take a dependable radio for updates on hurricane watches and warnings. Before you leave for your trip you may wish to call your local weather station for the nearest Weather Trak station, or call the Weather Channel Connection, (900) 932-8437.

To prevent accidents while swimming, never swim alone; know the water conditions (currents, tides, and undertows); do not swim if impaired by alcohol or medication; and remember, feet first first time. In a rescue attempt, row a boat to assist the victim, throw a life-preserving object with a rope attached, call out to bystanders for help, and know CPR (cardiopulmonary resuscitation). A scuba-diving license may be required to explore some of the spring caverns: call the Florida Division of Tourism, (904) 487-1462.

Vehicle vandalism has increased; lock all valuables out of sight, and if you will be gone overnight, leave your vehicle in a protected area or arrange a shuttle.

### Mosquitoes and Biting Flies
Mosquitoes (including the tenacious Asian tiger mosquito) are part of Florida's wildlife, an unpleasant part for outdoor adventurers. Florida's bug season is usually between the first of March and late autumn in the northern half of the

state, but it lasts year-round in the southern half. The state spends about $40 million annually to combat the pest, but if it were to become extinct, an essential link in the food chain for birds and fish would be destroyed. The mosquito is a bloodsucking insect, but only the female bites. Almost sightless, mosquitoes follow a hunting corridor when they sense carbon dioxide, moisture, and warmth. To avoid them, refrain from hiking and camping along streambeds or boggy ground, in marshes and mangrove swamps, and near shady, stagnant water during bug season. Instead, choose a high, dry, windy area whenever possible and hike or canoe in a winter season. Another strategy is to wear bugproof, light-colored clothes and a head net effective enough to keep out the no-see-ums. The most effective chemical repellent is high in deet (N-diethylmeta toluamide, to which you may be allergic) or permethrin. Also available is a natural repellent, Green Ban, available from Mulgum Hollow Farm of San Francisco. To treat itching bites, use a menthol phenol compound or an antihistamine cream. An aggressive mosquito, "Asian Tiger" with black and white stripes, was sighted in the Jacksonville area in the early 1990s. Repellents may be ineffective.

Among other insect pests are the deerflies (yellow flies) that frequent shaded woods; black flies (beach flies) that are more coastal; sand gnats (no-see-ums) that love you at the beach and in sandy, moist areas; and horseflies, whose habitat is chiefly prairie and open woods. Insect repellents, petroleum jellies, oils, protective clothing, and avoidance of habitat make dealing with the bugs easier.

### Poisonous Animals and Plants

In planning your outdoor excursions, you should know what poisonous animals and plants to avoid, and to what you are allergic. The most dangerous poisonous animals in Florida are pit vipers (pigmy and eastern diamondback rattlesnakes and the cottonmouth moccasin) and the coral snake. The canebrake rattlesnake and the copperhead appear infrequently and only in upstate Florida. Diamondback habitat is statewide, but the snake favors a dry to semidry pine-palmetto area. The pigmy (ground) rattler, in contrast, prefers a wet habitat near lakes and swamps; the cottonmouth also likes watery areas and streambanks (it can bite underwater); and the coral snake prefers upland woods. As precautions against snakebite, always look where you step, do not place your hands in places where you cannot see, do not go barefoot, and do not sleep exposed to the ground. If bitten, administer first aid and immediately transport the victim to an emergency facility for an injection of antivenin. Do not apply a tourniquet. If you are alone, go for help, but refrain from exerting yourself. If you are bitten by a scorpion fish while scuba diving, treat much as you would a snakebite. Emergency treatment at a facility is necessary for an extreme sting by a Portuguese man-of-war or a stingray.

Much less dangerous is the bite of the black widow spider, which lives near buildings, picnic tables, dead logs, and benches. Still, the patient should be taken to an emergency treatment center. Other less dangerous insects with venomous bites are the paper wasp scorpion, the fire ant, and the honeybee. A calamine lotion or antihistamine may suppress the pain. Emergency treatment is not usually necessary unless the victim has an allergy or has received profuse bites. The poisonous bites of chiggers (red bugs), a hard-to-see mite, are more of an irritant than a danger. Chiggers are found statewide and are prolific on dense bushes and vines in the summertime. As a preventive, use insect repellent on the boundary areas of your clothes. Calamine or caligesic ointments may relieve itching. To combat ticks (out mainly in the summertime), use a drop of kerosene or gasoline to loosen the bug's grip. Small seed ticks are common in piney woods and around Spanish moss. A good preventive is Permanone tick repellent used on your clothes; powdered sulphur also works.

Approximately sixty plants in Florida are poisonous if digested, including mushrooms, of which 50 percent are not native. At least fifteen plants cause coma or death; they include water hemlock, rubber vine, metel, jimsonweed, false poinciana, golden dewdrop, yellow jessamine, glory-lily, sandbox tree, physic nut, lantana, wax privet, chinaberry, oleander, castor bean, and black nightshade. To prevent illness, simply do not experiment with eating any plant off the land unless you know for sure that it is nontoxic. To treat someone, immediately have him or her drink at least two glasses of water to dilute the poison, induce vomiting with pharmaceutical syrup of ipecac, and take the victim to a medical facility. The leaves or sap of another twenty-five Florida plants can cause skin rashes. These include ragweed, wild poinsettia, punk tree, Brazilian peppertree, and poison ivy. Florida's main Poison Control Center has a 24-hour answering service, (800) 282-3171, which gives information on the nearest medical centers.

### OUTDOOR ACTIVITIES

#### Camping

Camping at developed campgrounds has been covered under *Accommodations,* but camping in the wilderness requires entirely different preparation and skill. The romance of backpacking all your gear to a wild, secluded campsite can become unpleasant if rainy weather floods your tent and soaks your down sleeping bag and potential firewood. My suggestion is to get out the *Boy Scout Handbook* or the *Girl Scout Handbook* again if necessary and "be prepared," choose your camping companions and campsites wisely, follow "no-trace camping" policy, and "pack out what you pack in." In preparing for your backwoods camping you may find the following books helpful: *Cooking for Camp and Trail* by Hasse Bunnelle and Shirley Sarvis; *Land Navigation Handbook* by W. S. Kawls; and *Harsh Weather Camping* by Sam Curtis. For your journeys, I describe some good campsites and list areas where camping is not allowed. Camping information is available from the Florida Campground Association, 1638 N. Plaza Dr., Tallahassee, FL 32308, (904) 656-8878.

**Hiking and Backpacking**

The state has more than 7,582 miles of trails: 1,721 miles of hiking trails; 611 miles of nature trails; 962 miles of multiuse trails for walking, jogging, and bicycling; 2,378 miles of bicycle trails; 394 miles of equestrian trails; 1,355 miles of canoe trails; and 161 miles of rails-to-trails for hiking, bicycling, and horseback riding. (The state's system is officially called the Florida Rails-to-Trails Program, but you will notice signs and literature with variant titles such as "rail-trail," "rail-trails," and "rails-to-trails.") The longest trails are in the national and state forests, where there are excellent opportunities to backpack from 1 to 2 weeks and camp along the way. For a challenge in long-distance hiking, try the mainline Florida National Scenic Trail (FT), the longest in the state. The FT includes a number of trails that have retained their original names. Among the longest continuous sections of the FT are a circuit around Lake Okeechobee and linear routes through the national forests. The Florida Trail Association either maintains or assists in maintaining the FT and many other trails for a total of nearly 1,000 miles.

The state has five major linear rails-to-trails. The two longest, each 47 miles, are Pinellas Trail, a route from St. Petersburg north to Tarpon Springs, and Withlacoochee State Trail, a route from Tribly north to Citrus Springs. General Van Fleet State Trail opened in 1992 and is 27.5 miles from Polk City north to Mabel. Gainesville–Hawthorne State Trail is 18.5 miles east-west, and Tallahassee–St. Marks Historic Railroad State Trail is 16 miles north-south. A sixth major trail of 21 miles is planned east of Mabel, near SR 50 toward Apopka.

Many beach trails are neither named nor marked, but I have described their locations in the chapters ahead. Also described are trails in preserves, botanical gardens, wildlife management areas, national wildlife refuges, and special or historic sites. Winter is the best time to hike and backpack in Florida; the climate and temperature then is ideal and the mosquitoes and biting flies are least aggressive or have disappeared. Access and addresses to the trails are given in each adventure. If you are a beginner, a couple of basic books may be of assistance: *The Complete Walker III*, by Colin Fletcher, and *Backpacking — One Step at a Time*, by Harvey Manning. For a guidebook about the major state trails, consult *A Hiking Guide to the Trails of Florida*, by Elizabeth Carter. Information on state trails is available from the Trails Coordinator, Division of Recreation and Parks (3900 Commonwealth Blvd., Tallahassee, FL 32303, [904] 487-4784).

### Birding

Florida is a state with a diverse birdscape that changes constantly. In parks, preserves, forests, and sanctuaries there are brilliant displays of migrant birds, some native and some off course, arriving in September and October and leaving in April and May. Some birders say if you can only come in one month, mid-May is best. Of the 450 species of birds, about one fourth are seashore and wading birds. Some will be listed in the chapters ahead. Birding is best in the early morning. Go quietly and slowly, even being sedentary, and take your binoculars, your birdbook, and some notepaper. Contact the Florida Audubon Society (Drawer 7, Maitland, FL 32751, [305] 647-2615) for a list of the forty-five or more state Audubon chapters, which can assist you with information about locations, birdbooks, and bird-watches.

### Bicycling

With nearly 2,400 miles of bicycle trails, you can see Florida on easy riding routes through historic cities and towns, along beaches, by pastoral farms, and on backcountry roads. Some cities and towns have bicycle trails that parallel streets, and other routes follow old railroad grades. In descriptions ahead, I give distances, beginning points, and general directions if the bicycle trails pass through or near other adventure routes. The best pedaling season is between Labor Day and Thanksgiving, a period with fewer tourists.

Florida's Department of Transportation has mapped seven routes, three of which connect with each other, which range from 90 miles to 300 miles each. They are Route A: Sugar Beaches (90-mile loop from Pensacola); Route B: Canopy Roads (100-mile loop from Tallahassee); Route D: Crystal Springs (100-mile loop from Gainesville); Route E: Healing Waters (300-mile loop, including Gainesville, Saint Augustine, Daytona Beach, De Land, and De Leon Springs); Route F: Lakes-N-Hills (100-mile loop in northcentral Florida that includes horse farms and orange groves); Route G: Withlacoochee Meander (120-mile loop from Crystal River to Brooksville); and Route H: Land-O-Lakes (155-mile loop from Kissimmee to Lake Wales). The maps describe points of interest, roadway conditions, and service locations and include regulations and safety tips. For a Touring Guide, contact the State Bicycle Program, Florida Department of Transportation (605 Suwannee Street, MS 19, Tallahassee, FL 32399, [904] 488-4640). The guide will include an order form with a price list. Request a directory of the state's bicycle clubs.

You may wish to seek faster map delivery from the American Youth Hostels (Florida AYH, P.O. Box 533097, Orlando, FL 32853, [407] 649-8761). This nonprofit organization has gleaned considerable information about bicycling. The Florida AYH also has other trail maps for the state, particularly in the southwest and southeast Florida, areas yet to be covered by the Department of Transportation map routes. For a one-week guided bicycle trip, choose the Florida Bicycle Safari, usually in November. It covers about 400 miles from coast to coast, is planned with great care, and ensures the best facilities for camping (or motels at discount rates). It is sponsored by WMFE-TV/FM 90.7 in Orlando (11510 East Colonial Drive, Orlando, FL 32817, [407] 273-2300). A guidebook that lists bike shops, bike clubs, and places to stay is *The Florida Bicycle Book,* by Native American Press. For general information on products and services, see *Bicycling* magazine (33 East Minor Street, Emmaus, PA 18098, [215] 967-5171).

Gaining in popularity are all-terrain bikes (ATBs), which are more ruggedly constructed than coaster and racing bikes. The ATBs (also called trail bikes, mountain bikes, or city bikes) have multiple-ratio gears and are better suited for sandy, rough roads. Because ATBs have heavy-duty tires that can cut deeply into soft earth, they should not be used on sensitive hiking trails. Cyclists will notice signs that prohibit the use of ATBs on hiking and equestrian trails in some parks, gardens, and at historic sites.

### Horseback Riding

Horseback riding is one of the more exciting ways to explore the state and there are ample opportunities for the rider in most of the regions of Florida.

Equestrians have access to about 450 miles of designated horse trails on public property, 106 of which are in the Withlacoochee State Forest in central Florida. Other major trails are in the Blackwater State Forest, Ocala and Apalachicola national forests, and Big Cypress National Preserve. In a class all by itself, the Florida Cracker Trail has a 150-mile ride in late April from Bradenton to Fort Pierce. This extraordinary trail will take you over country roads, farms, forest, and ranches from the Gulf of Mexico to the Atlantic Ocean. It crosses four of the most scenic rivers in the state (the Manatee, Myakka, Peace, and Kissimmee) and skirts the small towns of Zolfo Springs and Lorida. See Chapter 5 for more details. Among the state parks containing trails are O'Leno, Paynes Prairie, Wekiwa Springs, Myakka River, and Jonathan Dickinson. Shorter trails are in nearly a dozen state and county parks, and many backcountry roads go through public wildlife management areas, private ranches, and horse farms. In 1982 the Affiliated Horseman's Organizations of Florida (AHOOF) was organized, and the next year the legislature passed a horse safety bill that gave riders a measure of protection on roadways. For information on equine riding, campsites, ranches, trail maps, liveries, and supplies, contact AHOOF (P.O. Box 160145, Snapper Creek Branch, Miami, FL 33116, [305] 596-3998). Wherever you take your horse, be sure to have proof of a negative Coggins test for equine infectious anemia. The Florida Department of Agriculture, Division of Animal Industry, requires a negative test within 12 months.

## Boating

The art and skill of Florida canoeing is as old as its Indian culture. From huge cypress the Native Americans carved canoes that were used not only for inland rivers and coastal areas but for exploring throughout Florida Bay and the Keys. The Florida Department of Natural Resources promotes this outdoor sport today with a Florida Canoe Trail System that currently includes thirty-six designated rivers or sections of rivers for 1,300 miles. (Some of these and other canoe trails are described ahead in the adventures.) State designation of a river does not always confine its use to canoes or sailboats; since these are public waters, motorboats, jet-skis, and other craft may also be used. In most cases, banks and shorelines are private property except at access points, which means that canoeists must avoid trespass. The state requires a life jacket or other flotation gear for each occupant and has exempted from registration and titling canoes that are not motor powered and that are less than 16 feet in length. The state also distributes a map and description for each canoe trail, a *Canoe Liveries and Outfitters Directory,* and *Canoe Information Resources Guide* (canoe regulations and safety tips), and a listing of organizations that offer canoeing activities. For copies, contact the Division of Recreation and Parks (3900 Commonwealth Boulevard, Tallahassee, FL 32399, [904] 487-4784). In addition, there is canoe information from the Florida Association of Canoe Liveries and Outfitters (FACLO): P.O. Box 1764, Arcadia, FL 33821, (813) 494-1215. A county map is useful. It shows all road access points to the river, population areas, and the natural areas such as tributaries, swamps, and lakes. In some remote areas, a topographic map would be helpful. (See *Maps and Guidebooks,* this Chapter.)

Motorboating requires safety gear and state registration of your boat. If your boat is registered in another state, its certificate is valid in Florida for 90 days. Beyond that period you must register your vessel in the county where you reside. If you purchase a motor-powered vessel in Florida, or need information on boating regulations and safety, contact the

Florida Marine Patrol, (904) 487-3671, or the Bureau of Vessel
Titling and Registration (3900 Commonwealth Boulevard,
Tallahassee, FL 32399, [904] 488-1195). There are speed limits
in specific locations and sometimes only an electric motor
may be used. Boaters who need navigational charts (particu-
larly for the Intracoastal Waterway) may purchase them at
local marine supply stores, or order from Division C44,
Nautical Ocean Survey (Riverdale, MD 20840, [301] 436-6990).
Sailing and waterskiing are popular sports on many of the
lakes and bays year-round. Check at local marinas about
restricted areas. Suggested guidebooks are *A Canoeing and
Kayaking Guide to the Streams of Florida: North Central
Peninsula and Panhandle* (Vol. I), by Elizabeth Carter and
John Pearce, and *Central and South Peninsula* (Vol. II), by
Lou Glaros and Doug Sphar (Menasha Ridge Press, Birming-
ham, Alabama). For Florida's annual tide tables, fishing
regulations, boat licenses, organized camping, and diving
information, consult the *Florida Outdoor Guide* published by
*The Miami Herald Tribune*, (305) 376-2617.

### Fishing

The legendary "bass capital of the world," as some of the
state's citizens call their favorite local lakes and rivers, Florida
is an angler's paradise for fresh- and saltwater fishing. Among
the most popular freshwater fish are the largemouth bass,
sunshine bass, striped bass, bluegill, black crappie, sunfish,
and catfish. (See *Wildlife*, Chapter 1, for a more detailed listing
of Florida fishes.) Prominent localities that include one or
more of the above fish are Hurricane Lake, Juniper Lake, Lake
Talquin, Lake Jackson, and the Apalachicola River in the
Panhandle; and in the north, Suwannee, Santa Fe, and
Oklawaha rivers, Newnans Lake, Orange Lake, Lake Lochloosa,
and Lake George. Central locations are Tohopekaliga Lake,
Winter Haven Chain of Lakes, Lake Pierce, Lake Kissimmee,
Blue Cypress Lake, Reedy Lake, and Lake Istokpoga. In the
south are Lake Okeechobee (famed for speckled perch), Lake
Osborne, Lake Trafford, and the upper Everglades. Saltwater

*Suwannee River.* PHOTO BY Florida Dept. of Commerce.

fishing seasons are summer and fall in the upper half of the state and year-round elsewhere. The state has numerous saltwater fishing tournaments. Crabbing and shellfishing are also popular. For information on saltwater fishing contact the Department of Environmental Protection, Office of Fisheries Management (Mail Station 240), 3900 Commonwealth Blvd., Tallahassee, FL 32399, (904) 488-7326. Books on fishing are available from Great Outdoors Publishing Company (4747 28th Street, N, Saint Petersburg, FL 33714, [813] 525-6609). The *Florida Fish Finder* magazine (1233 W. Jackson Street, Orlando, FL 32805, [407] 425-0045) is published monthly. For free literature on fishing locations, licenses, laws, and the five regional offices, contact the Florida Game and Fresh Water Fish Commission (620 South Meridian Street, Tallahassee, FL 32399, [904] 488-1960). Also available from the commission is information about the public Wildlife Management Areas for hunting game animals in more than sixty wildlife areas, and *Florida Wildlife,* a bimonthly magazine of high-quality articles and photography.

### Snorkeling, Scuba Diving, and Surfing

The popularity of snorkeling and scuba diving (skin diving) in Florida has increased greatly in the past few years. Thousands are receiving diver training by professional instructors, diving clubs are multiplying, and commercial diving stations, stores, and rental equipment shops and new diving sites are being established. An adventurous trip to Florida is not complete without a view of its underwater world. It is a magnificent world of multicolored millions of marine animals and plants. In the clear warm water of the Atlantic and Gulf you will see schools of grunt, spadefish, porgy, squid, sea fans, sea whips, sea urchins, serpulid plume worms, gorgania, sponges, jellyfish, moray eels, and, in the more tropical waters, the beautiful parrot fish, angelfish, and butterfly fish. In addition, there are varied coral formations, reefs, fossils, treasure sites, and shipwrecks to explore. For diving activities, there are shelling, spearfishing, and lobstering (the latter two governed by state laws).

Freshwater diving is prominent at the major springs in the central and northern parts of the state. Water temperature and water currents remain stable, and night diving is safer there than in salt water, where ocean sharks and Portugese man-of-war are difficult to see. The springs, however, have multiple channels to caverns, a challenging environment that poses a hazardous risk to the diver. If you are a beginning snorkeler, train yourself with a guidebook and equipment. But scuba diving is different. Some of the equipment is the same as in snorkeling, but scuba involves breathing through a regulator tank of pure compressed air. Training at a YMCA or YWCA, resort hotel, or college that offers a certified course (which may require as many as 35 hours of time) is necessary. Even after you are certified, you may have to take advanced courses to qualify for exploring specific or dangerous sites or caves. For information on maps of specific sites (showing shipwrecks and treasure sites), purchase *Diver's Guide to Florida*, by Jim Stachowicz. Another book on exploring underwater is the *Sierra Club Guide to Scuba and Snorkeling*, by John L.

Culliney and Edward Crockett. For the most extensive information on equipment and supplies, consult the *Divers Supply News* (5208 Mercer University Drive, Macon, GA 31210, [912] 474-6790). Divers Supply stores are located in Jacksonville, West Palm Beach, and Gainesville in Florida, and in Savannah/Pooler and Macon in Georgia. For information on diving contact the Florida Association of Dive Operations (335 Beard St., Tallahassee, FL 32303 [904] 222-6000).

The high-energy seashores recommended for surfing are North Jetty and Pier (Jacksonville Beach), Mantanzas Inlet (Saint Augustine), Ponce de Leon Inlet (New Smyrna Beach), Playalinda Beach, Cocoa Beach, Indialantic (Melbourne), Sebastian Inlet, Stuart, and Jupiter Inlet on the Atlantic. On the Gulf Coast are Siesta (Sarasota), Lido and Longboat Keys, Saint Andrews State Recreation Area, Panama City Beach, Fort Walton Beach, and Gulf Beach (Pensacola). Shorter and broader boards are better suited for Florida, where the currents have less energy than in California. For more information, contact the Division of Tourism, (904) 487-1462.

### Guided Adventures

Commercial outfitters offer a wide range of guided adventure tours that last from 2 days to 2 weeks for a variety of age groups. Examples are canoeing trips into the Everglades and Okefenokee Swamp, sea sailing and sea kayaking, parasailing, deep-sea diving, long-distance cycling, island exploring, and houseboating. For information about some of these activities, contact Southeast Wilderness (711 Sandtown Road, Savannah, GA 31410, [912] 897-5108). Other canoeing tours are provided by Suwannee Country Tours (P.O. Box 247A, White Springs, FL 32096, [904] 397-2347), and Florida Outback Safaris (6446 SW 42nd St., Davie, FL 33314, [305] 792-7393 or [800] 423-9944). For island exploring, contact Tortugas Rowing Expeditions (Box 902, Summerland Key, FL 33042, [305] 872-3536). For a coast-to-coast Bicycle Safari in central Florida, contact WMFE-TV/FM Public Broadcasting (11510

Colonial Drive, Orlando, FL 32817, [407] 273-2300). For information on houseboating, saltwater laws, and marinas on the Intracoastal Waterway, contact the U.S. Army Corps of Engineers (P.O. Box 4970, Jacksonville, FL 32201) or the Florida Inland Navigation District (2725 Avenue East, Riviera Beach, FL 33404, [305] 848-1217). To help you catch the freshwater fish that got away, there are many guides: two are Slim's Fish Camp (P.O. Box 250, Belle Glade, FL 33430, [305] 996-8750/3844) and Thurmonds (P.O. Box 309, Orange Springs, FL 32682, [904] 546-2286). Diving to ancient shipwreck sites is provided by Promethean Adventures Charters (1221 Duval Street, Key West, FL 33040, [305] 294-2772, or [800] 323-DIVE). Adventures for parasailing and windsurfing safaris are offered by Sunset Water Sports (Smathers Beach, Key West, FL 33040, [305] 296-2554). Senior citizens who want information about tours and discounts may contact American Association of Retired Persons (601 E St. NW, Washington, DC 22049, [202] 434-2277). For families with children, contact Travel With Your Children (45 W. 18th St., New York, NY 10011, [212] 206-0688). For singles without companions contact Travel Companion (P.O. Box P-833, Amityville, NY 11701, [516] 454-0880). For other information on fully escorted or independent package tours, consult your local travel agent.

For those with physical limitations, but who wish to experience the outdoors, contact the Advocacy Center for Persons with Disabilities (2661 Executive Center Circle, W. Tallahassee, FL 32301, [800] 342-0823).

At the end of each adventure description is a listing of *Services and Amenities* under Information. Coverage may include addresses and telephone numbers for bed and breakfast homes, commercial campgrounds, motels, restaurants, ferry schedules, canoeing and boating guides, equestrian liveries, diving outfitters, sports rental services, fishing guides, sailing guides, bicycle centers and services, supply and equipment services, and much more. Because these services may change addresses or telephone numbers, the author would appreciate receiving corrected information.

# 3

## North Region

North Florida, once the home of the peaceful Timucuan Indians, is promoted as Florida's "First Coast," its "Crown," and its birthplace. Here the Spanish founded the nation's oldest city, Saint Augustine, in 1565. Historically supporting Florida's corona is the city of Jacksonville (founded in 1822), considered the "undisputed vacation capital of America" in the 1880s when it served as the gateway for northern travelers to health spas at warm springs, steamboat cruises on the Saint Johns River, hunting and fishing at sports resorts, and hotels at wide, sunny beaches. During this period in the late nineteenth century Standard Oil tycoon Henry M. Flagler spent his second honeymoon on a steamboat trip up the Saint Johns River and on a pioneer railroad to Saint Augustine. He was so emotionally inspired by Florida's potential for development that he spent the remainder of his life financing a coastal railroad and resort hotel chain from Jacksonville to Key West.

Jacksonville, the state's largest city in both population and acreage, continues to be a gateway and serves as a shipping, banking, and insurance center where skyscrapers are reflected in the Saint Johns River. With universities, art galleries, museums, and 200 parks, it offers many options to travelers who wish to stop over before adventuring into the more natural Florida. The Museum of Science and History exhibits displays of natural and physical sciences, wildlife, the archeology of Florida's Indians, and the state's pioneer life. A city of business and industry, Jacksonville has been described in brochures as the "working son in the Florida family of playboys." Other cities in north Florida are Gainesville (1830), home to the University of Florida (1853) and the Florida State Museum; Ocala (1827) in the central highlands of famous horse farms; and Daytona Beach (1870), one of the state's oldest resorts, internationally famous for its 23 miles of beach speedway and its year-round tourist communities.

Highlighting north Florida's natural history are the state's two largest rivers; a segment of the Okefenokee Swamp in Baker County; two national forests; more than thirty state parks, forests, and historic sites; and the largest concentration of springs in the state. The Saint Johns River, which begins in central Florida, flows north for 273 miles, and the Suwannee River, immortalized by songwriter Stephen Foster, flows south 177 miles (plus another 58 miles in Georgia) to the Gulf of Mexico. Both rivers are popular for fishing and water sports. A third river, the fourth longest in the state at 127 miles, is the Saint Marys, which forms a state boundary north of Jacksonville and drains from the Okefenokee Swamp. The Florida Trail winds 150 miles through the Ocala and Osceola national forests, and 100 miles of equestrian trails traverse the Ocala.

As you explore this section of the state you will find pristine coastal environments and hardwood hammocks, clean lakes and creeks, clear lagoons, remote forests, dry scrublands, bottomwoods and wetlands, salt marshes, estuaries, and islands. En route are old forts like Clinch, Carolina, and Matanzas; historic homes in Fernandina Beach, Saint Augustine, and Micanopy; ghost towns like O'Leno; preserved plantations like Kingsley; beaches like Amelia and Anastasia; springs like Silver in Marion County, Holton in Hamilton, and Ichetucknee in Suwannee; prairies like Paynes; and deep sinks like the Devil's Millhopper. Through the middle of all this is the De Soto Trail, now a string of highway routes with roadside markers to describe where de Soto and his army marched on an ill-fated attempt to find advanced Indian civilizations and riches.

A fit beginning to your adventures in the Sunshine State is at Florida's Crown, at the northeasternmost tip of Fernandina Beach. Follow the Buccaneer Trail, an oceanside highway that touches the soil on which French and Spanish explorers first walked in Florida.

## THE BUCCANEER TRAIL

The Buccaneer Trail is a 125-mile seashore auto route on state road A1A from Fernandina Beach to Daytona Beach. Treasure hunters once exploited each other and the native Timucuan Indians along this former perilous coastline, an area of pillage and ransom for buccaneers like Sir Francis Drake (1586), Edward Teach, alias Blackbeard (the early 1700s), and Jean Lafitte and Luis Aury (the early 1800s). Today as you drive by peaceful islands, inlets, forts, and ferries, you would hardly suspect the turbulence of those early days. But a short stay on Amelia Island, with its 4 centuries of history, or at Saint Augustine, the nation's oldest permanent settlement, will quickly transport you to the past. You will also see large preserves of beaches at the silver blue Atlantic, aquatic preserves, coastal wildlife sanctuaries, salt marshes, the state's oldest live oak forest, and nine state parks. (The trail is described, as are all adventure routes in this book, in order of the counties listed under *Information*.)

*What to See and Do:* Adventure options are camping near the sea; hiking coastal hammocks and the seashore; canoeing on estuaries and rivers; scuba diving and surfing in the ocean; windsurfing and sailing in the lagoons; fishing; bicycling; horseback riding; and birding.

*Where to Begin:* Begin at Fort Clinch State Park at Fernandina Beach. Access from I-95, Exit 129 north of Jacksonville, is east on SR A1A. (Highway A1A is Florida's longest state road; it follows the east coast for 328.6 miles.)

*About the Adventures:* The 1,086-acre Fort Clinch State Park is at the northeasternmost corner of Amelia Island, where Spanish moss hangs thickly from gnarled live oaks and cabbage palms and red cedars grow tall in search of sunlight. The island has had a rousing history under eight flags, the first French when Jean Ribault arrived in May 1562 and named it

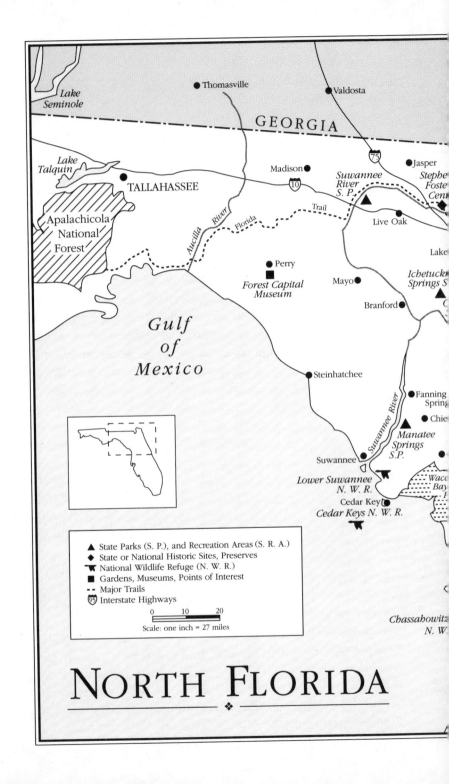

Lake
Seminole

● Thomasville

● Valdosta

GEORGIA

Lake
Talquin

🛣️75

Madison ●

Suwannee
River
S. P. ▲

● Jasper

Stephe
Foste
Cen

TALLAHASSEE

🛣️10

Trail

Live Oak

Apalachicola
National
Forest

Aucilla  River

Florida

Lake

● Perry

Ichetuckn
Springs S

Forest Capital
Museum

Mayo ●

▲

Branford ●

Gulf
of
Mexico

● Steinhatchee

Suwannee River

● Fanning
Spring
● Chie

▲
Manatee
Springs
S.P.

Suwannee ⌐

Lower Suwannee
N. W. R.

●

Waco
Bay

Cedar Key ●

Cedar Keys N. W. R.

🦅

▲ State Parks (S. P.), and Recreation Areas (S. R. A.)
◆ State or National Historic Sites, Preserves
🦅 National Wildlife Refuge (N. W. R.)
■ Gardens, Museums, Points of Interest
-- Major Trails
🛣️ Interstate Highways

0    10    20

Scale: one inch = 27 miles

Chassahowitz
N. W.

# NORTH FLORIDA

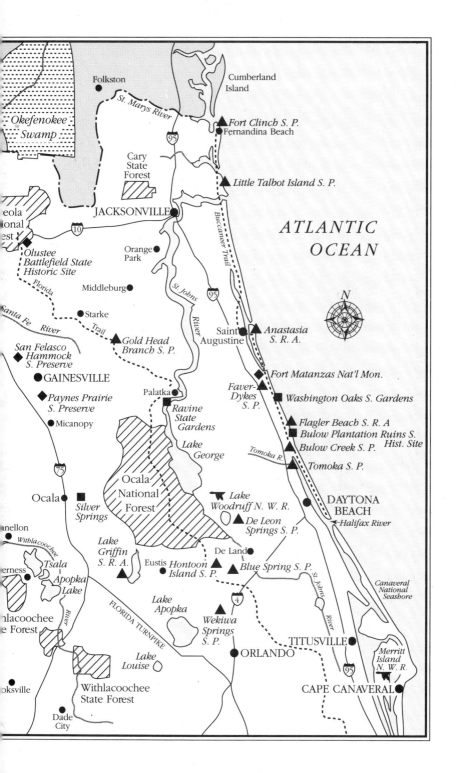

the  Isle of Mai. The Spanish captured it 3 years later, and the English acquired it in 1735, later naming it in honor of Princess Amelia, sister of George II of England. The island's oldest town is Fernandina Beach , settled in 1686 and named for King Ferdinand VII of Spain in 1811. Fort Clinch, the park's major attraction, was constructed in 1847. Later it was used as a Civil War outpost, from which the Confederates withdrew in 1862. Reactivated briefly in 1898 during the Spanish American War, the pentagonal brick fort with corner bastions has been preserved and is open for exploration.

The park has two full-service campgrounds, one behind a large foredune near the long fishing pier and the other more secluded in a coastal hammock by the Amelia River. The park accepts advance campground reservations. Other facilities are beaches, bathhouses, picnic areas, a youth camp, hiking trails, and a boat ramp to the Intracoastal Waterway. If you fish, expect to catch speckled trout, flounder, pompano, and drum. To see coastal wildlife, take the park's short Willow Pond Nature Trail and Magnolia Loop Trail on the west side of the entrance road to the fort. For a longer day hike, ask the park ranger for a map of the 10-mile Fort Clinch Historic Trail, a trail often used by Boy Scouts for hiking badge credit. The trail runs partly in the park but mainly outside it, through Old Fernandina and the downtown historic district of Fernandina Beach. Begin the hike at the Youth Camp in the park, cross Egans Creek bridge at 0.6 mile to turn south on 14th Street. Pass a historic marker at Estrada Street. At 1.7 miles is McCluse's Hill, the site of the Battle of Amelia fought by the Republic of Florida and Spain in 1817. Pass the entrance of the expansive Container Corporation of America at 2.3 miles and reach Bartram Trail historical marker at 3.5 miles near the Amelia River. Continue on the trail through Fernandina Beach's historic district of churches, homes, shops, and restaurants to where it turns into Atlantic Boulevard, east. Pass the entrance road to the park at 5.7 miles and continue east to the beach. The trail then turns north for a return to the park. Re-enter the park at 7.2 miles and at the fishing pier turn west at the parking lot. Follow an exit road to cross the main park road to return to the Youth Camp. (If you wish, you can hike another 2 miles on the beach to the fort and the interpretive center, where a return is made on the main park road to the Youth Camp road.)

While downtown on the trail (or, if you prefer, on a 2-hour guided tour of the fifty-block historic district), notice the port town's restored nineteenth-century Victorian buildings, featuring gables, turrets, and Tiffany windows. Places you might wish to explore are the Florida Museum of Transportation and History; the Amelia Island Museum of History; the Florida Marina Welcome Center; and the scenic shrimp fleet marina, known as the birthplace of modern shrimping. In early May, the town hosts the Isle of Eight Flags Shrimp Festival with food, folk music, mock pirates, and fishermen who welcome you aboard to examine their crafts.

After leaving the Fort Clinch State Park area, drive 13 miles south on A1A to Amelia Island Beach, the island's southern tip. The beach is wide, with sections that are remote, uncrowded, and excellent for horseback riding, hiking, surfing, and scuba diving. (See *Information* for liveries and outfitters.) Saltwater anglers line the causeway, as they frequently line the coast from Nassau Sound to Big Talbot Island. From here, another 7 miles takes you to Little Talbot Island State Park, an undeveloped hammock preserve of 2,500 acres. This park, like Fort Clinch, accepts advance campground reservations.

A 4-mile Island Hiking Trail leads you into three distinct stages of plant succession. (Inquire at the gate entrance for a required hiking permit.) The forest zone has huge live oak, magnolia, and sabal palm; the scrub zone has saw palmetto, myrtle, yaupon, and yucca; and the pioneer zone has mainly dune builders such as railroad vine, sea oats, and panic grass. Among the outdoor activities are camping, swimming, and surfing.

Drive along the Fort George River causeway to Fort George Island, where a side trip east leads to Huguenot Memorial Park, which is frequently crowded but has free beach camping without amenities. (Near here, at the mouth of the Saint Johns River, Frenchman Jean Ribault held the first Protestant worship service in America in 1562.) Another side trip from A1A is north to the Kingsley Plantation, Florida's oldest, on Spanish-moss-draped Fort George Road. After leaving the plantation, cross the Saint Johns River on a fifty-two-car ferry. Both the *Buccaneer* and the *Bluebeard* run to the fishing village of Mayport every half hour from 6 A.M. to 10:30 P.M.

In charming Mayport, picturesque Ocean Street has seafood restaurants, shops, and a shrimp fleet that returns late afternoons. On Wanderwood Road, at the south end of the U.S. Naval Air Station (which has weekend tours), is the large Kathryn Hannah Park, a recreation area with full-service camping, supplies, and bicycle, surf, and boat rentals. Miles of foot trails lead through the park's coastal forest.

The next 15 miles will take you through a beach area that is heavily populated, particularly around Jacksonville Beach. Along the way are three busy routes into Jacksonville: SR 10, SR 212/US 90, and SR 202. At the first traffic artery, SR 10 (Atlantic Boulevard), detour from A1A west to Fort Caroline National Memorial. After driving 3 miles from A1A, turn right (north) on Girvin and Mount Pleasant roads to the visitor center. A museum near the Saint Johns River depicts sixteenth-century tools, pikes, harquebuses and other armaments, and details the fort's tragic history of French and Spanish settlements, massacres, and resettlements, that began in 1564. There is a 1.2-mile roundtrip Nature Trail, which includes the short Old French Trail, to the fort at St. Johns River.

One mile southeast on Mt. Pleasant Road from the memorial park is Theodore Roosevelt Area of the Timucuan Ecological and Historic Preserve. It has three connecting trails–Willie Browne Trail, Two Pond Trail, and Bluff Trail–for a total of 2.5 miles. In 1969, Henry Browne III, a former owner, donated 342 acres to the Nature Conservancy for perpetual protection. His gravesite and old homesite are beside the main trail. In a mature maritime forest of oaks, palmetto, pines, ferns, and beauty bush, the trails lead to observation areas of marshes near Colorina Creek. A trail map is available at the preserve office.

At Mickler Landing, south of Ponte Vedra Beach, the highway follows the shoreline for 18 beautiful miles to Vilano Beach. After you cross Tolomato River Bridge, you will be in Saint Augustine, the oldest permanent European settlement in the nation. Some writers consider this city the Spanish equivalent of the English Williamsburg. At the junction of SR 5A, turn left (south) on San Marco Avenue and go to the Visitor Information Center between Castillo and Orange streets. From here you can visit historic houses and museums (particularly the Alcazar, a former 330-room luxury hotel constructed by railroad magnate Henry M. Flagler in 1888); festivals and drama; and fishing tournaments. If you would prefer a bed-and-breakfast hotel in Saint Augustine, try historic Kenwood Inn. (See *Information*.) At the highway junction of A1A and SR 214, the 300-mile Healing Waters Trail (Route E) for bicyclists passes through Saint Augustine on its way west to Gainesville on SR 214, and follows south on A1A to Ormond Beach before turning right (west) on SR 40 to complete its loop in Gainesville. (See the *Ocala National Forest* and *Ocean Pond to Paynes Prairie* adventures, this Chapter.)

In 1565 the Spanish religious zealot Pedro Menéndez de Avilés brought a colony ashore and named the outpost Saint Augustine because he arrived on the Spanish festival day of San Augustín. (Frenchman Ribault had earlier named the area River of Dolphins.) Remarkably, the outpost survived all military attacks, sieges, pillages, and burnings. Nine wooden forts perished, but the massive, symmetrical Castillo de San Marcos, built between 1672 and 1695, saved the colonists. The king of Spain invested what now amounts to $30 million in a fort of coquina stone, which protected the Spaniards against such buccaneers as Sir Francis Drake. In 1924 it became a national monument, the most visited historic site in all of Florida.

From the Castillo, the Buccaneer Trail crosses the Matanzas

*Castillo de San Marcos, Saint Augustine.* PHOTO BY Florida
Dept. of Commerce.

River bridge to Anastasia Island, where you can camp at the
Anastasia State Recreation Area. Anastasia, a wilderness host
to naturalists John and William Bartram in the eighteenth
century, has many appealing natural features. You can
explore 4 miles of beach and a haunting nature trail that takes
you among live oak, red bay, and sea grape. Within the park's
1,035 acres is the state's northernmost black mangrove swamp
and 35 other species of trees, including devilwood, shining
sumac, sand pine, and marlberry. Unique among its abundant
wildlife is the Anastasia beach mouse. Bird lovers can watch
160 species of shore, water, and roadside birds (best in the
wintertime), and lovers of windsurfing have a superb lagoon
in Salt Run. Quarried slabs from the island's ancient coquina
base were used to construct the Castillo de San Marcos.
Campground reservations can be made in advance.

Six miles south from the Anastasia Recreation Area park
you will arrive at Crescent Beach, from which you can take a
side trip on SR 206 (west) to US 1 and south 6 miles on US 1

to Faver-Dykes State Park. Remote and quiet, this biologically diverse campground retreat has hammocks and bayheads with wading birds, alligators, raccoons, and bobcats. Partly a former plantation, it now has pine and hardwood forests for camping and hiking. On Pellicer Creek you can canoe and fish west to US 1 or east through an aquatic preserve to the Intracoastal Waterway.

When you return to Anastasia Island and A1A, you are only 4 miles from Fort Matanzas National Monument. The 298-acre park is on the island's south tip at Matanzas Inlet; Rattlesnake Island, the site of the fort, is in the inlet. From the park's visitor center, a small park passenger ferry crosses to the island continuously each day except Tuesday. Originally, in 1569, the Spanish built the fort, a wooden watchtower with a thatched roof, to help them sight enemy ships. If a frigate was seen, a soldier could canoe north to warn the colony at Saint Augustine. Two hundred years later, in a war with the British, Spanish Governor Manuel de Montiano constructed a tower, which is still standing, of coquina stone quarried from Anastasia Island. On your return from the fort, you can follow an interpretive nature trail through red bay, sabal palm, red cedar, and scarlet gilia. Behind the dunes at the inlet, Menéndez slaughtered (*matanzas*) 245 French Huguenots, shipwrecked victims of a hurricane in 1565.

Across the inlet is the community of Summer Haven, a narrow thread of lagoons and dunes where fishing and crabbing are good, least terns are prominent, and sunsets and sunrises are incomparable. Another mile on the Buccaneer Trail brings you to Marineland, the first of its type in the world (1938). It has major aquatic displays of hundreds of fish, porpoises, sharks, seals, sea lions, moray eels, and dolphins (including the rare champagne). Adjoining the center are a hotel, a restaurant, and the University of Florida Graduate School of Marine Biology.

Your next stop is 2.5 miles south at Washington Oaks State Gardens. Different from any other park you have seen on A1A, this 390-acre park has an area called The Rocks with the world's largest coquina rock outcroppings sculpted by the sea. On the west side is the former nineteenth-century Belle Vista Plantation, now a formal horticultural center with roses, camellias, tropical gardens, and natural springs and pools. The plantation is also the site of one of Florida's first orange groves.

After another 14.5 miles along public beaches and picnic shelters by the sea you will arrive at Flagler Beach fishing pier and Flagler Beach State Recreation Area. The park is well known for its unique campground overlooking the Atlantic from the top dune level. On the west side of A1A, a manicured nature trail tunnels through dense live oak, saw palmetto, and yaupon to the Intracoastal Waterway. The park accepts advance campground reservations.

The Buccaneer Trail continues on A1A through highly urbanized Ormond Beach and Daytona Beach and ends at Ponce de Leon Inlet, but I recommend a detour to Tomoka State Park, where you can stay at the campground and take a day trip back to the beach. (This detour is also the route for the Healing Waters Trail for bicyclists.) To reach Tomoka, backtrack 3 miles from Flagler and turn left (west) on SR 100. Drive 3.2 miles to the Old Kings Road, turn left (south), and go 3.4 miles on CR 2001 to the entrance road of Bulow Plantation Ruins, a state historic site. After 0.8 mile on the entrance road you will notice the north terminus of the 5.8-mile Bulow Woods Trail on the right. Another 0.2 mile on the road takes you to a parking area near Bulow Creek and a road loop to the sugar mill ruins and interpretive center. The sugar mill was partially destroyed by Seminole Indians in late 1835, but it is still an outstanding open-air museum.

The ruins are on the north edge of Bulow Hammock where, in 1821, Maj. Charles W. Bulow of South Carolina acquired 4,675 acres of lush wilderness from Englishman James Russel. With slave labor Major Bulow cleared 2,200 acres for sugarcane and cotton, built a sugar mill, and developed Bulow Ville (the family "Big House") and a community with more than fifty buildings. Major Bulow died in 1826, leaving Florida's largest plantation to his sixteen-year-old son, John. While trustees managed the property, young John attended school in Paris for 5 years. In the year of his return he hosted John James Audubon on a 3-week exploration of Bulow Creek and Halifax River near the coast. Audubon later praised Bulow for his hospitality, but was less complimentary of the failure to snare waterfowl in the murky and mucky Halifax marshes. From the creek dock you can take a 13-mile canoe trip to the Halifax River, the route followed by John Bulow and Audubon.

During the early 1830s Bulow had a friendly relationship with the Seminole Indians and the plantation prospered. He so strongly opposed the U.S. government's efforts to force the Indians west of the Mississippi that he set up a 4-pound cannon to prevent Maj. Benjamin Putnam's state militia from searching the plantation for the Indians in 1835, the beginning year of the Second Seminole War. Major Putnam temporarily took Bulow prisoner, and when hostile Indians turned on the military and the settlers, the settlers fled with the major's troops north to Saint Augustine. By the end of the year the Seminoles had torched all the buildings on the plantation. The loss so discouraged Bulow that he went to Paris for solace, but he died 3 months later at the age of 26.

The Bulow Woods Trail connects the Bulow Plantation Ruins and Bulow Creek State Park. Maintained by the Florida Trail Association, the white-blazed trail crosses a few meandering streams and old plantation roads, passes marshes, and goes through stands of loblolly pine, magnolia, and live oak groves at least 200 years old. A short cut at 1.5 miles saves 1.5 miles on the route but bypasses Marsh Point, a major feature of the trail with splendid views of the Bulow Creek marshland. At 4.4 miles a blue-blazed spur trail leads 0.5 mile to an isolated campsite. During your quiet walk on the trail you may see deer, otters, armadillos, anoles, white ibis, and turkeys. With careful observation you can see large golden silk spiders and stick insects. Plants of particular interest are the floral clustered groundsel, the thorny Devil's walking stick, and the leafless, tiny bulbous whiskfern (*Psilotum nudum*). More ancient than a true fern, the short, creeping whiskfern is epiphytic and terrestrial; it grows at varied locations in the forest. Childhood exploring and subsequent hikes in the hammock during a 35-year period inspired naturalist David Raines Wallace to write *Bulow Hammock* in 1988. He stated that in finding things, such as the whiskfern, he found cultural and innate parts of himself. Perhaps on this trail you can experience the same pleasure Wallace did, or imagine what the plantation was like in 1831.

After you return to CR 2001 from the Bulow Plantation, turn left (south) to join and follow the scenic forest route of the Old Dixie Highway for about 8 miles to Bulow Creek State Park. This developing park, established in 1981, has the original forest, with the famous Faircloth Oak signed as being 2,000 years of age. (Botanists say it is more likely between 700 and 800 years old.) Other huge live oaks are also here, and a short nature trail takes you into the hardwood hammock. At the small coquina building is the south terminus of the Bulow Woods Trail from the Bulow Plantation.

Another 4.7 miles south is Tomoka State Park, which accepts advance camping reservations. On your way, stop at the Tomoka River to admire the habitat of waterfowl: ibis, herons, egrets, and wood storks. The park is on a peninsula, once the Indian village of Nocoroco, which the Spanish expedition of Alvaro Mexia saw in 1605. Remote and wild, the Tomoka basin has a boat ramp near the confluence of the Tomoko and Halifax rivers. Trails lead into a forest of pine and oak, part of which was once the indigo and rice plantation of wealthy English merchant Richard Oswald. Here you can rest and relax near fish-filled lagoons or take walks among little butterfly orchids, wild poinsettia, tread-softly, fernrose, and seaside verbena. Warblers and other songbirds cheer you in the day and owls call at night. Secluded in your quiet campsite, you will hardly believe you are less than 2 miles from densely populated Ormond Beach.

To see the end of the Buccaneer Trail, drive south on

North Beach Street from Tomoko State Park to SR 40, turn left to the beach, and rejoin A1A. In Ormond Beach is the Casements, a historical site of J. D. Rockefeller's former home and gardens (25 Riverside Drive) and the regal and nostalgic Ormond Hotel (15 East Granada, built in 1888). Daytona Beach is the world's most famous beach for swimming, sunning, sailing, surfing, bicycling, and fishing. Nearly 23 miles long and 500 feet wide in low-tide sections, the glistening sand beach is hard and fine. The Museum of Arts and Sciences at Tuscawilla Park Reserve offers glimpses of the area as it was in prehistoric times, and Indian artifacts are on display at the Halifax Historical Society Museum and at the Green Mound State Archaeological Site on A1A.

Ten miles south of the city you will arrive at the restored historic Ponce de Leon Inlet Lighthouse, built in 1883. A 175-foot climb on the spiral staircase will reward you· with magnificent views of the Atlantic and the inlet. While gazing out to sea, you can easily imagine a frigate or galleon with privateers or buccaneers sailing toward you.

### *Information*

Counties: Nassau, Duval, Saint Johns, Flagler, Volusia

Average Temperatures: January, 46°F (low), 67.6°F (high); August, 71.1°F (low), 88.8°F (high)

National Properties: Fort Caroline National Memorial, 12713 Fort Caroline Rd., Jacksonville, FL 32225, (904) 641-7155; Timucuan Ecological and Historic Preserve, 13165 Mt. Pleasant Rd., Jacksonville, FL 32225, (904) 221-5568; Castillo de San Marcos, 1 Castillo Dr. E., Saint Augustine, FL 32084, (904) 829-6506; Fort Matanzas National Monument, 1 Castillo Dr. E., Saint Augustine, FL 32084, (904) 471-0116

State Properties: Anastasia State Recreation Area, 5 Anastasia Park Dr., Saint Augustine, FL 32085, (904) 471-3033; Bulow Creek State Park, 3351 Old Dixie Hwy., Ormond Beach, FL 32074, (904) 667-3931; Bulow Plantation Ruins Historic Site, P.O. Box 655, Bunnell, FL 32010, (904) 439-2219; Faver-Dykes

State Park, Rte. 4, Box 213–J–1, Saint Augustine, FL 32086, (904) 794-0997; Flagler State Beach Recreation Area, 3100 South A1A, Flagler Beach, FL 32036, (904) 439-2474; Fort Clinch State Park, 2601 Atlantic Ave., Fernandina Beach, FL 32034, (904) 261-4212; Kingsley Plantation, P.O. Box 321, Fort George, FL 32226, (904) 251-3122; Little Talbot Island State Park, 12157 Heckscher Dr., Fort George, FL 32226, (904) 251-3231; Tomoka State Park, 2099 N. Beach St., Ormond Beach, FL 32074, (904) 677-3931; Washington Oaks State Gardens, Rte. 1, Box 128–A, Saint Augustine, FL 32086, (904) 445-3161

Other Historical Attractions: Amelia Island Museum of History, 233 S. Third St., Fernandina Beach, FL 32034, (904) 261-7378; Halifax Historical Society Museum, 252 S. Beach St., Daytona Beach, FL 32104, (904) 255-6976; Marineland of Florida, Rte. 1, Box 122, Saint Augustine, FL 32086, (904) 471-1111, or (800) 824-4218 in Florida, or (800) 874-0492 outside the state; Museum of Arts and Sciences, 1040 Museum Blvd., Daytona Beach, FL 32104, (904) 255-0285; Ponce de Leon Inlet Lighthouse, 4931 South Peninsula, Point Inlet, FL 32127, (904) 761-1821; Port Orange Sugar Mill Gardens, 950 Old Sugar Mill Rd., Port Orange, FL 32019, (904) 767-1735; The Casements, 25 Riverside Dr., Ormond Beach, FL 32074, (904) 673-4701

Chambers of Commerce: Amelia Island CC, P.O. Box 472, Fernandina Beach, FL 32034, (904) 261-3248; Daytona Beach Shores CC, 3048 S. Atlantic Ave., Daytona Beach, FL 32118, (904) 761-7163; Flagler County CC, Star Rte. 18–N, Bunnell, FL 32010, (904) 437-0106; Jacksonville CC, Three Independent Dr., Jacksonville, FL 32202, (904) 366-6600; Ormond Beach CC, Box 874, Ormond Beach, FL 32175, (904) 677-3454; Port Orange–South Daytona CC, 3431 Ridgewood Ave., Port Orange, FL 32119, (904) 761-1601; Saint Augustine–Saint Johns CC, 1 Ribera St., Saint Augustine, FL 32084, (904) 824-8142.

Services and Amenities: *Bed and Breakfast:* Bailey House, 28 Seventh St., Fernandina Beach, FL 32034, (904) 261-5390; Kenwood Inn, 38 Marine St., Saint Augustine, FL 32084, (904) 824-2116

*Bicycle Maps:* State Bicycle Program, (904) 488-4640; *Boat Rentals:* Club Nautico, 999 First Coast Hwy., Fernandina Beach, FL 32034, (904) 261-6998; *Horse Rentals and Stables:* Seahorse Stable, A1A South, Fernandina Beach, FL 32034, (904) 261-4878; *Scuba Diving:* Division of Tourism, 126 W. Van Buren St., Tallahassee, FL 32399, (904) 488-4952/487-1462; *Windsurfing:* Surf Station, 1002 Anastasia Blvd., Saint Augustine Beach, FL 32084, (904) 471-9463

## OCALA NATIONAL FOREST

Established in 1908, the 381,930-acre Ocala, between the Oklawaha and Saint Johns rivers, is the oldest national forest east of the Mississippi River. On Florida's central ridge of rolling sandhills and stands of sand pine and turkey scrub oak, the forest is known as scrub country, or "Big Scrub." Melrose naturalist-writer Al Burt described it as dry and delicate, a region struggling to remain "a desert outlaw." And part of Marjorie K. Rawlings' Pulitzer Prize winning novel *The Yearling* was filmed here. Other stands on the high ground are longleaf, slash, and loblolly pines, and in the flatlands grow red maple, cypress, and palmetto. Winding through the heart of the forest is the 67-mile Ocala National Recreation Trail (part of the Florida National Scenic Trail), which connects to warm lakes, springs, and campgrounds. The Ocala has a number of famous springs, the largest of which is Alexander Springs with a flow of 80 million gallons daily. Other major springs are Salt Springs and Juniper Springs, both with constant temperatures between 72 and 74 degrees Fahrenheit. Sixteen campgrounds, four wilderness areas, and eleven special-interest areas emphasize history, geology, archeology, and botany.

*What to See and Do:* Your adventure options are hiking and backpacking; camping in remote hammocks; fishing and boating in Lake George, the state's second largest lake; horseback riding on a 100-mile trail; backcountry bicycling; scuba diving, snorkeling, and swimming; and birding. Near the Ocala National Forest you can also visit natural gardens, floating islands, manatee habitat, historic towns, and a wildlife refuge.

*Where to Begin:* Two state roads intersect the forest: north-south SR 19 between Palatka and Eustis and east-west SR 40 between Daytona Beach and Ocala. State road 42 from De Land west to US 27/441 also connects with SR 19 on the south boundary of the forest.

*About the Adventures:* I have chosen to describe the north entrance of SR 19 from Palatka but will begin at Gold Head Branch State Park and include some side trips en route. If you approach from Jacksonville on I-295, take Exit 4 on SR 21 and drive south to the park, 16 miles south of Middleburg. After Middleburg the population thins, fire anthills are more frequent, and thick groves of turkey oak shine bronze red in December. A special natural feature of the 1,562-acre park, a deep, damp ravine in which a spring bubbles to form a stream, contrasts to the dry upper terrain. A graded trail descends to the branchhead among tall oaks, magnolia, and black tupelo. The park gets its name from the gold reported to have been mined here at the turn of the century. A longer trail ascends southeast to Glisson Mill, near the Sandhill and Turkey Oak campgrounds. Another natural feature across the road from the ravine is Sheeler Lake, round, pure, and blue. A bench beneath a live oak invites you to rest and listen to the yellow-throated warbler and white-eyed vireo, 2 of 125 species of park birds. Near the campgrounds by Lake Johnson are rental cottages, all named after trees. You may see deer, fox, or a raccoon or a squirrel at your back door, or catch bass, bream, or perch in the lake. Hikers may explore 30 miles of old backroads, including the Florida Trail and a section of historic tram road. The park is likely to be crowded in the summertime.

From the park, drive 6 miles south to Keystone Heights and take SR 100 east. After about 20 miles you will arrive at Rice Creek Sanctuary. Turn right to a remote property of the Georgia Pacific Corporation (5 miles west of US 17 junction in

Palatka), a day-use area with picnic tables. Cedar Swamp Trail and two other trails form a 3-mile loop on dikes of an eighteenth-century rice plantation, with boardwalks rising over the cypress swamps and streams of black water and with animal tracks indicating frequent use by wildlife. The trails adjoin the Florida Trail that enters and leaves the sanctuary on other private property.

In Palatka (an Indian name meaning "crossover") you can tour thirty-three blocks of two historic districts by the bass-filled Saint Johns River. Well known as a fishing center, the area hosts some fifty fishing camps and marinas. Within the city, off Moseley Avenue on Twigg Street, is the Ravine State Gardens. Here is another spring-fed deep ravine with nature trails. Thousands of azaleas and ornamental plants make a magnificent display of color in February and March, and coontie (also called arrowroot, from which the Indians made flour), bumelia, epiphytes, and hundreds of other plants are native. The gardens can also be viewed from a 2-mile one-way auto loop road.

Leave Palatka and drive south 20 miles on SR 19 to Salt Springs Recreation Area in the Ocala National Forest. From here you can organize and plan your stay in the forest. Open year-round, the campground has electric hookups and a nearby restaurant, grocery and gasoline store, and laundromat. Adventuring includes fishing (for bass, crappie, bream, and mullet), boating, and canoeing on the 4-mile Salt Spring Run to Lake George; and scuba diving and snorkeling in the springs. Flatboats and canoes are available for rent. A 3-mile spur trail connects to the Ocala Trail (described below). Ask campground staff for a multicolored forest map and descriptions of hiking trails and backcountry roads for bicycling. (The 300-mile loop Healing Waters Trail for bicyclists passes through here on SR 19 from the south and follows west on CR 316 on the north side of Lake Kerr.) The Lake George Ranger District office is 12 miles east of Silver Springs on SR 40.

If you wish to backpack on the Ocala Trail, drive north from Salt Springs on SR 19 for 8 miles to forest road 77 and turn

*Florida National Scenic Trail, Ocala National Forest.*
PHOTO BY Allen de Hart.

left to reach the north trailhead. (If you cross the Oklawaha River bridge you have gone too far.) Follow FR 77 to FR 88, turn right, and join the trail on the left at the Rodman Dam of Lake Oklawaha. On an easy, orange-blazed trail over slightly rolling hills of pine and southern hardwoods you will arrive at Lake Delancy, a primitive camping area, after 7.5 miles. At 11.8 miles you may find drinking water (if the hand pump is functioning), and at 13 miles, where you cross CR 316, a forest service facility should have drinking water. Treat all drinking water. When you reach SR 314 at 18.7 miles, go left for 4 miles east to Salt Springs Campground; along the highway are restaurants, small stores, and a motel. If you continue on the Ocala Trail you will soon cross FR 88, a paved road that leads south to SR 40, and enter a spectacular section of an open forest with tall longleaf pines, grassy rolling hills, and red-cockaded woodpeckers. Pass a junction with the blue-blazed spur trail to Salt Springs Campground at 22.6 miles, and later reach the northwest edge of beautiful Hopkins Prairie at 24 miles with its lakes and grasses, beds of sundews, and ducks, ibis, egrets, herons, and other wading birds. Owls call in the daytime from nearby wooded areas. At 28 miles you will arrive at a primitive camping area with a restroom and hand water pump. (Dirt FR 86 crosses the trail here to connect FR 88 west and SR 19 east.) When you cross FR 10 at 33 miles, you enter the Juniper Prairie Wilderness Area, in which you will remain until you reach Juniper Springs. You will see a number of fine places to camp, and cross Whiskey Creek at 35 miles. After another mile you may have to wade Whispering Creek. After passing through groves of sand pine, some recently clearcut, you will arrive at Juniper Springs Campground at 39.5 miles. Here are tent and trailer campsites, concessions, and hot showers.

Before continuing on your hike you may wish to stay an extra day or more at Juniper Springs to swim in the springs, hike the nature trails in a lush, semitropical forest, and rent a canoe for a 4-mile trip on Juniper Creek. Shuttle service is provided. Along the creek you will find dense palms, wildflowers, swamp growth, and, possibly, alligators. Your shuttle exit is near Sweetwater Springs on SR 19, 4 miles north of SR 40.

After Juniper Springs, continue on a white-sand footpath, boardwalks under palmetto, and sand under longleaf pine and around grassy prairies and dazzling, shallow ponds. At 47.5 miles, Farles Prairie has a campsite and drinking water, and at 49.5 miles is a camping area with drinking water and a short blue-blazed spur trail to Buck Lake. You will cross SR 19 at 52.2 miles and arrive at the south boundary of Billies Bay Wilderness Area after another 4 miles. When you cross SR 445, you will soon see a blue-blazed spur left to Alexander Springs Campground, which has concessions, hot showers, swimming, a nature trail, and a canoe trip. Year-round canoe rentals and shuttle service are available. The one-mile Timucuan Indian Trail near the springhead leads through a scenic forest of tall palms.

If you are canoeing on the 7-mile Alexander Springs Creek run, you will paddle through paths of water hyacinths on a slow-moving stream. A few tributaries—including Billies Bay Branch and Ninemile Creek—join the route from the west. Your take-out at the end of FR 552, a dirt road off SR 445, might be difficult in wet seasons. You may also canoe beyond that take-out into the wild and isolated Alexander Springs Wilderness Area. But be aware that you could easily be lost here without a forest or topographic map. Camping is allowed, though there are no designated sites. After about 2.5 miles, you will come to your last take-out at FR 540, from SR 42. Another 3 miles will take you to the Saint Johns River, with the remote Lake Woodruff Wildlife Refuge on the east side of the river, from which you must backtrack to take out. If you continue exploring downstream on the Saint Johns you will come to Stagger Mud Lake, Lake Dexter, and large Lake Woodruff (where camping is prohibited).

In the early 1990s construction began on Alexander Springs Wilderness Trail, approximately 12 miles long. In a rugged, remote, rarely seen section of the Ocala Forest, the blue-blazed trail parallels the Alexander Spring Creek for almost half the northwest route. Blazes and signs are not used in the wilderness section. The northwest terminus at SR 445 connects with the Ocala Trail, and the southeast terminus is at River Forest Campground by the Saint Johns River and the junction with SR 42/44. The trail passes lakes, wanders through cabbage palm, hardwood, and pine hammocks, and connects with FR 552, FR 540–2, FR 41, and other more primitive roads. Trail construction is a joint project of the U.S. Forest Service, the Florida Trail Association, the Halifax Audubon Society, civic clubs, and private businesses.

As you continue on the Ocala Trail you will cross a succession of dry ground and boardwalks that wind through oaks, gums, pines, cabbage palmettos, saw palmettos, and wildflowers and pass Paisley fire tower at 66 miles. Another mile will bring you to the end of your journey at Clearwater Campground by SR 42, 6 miles east of Altoona. Here you can swim, fish, hike a nature trail, and take a hot shower. From the Altoona crossroads with SR 19, it is about 7 miles south to the forest's Seminole Ranger District office.

The forest's longest canoe run, the 19.5-mile Oklawaha Canoe Trail on the Oklawaha River, is between Sharps Ferry and Eureka Dam along the forest's west boundary. (The Forest Service does not rent or provide shuttle service for this run.) This river runs about 60 miles from Lake Griffin north to the Saint Johns River, with the last few miles diverted as a part of the incomplete Cross-Florida Barge Canal. (Instead of putting in at Sharps Ferry, you could choose another put-in upstream about 10 miles at Moss Bluff lock and dam at the intersection of SR 314 and SR 464, 2 miles west of private Camp Oklawaha. Sections of this run have been dredged, and embankments sometimes prevent you from seeing the original woodlands.) Your first take-out is 3 miles past Sharps Ferry at SR 40, the site of a public park and boat launch at the southwest side of Delks Bluff bridge. A few yards before the bridge is the confluence of the light green Silver River, which originates 4 miles west from the famous Silver Springs in Ocala. From here the

Oklawaha River meanders through marsh, swamp, hardwood forests, and some embankments. Fishing for speckled perch, shellcracker, and catfish is excellent. After 10 miles you can take out at Gores Landing on the west side. Access is from SR 40 (2 miles east of Silver Springs) on SR 315 for 5.5 miles north to the first paved road to the right (east). The take-out at Eureka Dam is on SR 316 (between Fort McCroy on SR 315, west, and Salt Springs at SR 19, east). Although you could paddle farther downstream, the river becomes wider and less scenic as it flows to Lake Oklawaha.

Florida's longest national forest equestrian trail, in the southwest area of the forest, is made up of three loops—the 20-mile blue-blazed Baptist Lake Trail, the 40-mile red-blazed Flatwoods Trail, and the 40-mile white-blazed Prairie Trail—all leaving west from SR 19 at Altoona (4 miles north of Umatilla). The trails, old roads through the woods, offer excellent exposure to pinelands and hardwoods. The Forest Service does not provide stables, corrals, horse rentals, or guide service, but the Rocking Horse Ranch on SR 19, near the trailhead, provides short-term boarding, and Live Oak Ranch rents out horses. (See *Information.*)

Outside the southeast corner of the Ocala Forest, near De Land, are three state parks—De Leon Springs, Hontoon, and Blue Spring—and Lake Woodruff National Wildlife Refuge. After you cross the Saint Johns River on SR 40, drive to Barberville and then go 5 miles south to De Leon Springs on US 17. Major features at the springs are Old Methuselah, an enormous bald cypress on a nature trail of Florida elm, oaks, and gums, and the "Fountain of Youth" springs, which are a constant 76 degrees Fahrenheit, and have a daily 16-million-gallon surge. Swimming, canoeing, and scuba diving are popular. Adjoining the park on the south is the 18,500-acre Lake Woodruff National Wildlife Refuge, a preserve of rivers, marshes, timbered swamps, and uplands. Nonmotorized boating, fishing, and trail hiking are allowed, but not camping. Guided tours may be arranged by reservation (best from November through February). Continue 7 miles south on US

17 to historic De Land, the "Athens of Florida," and turn west on SR 44 (New York Avenue) toward Hontoon State Park. Turn left (south) on Old New York Avenue to River Ranch Road (only 2 miles east of Saint Johns River and Ocala National Forest). The 16,000-acre park is accessible only by boat; a ferry runs during the day and is free of cost. An excellent preserve where you may fish, tent camp, or stay in a rustic cabin, the island was once home to the Timucuan Indians, whose ceremonial mound you will see on a pristine forest nature trail.

From De Land drive south 5 miles on US 17/92 to Orange City and turn west for 2 miles on West French Avenue to Blue Spring State Park. On the east banks of the Saint Johns River, the clear, warm water teems with fish; from November through April your chances of seeing manatees are good. Scuba diving, snorkeling, fishing, and swimming are popular, and an overnight canoe-camping tour from Blue Spring to Hontoon can be arranged, possibly with a ranger as your guide. Boardwalk trails and a 4-mile hiking trail offer views of the spring, flatwoods, and sand pine scrub. Advanced reservations can be made for campground sites and family cabins.

For a trip outside the forest on the southwest boundary, drive west 8 miles on SR 42 from the Big Bass Lake Campground to a junction with SR 25 in Weirsdale. Drive south another 8 miles to Fruitland Park and turn east into Lake Griffin State Recreation Area. The 427-acre park has a campground and boat-ramp access for fishing and exploring the Dead River Marsh, where marsh peat forms floating grassy islands. You will see one of the state's largest live oaks on the nature trail. If you have time, drive west on SR 466–A, a few miles toward Wildwood to see some of Florida's most beautiful ranchland on rolling hills.

### *Information*

Counties: Clay, Putnam, Marion, Volusia, Lake
Average Temperatures: January, 46.8°F (low), 68.2°F (high); August, 72.8°F (low), 89.3°F (high)

National Properties: Ocala National Forest: Lake George Ranger District, Rte. 2, Box 701 (SR 40), Silver Springs, FL 32688, (904) 625-2520; Seminole Ranger District, 1551 Umatilla Rd. (SR 19), Eustis, FL 32726, (904) 357-3721; Lake Woodruff National Wildlife Refuge, P.O. Box 488, De Leon Springs, FL 32028, (904) 985-4673

State Properties: Blue Spring State Park, 2100 W. French Ave., Orange City, FL 32763, (904) 775-3663; De Leon Springs State Recreation Area, P.O. Box 1338, De Leon Springs, FL 32130, (904) 985-4212; Gold Head Branch State Park, 6239 State Rd. 21, Keystone Heights, FL 32656, (904) 473-4701; Hontoon Island State Park, 2309 River Ridge Rd., De Land, FL 32720, (904) 736-5309; Lake Griffin State Recreation Area, 103 Hwy. 441/27, Fruitland Park, FL 32731, (904) 787-7402

Chambers of Commerce: De Land Area CC, P.O. Box 629, De Land, FL 32721, (904) 734-4331; Greater Eustis Area CC, P.O. Box 1210, Eustis, FL 32727, (904) 357-3434; Ocala–Marion County CC, P.O. Box 1210, Ocala, FL 34478, (904) 629-8051; Putnam County CC, P.O. Box 550, Palatka, FL 32178, (904) 328-1503; Umatilla CC, P.O. Box 300, Umatilla, FL 32784, (904) 669-3511

Services and Amenities: *Horse Rentals:* Live Oak Ranch, Rte. 2, Box 147, Umatilla, FL 32784, (904) 669-3446; *Houseboat Rentals:* Go-Vacations, 2280 Hontoon Rd., De Land, FL 32722, (904) 736-9422

## OCEAN POND TO PAYNES PRAIRIE

Two miles in diameter, the circular Ocean Pond is center attraction in the piney Osceola National Forest. The source and outflow of this clean, blue green pond are known only to carp, catfish, sunfish, and eel. Begin at the shaded, secluded campground on the pond's north edge and journey south toward Paynes Prairie, one of the state's most significant natural areas. Before you leave, backpack the 20.4-mile Osceola Trail and visit Olustee Battlefield Historic Memorial. Then follow your route through a backcountry pine forest to the ghost town of Old Leno by the springs and sinks of the Sante Fe River, where you can get a lunch of tofu marinated in tamari at the Great Outdoor Trading Post in historic High Springs. After hiking through the distinguished ranch and farm country of Alachua County, you will come to the Devil's Millhopper, where you can descend 150 feet to a lush garden in Florida's limestone skeleton. Visit the Florida State Museum in Gainesville, dubbed Florida's most liveable city; historic Micanopy; and Cross Creek, the farm home of novelist Marjorie K. Rawlings. When you finally arrive at Paynes Prairie and explore the wildlife sanctuary you may wish to stay a long time.

*What to See and Do:* Adventure options on this trip are backpacking and primitive camping in the Osceola National Forest and Paynes Prairie; canoeing and fishing on the Santa Fe River; scuba diving and snorkeling at Ichetucknee Springs; and birding at places like Morningside Nature Center.

*Where to Begin:* From Jacksonville, take I-10 for 50 miles, taking Exit 45 to US 90 because I-10 underpasses Osceola National Forest roads; drive west to Olustee and then go 4.9 miles north on FR 250A to Ocean Pond Campground. If arriving from Lake City, drive east on US 90 to Olustee. The nearest international airport is in Jacksonville.

*About the Adventures:* Northeast of Lake City is the 157,655-acre Osceola National Forest, named for the Seminole Indian rebel who led a guerilla war for his people against the U.S. government in the Second Seminole War. The forest adjoins the Impassable Bay and other swamps south of the Okefenokee National Wildlife Refuge. In a flatwoods forest, longleaf and slash pines grow tall over gallberry, saw palmetto, and fetterbush. There are also sections of maple, willow, and oak; titi bogs; and swamps over huge phosphate claims. On a typical day or night you are likely to hear tree frogs (green, pinewood, pepper, and ornate chorus) in cacophony with aquatic frogs (bull, bronze, and leopard), only a few of the 50 species of amphibians. You might also see some of the 200 species of birds and 50 species of mammals, including beavers, black bears, and bats. A network of forest roads (849 miles) makes it possible to explore and ride horses deep into isolated, dense areas like the Big Gum Swamp Wilderness north of Ocean Pond. Ocean Pond is the only forest campground with restrooms, drinking water, and picnic tables. (It may be crowded in late spring and the summertime.) Across the pond from the campground is a day-use recreation area for boating and swimming. A forest map of all the back roads and cattle-grazing sections is available from the district ranger's office on the south side of US 90, west of Olustee. You will find a post office, country store, and telephone in Olustee and large shopping centers in Lake City.

The Osceola Trail, part of the Florida National Scenic Trail, has a south trailhead at the Olustee Battlefield on US 90, 1.5 miles east of Olustee. Florida's major Civil War victory—with heavy casualities—was fought here in February 1864 in an open forest. The battle is reenacted each February at an interpretive center on the site. After following the orange-blazed trail through a pine forest for 5.6 miles you will join a blue-blazed spur trail that takes you on a smooth, grassy trail to the Ocean Pond Campground. After another mile on the main trail, cross I-10 on a bridge (a jolt to forest tranquility from the noise of interstate traffic in the heart of the forest). You will cross a number of forest roads and stream footbridges and pass near old canals and through cattle stiles. Even in dry weather, you will probably find pockets of standing water on the trail. You may see deer and armadillos in the daytime and raccoons and skunks at night. The forest also hosts 53 active colonies of red-cockaded woodpeckers (and 7 other species of woodpeckers). In addition, you will see flycatchers, thrushes, warblers, purple finches, and painted buntings. Among the 30 or more species of wildflowers are bluestem, sundew, marsh pink, pipewort, and poor-joe. At 16.4 miles, pass a primitive campsite, the West Tower, which may have drinking water and a latrine. At 20.4 miles, an old jeep road will lead you to a forest gate and stile at Drew Grade Road, the end of the forest. (The Florida Trail continues west 0.7 mile to US 441 and, on other roads, to White Springs. See *Suwannee: River of Deer*, this Chapter.)

When you leave Ocean Pond, drive back to Olustee at the Osceola Experimental Forest and look for County Line Road. Follow it southwest for nearly 10 miles through a remote pine forest. At the community of Lulu, cross SR 100 and follow CR 241 to the junction with CR 18. (At the intersection the 100-mile loop Crystal Springs Trail for bicyclists passes south on CR 241 to its connection with the 300-mile loop Healing Waters Trail bicycle route, northwest of Gainesville. West on CR 18 the Crystal Springs Trail goes to Fort White.) Continue your drive west on CR 18 to US 41/441, turn left (south), and after 2.5 miles you will reach O'Leno State Park. The 1,716-acre park on the banks of the Santa Fe River is at the former lumber town of Leno ("Old Leno"), which became a ghost town soon after the beginning of the twentieth century. Its major natural features are a climax hardwood forest, a river rise, and sinkholes. Although the park is in a tranquil environment, you can hear the droning of traffic from I-75 in the east. Activities include swimming, canoeing, horseback riding, hiking, and birding. The park has four unique trails: the 0.5-mile Limestone Trail (a loop from the park road through a transitional forest to a limestone outcropping) and three trails that connect to form loops and lead to a primitive campsite. Begin at the swimming area on the 1-mile River Sink Trail which leads across the Santa Fe River on a suspension bridge built by the Civilian Conservation Corps in the 1930s. You will have an impressive view of the rapids before you loop through hammocks and flatwoods to the River Sink, where the Santa Fe flows underground for about 3 miles. North of the River Sink is a junction with the 3.5-mile Pareners Branch Trail. Well marked and designed, the trail goes to ponds, sinks, and sandhills before returning on the Old Wire Road, an early settlers' wagon route. En route, the 13-mile River Rise Trail connects to it. The River Rise Trail follows the Natural Bridge, the upland between the River Sink and the River Rise, and crosses the Bellamy Road, which was completed between

Saint Augustine and Tallahassee in 1826. (See *The Human Florida*, Chapter 1.) The trail passes the camping area at Sweet Water Lake, loops at the River Rise, and passes Black Lake before it returns. Ask the park ranger for a trail map. Campground space and cabin facilities can be reserved; pets are not allowed at either of the two campgrounds.

After leaving O'Leno State Park, drive south 6 miles to historic High Springs. The Santa Fe River curls around the northwest edge of the town, and 2 miles north on US 41/441 is a boat-ramp put-in for a 26-mile (or shorter) canoe trip. The Santa Fe Canoe Outpost will provide everything you need for a few hours to 3 days on the river. The outpost also furnishes equipment for snorkeling, camping, and fishing. (See *Information*.)

After 3 miles on your canoe trip you will pass under US 27, your first take-out point, and begin traveling through a beautiful area of pools, thick forest, and clear, bubbling springs. Nearly 6 miles after US 27 you will arrive at Ginnie Springs, famous for its deep spring cavern system, a challenge to scuba divers. The Ginnie Springs Campground is a large commercial outpost with standard facilities. There you can get diving instruction and diving equipment, either rental or for sale. (See *Information*.) About one mile after Ginnie Springs you will come to a few rocky shoals, and 10 miles from US 27 you will reach SR 47, where you may take out. If you opt to continue, you will find the first 3 miles of the next 13 generally limited to canoes, but after you reach the confluence with the Ichetucknee River, motorboat traffic will increase and the river will widen to your take-out at US 129.

While in High Springs, take a spur auto trip west on US 27 to day-use Ichetucknee Springs State Park, one of Florida's most unique. It covers half the length of the 6-mile river that begins at SR 238. Along the way you may see turtles, otters, and limpkins. The park provides a shuttle to four launch and take-out points.

To continue your journey, leave High Springs on US 41/27 south, go 7 miles to the junction with CR 232, and turn east through farm and ranch country. After 6 miles, turn right on SR 241 for 0.5 mile before turning east again on CR 232. Pass under I-75 and through San Felasco Hammock State Preserve, a diverse hardwood plant community of 6,500 acres with sinkholes, small springs, and streams. The longest of two trails, on the north side, is 8 miles long. During the months of October through April the rangers provide guided tours for hikers and horseback riders. On the third weekend in November, January, and March, they guide overnight back-packing trips. (See *Information.*) Three miles ahead, on the left, is the Devil's Millhopper State Geological Site, exposing 20 million years of life. Near the trail entrance to the rim are an exhibit area and information center. (The 100-mile loop Crystal Springs Trail for bicyclists begins here. Cyclists can park overnight if they contact the park ranger in advance.)

After you follow SR 232 east to US 441 south you will come to Gainesville. At the junction of SR 26, turn left on east University Avenue and go 5 miles to Morningside Nature Center, which will be on your left. It is a 278-acre day-use sanctuary open from 8 A.M. to 6 P.M. that takes you back 100 years to an authentic living history farm. Turkey Oak Trail, Blueberry Trail, and Tupelo Marsh Trail offer up to 3 miles for nature study, bird watching, and wildlife observation. On your return, turn left (south) on US 441, which is also 13th Street NW, and go 5 blocks. Turn right (west) on Museum Road and go one block to Newell Drive. Here is the Florida State Museum, the largest natural history museum in the South, and among the top ten in the nation. It is open daily from 9 A.M. to 5 P.M. and Sundays and holidays from 1 P.M. to 5 P.M. Two other city parks may interest you: the Bivens Arms Nature Park at 3650 South Main Street, an oak hammock sanctuary with a boardwalk trail; and Kanapaha Botanical Gardens at 4625 Southwest 63rd Boulevard, which has the South's largest herb garden. (See *Information.*)

The longest hiking trail in the Gainesville area is the 17-mile Gainesville–Hawthorne State Trail, a former railway constructed in the 1850s. Open for daytime use only, the asphalt surface section is for hiking and biking, and the dirt section includes horseback riding. The one-mile La Chua Trail, a side trail one mile east from the Gainesville trailhead, follows a grassy dike from the site of old Camp Ranch. The ranch is now headquarters for a district office of the Department of Environmental Protection. The La Chua Trail passes Alachua Sink, which clogged in 1971 and created Alachua Lake. Twenty years later the sink suddenly drained and the prairie developed. At the end of the trail is an observation deck for viewing wildlife.

To access the west trailhead of the Gainesville–Hawthorne State Trail from the junction of US 441 and SR 331, go 2.1 miles on SR 331 to SE 4th Street, turn right, go 0.9 mile to 15th Street, turn right, and go 0.7 mile to the parking area on the right. To access the east trailhead in Hawthorne, from the junction of CR 2082 and US 301, drive west one mile on CR 2082 to Southeast 200 Drive. Turn left to a parking area, also on the left, near Hawthorne Road High School. Access from side roads of SR 20 is also available. Before hiking the trail request a map from Paynes Prairie State Preserve.

After driving south on US 441 for about 10 miles you will arrive at Paynes Prairie State Preserve, which will be on both sides of the highway. The full-service campground is usually not crowded, but if it is filled, you will find a commercial campground a few miles south at MacIntosh. (See *Information.*) The 18,000-acre preserve is home to 720 species of vascular flora and at least 350 vetebrates. Amid a sea of willow, lotus, and soft rush, other wildlife present are mudfish, pigfrog, and water rat. Before you start your hike, check with a ranger for information on guided trips. For example, there are trips on the 2-mile Wildlife Walk and the 4-mile Rim Ramble the first three weekends of each month. On the last weekend of each month, a guide will take you on an overnight backpacking trip to scenic Persimmon Point. At other times a ranger will accompany you on a 2-mile round-trip adventure to the Alachua Sink and Alachua Lake, where you are guaranteed to see alligators and other wildlife. Other trails are the one-mile Bolen Bluff Trail to an observation platform not far from Alachua Lake, the 8-mile multiple-loop Chacala Trail (which features birding), the nature-study Wachoota Trail, and the remarkable Cone's Dike Trail of 5 miles into the heart of the prairie to see bison. (Call [904] 466-4100 for ranger-led tour reservations.) At Paynes Prairie you can also go fishing, boating (electric motors only), sailing, canoeing, swimming from a grassy bank, and horseback riding (by appointment). (The 300-mile loop Healing Waters Trail for bicyclists begins at the Gainesville Municipal Airport and follows roads south to the preserve on its way east.)

Before you complete this adventure, take a side trip to the Marjorie Kinnan Rawlings State Historic Site. Begin by going one-mile south on US 441 to Micanopy, the location of an ancient Indian settlement by Tuscawilla Lake, currently a 16-block historic district. From Micanopy take CR 346 4 miles east to CR 325 and turn south for 3 miles. The Rawlings House is at Cross Creek, a short stream between Orange Lake and Little Lochloosa Lake. It is open daily from 10 A.M. to 4:30 P.M. except for Tuesdays and Wednesdays; tours are guided. *The Yearling*, her compelling novel of a boy, Jody, and his adopted fawn, Flag, earned her the 1939 Pulitzer Prize in fiction and propelled her to international honors. A visit to her simple Cracker home will give you a vivid sense of both her and her characters.

### *Information*

Counties: Baker, Columbia, Union, Alachua

Average Temperatures: January 46°F (low), 67.8°F (high); August 72.6°F (low), 89.2°F (high)

National Properties: Osceola Ranger District, P.O. Box 70, Olustee, FL 32072, (904) 752-2577

State Properties: Florida State Museum, University of Florida, Gainesville, FL 32611, (904) 392-1721; Devil's Mill-hopper State Geological Site, 4732 Millhopper Rd., Gainesville, FL 32606, (904) 336-2008; Ichetucknee Springs State Park, Rte. 2, Box 108, Fort White, FL 32038, (904) 497-2511; Marjorie Kinnan Rawlings State Historic Site, Rte. 3, Box 92, Hawthorne,

FL 32640, (904) 466-3672; O'Leno State Park, Rte. 2, Box 1010, High Springs, FL 32643, (904) 454-1853; Olustee Battlefield State Historic Memorial, P.O. Box 2, Olustee, FL 32072, (904) 752-3866; Paynes Prairie State Preserve, Rte. 2, Box 41, Micanopy, FL 32677, (904) 466-3397; San Felasco Hammock State Preserve, same as Devil's Millhopper, above (call in advance for reservations)

Other Properties: Bivens Arms Nature Park, 3650 S. Main St., Gainesville, FL 32601, (904) 374-2056; Kanapaha Botanical Gardens, 4625 SW 63rd Blvd., Gainesville, FL 32601, (904) 372-4981; Morningside Nature Center, 3540 E. University Ave., Gainesville, FL 32601, (904) 374-2170

Chambers of Commerce: Alachua CC, P.O. Box 387, Alachua, FL 32615, (904) 462-3333; Gainesville Area CC, P.O. Box 1187, Gainesville, FL 32602, (904) 336-7100; High Springs CC, P.O. Box 863, High Springs, FL 32643, (904) 454-3120; Lake City–Columbia County CC (15 E. Orange St.), P.O. Box 566, Lake City, FL 32055, (904) 752-3690

Services and Amenities: *Commercial Campgrounds:* Ginnie Springs Campground, below; Sportsman Cove Campground, P.O. Box 107 (Ave. South and Second St.), MacIntosh, FL 32664, (904) 591-1435; Travelers Campground, Rte. 1, Box 231, Alachua, FL 32615, (904) 462-2505

*Bicycle Maps:* State Bicycle Program, (904) 488-4640; *Canoe Rentals and Supplies:* Ginnie Springs Campground, 7300 NE Ginnie Springs Rd., High Springs, FL 32643, (904) 454-2202; Great Outdoors Trading Company, 65–85 N. Main St., High Springs, FL 32643, (904) 454-2900; Sante Fe Canoe Outpost, P.O. Box 592, High Springs, FL 32643, (904) 454-2050; *Restaurants:* Oaks Restaurant, (904) 454-2940; *Scuba Diving and Snorkeling:* Ginnie Springs Campground, above

## SUWANNEE: RIVER OF THE DEER

Of all of Florida's rivers, none has the romantic appeal, multiple geological areas, variety of exploratory options, and clear natural springs of the Suwannee, Florida's "Queen of the Rivers." Immortalized in 1851 by Stephen Foster's "Old Folks at Home" (also known as "Suwannee River"), this historic and legendary river flows 235 winding miles south from Okefenokee Swamp in Georgia to the village of Suwannee at the Gulf of Mexico. It has lengthy sections of unspoiled natural beauty with one of the state's largest whitewater rapids, steep limestone banks, and calm, low currents. Enhancing its beauty are scenic tributaries, thick drapes of Spanish moss, preserved forests, wildlife habitats, indigenous plants and fish, zebra butterflies, and multihued phlox, swamplands, pastoral fields, and underwater cave systems. Sites to visit along this adventure route are the Stephen Foster State Folk Culture Center and two outstanding state parks: Suwannee, with the ghosts of a nineteenth-century town, and Manatee Springs, with a natural aviary.

*What to See and Do:* Adventure options are canoeing, boating, diving, hiking, birding, and fishing. Canoeing is emphasized, but you can also hike the park trails and the 49 miles of the Florida Trail that parallel the west side of the river from White Springs to Suwannee River State Park. The state has mapped the first 120 miles of canoeing for you; the real challenge is to paddle the entire canoeing distance of about 213 miles.

*Where to Begin:* For a canoe trip, put in at Fargo, Georgia, at the US 441 bridge, 40 miles north of Lake City; most of the other highway bridges under which the river flows (described ahead) also make good put-ins. Your last put-in option is at Fowler Bluff by SR 347, and your last take-out is at the village of Suwannee on SR 349. The nearest municipal airport is Lake City, and the nearest international airport and Amtrak are in Jacksonville, 55 miles east of Lake City on I-10.

*About the Adventures:* Suwannee is the name of more than a river; it is also a valley, reef, sound, spring, wildlife refuge, park, village, and county. The origin of the word may be *sawani*, a Creek Indian word for "echo," or it may be "San Juanee," a colloquial pronunciation of the Little Saint Johns

River that distinguishes it from the east Saint Johns River. The river was also called the *Guasaca Esqui*, "River of Reeds," by the Timucuan Indians. De Soto described building a bridge of "three pine trees in length and four in breadth" across the Suwannee, "the River of the Deer," September 23, 1539, to allow his army to pass about 5 miles downstream from the present Dowling Park. Originally, Stephen Foster, who never visited Florida or the river, wrote of Peedee River (from the Peedee Indians in South Carolina), but he changed it to "Swanee" (his spelling) in his second version for a more melodic sound. In 1935 Florida made "Suwannee River" its official state song.

The Timucuan Indians inhabited the Suwannee River basin when it was first explored by the Spanish in the sixteenth century. After de Soto's "Spanish Trail" through Florida, a series of Spanish missions were established; all were eventually abandoned or destroyed by native or emigrating Indians or by the English. Until the early 1800s the basin remained an unexplored wilderness, but in the 1830s steamers began navigating the river upstream to Ellaville, a distance of nearly 130 miles. Paddlewheel boats were commonplace by the 1890s but disappeared by the early 1920s. The few towns presently along the river are small; White Springs, with a population of about eight hundred, is the largest. The counties through which the river flows also have small populations, ranging from fifty-two hundred in Lafayette County to forty-four thousand in Columbia County (which includes Lake City, the largest municipality).

The Suwannee is the state's second largest drainage area in square miles (9,950 of which 5,720 are in Georgia). Both the Alapaha River and the Withlacoochee River (unrelated to another river by the same name in Florida) are major tributaries from Georgia that join the Suwannee in the southwest boundary of Hamilton County. The third major tributary is the Santa Fe, south of the town of Branford. At its beginning with the Big Alligator Creek in the Okefenokee Swamp, the Suwannee is a small, slow-current stream filled with dark tannin; the river remains dark except in localized areas with large natural springs. It is shallow in its upper sections but deepens to about 7 feet in its central and lower sections. It is about 60 feet wide at Fargo and gradually widens to 650 feet at the mouth. Shaped like a huge yellow fan, its delta of two main channels has dense grasses and islands. Its meandering has caused oxbow lakes, islands, and S-shaped designs. At least eighty individual springs discharge into the river, contributing to its good water quality. Only Swift Creek, about 4 miles west of White Springs, discharges a significant concentration of phosphates into the Suwannee. The river flows across clayey, unconsolidated deposits in the upper area, changes to a limestone base that is porous and fossiliferous in the central region, and crosses extensive marshland, known as the Ocala Formation, in the lower section.

Among the most common freshwater fish in the Suwannee are largemouth bass, redbreast, shellcracker, stumpknocker, bream, black crappie, pickerel, white and mud catfish, and the elusive Suwannee bass. High water is most likely in March, April, August, and September, with low water in the wintertime and June. Major floods have occurred and are the most likely in the spring and during the late summer hurricane season. Temperature averages are about 70 degrees Fahrenheit for spring and fall, 80 degrees in the summer, and 55 degrees in the winter. Mosquitoes are most prominent in the summertime and are the biggest nuisance in the Georgia area and from Branford to the Gulf.

In the 1960s the state attempted to have the Suwannee included in the nation's Wild and Scenic Rivers program, but citizens wanting to avoid restrictions created a public outcry so great that it was excluded. In 1973, a federal government study showed it needed protection. Then, in 1981, the state created the Water Management Lands Trust Fund, whose mission, among other things, was to protect the water and related land resources and freshwater springs as unique hydrological sites. Since then the state has purchased thousands of riverfront acres in an effort to save the rivers, and the

Florida branch of The Nature Conservancy has purchased miles of river boundary. According to Carolyn Mobley, public information director of the Suwannee River Water Management District, continuing efforts are necessary to keep the Suwannee "an outstanding Florida water," judging from the fast development of private vacation and campsite homes on the scenic banks, especially between US 129 and Suwannee River State Park.

When planning your trip, allow at least a week to paddle from Fargo to Suwannee River State Park, a distance of about 84 miles. Such a casual journey will allow time for observing the wildlife and topographical and historical features, and for preparing campsites. Allow an additional 2 weeks for the remaining 130 miles, so you can explore the scores of springs, make side trips in the tributaries (particularly the Santa Fe River), and fish. While planning, contact the Suwannee River Water Management District headquarters for state river maps (which cover from SR 6 near the Georgia state line to Branford at US 27), general guidelines on restrictions and flooding conditions, safety instructions, and a suggested camping list. You might also contact an outfitter to serve  as a guide or provide canoe rentals. (See *Information*.) It is wise not to leave your vehicle at an isolated put-in; instead arrange a shuttle, or leave your vehicle with a local contact. The full-service campground nearest to Fargo is the Stephen C. Foster State Park at the end of Georgia SR 177 in the Okefenokee Swamp; at the mouth of the river is Miller's Marine Campground at the end of SR 349 in Suwannee.

**Fargo (US 441) to White Springs (US 41), 45 miles:** Leave Fargo at the paved boat ramp. Unless the water is high, you will find a number of campsite options on the river, but do not camp on the private Saint Regis Paper Company property on the right side of the river. Between low banks you will see massive cypress, some of which rise from the center of the river. Ogeechee tupelo and other hardwoods are adjacent at the riverbanks. Wildlife species you may see are deer, river otters, wild hogs, beavers, gray squirrels, warblers, and wild turkeys. Because of the acidic water, fishing is not good in the first 25 miles or more. After 20.8 miles there is a take-out at the SR 6 bridge, 2 miles west from US 441 on the road to Jasper. Notice that the riverbanks ahead become higher and the limestone outcroppings more frequent. After 10 miles from SR 6 you will pass Cone Bridge Road, left, where you will find a public boat ramp and a potential campsite. (About 2 miles east from here is US 441.) Between here and the Big Shoals, the state's best whitewater rapids, you may see an alligator or the more rare Suwannee cooter. To the east will be the mouth of Deep Creek, unique because it drains from a large hardwood section of the piney Osceola National Forest. About one mile before the rapids is a take-out on the right, and the old Godwin Bridge Road that leads 1.5 miles out to SR 135 and White Springs. The Loop Trail and the Big Shoals Trail (a walking route to the rapids) begin here at the take-out. After the warning signs and the approach to Big Shoals, paddle toward the left side and beach your canoe at a safe place. After scouting, arrange for portage on the left side. (The ragged rocks can make this a dangerous run; if you run the rapids, use your life jacket and make your shoot in an unloaded canoe down the right side of the river.) Within one mile before White Springs and US 41 you will run Little Shoals, a series of cascades. At White Springs you have two take-outs 2 miles apart: US 41 and SR 136. Between them are a canoe livery and campground. Grocery and other stores are on US 41. For a step back in time to 1903 and a break from sleeping on the ground, bed and breakfast is available at the Telford Inn on River Street. (See *Information*.)

**White Springs (US 41) to Suwannee Springs (US 129), 19.2 miles:** After passing under the SR 136 bridge, you will see the foundation of the White Sulphur Springs Colonial Hotel and Springhouse on the right. Warmed by the spring, the river is popular for swimming. Just beyond the spring is a paddle wheeler and the dock of the Stephen Foster State Folk Culture Center. Open daily, the center has a 200-foot carillon tower with Degan tubular bells that play Foster music daily, animated dioramas, and a museum of Foster memorabilia. Born in Pittsburgh in 1826, Foster wrote 201 songs and received large royalties; indebtedness and separation from his family, however, contributed to his dying alone and with only 38 cents in his pocket in New York City in 1864. The center sponsors a number of cultural events, including the Florida Folk Festival, which emphasizes traditional music and arts and crafts, each Memorial Day weekend. The center is also a trailhead for the 49-mile Suwannee River section of the Florida Trail. It has drinking water and picnic tables, but camping is not allowed. Because the trail is on private property, you will need a Florida Trail ID card to hike this section.

For the next 36 miles on the river you will pass through sections of corridor with high limestone walls that have crevices and grottoes, where surface water drips through fissures and mosses grow thick and green. Snakes coil on the dry outcroppings in the sun and warblers and screech owls inhabit the upperstory of oaks and pines. You will go under I-75 (no take-out here) and pass the 1,189-acre Mattair Spring Tract, left, about 3 miles before approaching US 129. As part of its acquisition plans for protecting the river, the state intends to improve the area for a gopher tortoise habitat.

On the approach to the town of Suwannee Springs, notice the six springs, left, and a rock retaining wall housing the main spring. The site of an elegant resort hotel in the 1880s, the springs are now a popular swimming and sunning area and a take-out point. Access is off US 129, south of the bridge.

**Suwannee Springs (US 129) to Suwannee River State Park (US 90), 21.6 miles:** Pass under the abandoned and current US 129 bridges and reach another take-out, left, within one mile. Here you will find the Spirit of the Suwannee Campground, with full-service camping, and the Canoe Outpost, which offers complete outfitting and shuttle service on the Suwannee, Alapaha, and Withlacoochee rivers. Groceries can be purchased in the village.

Continuing downstream to the SR 249 bridge, you will pass Ratliff, Mill, and Mitchell creeks, all right. On the left, about 7 miles from US 129, is the Florida Sheriff's Boys Ranch for dependent youth. About 4 miles farther you will see the mouth of Holton Creek, right, the outlet from Holton Spring one-mile up the spring run. Here are some of the best karst topography in the state and the largest known population of cedar elm in Florida. About one mile farther on the Suwannee, left, is the only abundant trillium on the river. Because a residential subdivision threatens the area, the state plans to acquire it. Soon you will see Alapaha Rise, a first-magnitude spring, on the right. Some geologists say it is probably an underground flow of the Alapaha River, which joins the Suwannee about 0.5 mile downstream. When you pass under the SR 248 bridge you will see a boat ramp to the right and Hamilton County's Gibson Park, an area for simple camping.

The Suwannee River State Park is 7.5 miles from here; and for nearly the first 3 miles, steps lead up the riverbanks from private docks on both sides. Here, too, motorboat traffic will increase. When you see Lime Spring, left (also called Dry Branch), continue paddling to the take-out, left, in Suwannee River State Park. The park has a full-service campground and is a good place to leave a shuttle car. (Two miles east on US 90 is a grocery store.) A historic area, the park was the town of Columbus, population six hundred, and a railroad station in the nineteenth century. It also served as a defensive area to protect the railroad during the Civil War. The short Sandhills Trail leads to the Columbus cemetery and to the old Pensacola and Jacksonville stagecoach road; the Suwannee River Trail makes a loop across the rocky and mossy Lime Sink Run. Also worth a visit is the gushing Swannacooshee Spring on the west bank, near the confluence with the Withlacoochee River. Access to the park is on US 90, 14 miles west of Live Oak.

**Suwannee River State Park (US 90) to Luraville (SR 51), 29.5 miles:** For the next 130 miles, described in four sections, the river becomes broader and slower and hosts increasing numbers of power boats and water skiers. It is best to stay close to the right bank, attach an outrigger, or securely attach your canoes in a catamaran form. The major features in this section are the springs, remote riverscapes, and wildlife. Access points are plentiful, but sandbars for camping become less common and disappear entirely after Fanning Springs.

After leaving the Suwannee River State Park boat ramp you will pass Ellaville Spring, left, between the railroad bridge and the abandoned US 90 bridge. The spring surges from a limestone cave. Soon you will see the intake and outtake ditches of the Florida Power Company, left. After 2 miles, pass under the I-10 bridge (no take-out) toward long stretches of undisturbed bottomland. Here are well-developed riverine berms with live and post oaks, palmetto, and cypress draped with Spanish moss. Dowling Park, 15 miles from Suwannee River State Park, is a wayside park with a boat ramp and campsite; a grocery store is east on SR 250. Two miles downstream is Christian Park, left, with a canoe launch and a nature trail that leads to an iron spring. Home to raccoons, gray squirrels, and bobcats, the park has mossy oaks and, on its eastern elevation, longleaf pine and turkey oak. Along the river you are likely to see swallow-tailed and Mississippi kites and Cooper's hawks. Along the next 4 miles are Cork Springs, right, and Flynn and Charles springs, both left. The latter has a good campsite and two erupting springs divided by a short limestone natural bridge. About one mile farther is Allen Mill Pond Spring, right, but you will have to paddle about 0.5 mile up the spring run to see its source from multiple vents. After another mile is Thomas Spring, left, followed by Blue Springs, right, which has two pools of blue water. Blue Springs, also called Yana Spring and Lafayette County Park, has a campground and bathhouse. (Access is off CR 251B from US 27, northwest of the town of Mayo.) Perry Spring, right, is the last spring before you arrive at SR 51. Pass under the bridge to a wayside park, left, with a boat ramp and campsite. A grocery store is about one mile north on SR 51.

**Luraville (SR 51) to Branford (US 27), 22 miles:** When you leave Luraville you will notice the Irvine Slough, left, a swampy area that drains from Luraville Springs and Telford Spring. About 1.5 miles from SR 51 is Peacock Slough, also left, which has as its source a number of springs with a lengthy underwater cave system. These springs include Peacock Springs and Bonnett Spring, both preserved by The Nature Conservancy. From here to Troy Springs is about 15 miles. Along the way are a few islands and many springs including Cow Spring, an oval pool; Running Springs, in a network of limestone and a good campsite; Convict Spring, encased by a concrete wall and at a private campground; Suwannee Blue Spring, fenced; Owens Spring, an oval aquamarine pool; and Mearson Spring, a pool among high banks. Convict, Owens, and Mearson are on the right (west) bank, and the others are on the left. Soon after Running Springs is the remains of Drew Bridge, a railroad bridge that was left open when abandoned in the 1920s. At Owens Spring and Fort McComb Island is a boat ramp at CR 251. (Access from Mayo is east on US 27 for 6 miles to CR 251, left.) At Troy Springs, right, is an 80-foot-deep first-magnitude spring, 66 million gallons daily, in an elongated pool. The submerged hull of the *Madison*, a Confederate Army supply ship, can be seen here. Experienced scuba divers have described spectacular cliff formations in the depths. (Access from Branford is 4.5 miles west on US 27 to CR 425.) Less than one mile below Troy Springs is Ruth Springs Tract, right, which surrounds Lafayette County's Ruth Springs Park. The area has a boat ramp and nature trails, open only during daylight hours. Among the oak, gum, river birch, and cypress are fox, raccoon, otter, quail, and wild hog. (Access from Branford is the same as for Troy Springs.) Within one mile of Ruth Springs, in a dense forest, is light blue Little River Spring, left, which emerges from a long, deep, dangerous cave system. Experienced scuba divers can make a first-class dive in the spring to tunnels and rooms, including the "Florida Room," claimed to be the state's largest known underwater cave. (Access is 3 miles north of Branford on US 129, left on SR 248.) Pass under the US 27 bridge in Branford for a take-out ramp at Branford Springs Recreation Park, left. The town has grocery stores and the Suwannee River Cove, a down-home restaurant representative of an era gone but not forgotten, open Thursday through Sunday. Eight miles east on US 27 is River Run Campground, a full-service campground and canoe outfitter, with guide and shuttle service. (See *Information.*)

**Branford (US 27) to Fanning Springs (US 19/98), 43.5 miles:** From Branford, canoe 10.5 miles to the confluence of the Santa Fe River, left, where you will find a good campsite and have the option of paddling upstream on the Santa Fe. This is an undisturbed area of cypress, cedar, elm, bottomland hardwoods, and the river's largest heronry. Two miles downstream on the Suwannee is Turtle Spring, right, in a swampy area where it vents from Fletcher Spring, a nearby greenish oval pool. After passing through a developed area on both sides of the river, reach privately owned Rock Bluff Springs, left, a large pool with a 27-million-gallon daily flow. Here lives the Suwannee cooter, a threatened species. Shortly you will reach the SR 340 bridge at a take-out ramp and wayside park, left. A grocery store is 300 feet east on SR 340.

Between here and Fanning Springs 23 miles downriver are four parks with camping facilities; Fanning Springs also hosts a campground. The first site is about 2 miles from SR 340 at Guaranto Spring, right, the site of a Dixie County Park. The spring is a long, oblong swimming pool. After paddling another 4 miles you will see a boat ramp, left, to the residential subdivision of Wannee; after an oxbow bend in the river past Big Cypress and Cooper springs, right, you will arrive at another boat ramp at blue green Sun Spring, left. Ahead is Jack's Run Spring, left, and another Cooper Spring, right, which has a sulfuric odor.

Gilchrist County Recreational Area, another county park, also permits camping. In the park, enclosed in a swimming pool, are two vents of Hart Springs. Access is 5.5 miles from Fanning Springs on CR 232, left on CR 344. In this area are varied floodplain landforms and forests. The rare cedar elm, found only on the Suwannee River, reaches its southernmost extent here; large populations of water tupelo and overcup oak also approach their southernmost limits in North America.

Herons, swallowtail kites, wild turkeys, and river otters are frequently seen along the riverside. About 3 miles downstream from Hart Springs is Otter Springs, left, at the Otter Springs Resort and Campground with cabins, RV sites, tent sites, and canoe rentals. A special feature of Otter Springs is the *Suwannee Belle*, the only authentic paddleboat on the river. Access is off SR 232 west, 3 miles north of Fanning Springs.

The Suwannee River KOA, about one mile downstream from Otter Springs on the right, has full service and Old Town Spring for a swimming pool. The last spring on this section is Bell Springs, left, within one mile of your approach to the US 19/98 bridge, the river's "Big Bend," at Fanning Springs. Take out past the bridge at a wayside park and boat ramp, left. In the Fanning Springs–Old Town Community are another campground (called Suwannee River on US 19 Campground), restaurants that specialize in Suwannee River fish, and grocery stores.

**Fanning Springs (US 19/98) to Suwannee (end of SR 349), 30.5 miles:** The last miles of the Suwannee River are wide, have low swamp banks, are exceptionally remote after Fowlers Bluff, and become tidal among islands, creeks, and passes. At least 90 percent of the river frontage, including the area that is part of the Lower Suwannee National Wildlife Refuge, is either protected or planned for protection by the state. On the riverside are mature bottomland hardwoods with green-legged spiders, hawks, owls, and ospreys; and water lilies grow in some of the passes and coves. Mopping up the river floor like a living vacuum cleaner are sturgeons, channel catfish, and striped mullet. It is not unusual to see the Pensacola cooter, clumsy on a log but fast in the water; red-belly and snapping turtles; alligators; limpkins, which catch the apple snails; and herons, which catch fish. Manatees are rarely seen.

After a visit to Big Fanning Spring and Little Fanning Spring, which have a combined flow of 70 million gallons daily, your first access point is New Pine Landing, a Dixie

County Park with campsites, right, 5 miles from US 19/98. The next access is 4 miles ahead at Manatee Springs State Park, left, where 116.9 million gallons emerge daily from an extensive underwater cave system. A high boardwalk at the river's confluence with the spring run makes Manatee Springs easy to recognize. You will find nature trails, a boat ramp, and a full-service campground. Birding is popular in the 2,075-acre park of hammocks and sandhill communities. Of at least one hundred identified birds, the majority are permanent residents. Access the park from Chiefland 6 miles west on SR 320.

After another 8 miles you have access to Fowler Bluff, left. Beyond are Little Turkey Island and Turkey Island, and on the right of the river, in the second canal, is your final take-out, the end of your canoeing adventure at the town of Suwannee. (To see fully the Gulf of Mexico at Alligator Pass, you would need to paddle about 3 more miles among the islands.)

Awaiting you in Suwannee, home to frequent commercial and sports fishermen, are motels, stores, a laundromat, restaurants (one the home-style Suwannee Cafe), and Miller's full-service campground and marina. Miller's is also known for its rental houseboats, which can be used to cruise upstream as far as Branford. Like other small communities along the Suwannee River, Suwannee is accommodating and peaceful.

### *Information*

Counties: Clinch County, Georgia; Hamilton, Columbia, Madison, Suwannee, Lafayette, Gilchrist, Dixie, Levy

Average Temperatures: January, 44°F (low), 68°F (high); August, 71.3°F (low), 89.2°F (high)

National Properties: Lower Suwannee National Wildlife Refuge, P.O. Box 4139, Homosassa, FL 32647, (904) 382-2201

State Properties: Manatee Springs State Park, Rte. 2, Box 617, Chiefland, FL 32626, (904) 493-6072; Stephen Foster State Folk Culture Center, P.O. Box G, White Springs, FL 32096, (904) 397-2733; Suwannee River State Park, Rte. 8, Box 297,

Live Oak, FL 32060, (904) 362-2746; Suwannee River Water Management District, Rte. 3, Box 64, Live Oak, FL 32060, (904) 362-1001, or (800) 342-1002 in Florida

Chambers of Commerce: Gilchrist County CC, P.O. Box 186, Trenton, FL 32693, (904) 463-6327; Madison County CC, 105 N. Range St., Madison, FL 32340, (904) 973-2788; Mayo/Lafayette County CC, P.O. Box 416, Mayo, FL 32066, (904) 294-2704; Hamilton County CC, P.O. Box P, Jasper, FL 32052, (904) 792-1300

Services and Amenities: *Bed and Breakfast:* Telford Inn, River St., White Springs, FL 32096, (904) 397-2045; *Commercial Campgrounds:* Hollis' River Rendezvous, Rte. 2, Box 60, Mayo, FL 32066, (904) 294-2510; Miller's Marine Campground, P.O. Box 280, Suwannee, FL 32692, (904) 542-7349 or (800) 458-BOAT; Otter Springs Resort, Rte. 1, Box 1400, Trenton, FL 32693, (904) 463-2696; River Run Campground, Rte. 2, Box 811, Branford, FL 32008, (904) 935-1086; Shady Oaks RV and Motor Home Park, Rte. 3, Box 726–A, Old Town, FL 32680, (904) 498-7276; Spirit of the Suwannee Campground, Rte. 1, Box 98, Live Oak, FL 32060, (904) 364-1683; Suwannee River KOA, P.O. Box 460, Old Town, FL 32680, (904) 542-7636

*Canoeing Outfitters:* River Run and Spirit of the Suwannee, above; River Road, Rte. 1, Box 93–K, White Springs, FL 32096, (904) 397-2945; *Diving:* Hollis' and Miller's, above; Florida Division of Tourism, 126 W. Van Buren St., Tallahassee, FL 32399, (904) 448-1462; *Emergency Telephone Numbers:* County Sheriffs: Hamilton, (904) 792-1001; Columbia, (904) 755-3222; Suwannee, (904) 362-2222; Madison, (904) 973-4001; Lafayette, (904) 294-1222; Gilchrist, (904) 463-2245; Dixie, (904) 498-3383; Levy, (904) 486-2111

## CEDAR KEYS

Ask some local residents where Cedar Keys is and you might hear answers like "On Way Key because it's way out," "At the end of the swamp road," or "Halfway between Tampa and Tallahassee but a world apart." The Cedar Keys are a group of forty small barrier islands in the Gulf of Mexico. Some are sun bleached, raw, and snake infested; only the fishing village of Cedar Key is a town. A 3-mile causeway ties the town to the mainland for its fresh water and electricity. It is a small community but large in hospitality, modern but symbolically the "Old Florida," and enterprising but relaxed. With more pelicans than people, and with oyster beds as close as backdoor gardens, the town has a reputation as the storybook setting of pioneers, fishermen, artists, writers, and nature enthusiasts. Within sight of Cedar Key is Cedar Keys National Wildlife Refuge—a haven for porpoises, mullet (which hop up and down like grasshoppers), and 238 species of water-fowl—and islands like Seahorse Key, with the highest dunes in the keys. Only a few miles away, on the mainland, are the mystical Lower Suwannee National Wildlife Refuge and the remote Waccasassa Bay State Preserve.

*What to See and Do:* Cedar Keys is ideal for saltwater fishing, canoeing, birding, and marine studies. On the mainland are unspoiled forests, bays, creeks, and swamps for canoeing, birding, hiking, and exploring.

*Where to Begin:* From the Otter Creek intersection of US 98/19 and SR 24, drive west 21 miles on SR 24. The nearest airport is Gainesville Municipal Airport, 55 milers northeast. (Cedar Key has a small, 2,400-foot private airport.)

*About the Adventures:* The colorful history of Cedar Keys is one of prosperity and failure, of storm and ruin, of tenacity and endurance. The Keys' first commercial settlers, led by Augustus Steele, came in the 1840s to harvest shellfish and to cut forest. Prosperity followed, with the first cross-state railroad from Fernandina in 1861 made possible by the U.S. Senator David Levy Yulee; the rails would serve as a shuttle for cotton, salt, timber, and naval-store supplies between Cuba, Mobile, and New Orleans and the eastern Atlantic seaboard. Swarms of tourists rode the rails, and the town flourished, becoming the second largest city in the state during the 1880s. Manufacturers marveled at the virgin cedar, cypress, and pine, and made Eagle pencils until every tree was gone. Not to be defeated, the "Venice of America" bounced back with a harvest of oysters and fish. Once again the resources were destroyed by overharvesting; ships no longer docked, and tourists turned to new railroads and new towns. Then, in 1896, a merciless hurricane devastated almost everything but the human spirit, ending the glory of nineteenth-century Cedar Keys. Tenaciously, some residents returned, and by 1910 a new business of palmetto brooms and brushes thrived. But that, too, was soon brushed away, this time by competition with plastics. For the next 50 years the islands were the Rip Van Winkle at "the end of the swamp road"—yet throughout its undulating history, Cedar Key never lost its charm. It now offers a number of worthwhile opportunities.

First, simply ruminate in this town of about eight hundred hardy residents; sleep in the hand-hewed cypress and tabby Island Hotel, vintage 1861, which has withstood hurricanes and is on the National Register of Historic Places. From its breeze-weathered rocking chairs on the second-floor porch with frontier colonnades, you can smell the sea, an enticement to the town's poached and broiled seafood, fresh smoked mullet, oysters, and blue crabs. You can walk to the Cedar Key Historical Society Museum (open parts of every day except Saturday), shops, restaurants, hotels, motels, art galleries, and boat docks. At the Cedar Keys State Museum (open all day Thursday through Monday) are a shell collection by former resident Saint Claire Whitman and information on John Muir, who hiked 1,000 miles from Indiana to Cedar Keys in 1867 at the age of 29. You can easily meet the islanders, who will guide you for fishing, boating, and hiking. They can ferry you on the *Island Hopper* to Seashore Key, and hiking guides, like "bird-lady" Harriet Smith, can recommend a score of unforgettable self-guided walks and boat trips.

Your second experience is to paddle or row a shallow-draft boat among the bays and marshes, around tiny islands, through causeway channels, by oyster beds, and perhaps completely around Way Key. Regardless of your adventure, begin early in the morning or at the first rising tide. Wear knee-high boots to protect you if you wade in the mud or shallow waters. Greeting you will be sandpipers, dowitchers, egrets, herons, clapper rails, marsh wrens, and warblers. If you go saltwater fishing, you will find plenty of mangrove snapper, redfish, grouper, snook, and sea trout year-round, kingfish in the spring and fall, and tarpon in late spring through summer. Rental sailboats, with instructions, are available for guests of the Faraway Inn. (See *Information.*)  For another kind of excitement, ask a guide to take you to see the edges of historic Atsena Otie Key, and to Seahorse Key (leased by the University of Florida for marine and ornithological studies) in the Cedar Keys National Wildlife Refuge. Ranked as one of Florida's largest nesting areas, the refuge has between 50,000 and 100,000 white ibis, egrets, cormorants, herons, pelicans, and other birds. Beaches are open to the public, but island interiors are closed to the public, and perhaps just as well; an average of twenty cottonmouth moccasins inhabit each acre on Seashore, Snake, and North keys.

East of Cedar Keys, along Waccasassa Bay and all the way to Yankeetown, is the 30,784-acre Waccasassa Bay State Preserve. Consisting mainly of salt marshes, wooded islands, and inland forests of bottom hardwoods and cypress, it is home to raccoons, otters, bald eagles, and black bears. You can paddle and explore in more than one hundred tidal creeks and at the mouth of the Waccasassa River and see plenty of wading and shorebirds, speckled trout, redfish, and mullet. If you wish to camp, paddle upstream on the Waccasassa River to the designated campsite. (You may also reach the Waccasassa River at a boat ramp on CR 326 from US 98/19, 5.5 miles south from the intersection of US 98/19 and SR 24.) Rangers lead canoe tours in the spring and fall.

On the mainland, wildlife abounds at the 4,000-acre Cedar Key Scrub Preserve, Shell Mounds, and the 35,620-acre Lower Suwannee National Wildlife Refuge. From Cedar Key drive northeast on SR 24 and turn left on CR 347. After 1.2 miles, look for a primitive road on the left. Here you can hike about 2 miles through sand oaks where the Florida scrub jay reigns. After another mile on CR 347, turn left on CR 326, Shell Mound

Road, to pass Shell Mound Park, right, and continue to the end of the road, where you will find a boat-launching area into the Suwannee Sound marshes. Along the road are the Indian Shell Mounds, left, the major one at the refuge boundary marker. You are likely to see or hear ospreys, armadillos, nuthatches, pine warblers, and red-shouldered hawks among the scrub, live oaks, pines, and palmettoes.

Farther north on CR 347, about 6.5 miles from the CR 326 junction, look for a gate on the left in the Lower Suwannee National Wildlife Refuge. From here you can hike at least 3.5 miles into a labyrinth of old forest roads to see deer, wild hogs, and armadillos. Prominent wildflowers include long-leaf violets, glades lobelia, purple flag, duck potato, and dozens of other species. Finally, farther north, about 4 miles on CR 347, look for another forest road, left at gate No. 3. You can hike into the frequently wet depths of the forest on a straight road for about 2.5 miles and then make a left at a cable gate among the pines, wildflowers, yellow-rumped warblers, and white-eyed vireos. On this, as on all old roads you explore, you are likely to see signs of bobcats, raccoons, and deer. During hunting seasons the gates may be open, but those are not good times for you to go hiking. Check with the ranger about hunting seasons and other old paths for exploring.

### *Information*

County: Levy

Average Temperatures: January, 52°F (low), 73.1°F (high); August, 73.6°F (low), 89.8°F (high)

National Properties: Cedar Key National Wildlife Refuge, Rte. 2, Box 44, Homosassa, FL 32646, (904) 628-2201; Lower Suwannee National Wildlife Refuge, Rte. 1, Box 1193C, Chiefland, FL 32626, (904) 493-0238

State Properties: Cedar Key State Museum, P.O. Box 538, Cedar Key, FL 32625, (904) 543-5350; Waccasassa Bay State Preserve, P.O. Box 187, Cedar Key, FL 32625, (904) 543-5567

Chamber of Commerce: Cedar Key Area CC, P.O. Box 610, Cedar Key, FL 32625, (904) 543-5600

Services and Amenities: *Commercial Campground:* Cedar Key RV Park, 6th and G Sts., Cedar Key, FL 32625, (904) 543-5150; *Lodging:* Island Hotel, 2nd and B Sts., Cedar Key, FL 32625, (904) 543-5111; Faraway Inn, 3rd and G Sts., Cedar Key, FL 32625, (904) 543-5330

*Boating Guide: Island Hopper,* (904) 543-5889/5622; *Broiled Seafood:* The Captain's Table, Dock St., Cedar Key, FL 32625, (904) 543-5441

## AUCILLA SINKS AND WACISSA SPRINGS

Remote and mysterious, the Aucilla River, with its "Big Rapid," has 19 miles for canoeing; its companion river, the spring-fed swift Wacissa, has 14 miles. For 5 miles the secretive Aucilla is subterranean, with large, deep, dark sinkholes revealing parts of the meandering underground channels. Although canoeists must leave the Aucilla 2 miles before the sinks, hikers can see them from the Florida Trail, which twists through an ominous forest and over ragged limestone. Because the Aucilla has hazardous rapids and man-made dams, the run is recommended only for experienced canoeists.

*What to See and Do:* In addition to canoeing, hiking, and camping, your options on this journey are scuba diving at Wacissa Springs, bicycling the wildflower-bordered historic Canopy Roads, and studying wildlife in the Aucilla Wildlife Management Area.

*Where to Begin:* Canoe access to the Aucilla River is on US 27/19 at the east edge of Lamont (16 miles south of Monticello) 12 miles south from I-10, Exit 33, on US 19/SR 57 and US 27/19. Access to the Wacissa River is at Wacissa Springs Recreation Park and boat ramp (16 miles south of Monticello) 11 miles south of Lloyd and I-10, Exit 32 on CR 59. For air travelers, the nearest airport is the Tallahassee Municipal Airport, 30 miles west of Lamont. Trailheads for hikers and bicyclists are described below with the trail routes.

*About the Adventures:* Before you canoe either river you may wish to set up base camp at Camper's World or at the KOA at the junction of I-10 and US 19, Exit 33. (See *Information.*) They have full service and are only 5 miles from restaurants and shopping centers north in Monticello and 12 miles north of the rivers. Only primitive camping is permitted along the rivers.

The Aucilla River has its nebulous headwaters a few miles east of Thomasville, Georgia, and seeps south with uncertain direction. Branches and creeks lose their names when they join it, and all may disappear before emerging at ponds, sinks, and swamps. The water flow finally becomes defined in Florida at Sneads Smokehouse Lake, east of Monticello on CR 146. After a few miles it becomes the boundary between Jefferson and Madison counties and farther downstream between Jefferson and Taylor counties. All the counties are 50 percent or more wetlands. In its journey between US 90 and I-10 the Aucilla is joined by the Little Aucilla River from the northeast, whose swamp origins imitate the vanishing acts of the Aucilla. The Little Aucilla's defined route is near Blue Sink, north of Greenville. Tributaries Wolf Creek and Alligator Creek join the tannin-colored Aucilla and make it large enough for a canoeist to begin an exciting trip by Lamont. The 19-mile trip has an upper section of 13 miles to the bridge at CR 257/14, and a 6-mile lower section. The upper section generally requires moderate paddling in slow water with light drops over occasional rocky shoals. Both sections are scenic, with strands of oak, pine, palmetto, cypress, and magnolia above varied layers of limestone on the riverbanks. You can find campsites in the woods, but use care to prevent forest fires. Your first take-out is at CR 257, 7 miles south of Lamont. The lower section is more exciting; about one mile south of the Jones Mill Creek confluence is the "Big Rapid," claimed by some canoeists to be the state's best whitewater. The drop is about 8 feet in a distance of 25 yards. Scouting before the run is essential and easy from the east bank. The run is usually made on the east side of the river. After another mile you will come to an abandoned bridge, your take-out point, on the east bank. (The river goes another 2 miles before silently disappearing underground and does not emerge again for about 6 miles, when it joins the Wacissa River north of the US 98 bridge.) Access to the take-out from the CR 257 bridge becomes CR 14 once you cross the bridge south in Taylor County. Drive 4.6 miles on a rough road to Cabbage Grove near the fire tower. Turn right, and in about 0.7 mile turn right again on a graded dirt road that goes straight, 2.5 miles, to the river at the abandoned bridge.

The Wacissa River provides a challenging 14-mile canoe route from Wacissa Springs to US 98. At the beginning of the head spring, and for nearly 3 miles, there are a dozen beautiful natural springs that have a constant temperature of 69 degrees Fahrenheit and an average flow of 374 cubic feet per second. For scuba diving, the Big Blue Spring, about one mile downstream, is one of the largest; it is about 45 feet deep and has a cavernous limestone bottom. Two miles farther is Cedar Island Spring, the last of the group. After about 6 miles, the river narrows, with a number of small channels to the right; stay left. After about 2 miles it becomes wider. When you reach the primitive Goose Pasture Campground, left, you can take out. (See *Florida National Scenic Trail,* Chapter 4.) For the next 5 miles it is advisable to have a guide, a county or topographic map, or someone who knows the river. (See *Information.*) Paddle through pickerel weed and wild rice, and after about 2 miles watch for a metal post. Follow an opening of a channel, right of the post, to what becomes a narrow but defined channel, the Slave Canal. You must follow the canal, because the river disperses into a sinister swamp. From here to the take-out you will slip under a jungle of cypress, gums, and ashes, where you will likely see wildlife. When you pass the confluence of the Aucilla from the left, keep right, and do not go under the US 98 bridge. Turn right upstream on another channel to the take-out and boat launch. On US 98, you are 15 miles east of Newport. (No longer hiding underground, the Aucilla River calmly flows to the Gulf on an old 5-mile channel made by the Wacissa and Aucilla Navigational Company in the early 1930s. After making its way through an impenetrable morass of wetlands, it ends in Florida's Big Bend much as it started in Georgia—secretively.) While you are in this area, if you take US 98 about 25 miles east to Perry you can visit the Forest Capital State Museum, "The Tree Capital of the South," on US 98/27A in the south section of town. In tribute to forestry, it emphasizes the value and uses of the 314 known species of trees in the state. Also at the center is a nostalgic Cracker cabin. The museum may be closed on Tuesdays and Wednesdays; call in advance.

The Florida Trail, on its route between the Suwannee River and the Saint Marks Wildlife Refuge, meanders through the Aucilla Wildlife Management Area and passes by many sinks of the Aucilla River. Huge oaks, gums, and magnolias tower over patches of dense wax myrtle, titi, ironwood, and beauty-berry. Large coiled and draping grapevines intertwine like snakes from *Raiders of the Lost Ark*. When the leaves are on the hardwoods, a darkness permeates the path and makes the cypress knees in the water-filled sinks look like denizens of a black underworld. Beside them are sparkling blue reflections when the sun penetrates the forest. From one surprise sink to another, the trail skirts dangerously close to the limestone edges. The sinks have unposted names: Mosquito Slap, Long Suffering, Dragonfly, Sunshine, and Vortex. Hiking this section during high water is hazardous.

The easiest access to the Florida Trail is from US 98 on the Powell Hammock Road, 2 miles east of the Aucilla bridge. Drive north 4.3 miles on the Powell Hammock Road and turn left on the dirt Goose Pasture Road. After one mile park on the right, near Roadside Sink. The orange-blazed trail crosses the road near the cattle grate. A south route is 4.2 miles one way and passes sixteen sinks. A north hike is 4.7 miles by four sinks and to the Aucilla "Big Rapid" where you canoed. (Ahead 2.5 miles on Goose Pasture Road is a public primitive campground on the banks of the beautiful Wacissa River. This is an isolated area, though usually crowded in summer and closed during the hunting season. You will find picnic tables but no drinking water here.) Acquire information on this wild area from the rangers at the Cabbage Grove state forestry station, 2.1 miles north on the Powell Hammock Road. If you are interested in more remoteness on the Florida Trail (FT), continue north on rough CR 14 for 3.2 miles from the forestry station to the FT sign. (You will recognize the road from your canoe shuttle.) Your backpacking trip, right, is 16.7 miles on property of the Buckeye Cellulose Corporation to US 19/27, 11 miles northwest of Perry. The route follows open pine forest roads through both dry and wet areas. Camping is prohibited during the hunting season, and drinking water should be treated. A compass and county map are recommended. You will see wildlife.

One of Florida's major bicycle routes—the 100-mile Route B: Canopy Roads—loops east in Jefferson County from its western trailheads in Tallahassee. A beguiling route over rolling hill country through stately oaks and wildflowers, the 30-mile section, called the Tallahassee Hills, passes the Wacissa Springs and goes north on CR 259 to Wacissa Tower, the site of the old Spanish Missions of San Francisco de Oconi and La Conception de Ayubale. Ahead it passes near the KOA at CR 158B, where your base camp was recommended, and to Monticello, the county seat. The city has a 27-block historic district with a number of properties in the National Register of Historic Places, one of which is the acoustically perfect Perkins Opera House on Washington Street and Courthouse Square. Both the county and the city honor Thomas Jefferson, and "The Keystone County," is the state's only one that extends from Georgia to the Gulf.

### Information

Counties: Jefferson, Madison, Taylor
Average Temperatures: January, 44.8°F (low), 67.2°F (high); August, 71.1°F (low), 90°F (high)
State Properties: Cabbage Grove State Forest Fire Tower,

Rte. 1, Lamont, FL 32336, (904) 584-6371; Forest Capital State Museum, 204 Forest Park Dr., Perry, FL 32347, (904) 584-3227

Chambers of Commerce: Monticello–Jefferson County CC, 420 W. Washington St., Monticello, FL 32344, (904) 997-5552; Perry–Taylor County CC, P.O. Box 892, Perry, FL 32347, (904) 584-5366

Services and Amenities: *Commercial Campgrounds:* Camper's World, Rte. 1, Box 164B, Lamont, FL 32355, (904) 997-3300; Monticello KOA (Tallahassee East), Rte. 3, Box 25, Monticello, FL 32344, (904) 997-3890

*Bicycle Maps:* State Bicycle Program, (904) 488-4640; *Guided Canoe Trips:* Down River Canoe Trip, P.O. Box 837, Tallahassee, FL 32302, (904) 222-5546

# 4

# NORTHWEST REGION

Northwest Florida—the Panhandle—with two time zones, is distinctly different from other regions of the state in topography, agriculture, and history. Its east-west boundary is from the Aucilla River to the Perdido River, and its north boundaries are Alabama and Georgia, from which settlers migrated rapidly after Florida became a U.S. territory in 1821. Between 1835 and 1850 the area around Tallahassee and from Georgia to the Gulf was the most populated in the state. The new migrants brought with them the culture and life-style of the Old South, the slave plantation system. They built mansions, many that remain today in Jefferson, Leon, and Gadsden counties. The 1860 census revealed the seaports of Pensacola and Apalachicola as some of the state's most "urban places" at the time. Now, in the 1990s, the northwest region is the lowest in population—an advantage for citizens who wish to retain much of the Old South charm and flavor of the original, traditional, natural Florida.

Previous to the arrival of the first inland Spanish explorer, Pánfilo de Narváez, in 1528, Florida's northwest region was inhabited by Apalachee Indians, a horticulturally minded tribe in the Tallahassee area; the Chatot group in the Marianna area; and the Panzacola in the Perdido River basin. In the late seventeenth century the Spanish converted some of the Indians to Christianity and built missions for them; between 1704 and 1710 the British colonists burned the missions. Between 1763 and 1783, British colonial rulers created two separate Floridas: the peninsula was East Florida, and the present-day Panhandle, all the way to the Mississippi River, was West Florida. In the First Seminole War (1817–1818), U.S. Army Col. D. L. Clinch invaded Spanish Florida from Fort Scott, north of Tallahassee. General Andrew Jackson killed or captured what Indians or escaped slaves had been spared when he invaded the Panhandle in 1818. It is no wonder that the Apalachee named their last central village Tallahassee, which means "abandoned village."

Tallahassee is the largest city of the Panhandle, the seat of government since 1824, the home of Florida State University, founded in 1857, and the center of museums and historic buildings. Pensacola and Panama City are the second and third largest cities, respectively, with the summer-crowded 100-mile "Miracle Strip" of commerce and tourism between them. Pensacola, with its Old Spanish and Old South atmosphere, is the state's largest landlocked deep-water harbor and the birthplace of American military aviation. Panama City has long been known as a vacation and fishing mecca.

The Panhandle is home to Eglin Air Force Base, which has the world's largest climatic laboratory; a major Indian temple mound in Fort Walton Beach; the state's first constitution convention site (1838) in Port Saint Joe; the state's first chartered railroad route (1836), between Tallahassee and Saint Marks; and a shrine in Apalachicola to honor Dr. John Gorrie, whose artificial ice-making machine led to air-conditioning (1845).

It is also home to some of the state's most cherished natural resources: the expansive Apalachicola Natural Forest, the state's largest; the remote Blackwater River State Forest; the Florida Caverns; Saint Marks and Saint Vincent wildlife refuges; Gulf Islands National Seashore; springs like Wakulla; rivers like Apalachicola; and twenty state parks. The northern half of this uncrowded landstrip features rolling hill farms of corn, soybeans, peanuts, watermelons, and tomatoes; headwaters of clean streams, longleaf-pine and hardwood forests; rangeland; and Florida's highest point in elevation, Lakewood (345 feet), in sight of the Alabama state line. Southward, the natural habitats are mixed hardwood and cypress hammocks, swamps, estuaries, bayous, and bays. Slender barrier islands

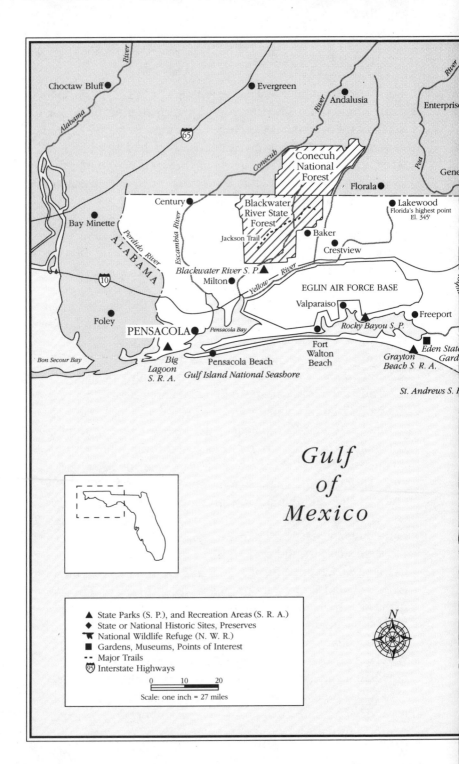

Choctaw Bluff●

●Evergreen

Andalusia

Enterpris

*River*

*Alabama River*

65

Conecuh
National
Forest

*Conecub*

*Pea*

Florala●

Gene

Century●

Blackwater
River State
Forest

●Lakewood
Florida's highest point
El. 345'

Bay Minette●

*Escambia River*

*Perdido River*

A L A B A M A

Jackson Trail

●Baker

Crestview

*Blackwater River S. P.*▲
Milton●

*Yellow River*

EGLIN AIR FORCE BASE

Valparaiso●

Foley●

10

PENSACOLA●

*Pensacola Bay*

Fort
Walton
Beach

*Rocky Bayou S. P.*▲

●Freeport

Eden Stat
*Grayton* Gard
*Beach S. R. A.*■

*Bon Secour Bay*

▲
*Big
Lagoon
S. R. A.*

Pensacola Beach

*Gulf Island National Seashore*

St. Andrews S.

*Gulf
of
Mexico*

▲ State Parks (S. P.), and Recreation Areas (S. R. A.)
◆ State or National Historic Sites, Preserves
🐾 National Wildlife Refuge (N. W. R.)
■ Gardens, Museums, Points of Interest
-- Major Trails
⑨ Interstate Highways

0      10      20

Scale: one inch = 27 miles

N

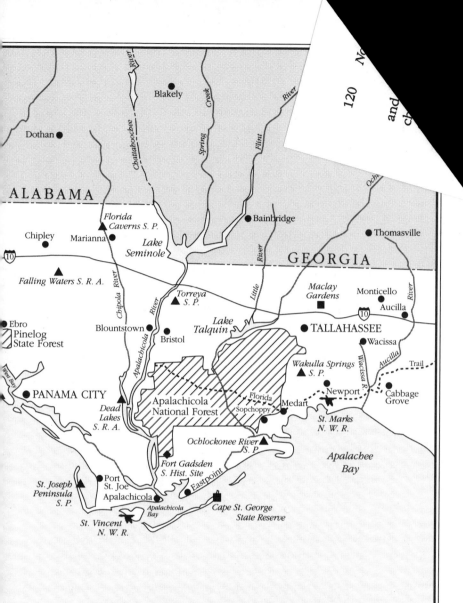

# NORTHWEST
# FLORIDA

❖

crystal white beaches garnish the mainland. Among your choices for outdoor exploration are 200 miles of bicycle trails, 275 miles of hiking trails (including the Florida Trail), 100 miles of equestrian trails, and 15 canoe rivers; or you can bird-watch (almost everywhere), scuba dive, fish, and, a rare option, go spelunking.

## APALACHICOLA NATIONAL FOREST

*Apalachicola* is an Apalachee Indian word meaning "friendly people who live on the other side." A river, town, bay, and forest carry the name. Once the domain of the Apalachee, the state's largest national forest (558,813 acres) borders the capital city, Tallahassee, to the northeast and the historic Apalachicola River to the southwest. Six expansive water-sheds support an exceptionally diverse plant and animal habitat, home to an estimated 10,000 deer, 2,000 turkeys, and 175 bears, in its swamps, savannahs, hammocks, and sandhills. Snake-shaped creeks and branches wind through the forest to the rivers like limbs on lengthy tree trunks. Hundreds of pools and lakes from ancient sinks dot the forest. Two isolated wilderness areas, the 24,000-acre Bradwell Bay and the 8,000-acre Mud Swamp–New River, are as inaccessible today as they were to the Apalachee.

The Trout Pond Recreation Area, unique to the forest, serves disabled individuals in addition to the general public; for example, its paved Discovery Nature Trail has signs in braille, and its swimming pool is constructed to serve mobility-impaired people.

*What to See and Do:* Your adventure options in this forest are to hike the 66-mile Apalachicola Trail, now the Florida National Scenic Trail (described separately in this chapter); horseback ride on the 30-mile Vinzant Riding Trail; fish for bream, bass, and perch; canoe the Sopchoppy and other rivers; and go birding along an incredible network of forest roads (2,049 miles) where there are, for example, six hundred active red-cockaded woodpecker colonies—twenty times as many as in north Florida's Ocala National Forest.

*Where to Begin:* From Tallahassee, access via US 319 and SR 373 south, and SR 20 west; from Bristol, use CR 12 south; from Apalachicola, take SR 65 north off of US 98; from Sopchoppy, use SR 375 north; and from Wakulla, take SR 267 west. The nearest airport is Tallahassee Municipal Airport, at the northeast edge of the forest. Once you are in the backcountry of this great forest, you will need a current forest map from either of the ranger district offices. (See *Information.*)

*About the Adventures:* The forest has eighteen recreational areas, ten of which are campgrounds that range from primitive (no drinking water) at Hitchcock Lake to developed (with a cold shower) at Silver Lake. None have hookups. To get to Silver Lake, which I suggest as your north base camp, go west 3.5 miles on SR 20 from its junction with SR 263 in Tallahassee and turn south on Silver Lake Road, SR 260. After 3.2 miles you will reach a campground of pine and cypress with a spring-fed lake, a swimming beach, nature trails, spacious campsites with picnic tables, and an RV dump station. Hickory Landing and Lake Wright, both picturesque and peaceful under moss-draped cypress at Owl Creek, make good south base camps. They have picnic tables, restrooms, and drinking water. Access is on FR 101, off SR 65, 2 miles south of Sumatra and 22 miles north from US 98 at Green Point. Those who prefer a full-service campground for a south base camp might try a commercial camp (no tenting) in Tallahassee, or try Ochlockonee River State Park 4 miles south of Sopchoppy on US 319. (See *Information.*)

The Apalachicola River, the boundary between eastern and central time zones, flows within a few miles of the western edge of the forest. A jungle of uninhabitable and inhospitable wetlands prevent walking access to the river for 40 miles downstream, except at Fort Gadsden State Historic Site. Exhibits at a kiosk describe the old British fort's violent, gruesome past and explain how Gen. Andrew Jackson used it as a supply base for destroying the Seminole settlements in

1818. Access to the fort, a former steamboat landing, is on FR 129, off SR 65, 2 miles south of Hickory Landing. The powerful, impressive river is wide, sometimes swift, and brown from flooded tributaries; it passes through hardwood forest, broad marshes of grasses with wildfowl, and unexplored swamps. Steamboats, ferries, and barges once used the Apalachicola for transportation north to Georgia and Alabama. Because of its remoteness, lack of access, and motorboat traffic, the river is not recommended for canoeing—but five canoe access points do make the challenge possible for the adventurous explorer. If you go, take a forest, county, or topographic map (of Orange, Kennedy Creek, and Forbes Island) because the intractable maze of backwater arms and connecting sloughs can easily have you lost. At Big Gully Landing, you can follow the Equaloxic Creek 5 miles, catching bass, catfish, and bream on the way. From the town of Bristol, access is 12.8 miles south on CR 12, right on CR 379 for one mile, and right again (west) on FR 133 for one mile. Within 2 miles of the river is White Oak Landing on the River Styx. Its entrance is 8 miles south of Big Gully on FR 115, west. Both Wright Lake and Hickory Landing on Owl Creek are within 2 miles of the river (access mentioned above). Cotton Landing, on Kennedy Creek, is a good stream for fishing; it is on FR 123, off CR 379, between White Oak Landing and Wright Lake. It is 5 miles on the creek to the Apalachicola River.

The U.S. Forest Service began restoring the Apalachicola Forest after it purchased the land in 1936; heavy logging and naval stores had damaged it after the turn of the century. Today, timbering is selective, with annual cuts averaging 30 million board feet. Of the gross revenue, 25 percent, or an annual average of $1 million, goes to the four counties in the forest. Ubiquitous groves of loblolly and slash pine provide the chief timber source. In the remote areas, particularly in the wilderness areas, are sections of undisturbed climax forest with slash pine and cypress up to 400 years old. On a space percentage, the Apalachicola has fewer inholdings than the Ocala. It also has twice the growing timber stock of the Ocala,

*Gray Fox, Apalachicola National Forest.* PHOTO BY Florida
Game and Fresh Water Fish Commission.

yet the Ocala sells and harvests twice as much timber. Nearly half of Apalachicola's acreage has been leased to oil and gas companies, but you will not see any active wells at this time; 1,298 acres are leased for cattle grazing.

Apalachicola has a larger percentage of wildlife than Ocala, including 85 percent more wild turkeys. (But the bald eagle is rare in Apalachicola, while as many as seventy-five adults and perhaps thirty-five fledglings live in Ocala.) Deer, turkey, squirrel, quail, rabbit, raccoon, fox, nutria, wild hog, armadillo, mink, otter, opossum, snakes, frogs, and many species of birds all inhabit the forest. Bear, bobcat, and coyote are also here but are more illusive. Because of game hunting in the forest, mainly from November through February, hikers are advised to camp only at designated campsites. (Secure a wildlife management list of hunting periods from the offices of the district rangers.) Although the Apalachicola has 150,000 more acres than the Ocala National Forest, it has only 20 percent as many visitor days (the equivalent of one person remaining at a site for 12 hours). As a result, your sojourn into this vast forest should provide you with a secluded respite in which to study the natural environment.

Some of the forest's scenic geological areas are River Sinks, Rocky Bluff, Morrison Hammock, and the Dismal and Leon sinks complex. The latter is only 5 miles south of Tallahassee off US 319, west, at the boundary of Wakulla and Leon counties. It has a 3.3-mile loop trail. River Sinks and Kini Spring are another 2 miles south off US 319, east. Rocky Bluff Scenic Area is on FR 390, 3 miles south of Bloxham on SR 375. The major forest spring is at Morrison Hammock Scenic Area off SR 399, east, 4 miles south of Sopchoppy on US 319. Some streams have small springs for headwaters; others, like Lost Creek, which flows for more than 30 miles before it vanishes underground southwest of Crawfordville, are less defined.

Canoeing options on the Ochlockonee River, the forest's longest canoe route, range from short day trips to overnights. One easy route is at cypress-bordered Lake Bradford at the southwest corner of Tallahassee on SR 263, toward the airport.

Because Bradford has no current, this is a good place for beginners to paddle in either direction. For best conditions, canoe when the water gauge is above 1.2 feet (100 feet east of the culvert on SR 263, north of the airport). About halfway, in the multiple lakes, you will encounter a narrow channel. In contrast to Lake Bradford, 10-mile Lost Creek is considered challenging because of its sharp bends, fallen trees, and cypress knees. The best season for canoeing is from June to September when the water is usually at its highest. To access the Lost Creek put-in from Crawfordville, go 7 miles on SR 368, west (which becomes FR 13), to FR 350. Turn right, go one mile, and put in at the bridge. Take out on SR 368, at the bridge, 2 miles west of Crawfordville. The water gauge at the take-out should register 4.5 feet or more for best conditions.

Another challenging canoe route is on the Sopchoppy River, which parallels the exceptionally wild and beautiful Bradwell Bay Wilderness Area. Although you can paddle for nearly 35 miles to US 319 south of Sopchoppy, the first 15 miles are exclusively through the forest and the last 10 flow through private inholdings before leaving the forest. The run can be strenuous, with sudden turns, narrow spaces, and tricky maneuvering among the cypress knees. Level bank tops and sandbars provide easy camping spots. The river flows through a forest of tall longleaf pine, magnolia, saw palmetto, yaupon, titi, blueberry, and wild azalea, and through the home of bear, bobcat, and otter. Before you attempt this trip you should check the water gauge at Mount Besser bridge on FR 343, 3 miles northwest of Sopchoppy, to be certain that you have adequate water, 10 feet or higher on the gauge. To access, take SR 368 (which becomes FR 13) from Crawfordville and go 11 miles to the Sopchoppy bridge. Your first take-out is 10 miles downstream at FR 329 at a cement bridge and junction with the Florida Trail. (It is about 9 miles from here to Crawfordville via FR 348 to FR 365 to SR 368.) If you continue downstream you will notice high banks of white sand, huge cypress, and constant growth of cypress knees. (The Florida Trail parallels the river on the west side, giving hikers a scenic view.) Your take-out after 5 miles is at FR 346, at the Oak Park bridge near a power line, north of Sopchoppy.

The Apalachicola's longest and most challenging river is the Ochlockonee, which flows 50 miles through the entire forest center, separating the Apalachicola Ranger District, west, and the Wakulla Ranger District, east. Six campsites have limited facilities (mainly hand water pumps and latrines); not all are at the riverbank, and you will need a forest map with some checkpoint guidance from a ranger or a canoe guide as to what side stream or backwater arm to take. Or put in at your take-out first, paddle the short distance to the river, and leave a ribbon on a tree limb or other recognizable marker. The Ochlockonee River begins in Worth County, Georgia, and flows 150 miles to the Gulf, but for the purpose of this trip, I recommend a put-in at Pine Creek Landing and a take-out 19 miles later at Mack Landing. The water depth is controlled by water released from the Talquin Lake dam at SR 20 in Bloxham; be certain there is enough water to make your trip enjoyable and worthwhile. For information, call the City of Tallahassee Utility Department, (904) 576-2572.

To reach Pine Creek Landing, drive 10 miles south from Bloxham on SR 375 to FR 335 and turn west for 1.5 miles to a boat ramp. For the first 2 miles the national forest boundary will be to your left, but for the remainder the forest will be only on your right because of inholdings. At about 3 miles the river divides; follow west of the island. Soon thereafter you will pass under the FR 13 bridge. (There is no access point here, but you are only 0.8 mile west from SR 375 and 0.6 mile east from Porter Lake Campground, which has picnic tables, water, and restrooms.) About 2 miles farther, a backwater route makes Porter Lake and Whitehead Lake campgrounds accessible to the right, but unless you know the river and have previously tied your ribbon to a tree you will have difficulty locating the access. After 13 miles you will reach Lower Langston Landing on the west bank for camping (without facilities) and a take-out on FR 152 to SR 67. Your take-out point is 6 miles farther on the east bank at Mack Landing, which has drinking water, restrooms, and tables. Access here is on FR 336, 1.5 miles out to SR 375. Below Mack Landing you could canoe another 12 miles to Wood Lake at FR 338, but the area is not as scenic and you will share the river with motorized craft.

The forest contains the largest population of red-cockaded woodpeckers, a threatened species in the Southeast. Hardly larger than a bluebird, both male and female are black with rows of white marks on the back and white cheeks. Only the male has a small red streak behind his eyes. Red-cockaded woodpeckers group in clans; each clan may have as many as nine birds, but never more than one breeding pair. Clan members nest and roost in a selection of cavity trees (usually less than ten trees) called a colony. They are the only birds that peck out living quarters in live pines, which are usually between 50 and 100 years old. It may take months or years to complete a cavity, around which they will peck resin wells that drain the pine bark. The resin protects the birds against small mammals, snakes, and other predators. To survive, the woodpeckers need a large pine forest for foraging, normally 100 acres for each clan; they diet almost exclusively on the larvae of wood-boring insects. Nesting is between April and July, when the female lays an average of three eggs in the breeding male's roosting nest. During the day the clan members take turns incubating the eggs, but the breeding male cares for them at night. During the nesting season resin matts the pair's plumage, but nature has its way with a postnuptial molt of new feathers. The red-cockaded's well-constructed home is the envy of some other birds, particularly of other woodpeckers, which physically compete to acquire it, and flying squirrels. To see their habitat, go quietly with your binoculars along forest roads 369, 307, 373, 367, and 360, which connect with SR 267 between SR 20 and US 319, about 7 miles southwest of Tallahassee. To assist you, the forest service has painted a double yellow band around colony pines.

Another threatened species in the Apalachicola is the

gopher tortoise, which burrows into the sandy soil of the piney forest. Like the red-cockaded woodpecker, the gopher tortoise builds a home that entices other animals to move in. You are likely to see gopher tortoises in a large section of the forest near Leon Sinks Geological Area, about 5 miles southeast of Tallahassee between US 319 and SR 373.

Equestrians will find well-maintained trails marked red, white, and blue for 30 miles on the forest's Vinzant Riding Trail. On this trail, open to the public without charge, you can ride your horse through open pinelands and lowlands of lush shrubbery and wildflowers. To parking and access, go west about 12 miles from Tallahassee on SR 20, past Fort Braden School, and turn left on FR 342 to the junction with SR 267.

Near the forest are other natural attractions—botanical gardens, Indian mounds, and a natural history museum—that you may wish to visit. One of the most scenic areas is 1,062-acre Torreya State Park, 12 miles north of Bristol on SR 12 and CR 270 or CR 271. The serene and beautiful park is on the high hills east of the Apalachicola River. Here the Apalachee Indians lived, General Jackson and his army crossed the river in 1818, famous steamboats stopped, the Jason Gregory plantation building has been moved, Confederate guns protected the steamboats plying the river, and the CCC manicured the landscape in the 1930s. You will find river swamps, hardwood and pine forest, and a waterfall on the steep Weeping Ridge Trail. Streams cascade over limestone shelves, and hard red clay bluffs line the 7-mile Apalachicola River Bluff Trail. Wildlife is prominent, with at least 140 species of mammals and reptiles and 125 species of birds. Color is intense in spring with dogwood, redbud, wild azalea, and yellow jessamine, and in autumn with hardwood foliage. The campground has full service and an overlook where you can sit on a bench under a sweet gum above the Apalachicola River Valley. Far in the distance are lights, like evening stars, on I-10, but they are too far away for you to hear the traffic— another reason to be at this tranquil place.

River Bluff State Recreation Area is on the south side of

Lake Talquin; access is on Jack Vausa Road, 10.3 miles west on SR 20 from the SR 263 junction in Tallahassee. Here are fishing for largemouth bass, speckled perch, and shellcracker in the lake, and a scenic loop nature trail on the bluff.

In Tallahassee, the Museum of Florida History offers intriguing displays of mastodons, Indian Artifacts, and Spanish doubloons and armaments—a glimpse at the state's evolution from prehistoric times to present. You can also see the San Luis Archaeological and Historic Site and the excavation grounds of ancient Indians. Begin your tour at the R. A. Gray Building, 500 South Bronough Street, in downtown Tallahassee. To visit the Lake Jackson Mounds, leave downtown on Monroe Street, US 27, and go north about 4 miles to an overpass of I-10 (Exit 29). Continue ahead 1.7 miles to Crowder Road and turn right. This is one of the most important historic sites of Florida Indians, estimated to have covered 81 acres between A.D. 1200 and A.D. 1500. The park is open daily. From the mounds, return to I-10 and follow it 4 miles east to Exit 30. Turn north on US 319, Thomasville Road, and in less than a mile you will be at Alfred B. Maclay State Gardens. The Big Pine Nature Trail offers scenic views of Lake Hall and the hillside woods. From mid-December to April 30 is peak blooming season.

An exciting rails-to-trails experience on the 15.8-mile Tallahassee/St. Marks Historic Railroad State Trail begins at the southwest corner of SR 283 (Capital Circle Highway) and SR 363 (Woodville Highway). Paved with asphalt for hikers, bikers, and skaters, it also has a parallel dirt trail for horseback riding. There are a few sites with picnic tables and drinking water. (A shelter is planned north of Wakulla.) Bicycles are available for rent at the north trailhead. The south trailhead is in the town of St. Marks where the Florida National Scenic Trail follows it for 1.7 miles from US 98. The railroad trail, which parallels SR 363 on the west side, passes through pine and hardwood forests, agricultural fields, and sparse residential areas. (See State Properties in *Information.*)

If you plan a bicycle trip, you have a 100-mile loop with

subloops on Route B: Canopy Roads. (See *Aucilla Sinks and Wacissa Springs,* Chapter 3.) You may begin the Moccasin Gap (B-1) section at the Maclay State Gardens on Maclay Road, west to Meridian Road. On its 38-mile route, it passes through the countryside to Miccosukee and Lloyd. From there you could take the Tallahassee Hills (B-2) section to Monticello, Waukeena, and the Wacissa Springs for 30 miles. The Bellamy Road (B-3) section takes you through more grazing pastures and beautiful countryside along the Old Saint Augustine Road for 15 miles. (The historic route was first constructed by John Bellamy and his slaves from Saint Augustine to Pensacola.) Along this route is Southwood Plantation, home of the late Edward Ball, financier, naturalist, and former owner of the Wakulla Springs. Your other two sections, Old Fort (B-4), for 3 miles, and Historic Mansions (B-5), for 5 miles, are within the city of Tallahassee. They include Old Fort Park (commemorating the Civil War), capital buildings, the historic district, and the governor's mansion. (See *Bicycling,* Chapter 2.) Another historic site is 12 miles southeast of Tallahassee. Take SR 363 6 miles to Woodville and turn east on Natural Bridge Road, SR 354, for 6 miles to Natural Bridge Battlefield, where the Saint Marks River once flowed underground to form a bridge. Two first-magnitude springs are here. Confederate troops, including Florida teenage cadets and elderly men, repelled Union troops here in March 1865, a month before the Civil War was over, keeping them from entering Tallahassee, the only Confederate capital east of the Mississippi not captured.

Twelve miles south of Tallahassee on US 319 and SR 61 is Wakulla Springs, one of the world's deepest springs, an expedient place for filming *Creature of the Black Lagoon.* Wakulla Springs, with an Indian name meaning "mysteries of strange waters," are at least 250 feet deep and have unknown linear distances (underground channels) from which gush 600,000 gallons of clear 70-degree water each minute. Now a 2,888-acre state park honoring Wildlife Foundation founder Edward Ball, it is a birding mecca, a habitat for thousands of waterfowl—gallinules, egrets, ibis, wigeons, and lesser scaups—seen mainly from guided tours on glass-bottom wildlife observation boats. Facilities include a picnic area, nature trails, a beach, and a swimming area. Lodging and meals are available at the Wakulla Springs Lodge, a Spanish-style inn with Tennessee marble floors, decorative arches and beams, and high-ceilinged rooms. (Call in advance for reservations.) Home-cooked dinners are served in a dining room with a large fireplace. The park restricts swimming except in designated areas. (In 1987, an alligator drowned a snorkler who entered restricted downstream waters.) Private boats, canoes, and fishing are not allowed.

### Information

Counties: Liberty, Franklin, Leon, Wakulla

Average Temperatures: January, 43.8°F (low), 67°F (high); August, 71.1° (low), 89.6° (high)

National Properties: Apalachicola Ranger District (SR 20), P.O. Box 579, Bristol, FL 32321, (904) 643-2282; Wakulla Ranger District (US 319), Rte. 6, Box 7860, Tallahassee, FL 32327, (904) 926-3561; Forest Headquarters, City Centre Bldg., 227 N. Bronough St., Suite 4061, Tallahassee, FL 32301, (904) 681-7265

State Properties: Alfred B. Maclay State Gardens, 3540 Thomasville Rd., Tallahassee, FL 32308, (904) 487-4556; Fort Gadsden State Historic Site, P.O. Box 157, Sumatra, FL 32335, (904) 670-8988; Lake Jackson Mounds State Archaeological Site, 1313 Crowder Rd., Tallahassee, FL 32308, (904) 922-6007; Lake Talquin State Recreation Area, 1022 De Soto Park Dr., Tallahassee, FL 32301, (904) 922-6007; Torreya State Park, Rte. 2, Box 70, Bristol, FL 32321, (904) 643-2674; Wakulla Springs State Park, Wakulla Springs Rd., Wakulla Springs, FL 32305, (904) 922-3633 (Wakulla Springs Lodge and Conference Center, [904] 224-5950); Ochlockonee River State Park (4 miles south of Sopchoppy on US 319), P.O. Box 5, Sopchoppy, FL 32358, (904) 962-2771; Museum of Florida History, 500 S. Bronough St., Tallahassee, FL 32399, (904) 488-1484

Chambers of Commerce: Florida CC, 136 S. Bronough St.,

Tallahassee, FL 32301, (904) 425-1200; Liberty County CC, P.O. Box 523, Bristol, FL 32321, (904) 643-2359; Tallahassee Area CC, 100 N. Duval St., Tallahassee, FL 32301, (904) 224-8116; Tallahassee Convention and Visitors Bureau, 200 W. College Ave., Tallahassee, FL 32302, (904) 681-9200 and (800) 628-2866

Services and Amenities: *Commercial Camping:* Bell's Campground (no tents; one mile west on US 90 from SR 283), 6401 W. Tennessee St., Tallahassee, FL 32304, (904) 575-5006

*Bicycle Maps:* State Bicycle Program, (904) 488-4640; *Canoe Liveries:* The Canoe Shop, 3102 S. Adams St., Tallahassee, FL 32301, (904) 877-1792; Down River Canoe Trips, P.O. Box 837, Tallahassee, FL 32302, (904) 222-5546

## FLORIDA NATIONAL SCENIC TRAIL

In 1988 the Florida Trail became the Florida National Scenic Trail, the eighth trail designated under the National Trails System Act passed by Congress in 1968. Unlike any other national trail, it extends through the nation's only subtropical region, making it accessible throughout the winter season. Of the 1,300 miles proposed and under sectional construction by volunteers of the Florida Trail Association, more than 500 miles are now continuous in the central and north regions of Florida and in part of the Panhandle region. Providing access to some of Florida's most unique natural environments, the trail begins in Big Cypress National Preserve, near the north edge of Everglades National Park, and will, when completed, end on the white sand beaches of Gulf Islands National Seashore at Pensacola. In Big Cypress the trail passes through miles of marshes, prairies, hardwood hammocks, and dwarf pond cypress adorned with bromeliads and orchids. After following the rim of Lake Okeechobee, it enters central Florida on the Kissimmee River Basin. In the Ocala National Forest the route is through the nation's largest stand of sand pine along clear, clean, natural springs. After crossing through stands of long-leaf pine in the Osceola National Forest, it turns westward to follow the limestone and high sand banks of the Suwannee River, en route to the Aucilla River area. Turning southwest, it passes through the Saint Marks National Wildlife Refuge and follows the former Apalachicola Trail through the Apalachicola National Forest to its end near Bristol and the Apalachicola River.

In the early 1960s, James A. Kern, a Miami wildlife photographer and real estate broker, hiked southern sections of the Appalachian Trail and returned to Florida with a desire to have a long trail in his home state. He discussed his dream with a few of the state's environmentalists—Marjory Stoneman Douglas, Archie Carr, Ross Allen, and Allan D. Cruickshank. To bring the trail idea to public attention, Kern led a well-publicized hike of 160 miles in 12 days from the Oasis on the Tamiami Trail Highway to Sebring in 1964. In the same year he prepared a charter for the establishment of the Florida Trail Association (FTA). Two years later, in September and October, he led other long hikes in the Corkscrew Swamp Sanctuary and from Fisheating Creek to Highlands Hammock State Park. By the end of October Kern and a friend, Cliff Edstrom, had rendezvoused with Tom Montoya, Ken Alvarez, Margaret Scruggs, and U.S. Forest Service officials at Clearwater Lake Recreation Area in the Ocala National Forest. Their purpose was to flag and blaze 70 miles of the "first" Florida Trail. "I doubt that any of the present trail through the Ocala lies on that route, but it was a start," says Scruggs, the association's historian. On December 3, 1966, the FTA held its first annual meeting. Since then it has grown to more than 5,000 members, and maintains more than 1,000 miles of trails that include the main route of the Florida Trail as well as local trails.

The FTA, "dedicated to developing and maintaining hiking trails," makes available to its members a guidebook with maps, *Walking the Florida Trail,* and publishes a public trail guide and a trail manual. (See *Information.*) The association tabloid, *Footprint,* publishes chapter news, directories, and information about trail changes, regional and state conferences, and weekly hiking activities throughout the state. There are 14 chapters of the FTA, located in such cities as Jacksonville, Tallahassee, Miami, Oviedo, Gainesville, Fort Lauderdale, De Land, Lake Wales, Melbourne, Lake Park, Panama City, Tampa, McAlpin, and Pensacola. Contact the main office for the names and addresses of the chapter leaders for the areas you wish to hike.

Although I and a few other hikers had sporadically completed all parts of the Florida Trail before Steve Sheridan, it was the 21-year-old musician from Tallahassee who brought national media attention to the trail in the spring of 1989. Considered the first through hiker, Sheridan completed 700 miles in 47 days from Big Cypress Swamp Preserve to the Camel Lake area of the Apalachicola National Forest.

*What to See and Do:* Sections of the Florida Trail are covered elsewhere in this book, but the 110 miles of the first three sections designated to national status are described below. The route crosses the Apalachicola and Wakulla ranger districts; crosses four canoeable rivers; passes through the remote Bradwell Bay Wilderness, the historic town of Saint Marks, and the ghost town of Port Leon; and follows dike passages in Saint Marks National Wildlife Refuge. You will see an extraordinarily wide variety of wildlife.

*Where to Begin:* Take Exit 22 or 25 from I-10 (west of Tallahassee) for 20 miles to Bristol. At the junction of SR 20 in Bristol, drive south on SR 12 10 miles to the trailhead on the left (0.6 mile north of the forest work center). The eastern trailhead is on US 98 (0.7 mile west of the Aucilla River bridge) 13.6 miles east of the Newport entrance to the Saint Marks National Wildlife Refuge. The nearest municipal airport is in Tallahassee, 45 miles east of Bristol.

*About the Adventures:* To acquaint yourself with the first 66 miles of this trek, read the adventures of the Apalachicola National Forest in the beginning of this chapter. The other 44 miles are in the Saint Marks National Wildlife Refuge. On this trip, plan 7 to 10 days to allow for nature study, changes in the weather, and side trips. Observing wildlife in Saint Marks National Wildlife Refuge can take at least a day or two, and the nearby areas of Otter Lake at Panacea Field can easily be another day. Other areas, such as Ochlockonee River State Park, Wakulla and Newport springs, and Wakulla Beach, are worth leisurely visits. If you are exploring the Apalachicola National Forest and canoeing in the forest or nearby rivers, or bicycling in and around Tallahassee, you will need another week or two.

The national forest does not require a permit or restrict where you can camp, but in the Saint Marks National Wildlife Refuge only through hikers are allowed to camp, with a permit, at the six designated wilderness-type campsites. You will need complete backpacking gear for this trip. There are no shelters, only one small town on the trail, and, for the first 66 miles, only three state roads leading to supplies or to help in an emergency. Potable water is at Camel Lake and Porter Lake campgrounds in the first 33 miles. Other sources are a store on US 98/319, the US 98 bridge over the Saint Marks River, the town of Saint Marks, and the refuge visitor center. All water from surface sources should be boiled or chemically treated. Groceries, restaurants, and lodging are available on the trail only in the town of Saint Marks, but are near the trail when you cross US 319, US 98, and SR 365. It is best not to hike alone, particularly through the Bradwell Bay Wilderness Area, where water in the rainy season can be to your waist and where titi groves impede your passage and block the visibility of orange blazes. It is advisable never to leave the trail in this remote wilderness. Take a current forest and refuge map and a compass, and if you do go alone, inform a ranger of your plans. It is also advisable to wear safety orange apparel during the winter hunting season, usually from mid-November to February 1.

Start at the west entrance on SR 12, 10 miles south of Bristol and 1.3 miles north of FR 105 (Camel Lake Road). Follow the trail east through a frequently wet savannah of wild orchids and other wildflowers and into a forest of hardwoods, pines, and cypress. Arrive at Memery Island on higher ground at 3 miles. An alternate blue-blazed trail follows a more eastern route to rejoin the Florida Trail between Camel Lake and Big Gully Creek. At 5 miles, the trail crosses FR 105, where 0.1 mile on the right is Camel Lake. It has a campground with drinking water, picnic tables, and restrooms. The campground also has a wide trail that circles the lake. From here, follow the trail through fox and gopher tortoise habitat of pine, palmetto, colicroot, and turkey oak. To the left you will notice the junction on the blue-blazed route to Memery Island.

When you come to a junction with FR 105, cross the Big Gully bridge; then turn right into the woods to join and cross other forest roads. Along the way you will experience damp areas with trumpet plants, sundews, and hat pins. A few sections of dense Saint-John's-wort turn the open piney areas into an expansive subcanopy of yellow gold in the springtime.

At 15.3 miles the trail meets SR 65; turn left here on the highway to cross the New River bridge. An immediate right leads you to the Apalachicola Northern Railroad and the former turpentine camp of Vilas, where turpentine was harvested from pine and shipped on the railroad to market. Among the weeds and forest are remnants of the buildings. For the next 13 miles you will go through a pine-palmetto forest with segments of titi and Saint-John's-wort. You will cross five different forest roads; notice that the trail has an affinity for FR 107, which it crosses and follows a number of times. At one section, near the crossing of Indian Creek, it follows more than 2 miles on the shadeless road. Another crossing of Indian Creek is at the SR 67 bridge and its tributary, Coxes Branch, 0.4 mile after the bridge at SR 67. After crossing Hickory Branch and FR 142, you will cross paved FR 13 and descend to Porter Lake Campground near the Ochlockonee River bridge. Here are picnic tables, restrooms, drinking water, and a cleared area under tall trees for campsites. (An emergency telephone is available at a private residence, north on FR 13, near the junction with SR 375.) The river is the boundary between Liberty and Wakulla counties, and between the Apalachicola ranger district, through which you have passed, and the

Wakulla ranger district, through which you will continue.

After crossing the FR 13 bridge, follow the trail up an embankment to an inholding, whose boundary is along the Ochlockonee River, and out of the forest across Smith Creek bridge on SR 375. This section of the trail is 3.6 narrow, twisting miles among hardwoods, by a huge sawdust pile, and near the dark, silent, sinister Ochlockonee River to your right. When you cross SR 375 again, you will be in a pine forest that becomes a mixed forest on its way to FR 314, the west boundary of the Bradwell Bay Wilderness Area. Turn right on SR 314 and follow it 0.6 mile to the wilderness entrance, left. In the next 11.6 miles the trail has two short spurs, the first after 5 miles and the second at 6.4 miles. Both are marked with signs off FR 329, the nearest parallel route on the south boundary. The bay is an immense saucer shape of lowlands surrounded by higher ground. It has virgin stands of high slash pine, spared from the loggers early in the twentieth century. An undergrowth of dense titi, saw palmetto, and grasses offers coverage for the small mammals, and clusters of oaks, black gums, and maples shade songbirds, owls, and hawks. Prominent in the wilderness are two species of titi: the fragrant black titi (*Cliftonia monophylla*), also called buckwheat, which flowers from March through April, and leatherwood (*Cyrilla racemiflora*), which flowers in May and June. Patches of carnivorous flora—pitcher plants, sundews, and bladderworts—are in wet areas.

Wildlife includes snakes, alligators, bears, deer, raccoons, sandhill cranes, wild turkeys, ospreys, eagles, woodpeckers, and other birds. Hunters have legendary tales about the bay's "wildcats and panthers and snakes as long as a man is tall." Perhaps the most legendary hunters were Carl Bradwell, for whom the bay is named, and his father. The story, as told in 1989 by 87-year-old Otha Anderson, is that Carl's father and a companion went bear hunting in a dry season of the bay. They became lost, wandered around for days without food and water, and finally made their way out in "poor condition." To avoid carrying any extra weight, they had left an old shotgun in the "crook of a tree," a gun for which, during his lifetime, Carl offered $10,000 if found. The Bradwells and other exploratory hunters have named the streams here and nearby for animals—Alligator, Little Owl, Mosquito, Tiger, and Monkey.

About 5 miles into the bay you will be near the defined headwaters of Monkey Creek, where the trail takes a more northeastern direction. Later the trail joins an old forest road that curves south to parallel the Sopchoppy River. Along this route you will see hardwoods, holly, blueberry, titi, and orange milkweed. Fragrant wild azaleas also enhance this part of the trail. When you arrive at FR 329, turn left and follow the road 0.1 mile to the Sopchoppy River. Without crossing the road bridge, turn right downstream on a high bank near huge cypresses; this is one of the most scenic routes in the forest. After 2.7 miles, cross Monkey Creek on a footbridge, and after another 3.5 miles you will reach FR 343 to cross a road bridge over the Sopchoppy River. From here head southeast, cross FR 365 in a pine and oak forest, and later cross FR 356 before arriving at US 319, the end of the national forest and 66 miles on the trail. To the left (east), it is 0.3 mile before the trail leaves US 319 and enters the Saint Marks National Wildlife Refuge. To the right (west), on US 319, it is 4.7 miles to the town of Sopchoppy.

The next 44 miles, through the Saint Marks National Wildlife Refuge, has a greater variety of forest types and wildlife zones than any other refuge or forest in northern Florida. Within its 96,700 acres (31,700 of which are waters in the Apalachee Bay) are hardwood swamps and uplands, pine forests, tidal marshes, freshwater impoundments, rivers, and islands. You will find exceptional opportunities for hiking and backpacking; fishing, hunting, and crabbing; boating; and studying the 295 species of birds, 65 species of reptiles, and 50 species of mammals. During your journey you are likely to see many species, particularly the most common: deer, squirrels, rabbits, armadillos, wild hogs, raccoons, grebes, herons, double-crested cormorants, teals, hawks, sandpipers, terns, woodpeckers, tree swallows, warblers, sparrows, alligators, turtles, and lizards such as the green anole and broadheaded skink. Venomous reptiles—eastern coral snake, Florida cottonmouth, and pigmy and diamondback rattlesnakes—are common in the refuge.

Harbored in the Apalachee Bay (part of the Gulf's Big Bend), the refuge spreads across the southern end of Wakulla and Jefferson counties and the southwest tip of Taylor County. South-draining rivers are the Ochlockonee and Sopchoppy on the west boundary, the Aucilla on the east, and the Saint Marks and Wakulla in the center. On the east and northeast is the vast Aucilla Wildlife Management Area, and at the western border, across US 319, the Apalachicola National Forest. The refuge is divided into three administrative units: Panacea, west; Wakulla, central; and Saint Marks, east, where the refuge's administrative office and visitor center are located. Also in the Saint Marks unit are 2,205 acres of freshwater impoundments for year-round fishing, a haven for migratory birds, including Canada geese.

This refuge is among the oldest in the nation (1931), and the area's history can be traced from the shards of Indian hunting camps of the Middle Archaic period (8000-4000 B.C.). Archeologists have also found many burial mounds, advanced pottery designs, and shell beads of the Fort Walton period (A.D. 1000–1500). Exploring Spaniards, led by Pánfilo de Narváez, first came in 1527, followed by de Soto and his six hundred men in 1539. About 100 years later the Franciscan Fathers from Saint Augustine started missions in the area at the mouths of the Wakulla and Saint Marks rivers. Fourteen years after the English destroyed one, San Marcos de Apalache, in 1704, the Spanish built a new fort. For the next century control shifted between the English and the Spanish until Spain ceded Florida to the United States in 1821.

The refuge has a number of points of interest, some of which are close enough to the Florida Trail for exploration or hiking. Others are distant enough to warrant a drive before or after your Florida Trail journey. One historic place, the 80-

foot-high Saint Marks Lighthouse at the end of CR 59, was constructed in 1813 by Calvin Knowlton, who chose his limestone block foundations from the ruins of the old Fort San Marcos de Apalache in the town of Saint Marks. At another point of interest, Otter Lake Field in the Panacea unit, trails take you into a mixed forest with white sand, lakes, and wildflowers.

In an effort to encourage coexistence with and protection of the environment, the refuge has a combination of at least fifty commonsense regulations, low-impact trail techniques, and restrictions. Only through backpackers are allowed to camp in the refuge, and only then at the six wilderness-type campsites, for no more than one night at any one site. Open fires, firearms, and swimming are prohibited. A use permit (which requires a small, nonrefundable fee) must be requested from the refuge office in person, by mail, or by telephone at least 15 days prior to your trip. Access to the visitor center is on CR 59, Lighthouse Road, 3.6 miles south from the US 98 junction at the state Division of Forestry fire tower in Newport. Office hours are Monday through Friday, 8 A.M.–4:15 P.M., and Saturday and Sunday, 10 A.M.–5 P.M. (See *Information.*)

To continue on the Florida Trail from the Apalachicola National Forest at US 319, enter the Saint Marks National Wildlife Refuge and go 1.2 miles through the woods to US 98. (To the left [north], 0.6 mile is Medart, where you will find a store and laundry. To the right [south] 3 miles is Panacea, for groceries, fresh seafood restaurants [Angelo's and Posey's Beyond the Bay], a motel and a post office.) Ahead on the trail are campsites Marshpoint, at 4.5 miles; Wakulla Field, at 10 miles; and River Hammock, at 15 miles. Along the way you will be in a longleaf pine and mixed hardwood forest with bracken, wild phlox, sensitive briar, penstemon, and cross and trumpet vines. You will pass three blue-blazed spur or loop trails that lead to other varieties of vegetation. At 8.2 miles the trail reaches CR 365. (To the right, 1.3 miles, are groceries; Spring Creek Restaurant, with its homemade rum-coconut-carrot cake and unique dry-mix salad dressing; and a motel.)

The trail follows north on CR 365 for 1.3 miles before reentering the forest. At 19.2 miles you will reach US 98, where the trail turns right to cross the Wakulla River bridge. After 2.3 miles on the highway, turn right on the Saint Marks Trail, a multiple-use paved historic route to Saint Marks and a rails-to-trails project between Saint Marks and Tallahassee. (See *Apalachicola National Forest* in previous section.) When you come to the first paved road that crosses the trail (near a Baptist church), you have an option of a commercial campsite with hot showers and tent sites, or cabins at the Shell Island Fish Camp by the Wakulla River. (Access to the camp is right [west] one mile.) Continue on the trail about 0.5 mile to the fishing port village of Saint Marks. All the restaurants here are inexpensive and have good food. Posey's is known for its smoked mullet, baked oysters, homemade hot sauce, and hearty fishermen's atmosphere. While in Saint Marks, be sure to visit the historic fort of San Marcos de Apalache on Canal Street, which has a visitor center and a short trail, partly on a boardwalk over the edge of the Wakulla River. At this point you have backpacked 23.5 miles in the refuge. For the remainder of your hike, you will find the campsites East River at 27.8 miles, Ring Dike at 34.8 miles, and Pinhook River at 39.5 miles.

Ask a local fisherman at the dock to ferry you across the Saint Marks River to rejoin the trail. After you cross, you will be in the Saint Marks Wilderness for 1.6 miles on a route that follows an abandoned railroad grade to Lake Leon, a ghost town since 1843, when it was battered by a hurricane. From here, a short, blue-blazed spur trail leads west to the Saint Marks River. When you arrive at the East River campsite, you will be only 0.1 mile from a junction with a blue-blazed road-trail to the visitor center. (The 0.8-mile spur trail is a wide grassy service road bordered with lavender ruellia. Tall pines, sabal palmetto, and live oak tower over yaupon. Hives of honeybees may be seen near the trailside.) When you reach CR 59, turn left (north) on the paved road, and after 0.3 mile turn right (east) on a dike road. (It is 2.2 miles farther north on CR 59 to the visitor center, and 4.3 miles south to Saint Marks Lighthouse.)

Follow the Florida Trail on the dike rims, parts of the Stoney Bayou and Deep Creek trails, along a completely open, grassy route among the impoundments. The major features here are wildlife: the migration of ibis and white pelicans in March, crabbing at its peak in May, alligator hatching in August, migration of swallowtail butterflies in September and monarch butterflies in October, waterfowl population at its peak in November, bald eagles nesting in December, and ospreys returning in February. Your fifth campsite, Ring Dike, is at the south side of the East Stoney Bayou impoundment.

From here, go northeast to a junction with the blue-blazed Deep Creek Trail, left, at 37.8 miles. Turn right on the old Aucilla tramway and, after 1.8 miles, cross the Pinhook River wooden bridge to the last campsite, Pinhook River. Your final 4.0 miles are partly on a grassy trail and into forests of oak, maple, gum, magnolia, sabal palmetto, and pine. The last 0.7 mile is on private property, and you may not find any trail blazes. Exit at a cable gate to US 98 0.7 mile west of the Aucilla River bridge. (The Florida Trail continues east on US 98 2.7 miles before turning left on Powell Hammock Road.)

If you did not drive through parts of the Saint Marks National Wildlife Refuge before your hike, you will find it worthwhile to spend some time at the visitor center there. Stroll the 0.3-mile Plum Orchard Trail by the Plum Orchard Pond with its grama grass, giant foxtail, rice rush, and aromatic dog fennel. Drive south on CR 59 to the 1.0-mile Mounds Pool Trail with its observation tower. This interpretive route was once a turpentine forest with pine, needlerush marshes, cordgrass, and waterfowl. Farther ahead are a picnic area, a boat launch, and the Saint Marks Lighthouse.

Other trails in the refuge are in the Panacea unit near Otter and Fox lakes, where there are facilities for fishing, boating, picnicking, and hiking on the 4.6-mile yellow-marked Ridge Trail and the 7.9-mile blue-marked Otter Lake Loop Trail. Access to the trails is 1.2 miles west on CR 372 from US 98 in Panacea, and the other facilities are another 0.8 mile on CR

372. These trails are easy walking and usually well maintained. The section through Panacea Field in a bed of soft grass and wildflowers, with water lilies on the lake, exemplifies the natural beauty on the trails.

## Information

Counties: Liberty, Wakulla, Jefferson
Average Temperatures: January 43.7°F (low), 67.1°F (high); August 71.2°F (low), 89.3°F (high)

National Properties: Apalachicola National Forest, see *Information* under *Apalachicola National Forest*, this Chapter; Saint Marks National Wildlife Refuge, P.O. Box 68, Saint Marks, FL 32355, (904) 925-6121

State Properties: San Marcos de Apalache, 1022 De Soto Park Dr., Tallahassee, FL 32301, (904) 922-6007; Tallahassee–St. Marks Historic Railroad State Trail (same address as San Marcos de Apalache); Newport Recreation Area, Division of Forestry, (904) 925-6171; see *Information, Apalachicola National Forest,* this Chapter

Chambers of Commerce: Liberty County CC, P.O. Box 536, Bristol, FL 32321, (904) 643-2359; Wakulla County CC, P.O. Box 598, Crawfordville, FL 32326, (904) 926-1848

Organizations: Florida Trail Association, P.O. Box 13708, Gainesville, FL 32604, (904) 378-8823, or (800) 343-1882 (offices at 5415 SW 13th St. in Gainesville, 32608); Saint Marks Refuge Association, P.O. Box 368, Saint Marks, FL 32355

Services and Amenities: *Commercial Campgrounds:* Holiday Park and Campground (full service) on US 98, east end of Ochlockonee River bridge, (904) 984-5757; Shell Island Fish Camp (full service and cabins), P.O. Box 115, Saint Marks, FL 32355, (904) 925-6226; *State Campground:* Newport Recreation Area (hot showers; no hookups), across US 98 from the entrance to Saint Marks National Wildlife Refuge Visitor Center, (904) 925-6171

*Restaurants:* Angelo's Seafood Restaurant, on US 98 in

Panacea, (904) 984-5168; Fishermen's Net Restaurant, Saint Marks, (904) 925-6323; Posey's Beyond the Bay (also has motel), P.O. Box 294, Panacea, FL 32346, (904) 984-5799; Posey's in Saint Marks, (904) 925-6172; Spring Creek Restaurant, Spring Creek, on CR 365, (904) 926-3751; Saint Marks Restaurant (candlelight atmosphere), in Saint Marks, (904) 925-6458

## ISLANDS OF THE SAINTS

In the southernmost part of the Panhandle are sparsely settled Gulf and Franklin counties. Only a few highways pass through their expansive swamps, wetlands, and forests with intriguing titles of Dead Lake, Indian Swamp, Tates Hell Swamp, and Crooked Creek. And only one, US 98, an east-west coastal route, connects the counties across the Apalachicola River and bay that divide them. The state's first constitution was written and its first territorial convention met in 1838 in Port Saint Joe, the seat of Gulf County. The county is also famous for the only white tupelo honey, which never granulates, from the Dead Lake swamps of the Chipola River basin. Franklin County has fewer than nine thousand residents, most of whom live in the villages of Apalachicola and Carrabelle. Apalachicola, the county seat, is mostly historic; it is headquarters for the Apalachicola National Estuarian Sanctuary, the largest in the nation, and for the Saint Vincent National Wildlife Refuge. Here succulent Apalachicola Bay oysters account for 90 percent of the state's harvest. Apalachicola was also once home to John Gorrie (1803–1855), a medical doctor who fathered the concept of modern refrigeration. In a county commited to conservation, the Islands of the Saints include Saint James, Saint George, and Saint Vincent.

*What to See and Do:* Within these two friendly and uncrowded counties, you will find sufficient beach hiking, canoeing, boating, fishing, and birding adventures to keep you active and content for weeks.

*Where to Begin:* East or west, US 98 takes you to the

islands, with spurs of SR 30 to Saint Joseph peninsula and Saint Vincent Island, and G1A bridge to Saint George Island. The nearest airports are in Panama City, 40 miles from Port Saint Joe, and Tallahassee, 60 miles from Eastpoint. If you are arriving from Port Saint Joe, leave US 98 and take SR 30 (SR 30A on some maps) to the peninsula and to Saint Joseph Peninsula State Park for your first night. You will find full-service campgrounds and fully furnished cabins with fireplace, heat, and air-conditioning. If you arrive from the east on US 98 at Eastpoint, take the G1A bridge to Saint George Island State Park for a full-service campground. Both parks accept advance reservations. Commercial campgrounds and bed-and-breakfast inns are listed under *Information.*

*About the Adventures:* The Saint Joseph park has 9 miles of enormous dunes that form a backdrop of glistening white beaches long enough that you can walk away from the campground to find a heavy aura of solitude. Some naturalists say that this is the most unspoiled barrier beach in the state; up and down it you will see Gulf mist hovering as white and pure as the sand. You can hike north on the spit and along 5 miles of Saint Joseph's wilderness beach to wild Saint Joseph Point. Be sure to register with the park superintendent before you go, and if you plan to primitive tent-camp in the 1,650-acre wilderness, secure a permit and hike the forested interior route of pine flatlands and hammocks. From the park entrance the Bay Trail leads through sabal palm, red cedar, and live oak to Saint Joseph Bay, and the Barrier Dune Trail loops through sand pine, yaupon, Spanish bayonet, and rosemary near Campground No. 1. A boat ramp in the park provides access for boating, sailing, and saltwater fishing for cobia, bluefish, redfish, and flounder. On the bay side, sea trout are plentiful in the grassy flats, and bay scallops and octopi are part of the varied marine life. Wherever you go you will see shore- and wading birds, as many as 209 known species. For birders, the migration of hawks here in the fall and spring is particularly pleasurable. Sharp-shinned, broad-winged, and other hawks pass here on coastal flights. Red-tailed and red-shouldered hawks occasionally dwell here permanently, and the northern harrier (marsh hawk) is common during the wintertime. Nocturnal visitors include cotton mice, striped skunks, and raccoons. While here, you must also see a sunrise across Saint Joseph Bay and a Gulf sunset from an overlook on the dunes or at surf side.

A day trip to Saint Vincent National Wildlife Refuge, a drumstick-shaped island in Apalachicola Bay, can be exciting. From the mainland, follow SR 30 east 3 miles and turn on SR 30B to Indian Peninsula where the staff at Indian Pass Campground can probably assist you in locating a boatman to take you across the Indian Pass to the island. (You should also contact the refuge headquarters at the west side of the town of Apalachicola for information, preferably well in advance. Refuge personnel do not provide ferry service to the island.) Make your plans with the boatman in advance to allow an early morning departure. Take a day pack with all the water and food you will need for the day, a first-aid kit, maps, and insect repellent. You may hike 14 miles of pristine beach and 80 miles of crisscrossing hard sand roads in the forest. You may need a refuge map to schedule your time. Refuge management allows hunting with permits (with primitive weapons) for sambar and white-tailed deer, wild hogs, and raccoons on a weekend in mid-December and in January and February. (Call the refuge for the exact dates.) No other visitors are allowed on the island during hunting days. Regional U.S. Fish and Wildlife Service policy precludes all types of camping and overnight stays on the island except for hunters, who are allowed to camp in order to help with wildlife management. The policy to allow an overnight stay for a blood sport but deny it to a naturalist with a camera is difficult to defend.

Dolphins may follow you across the 500-foot Indian Pass, and the moment you are on shore terns and willets will dart and scream if you go near their nesting areas. In the springtime you may see ospreys, you may watch soft-shelled turtles laying eggs, and you may hear turkeys clucking in clutch groves. In summer loggerhead sea turtles lumber up the wide beaches to lay eggs, while female alligators stay near their nests in marshes and lakes. Oystercatchers look for mollusks, preferably raccoon oysters. These black-and-white shorebirds with long orange bills usually nest in the spring. The precocial chicks, like the parents, can swim, dive, and swiftly run up and down the beach. Tricolor and little blue herons stay only a few feet away from you, double-crested cormorants fly low to observe you, and sandpipers run and then stop and watch both you and the waves. In September the shorebirds and waterfowl begin to migrate and by December and January they reach peak population. You need more than a day on this island: one to watch the birds, one to study the seashells, and another to spend in the forest.

After you enter the forest, the island world changes radically, becoming habitat for twenty-six mammal and thirty-four reptile species. Both the cottonmouth and the rattlesnake are here. Most of the wildlife is not friendly and gives you plenty of space, but ticks, chiggers, and mosquitoes love you and expect to emigrate from the island at your expense when you depart. Refuge botanists have catalogued eighty species of trees, shrubs, and vines. Bright orange sesban and beauty-berry sometimes lean from the roadside to greet you, and blue lupine covers the banks along with red coral bean. Oak, pine, willow, magnolia, and cabbage palm hover over matrimony vine, gallberry, and fetterbush.

While visiting the Apalachee Indians in 1623, Spanish Franciscan friars named the island Saint Vincent. Other Indians and some white settlers used the island for hunting and seafood harvesting until 1868, when George Hatch of Ohio bought it for $3,000. Hatch lived and died here; his gravestone is the only one here. In 1908 a new owner bought the island and imported European game animals. By 1940 the Saint Joe Lumber Company had removed the timber, and 8 years later ownership changed again. Zebra, eland, jungle fowl, and ring-neck pheasant were imported for a hunting preserve. Finally, in 1968, The Nature Conservancy saved the

12,348-acre island from further exploitation, purchasing it for $2.2 million, repaid by the U.S. Fish and Wildlife Service from duck stamp sales. Before you leave Indian Pass, you may wish to go oystering, cast-netting for mullet, or, if you are here in the late summer, crabbing for blue crabs on the peninsula sound side.

On your way to Saint George Island you will pass through Apalachicola, one of Florida's most desirable communities. Most of the town, 146 blocks, is a historic district. Fluted Doric and Ionic columns reach up to invite you in, much as they have invited the sea breeze for more than 150 years. You will find churches, sponge and cotton warehouses, an armory (one of two owned by the state), Indian mounds, inns, and, at Avenue D and 6th Street, the John Gorrie Museum. Get a map at the chamber of commerce at 128 Market Street and spend the day on a walking tour of history. After lunch at the restored Gibson Inn at 100 Market Street, you may decide to return there for dinner and stay all night. The staff may help you plan fishing trips and historic river tours and rent bicycles.

Flatboats laden with cotton docked in Apalachicola, at the mouth of the Apalachicola River, in the early 1820s, and all citizens went out to see the river's first steamboat in 1828. Soon the town was one of the three largest world cotton ports in the Gulf. Blockade runners, who supplied food and materials to the Confederacy, used the town during the Civil War. Its golden years returned in the late nineteenth century with the cypress milling boom that lasted until the 1920s. Since then, shrimping, oystering, and fishing have determined its economic health.

In Apalachicola you will find headquarters offices for Saint Vincent National Wildlife Refuge, the United Nations Biosphere Reserve, and the Apalachicola National Estuarine Research Reserve (ANERR). You can also rent boats from here to explore the bays and rivers, rent a sailboat to sail around the barrier islands, or go to Eastpoint and wade in the bay with a gill net to catch mullet, sea trout, and crabs. Coastal restaurants serve blue crab, shrimp, oyster, redfish, mullet, flounder, sea trout, and Spanish mackerel. Farther east, in Carrabelle, take a ferry to remote, preserved Dog Island. For the ultimate in seafood cuisine, attend the Florida Seafood Festival (the state's oldest) the first weekend in November. Among festival highlights are oyster-shucking and oyster-eating contests.

The ANERR encompasses 193,118 acres of environmentally sensitive Apalachicola Bay and portions of the Apalachicola River floodplains and barrier islands. Vital to the future of the fin and shellfish industry in the area is the environmental purity of the river and other streams flowing into the bays and of the surface water from human development in the bays and sounds. Seafood harvesting, of shrimp and oysters in particular, provides about 75 percent of the area's employment. The area is also significant for 904 known species of fish, which certainly makes it the most productive in the nation, and perhaps in the Northern Hemisphere. A number of endangered and threatened animal and plant species also live here. Since 1985 a plant-life study by the Department of Biological Science at Florida State University has documented 1,157 vascular plants within 50,000 acres of the ANERR. During the research one new species of daisy (*Boltonia apalachicolensis*) was found. Apiaries provide 750,000 pounds of tupelo honey annually.

Saint George Island is a rare 29-mile sand strip that is no more than one mile wide at any point. At the west end is a 10-mile-long island called Little Saint George, now Cape Saint George State Reserve. Little Saint George was separated from the main island when the U.S. Army Corps of Engineers cut a channel, Sikes Cut, in 1954 to provide access to Apalachicola Bay for commercial and fishing fleets. Primitive camping is permitted on the reserve at West Pass, Sikes Cut, or Government Dock. Access by private boat and take all necessary supplies with you. Park rangers patrol the reserve to protect it from misuse. An uninhabited island, you will find it ideal for solitude and natural beauty. During fall and spring migrations you will find a diverse and abundant bird population. You may see loggerhead sea turtles and snowy plovers in the summer. Plant communities include willow swamps, slash pine flatwoods, and cabbage palms in the savannahs. The island is home to the Cape Saint George Lighthouse, built in 1852 and still in service.

The central part of Saint George Island is becoming increasingly developed with private beach homes and low-density condos, but you will find a 9-mile stretch of undeveloped beach, Saint George Island State Park, on the eastern part of the island. You will find one campground under pines on the bay side, and a 2.5-mile backpacking trail leads to a primitive site at Gap Point. Other activities are fishing, surfing, and beach hiking to boardwalks and overlooks. At the east end are scenic windblown, wave-altered, ever-shifting sand-bars and shallow lagoons. Until 1965 the island was accessible only by boat; now a 4-mile waterscape causeway leads to the island's center. As early as the tenth century, Creek Indians lived here; after European settlers came, the claims shifted back and forth until 1803 when the Indians ceded the island to the John Forbes Company. Legend claims that pirates and privateers buried treasure on the island during the eighteenth century.

If you decide to take a break from the magic of sand and sea, you could visit the Constitution Convention State Museum in Port Saint Joe, or canoe and freshwater fish at Dead Lakes Recreation Area, 4 miles north of Wewahitchka on SR 71. At Dead Lakes you will see thousands of cypress, pines, and gums dead from a natural water elevation of the Chipola River. A remote campground offers full service; two nature trails take you around dark ponds where elderberry and bayberry bloom together and where huge cypresses are kings of the swamp. The park offers excellent fishing for bass, bream, perch, and catfish.

Also remote is the Fort Gadsden State Historic Site in the Apalachicola National Forest, 24 miles north on SR 65 from US 98, a few miles east of Eastpoint. (See *Apalachicola National Forest,* this Chapter.)

During your stay at the Islands of the Saints, you will

notice literature and signs that say "Florida's best kept secret," "Escape to an island that time forgot," or "Florida beaches without crowds." Help keep those slogans current. This is a region of history, an incomparably rich estuary and seascape, which has the best oysters in the world, good people, and peace of mind.

### *Information*

Counties: Gulf, Franklin

Average Temperatures: January, 44°F (low), 67.5°F (high); August, 70.8°F (low), 88.7°F (high)

National Properties: Saint Vincent National Wildlife Refuge, Box 447, Apalachicola, FL 32320, (904) 653-8808

State Properties: Constitution Convention State Museum, 200 Allen Memorial Way, Port Saint Joe, FL 32456, (904) 229-8029; Dead Lakes State Recreation Area, P.O. Box 989, Wewahitchka, FL 32465, (904) 639-2702; Fort Gadsden State Historic Site, P.O. Box 157, Sumatra, FL 32335, (904) 670-8988; John Gorrie State Museum, Ave. D and 6th St., Apalachicola, FL 32320, (904) 653-9347; Saint George Island State Park and Reserve. P.O. Box 62, Eastpoint, FL 32328, (904) 927-2111; Saint Joseph Peninsula State Park, Star Rte. 1, Box 200, Port Saint Joe, FL 32456, (904) 227-1327

Chambers of Commerce: Apalachicola Bay CC, 57 Market St., Apalachicola, FL 32320, (904) 653-9419; Gulf County CC, P.O. Box 964, Port Saint Joe, FL 32456, (904) 227-7522

Services and Amenities: *Bed and Breakfast:* Magnolia's, US 98 at 9th St., Apalachicola, FL 32320, (904) 653-8905; *Commercial Campgrounds:* Apalachicola Bay KOA, P.O. Box 621, Eastpoint, FL 32328, (904) 670-8307; Indian Pass Campground, Star Rte. 1, Box 750, Port Saint Joe, FL 32456, (904) 227-7203; *Inn:* Gibson Inn, 100 Market St., Apalachicola, FL 32320, (904) 653-2191/8282

*Boat Ferrying:* Captain Bob, Box 399, Apalachicola, FL 32320, (904) 653-9025; Captain Bud, P.O. Box 158, Port Saint

Joe, FL 32456, (904) 229-6284; *Florida Seafood Festival:* (904) 653-2219; *Restaurant:* The Seafood Shack, US Hwy. 98, Eastpoint, FL 32328, (904) 670-8031

## FLORIDA CAVERNS

Beneath Florida's surface is an unmeasurable network of limestone caverns, almost exclusively filled with water. Of these, about 370 caves are known to be dry, and none is comparable in geological significance to the Florida Caverns at Marianna. Here stalactites, stalagmites, terraced rimstone pools, pillars, columns, and thin flowstone have been formed by calcited dripping water that takes 100 years to form one cubic inch. The caverns are part of the 1,783-acre Florida Caverns State Park that also contains a unique natural bridge over the Chipola River, the truly blue water of Blue Hole Spring; Indian history; and the botanical marvel of Appalachian Mountain vegetation growing near subtropical species.

*What to See and Do:* Exploratory options include canoeing, hiking, fishing, nature study, and—especially exciting in this area—spelunking.

*Where to Begin:* On I-10 from the east take Exit 21 to SR 71, north; from the west, take Exit 20 to SR 276, north. Both state roads go to Marianna, from which SR 167, north, will take you 3 miles to the park entrance.

*About the Adventures:* You have two choices for caving. The first, most popular to the public, is a guided tour in the main Florida Caverns; the other is a specialized spelunking adventure. Walking tours of the main Florida Caverns usually leave every hour, daily, for a small fee. While waiting to begin you can see exhibits and attend an audiovisual program that interprets the caverns' history and geology. Here you will see evidence of a cave system that existed above the two present levels millions of years ago. The current lower level has more seepage during the rainy season, and below it, the underground water is carving yet another system of caves. Indians used parts of the caverns long before the Spanish reported them in

1693, and according to legend the Seminole Indians hid from Gen. Andrew Jackson here in 1818 when he passed through to use the natural bridge over the Chipola River. In the 1930s the CCC removed some of the barriers to allow access to some of the caves' spectacular areas, such as the Cathedral and Wedding rooms. For about 0.5 mile the route ascends and descends past naturally polished formations similar to those in the limestone caverns of Tennessee, Virginia, and West Virginia. Animal life in the caves includes the endangered gray bat (*Myotis grisescens*) and eyeless, colorless crayfish (which you probably will not see).

Your guided spelunking trip will last about 3 hours, including orientation. The trip begins at 1:30 P.M. Central Standard Time on the second or fourth Saturday of each month. Advance reservations are necessary, and you must sign a waiver of responsibility prior to the adventure. (If you are under 18 years of age, you must be accompanied by an adult accountable for your safety and conduct.) The trip requires a small fee and tours are limited to a safe number of persons. Because spelunking is strenuous and involves crawling, the park ranger requires that you be in good physical health with no back or limb impairments, without a history of heart disease, asthma, or diabetes, and that you absolutely do not have any symptoms of claustrophobia. You must have a dependable, battery-powered headlamp, sturdy, rubber-soled shoes, and a hard hat, and plan on getting dirty or muddy. A camera and flash units are not recommended; if you do bring them, pack then securely. For more information purchase *Caving Basics* from the National Speleological Society. (See *Information*.)

Florida Caverns State Park has nature trails, boat-ramp access for fishing and canoeing on the Chipola River above the river rise, and a full-service campground near the warm Blue Hole Spring. Advance reservations are accepted. The short nature trails—Beech-Magnolia, Flood Plain, and River Rise—are superb for nature study. Old and tall beech, magnolia, tupelo, cypress, shield fern, and oak-leaf hydrangea grow in parts of the lower elevation. On the upper hillside levels are redbud, columbine, saw palmetto, bloodroot, and trillium. Huge, fragrant southern magnolia trees blossom in late May around the visitor center.

Fishing and canoeing opportunities are best outside the park south on the Chipola River for 38 miles. Indigenous to the area is shad bass (a cousin to the redeye), also called Chipola bass. These fish prefer to harbor at the rippling rocky limestone shoals where they feed on crayfish and baitfish. Other catchable fish are catfish and bream. Characteristic of the route are bankside grottoes, pools, limestone bluffs, springs, shoals, and islands. Sometimes in the dry seasons the pools are exceptionally clear and green. Although you will see some populated areas and farmlands, the river generally runs through a wild area inhabited by azaleas, cardinal flowers, deer, turtles, alligators, and, on the overhanging hardwoods, songbirds. Canoes can be rented from Chipola River Canoe Trails. (See *Information*). The best upper upriver put-in for a 38-mile canoe trip is at the SR 167 bridge in Marianna. Take-out distances are 10 miles to SR 280, 10 miles to SR 278, 8 miles to SR 274, and another 10 miles to SR 20. Farther downstream the river becomes more swampy on its way to Dead Lake.

Occasionally the limestone surface over a cavern will collapse, forming a sink. One such sink is at Falling Waters State Recreation Area, about 15 miles southwest from Florida Caverns. To get there go west on I-10 to Exit 18, turn south on SR 77, and, less than a mile farther, turn left (east) on SR 77A. A distinctive feature at the park, the fern- and moss-lined cylindrical sink is 100 feet deep and 15 feet wide. A small surface stream falls into it and disappears in limestone caverns. Surrounding you on the interpretive trails are white oak, southern magnolia, dogwood, American beech, and longleaf pine, a haven for fox and squirrel. At a nearby lake are Osceola's plume, meadow beauty, and many species of songbirds. The park has a full-service campground, a youth camp, and a picnic area.

## Information

Counties: Jackson, Washington

Average Temperatures: January 39.8°F (low), 67°F (high); August, 71.1°F (low), 89.4°F (high)

State Properties: Falling Waters State Recreation Area, Rte. 5, Box 660, Chipley, FL 32428, (904) 638-6130; Florida Caverns State Park, 3345 Caverns Rd., Marianna, FL 32446, (904) 482-9598

Chambers of Commerce: Marianna CC, P.O. Box 130, Marianna, FL 32446, (904) 482-8061; Washington County CC, P.O. Box 457, Chipley FL 32428, (904) 638-4157

Services and Amenities: *Canoe Rentals:* Chipola River Canoe Trails, P.O. Box 621, Marianna, FL 32446, (904) 482-4948; Cypress Springs Canoe Trails, P.O. Box 726, Vernon, FL 32462, (904) 535-2960; *Speleological Information:* National Speleological Society, Cave Ave., Huntsville, AL 35810, (205) 852-1300

## BLACKWATER BACKCOUNTRY

Blackwater: The Choctaw Indians called it *okaloosa*, or "pleasant place." The Blackwater River flows through a supreme forest with rolling, sandy-clay hills and gleaming lakes. To preserve it, Florida established the Blackwater River State Forest in 1938, the state's largest (183,155 acres) and highest (90 to 291 feet in elevation) of its four forests. Primarily pristine, the Blackwater is famous for its stand of longleaf pine, one of the largest and most magnificent on the continent. It touches Alabama's Conecuh National Forest at the state line for 25 miles. In the Conecuh, established in 1936, are the remote headwaters of the Blackwater River and its clean tributaries—Sweetwater, Juniper, and East Coldwater creeks. Shallow, swift, and pure, they carry rich, tea-red tannin that consistently resculpts beautiful sugar white sandbars. Without surprise to canoeists, the state legislature in 1981 designated the stream network the state's "canoe capital." At the forest's southwest corner is an additional backcountry—the Blackwater River State Park—with remote oxbow lakes in magnolia and cedar forests.

*What to See and Do:* Adventure options are hiking the 21-mile historic Jackson Trail, canoeing 30 miles on the scenic Blackwater River, and horseback riding 20 miles on the Coldwater trails. Freshwater fishing and nature study can also be part of your adventure.

*Where to Begin:* The state forest headquarters is on SR 191, immediately south of the intersection in Munson with SR 4 (20.5 miles north of Milton and 13 miles west of Baker). To reach the state park, turn off US 90 ( 8 miles southeast of Holt and 10 miles northeast of Milton) and drive 3.5 miles north on FR 23. The nearest airport is in Pensacola, nearly 40 miles from Munson.

*About the Adventures:* The forest is composed of five vegetative types: longleaf pine–turkey oak, which monopolizes the dry areas; loblolly pine–hardwood, in upland areas; slash pine, mostly in damp areas with red maple, southern magnolia, sweet gum, and cypress; swamp hardwood of bay, gum, and ash, in wet or floodplain areas; and stands of Atlantic white cedar, spruce pine, and cypress that grow on the creek- and riverbanks. These fragrant conifers and hardwoods mix on rolling hills of sandy, red-orange clay and fine white sand formed by erosion more than 2 million years ago. During that same period, rich floodplains covered with wildflowers were also created.

The Division of Forestry manages the forest with timber harvesting through sustained-yield programs, bringing the state more than $3.5 million annually; selected seasons for hunting; wildlife, water, and soil protection; and public recreational facilities. The Division of Recreation and Parks manages the 390-acre Blackwater River State Park in the southwest corner of the forest. In the park, a protected area, hunting and timber harvesting are not allowed.

For hikers, the historic 21-mile orange-blazed Jackson Trail, part of a former Indian trail, meanders diagonally across

*White-top pitcher plants, Blackwater State Forest.*
PHOTO BY Allen de Hart.

the southeast section of the forest. By the late eighteenth century, the trail had developed from Escambia Bay (north of Pensacola) to the Chattahoochee River (near present-day Columbia, Georgia) as a trade route between the Creek Indians and the Spanish and later the English. In 1818 the impetuous Gen. Andrew Jackson journeyed along Florida's portion of the route to Pensacola to end the First Seminole War. Today the trail is called the Andrew Jackson Red Ground Trail (after the red sand-clay). A national recreation trail, also designated as part of the Florida Trail system, the Jackson Trail has its northern terminus at Karick Lake (7.4 miles north of Baker on SR 189). Its southern terminus is at scenic Red Rock Picnic Area by Juniper Creek (3.7 miles east on paved FR 72 from the Spring Hill Church on SR 191, 11.5 miles north of Milton).

If you hike from Karick Lake Campground, you will curve around the dam and follow a wide, bush-hogged footpath and sandy forest road through stately longleaf pines. Regardless of the season, breezes through the pines give a constant soothing sough. Sparkleberry and turkey oak give some shade over wire grass and saw palmetto. In the winter the wind rattles the stubborn, unfallen turkey oak leaves. A few streams along the way have sweet gums, oaks, and maples to shade the ferns and wildflowers. After 8 miles you will cross a bridge over the Blackwater River on FR 50. Ahead you will leave the road, left, and enter a low area of hardwoods. After passing the restored Peaden Cemetery you will reach a shelter under a canopy of live oaks. (A well here may not be functioning because the local health department requires chlorinators. See Chapter 2, *Health and Safety,* regarding drinking water.) Before crossing SR 4, you will notice a connector trail, the 4.5-mile Sweetwater Trail, which parallels SR 4 on its way to Bear Lake Recreation Area and then across a swinging footbridge over the Sweetwater Creek to the Krul Recreation Area. Along the way are outstanding colonies of wildflowers; if you are here in mid-May, you will see a sea of trumpets and the infrequent to rare insectivorous white-top pitcher plant (*Sarracenia leucophylla*). Among the other plants are yellow trumpets, white sedges, orchids, sundews, and cinnamon ferns. A shelter at 15.5 miles, like the first, does not have water or toilet facilities. Between FR 2 and FR 33 are brilliant orange gladioluses, which forest personnel think may have descended from an old homesite, now vanished. Other flowers along the trail are rattlebox, colicroot, yellow jessamine, and orange milkweed. Wildlife you may see are white-tailed deer, foxes, skunks, raccoons, armadillos, gopher tortoises, pine warblers, and hawks. The diurnal eastern coachwhip snake, which can grow up to 8 feet long, is common through the forest. It is usually black from its head nearly half way down its body and then becomes tan to cream. With long, smooth scales and a long, slender tail, it moves gracefully, with unusual speed, its head as much as a foot off the ground so it can view its prey: lizards, rodents, and birds. The black racer and southern hognose snake may also be seen. In the forest, but unlikely to be seen, are the poisonous snakes: rattlesnake, copperhead, cottonmouth, and coral. You are most likely to hear warblers, thrashers, and sparrows on the trail, but if you look carefully, you may also see a red-cockaded woodpecker. Game birds such as wild turkeys and quail are present (seasonal hunting is allowed in the forest; a Florida hunting license is required). You will complete the trail across the Juniper Creek bridge at Red Rock Picnic Area.

At the Blackwater River State Park you can hike three short nature trails—Oxbow Lake Trail, Blackwater River Trail, and the Chain of Lakes Trail. Access to the park from the Red Rock Picnic Area is east of Juniper Creek 6 miles south of FR 19, FR 86, and FR 23. These trails will invite you into a natural display of oxbow ponds and levees created by the river. Floodplain areas have sweet bay, red maple, Atlantic white cedar, magnolia, cypress, and swamp cyrilla. The pineland sections have slash and longleaf pines, fetterbush, crooked-wood, and sparkleberry. The park also has a picnic and swimming area by the river, and a campground on a hilltop. Birders can watch for the yellow-billed cuckoo, nighthawk, and orchard oriole in the summertime, and another seventy-five seasonal species.

Your visit to the forest will not be complete without a canoe trip on the Blackwater River. Exceptionally scenic, the Blackwater is one of the cleanest rivers in the United States. After passing through the forest, it empties into Blackwater Bay, near Milton. Choctaws and Creeks originally explored it; the first known foreign explorer was Don Carlos de Siguenza y Gongora, a Mexican scientist commissioned by the Spanish in 1693. He named the river Rio del Almirante, in honor of an earlier Spanish explorer, Admiral Pez, of the Pensacola area.

The put-in for the Blackwater River Canoe Trail is at Kennedy Bridge by a primitive campground on FR 24. (Some canoeists begin upstream in a more remote and wild area near the Alabama state line; inquire at the forest headquarters about directions and river conditions.) Although there are take-outs along the way, you can paddle 30 miles to the Deaton Bridge take-out at Blackwater River State Park. You could paddle another 14 miles to Milton, but the river becomes torpid, and you will meet motorboat traffic. The Coldwater Creek has desirable canoeing for about 20 miles between SR 4 and 191, and Sweetwater and Juniper creeks have about 15 miles of good water between SR 4 and FR 86. All the streams are scenic and generally easy to maneuver; many sandbars provide campsites, and a wide range of flora covers the high banks. Particularly noticeable are the cypress and white cedar. A few species of darters, sunfish, bass, and catfish inhabit the streams, but do not depend on them for your evening meal. You can canoe in any season; you will find ideal temperatures and avoid summer traffic in spring and fall, but the water may be low then. If you canoe without a guide, take a forest headquarters map that will show you forest road numbers, rivers, canoe trails, and campgrounds. (See *Infomation.*)

Equestrians will find seventy-two horse stables at the Coldwater Recreation Area and more than 20 miles in six blazed horse trails, including the linear Spanish Trail. These trails are particularly famous for leading through stands of longleaf pine. You will need proof of a current Coggins test for the horse before entering the Coldwater area and reservations to use the stable. Entrance is on FR 1, 4 miles south of SR 4, 0.5 mile east of Berrydale.

For other forest adventures, you might explore the 300-plus miles of remote sandy forest roads or study nature at the 900-acre Environmental Center. Anglers (with electric motorboats) can catch channel catfish, bass, and bluegill at Bear, Hurricane, and Karick lakes.

Five Blackwater River State Forest campgrounds (Krul, Bear, Hurricane, Karick, and Coldwater) have basic facilities, including hot showers, and five primitive campgrounds have only picnic tables. Tomahawk Landing, a commercial campground with full service on the west side of the forest, is 12.5 miles north of Milton off SR 87 for 4 miles east; it is open April to November 1 and by appointment in the winter. East of the forest (south of Crestview), Holiday Lake Trav-L-Park offers full service. Open all year, it is behind the Holiday Inn, on SR

85 at the I-10 intersection, Exit 12. From the forest, the closest grocery store, restaurant, and post office are in Baker on SR 89. The nearest towns for motels, shopping centers, and hospitals are Milton and Crestview. If you want something more luxurious, try the Exchange Hotel, an office building restored, for a bed and breakfast in Milton with a surprisingly reasonable price. (See *Information*.)

About 20 miles east of the Blackwater River, flowing parallel to it, is the larger and longer Yellow River. Also beginning in Alabama, the Yellow River drains the area hill country and empties into Blackwater Bay. The Yellow River is not as clear as the Blackwater River, its sand is not as white, and its environment is less wild. But its aquatic vegetation and fish are more abundant. The river does not pass through a public forest or park, thus camping is confined to the riverbank or sandbars. The most desirable put-in is at Oak Grove on SR 2. (The river can be canoed farther north, at least from Alabama SR 55 at the edge of the Conecuh National Forest, but strainers and swift, deep water make this section more dangerous for the inexperienced.) After canoeing 17 miles through a scenic area with wildlife, high bluffs, and forest vegetation, you can take-out at Milligan, east, on US 90.

The 84,400-acre Conecuh National Forest in Alabama adjoins the Blackwater River State Forest on the north side. The Conecuh has lakes for swimming, boating, and fishing, and the 20-mile Conecuh Trail, a trail much like the Jackson Trail described above. Access the forest from SR 189 and SR 181 north. (See *Information* for the headquarters address.)

Often unknown to the public are the outdoor recreation activities in the 720-square-mile Eglin Air Force Base, the nation's largest forested base, south of Blackwater River State Forest. In Santa Rosa, Okaloosa, and Walton counties, its north boundary is by the Yellow River and I-10, and its south boundary extends to the Fort Walton Beach area and Choctawhatchee Bay. (See *The Emerald Coast*, this Chapter.)

### *Information*

Counties: Okaloosa, Santa Rosa

Average Temperatures: January, 39.9°F (low), 67°F (high); August, 72°F (low), 89.8°F (high)

National Properties: Conecuh National Forest, Box 310, Andalusia, AL 36420, (205) 222-2555; Eglin Air Force Base, Natural Resources Branch, AD/DEMN, Eglin AFB, FL 32542, (904) 882-4164

State Properties: Blackwater River State Forest, Rte. 1, Box 77, Milton, Fl 32570, (904) 957-4201; Blackwater River State Park, Rte. 1, Box 57-C, Holt, FL 32564, (904) 623-2363

Chambers of Commerce: Crestview Area CC, 502 Main St., Crestview, FL 32536, (904) 682-3212; Niceville–Valparaiso Bay Area CC, 170 N. John Sims Pkwy., Valparaiso, FL 32580, (904) 678-2323; Santa Rosa County CC, 501 Stewart St., NW, Milton, FL 32570, (904) 623-2339

Services and Amenities: *Bed and Breakfast:* Exchange Hotel, 302 Elmira St., Milton, FL 32572, (904) 626-1500; *Commercial Campgrounds:* see Adventures Unlimited, below; Holiday Lake Trav-L-Park, (904) 682-6111

*Canoe Rentals:* Blackwater Canoe Rental, Rte. 16, Box 72, Milton, FL 32570, (904) 623-0235; *Canoe Guides and Rentals:* Adventures Unlimited–Tomahawk Landing, Rte. 6, Box 283, Milton, FL 32570, (904) 623-6197/ 944-4386; Bob's Canoes, Rte. 8, Box 34, Milton, FL 32570, (904) 623-5457; *Other Canoe Contacts:* Action Blackwater, (904) 537-2997; Jackson Trails Canoe Rentals, (904) 623-4884; Leisure Tyme, (904) 626-0850

## THE EMERALD COAST

Between Pensacola and Panama City are 100 miles of bays, beaches, and bayous unlike any others in Florida. Emerald-colored Gulf waters lap "The Emerald Coast," the natural home of pure, sparkling quartz sand from the ancient Appalachian Mountains; the sugar white coastal sand is of such fine texture that the oval-shaped grains squeak beneath your feet.

Hurricanes sometimes bruise these barrier shores, but the sand's timeless resilience and the gentle Gulf breezes heal the scars. Wildlife and human residents weather the storms, and sand dunes pile high again. Indians favored the Emerald Coast for its wealth of seafood, and Spanish explorers in the Bay of Ochuse (Pensacola Bay) would likely have made the first European settlement here in 1559 had a tropical storm not destroyed most of their fleet. Today, condos, shopping centers, and amusement parks crowd long sections of the coast, the Miracle Strip that fronts the emerald shores. Other sections are preserved, as you will find when you journey to the long Gulf Islands National Seashore, the Big Lagoon, Santa Rosa Island, Indian Temple Mound, Rocky Bayou, Choctawhatchee Bay, and the sanctuary of Pine Log State Forest.

*What to See and Do:* A mélange of adventures on the Emerald Coast includes hiking on pristine beaches and sequestered wildlife trails, scuba diving, snorkeling, sailing, parasailing, surfing, canoeing, crabbing, fishing, camping, bicycling, and exploring historic sites. Because vacationers usually flock to the beaches between Memorial Day and Labor Day, you may wish to choose other times to visit.

*Where to Begin:* To reach your base campground at Fort Pickens on Gulf Islands National Seashore, from I-10 take Exit 4 and follow I-110 to US 98 in Pensacola. Turn east on US 98, cross the Pensacola Bay Bridge, turn right on SR 399 to Pensacola Beach, turn right again, and drive 2.3 miles to the park's entrance station.

*About the Adventures:* While visiting the natural attractions of the Pensacola Bay area, do not overlook Pensacola, Florida's western gateway and a city of traditional Deep South hospitality, charm, and elegance. With 400 years of recorded history, Pensacola, named for the Panzacola Indians, is near natural environments and preserved landmarks. Diego Miruelo, a Spanish sea captain, was the first foreign explorer to discover the bay in 1516. In 1559 Spanish explorer Don Tristán de Luna formed a colony with fifteen hundred settlers, mainly from Mexico, which lasted 2 years. Other, longer-enduring settlements were established in 1698 and 1723. When William Bartram journeyed here in 1775 to discuss natural science with the settlers, he described the bay as "safe and large enough to shelter all the navies of Europe." Sprinkled with an international mixture of pirates, privateers, dons, and gentry, the settlements shifted thirteen times among Spanish, French, and English control until February 1821 when Florida became a U.S. territory. President James Monroe appointed as provisional governor Andrew Jackson, who moved in June to a large Spanish house north of the city. Governor Jackson denounced the heat and humidity and the dilatory efforts of the Spanish to transfer control. In contrast, the first lady was content and cheerfully praised Pensacola's cultural mix, calling it "the most healthful place" to which she had been.

For a week each mid-May the city celebrates its history with a costumed fiesta and the arrival of a heritage four-masted sailing vessel to mark de Luna's colonization attempt, an occasion characteristic of Pensacola's reverence for its history, restoration, and preservation. Historic sites include the downtown 20-block Seville Historic District; southern mansions among 404 homes in the North Hill Preservation District; Florida's oldest Protestant church, Old Christ Church, at the corner of South Adams and Zaragoza streets; French Creole architecture at 205 East Church Street; New World Landing Inn, 600 South Palafox Street; and the Hopkins' Boarding House (where inexpensive but sumptuous meals are served in the tradition of a southern grandmother) on North Spring Street. The city is also the birthplace of naval aviation and home to the intrepid Blue Angels and "the world's longest fishing pier" (old US 98 across the bay) for resolute anglers.

Of all the areas of natural beauty in the bay area, the Gulf Islands National Seashore merits special focus here. In 1971 Congress authorized the park, a 137,598-acre preserve of islands, parts of islands, sounds, and mainland tracts that stretch from the east end of Santa Rosa Island in Florida west to West Ship Island in Mississippi. (Ship Island was cut by Hurricane Camille in 1969 to form separate east-west islands.) The park is divided into two districts, one for each state. Between the districts is an appendage of Alabama, but none of the Alabama islands or seashores is presently included in the park. Florida has 65,816 acres in the park, of which 9,366 are on land and accessible by highways. Mississippi has one mainland-based area accessible by US 90 at Davis Bayou, and four offshore islands 10 miles from the mainland and accessible only by boat. In 1978 wilderness was designated on 1,800 acres of Horn and Petit Bois islands in the Mississippi district. Only the Florida district is described here, but if you have time to explore and wish true isolation, make Horn and Petit Bois part of your journey. Donald A. Schuler, author of *Adventuring Along the Gulf of Mexico*, describes these islands as "arguably the loveliest in the Gulf," and artist Walter Anderson calls them a "magic carpet, surrounded by inhabited space." (See *Information.*)

On the way to your campground in Gulf Islands National Seashore, stop for information at the Visitor Information Center at the north end of the Pensacola Bay Bridge, and at Naval Live Oaks, the park headquarters, 2 miles east of Gulf Breeze on US 98. Naval Live Oaks is open daily and has information on all park sections—Okaloosa, Santa Rosa, Naval Live Oaks, Fort Pickens, Pensacola city forts, and Perdido Key. Audiovisuals and natural and Indian history exhibits prepare you for adventures of fishing, boating, scuba diving, sailing, bicycling, and hiking in the park. Also at Naval Live Oaks are 1,378 aces of oaks, southern magnolias, pines, sweet bays, and myrtles. Snake, fox, raccoon, and squirrel inhabit the woodlands. On the sound side are striped mullet, speckled sea trout, and oysters. A youth campground is here, and one of the Sugar Beaches bicycle routes passes through. Live Oaks received its name from a congressional resolution passed in 1827 that required the U.S. Navy to increase its reserve of live oaks for shipbuilding. Live oak, the heaviest of oaks, resists disease and decay. Early U.S. ships of live oak include the *Hancock,* a Revolutionary War vessel; the USS *Constitution,* "Old Ironsides" of the War of 1812; and the *Constellation.* The need for the tall, tough, handsome trees diminished after iron and steel warships were introduced.

From park headquarters, continue to the two-hundred unit Fort Pickens Campground, which has a combination of sites with and without full service, a commissary, and a laundry. Reservations cannot be made, but you should call in advance to inquire about vacancies. (Another full-service base camp you could consider is Big Lagoon State Recreation Area, which accepts advance reservations. See below.) Beach camping at Fort Pickens is prohibited, but you may explore 9 miles of unspoiled beach. You will notice two short nature trails—Blackbird Marsh and Dune—near the entrance to the campground. Lantern bush, gallberry, myrtle, live oak, sand and slash pines, and pale, lavender, aromatic conradina (which blooms in early spring) grow on them. Other conspicious spring flowers are the brownish sheep sorrel, rose pogonia, yellow coreopsis, and white lizard's tail. Balduina honeycomb heads, purple gerardia, and woody goldenrod are colorful in the fall, and blooming through all seasons are the golden flower heads of camphor weed. You may see a ghost crab or a wolf spider on sandy trails, but the beach mice that burrow to escape the heat of day will likely elude you. Constantly looking for picnic crumbs are the fish crow, mockingbird, blue jay, and rufous-sided towhee. Tree frogs, terns, black skimmers, and double-crested cormorants are here with raccoons and striped skunks and with many other wildlife species.

Fort Pickens, constructed in 1829–1834, is the largest of four forts built by the U.S. Army Corps of Engineers to protect the Pensacola Harbor from foreign invasion after Florida became a U.S. territory. The large fort of brick and earth was obsolete by the turn of the twentieth century, but it has been preserved so that you can explore a labyrinth of casemates, chambers, bastions, and quarters, one of which held the shackled, exiled Apache Chief Geronimo and recreant followers from 1886 to 1888. Slaves built the structure of at least 21.5 million bricks; the defense design includes extensive passageways, dark gunpowder storage rooms (where a flashlight is needed), and pits for disappearing cannon. Near the fort are a museum, fishing pier, and access to the beach at the end of the island from which you can see Perdido Key. Ask the park ranger for information about where you can scuba dive and spearfish.

To reach the park's other forts and Perdido Key, return to US 98, cross the Pensacola Bay Bridge, and follow US 98 (Garden Street) to SR 292. Turn left (south) on a busy route that is first Barrancas Avenue but becomes Gulf Beach Highway. At Navy Boulevard (SR 295), turn left (south) to the Pensacola Naval Air Station, home base for the aircraft carrier USS *Lexington*, which, if in port, is open to the public. Signs will guide you to Fort San Carlos de Barrancas, restored between 1839 and 1845, and to the Naval Air Museum, the nation's largest and most comprehensive. It traces the history of U.S. naval aviation and houses the Naval Aviation Hall of Honor. Fort Barrancas was built by Spain in 1698, captured and recaptured by the French and British, and reclaimed by Spain 100 years later. It last saw military action during the Civil War.

Return to SR 292, turn left (west), and continue to Perdido Key. Along the way you will see the entrance (on the left) to Big Lagoon State Recreation Area, which has a first-class, full-service campground. Sixteen miles west of the Pensacola Visitor Center, this jewel of a park has a beach for swimming, access for sailing and waterskiing, and a deluxe, 500-seat, all-weather amphitheater. Three nature trails—Long Pond, Yaupon, and Grand Lagoon—take you by boardwalk along a mystical route of flatwoods, swales, and salt marshes where you will see mammals and reptiles, brown thrashers, nuthatches, great blue herons, clapper rails, and other birds. An observation tower at East Beach honors Francis M. Weston (1916–1969), ornithologist, and provides a panoramic view of Big Lagoon and Perdido Key.

*Big Lagoon State Recreation Area.* PHOTO BY Allen de Hart.

Two miles west on SR 292 are seafood restaurants on Sorrento Road and at Perdido Key Bridge Marina. After crossing the bridge, drive one mile to the junction (on the left) to day-use Johnson Beach on Perdido Key. This part of the Gulf Islands National Seashore has 7 miles of beach, dunes, and windswept vegetation. A short nature trail on the Big Lagoon bay side introduces you to some of the plants: black rush, saw grass, Florida rosemary, milkweed, slash pine, and live oak. Nearby, on the oceanfront, is a parking area for swimming and picnicking. You can hike east along the beach and spend the day on the slender key whose dunes were washed away like dust by Hurricane Frederick in 1979. Only the call of shorebirds and the reverberant sea will be your companions. Along the way you will see blue and speckled crabs where the waves break; this is an excellent place for crabbing. At the end of the key you can see Fort Pickens across Pensacola Pass.

Visit another part of the Gulf Islands National Seashore, the pristine Santa Rosa Recreation Area, on your way to Fort

Walton. Access, from Fort Pickens and Pensacola Beach, is 7 miles on SR 399. A dune-protecting boardwalk extends to both the Santa Rosa Sound and the seashore of this day-use facility, where you can picnic or stroll along unmarred white beaches in both directions.

Before leaving the Pensacola area, you may wish to try two other activities there: a canoe trip on the Perdido River and a 90-mile bicycle trip. The 29-mile canoe trip begins at Old Water Ferry Landing and goes south to US 90 (about 2 miles south of I-10 and 14 miles west on US 90 from Pensacola). To begin, travel 15 miles north on US 29 from I-10 in Pensacola to SR 182, and turn left (west). Follow SR 182 for 5 miles to CR 99 and turn right (north). After 4.7 miles on CR 99 turn left (west) on CR 97A at Bay Springs; go 4.5 miles to an unpaved road, turn left (west) to the put-in, Old Water Ferry Landing, at the river. Take-out options are at Barrineau Park after 10 miles, at Muscogee Landing after 9 miles, and at US 90 after 10 miles. Access at US 90 is at a private boat ramp on the northeast side of the bridge. (Ask permission to take-out here before you begin your downriver trip.) Your journey on the Perdido River will take you through everything from remote hunting preserves of deer and turkey to popular swimming and fishing holes used by local citizens. Framed by tall oak, sweet gum, maple, cypress, and red cedar, the river is usually shallow and has frequent sandbars for campsites. The river divides Alabama and Florida. (See *Information.*)

One of the state's bicycle program routes is Route A: Sugar Beaches, which is 90 miles long in three sections. The Five Flag (A-1) section is 5.6 miles one way through the historic district from the Pensacola Visitor Center to the Pensacola Airport. The 16-mile one-way, Shifting Sands (A-2) section leaves the Pensacola Visitor Center, crosses the 3-mile Pensacola Bay Bridge on US 98 to SR 399 and to Pensacola Beach, and turns west to Fort Pickens. It returns to Pensacola Beach. From here the Naval Live Oaks (A-3) section makes a loop of 50 miles east on SR 399 to Navarre, then goes north on SR 87, west on SR 399, and, finally, 8.8 miles on US 98. This scenic route follows the shoreline, passes by East Bay, and then goes through Naval Live Oaks preserve.

After you leave Santa Rosa Island through Navarre, your next stop will be Fort Walton Beach, a center for beach and bay water sports, regattas, fishing tournaments, ancient Indian history displays, and festivals. The excellent restaurants along the Miracle Strip include The Sound on US 98 at the western water-side edge of the city, (904) 243-7772; its specialities are fresh seafood and homemade pastries. Campgrounds are at Eglin Air Force Base and Rocky Bayou State Recreation Area. At Fort Walton's Indian Temple Mound and Museum on US 98, the large mound and artifacts tell the story of 10,000 years of Indian culture. The mound is open daily to visitors; the museum is open Tuesday through Sunday. The cities of Fort Walton and Destin sponsor the Billy Bowlegs Festival in late May or early June, in memory of the colorful Seminole Indian chief of "Bowlegs War." The chief, who reportedly left buried treasures, surrendered himself, his warriors, women, and children to the U.S. government for cash bounties in 1858 during the Third Seminole War.

For information about camping and other outdoor recreation at Eglin Air Force Base, drive north 13 miles on SR 85 from US 98 in Fort Walton to Jackson Guard. The base is located on the east side of SR 85 (near a Comfort Inn) after the junction with SR 20 in Niceville. The 460,800-acre base, the largest forested base in the nation, was formerly the Choctawhatchee National Forest (of which Apalachicola National Forest still manages 957 acres). Under the Emergency Land Act it was converted to Eglin AFB in 1939, but half of the vast territory is open to the public. Its natural communities are xeric and mesic uplands, rocklands, coastal uplands, wetlands, estuaries, lakes, and streams. Following the backcountry roads and seeing the wildlife (328 identified species of birds, more than 200 plants, and 170 mammals and reptiles) will give you more the feeling of a national forest than of a military base.

In the base are 52 miles of boat and canoe routes in eight

bayous and rivers; white sand beaches and some of the largest and most impressive dunes in the state; sixteen designated campgrounds (not full service); miles of backcountry routes for bicycling, hiking, and horseback riding; ponds and streams for fishing and gigging; open areas for nature study; and hunting. The base provides a free 2-hour (seasonal) tour, but permits are required for all activities. Permits are available at the Jackson Guard office Monday through Friday, open from 7 A.M. to 3:15 P.M. except for weekends and holidays. If you request permits by mail, apply at least 3 weeks in advance. (See *Information.*) The main base also has a worthwhile educational and historical exhibit of U.S. Air Force development at the Air Force Armaments Museum, located halfway between Niceville and Fort Walton Beach at the junction of SR 85 and SR 397.

On SR 20, 3 miles east of Niceville, is Rocky Bayou State Recreation Area. Rarely filled, even in the peak of summer, this quiet, rustic, beautiful area by the bayou has full-service camping, boating, fresh- and saltwater fishing, and a white sandy beach for swimming. Mature sand pines, oaks, and magnolias rise above turkey oaks, saw palmettoes, carpets of reindeer moss, and wildflowers such as standing cypress, a bright red herb, on the Sand Pine and Rocky Bayou nature trails. If you visit in late October, and enjoy mullet and allied foods, stop at the Boggy Bayou Mullet Festival at SR 85 and College Boulevard in Niceville, one mile north of the SR 85 and SR 20 junction, (904) 897-4986. Before you return to Fort Walton Beach, you may find the Historical Society Museum (115 Westview, Valparaiso) of interest. It houses a remarkable display of Civil War documents and Indian and pioneer settler artifacts.

Return to Fort Walton Beach and cross the bridge on US 98 to the Okaloosa Area, where you can visit the easternmost day-use facility of the Gulf Islands National Seashore, a picnic area and boat launch to the Choctawhatchee Bay. To continue your journey, cross the East Pass Bridge to Destin, called "the luckiest fishing village in the world" for its legendary fishing environment since Capt. Leonard Destin pioneered commercial fishing here more than a century ago. The town celebrates the seafood industry with an annual Seafood Festival and sailing regattas. Two miles east of Destin is the day-use Henderson Beach State Recreation Area, a 208-acre natural beach acquired under the state's Save Our Coast program of the 1980s. After another 10 miles on US 98, turn right on CR 30A for access to Grayton Beach State Recreation Area, which has a full-service campground, with reservations accepted between June 1 and Labor Day. Wind-sculpted high white barrier dunes, oaks, and slash pines make this park a distinctive work of art. A nature trail from the picnic area leads into a pine flatwoods close to sand dunes piled to the tree tops.

When you leave Grayton Beach, follow CR 283 out to US 98, turn right, and after 2 miles turn left on CR 395 to Point Washington. After 1.2 miles you will come to peaceful Eden State Gardens, the preserved home of legendary swamp lumber entrepreneur William Henry Wesley. The spacious home was built in 1897 and remained in the Wesley family until 1953. Tours through the heirloom-filled rooms and azalea-scented gardens take you back in history to sawmill settlement. The gardens are open daily; the house Thursday through Monday. Point Washington has its Wesley legends; it also has a *Crocodile Dundee* in reverse. If you have not called ahead, ask anyone about "Captain Carl." He can take you and five others in his 18-foot flat-bottom *Marsh Hen* on a 5-hour tour of the alligator-infested maze of bayous and interlocking delta channels of the Choctawhatchee River Swamp. (See *Information.*)

To reach your destination at Pine Log State Forest, backtrack 3 miles on US 98 to the junction with US 331 and take US 331 across the scenic Choctawhatchee Bay to SR 20. Turn right (east) on SR 20, take another right on SR 79 at Ebro, and after one mile turn right again. Of the twenty campsites here, five have electrical hookups. Reservations are not accepted, but call in advance for information about space availability. (Another option for a campsite is at Saint Andrews State Recreation Area in Panama City, where advance reservations are accepted.) Pine Log, purchased in 1935, is one of Florida's four major state forests. Operated under multiple-use guidelines for timber, wildlife, and game management, the 6,911 acres are also open for camping, fishing, boating, hunting, swimming, hiking, and birding. Pine Log is a superior place to relax and listen to the cicadas and crickets that have replaced the surf sighs of the Emerald Coast. Two natural lakes are near the tranquil campground, one with dark cypress shrouded with Spanish moss in a shadowy mist, the other grass bordered with tall pines effusing the sun's rays. Manicured by lawn mower, the 3-mile blue-blazed Pine Log Nature Trail loops from the ranger's driveway and shares nearly a mile with the Florida Trail. For a short distance the trail parallels Pine Log Creek among titi, sweet bay, juniper, and gum. Redroot and other wildflowers, warblers, woodpeckers, and sparrows are prominent in grassy open pine stands. For wilderness-type hiking, follow the Florida Trail either east or west for a few miles within the forest boundary.

For a side trip from your base camp at Pine Log, travel south on SR 79 to the popular Saint Andrews State Recreation Area on the Miracle Strip and take a boat trip to undeveloped Shell Island. For another side trip, drive north on SR 79, 3 miles past Vernon, for an adventurous rental canoe trip on Holmes Creek at Crystal Spring. (See *Information.*)

### Information

Counties: Escambia, Santa Rosa, Okaloosa, Walton, Bay
Average Temperatures: January, 43.8°F (low), 67°F (high); August, 74°F (low), 90°F (high)
National Properties: Gulf Islands National Seashore, Florida District, P.O. Box 100, Gulf Breeze, FL 32561, (904) 934-2604; Mississippi District, 3500 Park Rd., Ocean Springs, MS 39564, (601) 875-0821; Eglin Air Force Base, Natural Resources Branch, AD/DEMN, Eglin AFB, FL 32542, (904) 882-4164

State Properties: Big Lagoon State Recreation Area, 12301 Gulf Beach Hwy., Pensacola, FL 32507, (904) 492-1595; Eden State Gardens, P.O. Box 26, Point Washington, FL 32454, (904) 231-4214; Grayton Beach State Recreation Area, Rte. 2, Box 6600, Santa Rosa Beach, FL 32459, (904) 231-4210; Henderson Beach State Recreation Area, 17000 Emerald Coast Parkway, Destin, FL 32541, (904) 837-7550; Perdido Key State Recreation Area, c/o Big Lagoon State Recreation Area (above); Pine Log State Forest, Star Rte., Box 14A, Ebro, FL 32437, (904) 535-4185; Rocky Bayou State Recreation Area, 4281 Hwy. 20, Niceville, FL 32578, (904) 833-9144; Saint Andrews State Recreation Area, 4415 Thomas Dr., Panama City, FL 32408, (904) 233-5140

Museums: Historic Pensacola Village, 120 Church St., Pensacola, FL 32501, (904) 444-8905; Indian Temple Mound Museum, 139 Miracle Strip Pkwy., Fort Walton Beach, FL 32548, (904) 243-6521; National Museum of Naval Aviation, Naval Air Station, Pensacola, FL 32508, (904) 453-NAVY and (800) 327-5002; Museum of the Sea and Indian, 4801 Beach Hwy., Destin, FL 32541, (904) 837-6625; The Museum of Man in the Sea, 17314 Back Beach Rd., Panama City Beach, FL 32413, (904) 235-4101; T. T. Wentworth Jr. Museum, 330 S. Jefferson St., Pensacola, FL 32501, (904) 444-8586; U.S. Air Force Armament Museum, Eglin AFB, Valparaiso, FL 32542, (904) 882-4062

Chambers of Commerce: Bay County CC, P.O. Box 1850, Panama City, FL 32402, (904) 785-5206; Destin CC, P.O. Box 8, Destin, FL 32540, (904) 837-6241; Gulf Breeze Area CC, P.O. Box 337, Gulf Breeze, FL 32562, (904) 932-7888; Greater Fort Walton Beach CC, P.O. Box 640, Fort Walton Beach, FL 32549, (904) 244-8191; Navarre Beach CC, P.O. Box 5336, Navarre, FL 32566, (904) 939-3267; Pensacola CC, P.O. Box 550, Pensacola, FL 32593, (904) 438-4081; Santa Rosa County CC, 501 Stewart St., SW, Milton, FL 32570, (904) 623-2339

Services and Amenities: *Commercial Camping:* Cherokee Campground, 5255 Gulf Breeze Pkwy., Gulf Breeze, FL 32561,

(904) 932-9905; Island View Campground, Navarre Beach, Navarre, FL 32569, (904) 932-2530

*Bicycle Maps:* State Bicycle Program, P.O. Box 550 (9th and Chase Sts.), Pensacola, FL 32593, (904) 434-1234; *Boat Guide for the Choctawhatchee River:* Carl Forrester, Rte. 2, Box 181, Point Washington, FL 32454, (904) 231-4420; *Canoe Rentals and Guides for Perdido River:* AAA Canoe Rental, Rte. 2, Box 578, Cantonment, FL 32533, (904) 587-2366; Adventures Unlimited, Rte. 6, Box 283, Milton, FL 32570, (800) 239-6864; *Canoe and Diving Rentals and Instruction for Holmes Creek:* Cypress Spring Canoe Trails, Vernon, FL 32462, (904) 535-2960; *Home-Cooked Food:* Hopkins Boarding House, 900 N. Spring St., Pensacola, FL 32501, (904) 438-3979; *Parasailing, Surfing, and Waterskiing:* PBS Watersports, 1320 US 98E, Fort Walton Beach, FL 32549, (904) 244-2933; *Scuba Diving and Snorkeling, Rentals and Instruction:* Hydrospace Dive Shop, 3605 Thomas Dr., Panama City, FL 32402, (904) 234-9463; Surf and Sail Boardsailing, 11 Via de Luna, Pensacola Beach, FL 32561, (904) 932-SURF; *Water Sports Rental and Equipment:* Key Sailing Center, 500 Quietwater Rd., Pensacola, FL 32561, (904) 932-5520; *Wildlife Rehabilitation:* Wildlife Rescue and Sanctuary, P.O. Box 6123, Gulf Breeze, FL 32561, (904) 932-7768

# 5

## CENTRAL REGION

Central Florida is between the green Ocala National Forest and the blue Lake Okeechobee. In the center of this region are thousands of natural lakes, known Florida's Land of Lakes, one of which is Lake Kissimmee, from which the mangled Kissimmee River flows south to Lake Okeechobee. Another famous fish-filled river, Saint Johns, flows north from its headwaters in the marshes near Blue Cypress Lake. A third major river, the Withlacoochee, originates in the Green Swamp, a few miles west of Walt Disney World, and empties into the Gulf north of Crystal River. The Green Swamp area, particularly from Haines City and Lakeland to Brooksville, is a significant aquifer that supplies 70 percent of the state's underground fresh water. The Indian River, chiefly a saltwater system, runs along the entire eastern seashore between the mainland and a stretch of barrier islands that form the "space coast" in the Cape Canaveral area and the "treasure coast" south of Sebastian Inlet. Because the sun shines almost every day on the Gulf shore, it has been labeled the "sun coast." Sections and patches of hardwoods, wetlands, and pine forests with dense saw palmetto cover the region, but they are interspersed with ranchlands, citrus groves, and vegetable farms. On the coastal areas are mangrove thickets, bays, islands, and estuaries. To the dismay of environmentalists, a human population of 4 million has surrounded most of the natural areas and is rapidly altering the ecosystem.

Before the Seminole Indians and white southern immigrants settled in central Florida in the eighteenth and nineteenth centuries, the nonagricultural Ais Indians inhabited the eastern shoreline. On the western shore, the Tocobaga lived north of Tampa Bay, and the Calusa lived to its south. In April 1528, Spanish explorer Pánfilo de Narváez landed in Tampa Bay and marched north toward the Tallahassee area, a route generally followed by Hernando de Soto 10 years later.

The upper half of central Florida is the fastest growing area in the state. Orlando (1837), the railway and highway hub for massive development, is connected to the Tampa (1823)–Clearwater (1842)–Saint Petersburg (1876) corridor along I-4, which is expected to be Florida's first section urbanized from coast to coast. The Orlando area, which began as a simple U.S. soldiers' campground in the second Seminole War (1835–1842), now receives more visitors than any other metropolitan area in Florida. Economically sound with citrus, aerospace, and electronic industries, its magical source of attention is Walt Disney World, a cornucopia of pleasurable epics. But long before Mickey Mouse came to town and the amusement parks displayed ballerina killer whales, the city and county revealed their cultural heritage with natural science centers, botanical gardens and parks, and historic museums.

The merging population of Tampa–Clearwater–Saint Petersburg has made Pinellas County the most densely populated in the state. Its 28 miles of dazzling, sunny beaches pull visitors here like a magnet, much as the railroad and hotel magnate Henry Plant pulled them in during the 1880s, when he was the opulent Gulf Coast rival of Florida's godfather, Henry Flagler, on the eastern shore. Sunny, sophisticated, and industrially selective, this megalopolis shines with museums of art and natural history, seabird sanctuaries, botanical gardens, the largest collection of Dali art in the world, and a futuristic inverted pyramid at the end of a one-mile pier in Tampa Bay.

Some of the smaller cities are also historic and colorful: Winter Haven has its rose-perfumed Cypress Gardens (1936), Florida's lush and first theme park; Lakeland has the world's largest group of buildings designed by Frank Lloyd Wright at Florida Southern College (1885); elegant Winter Park, "Little

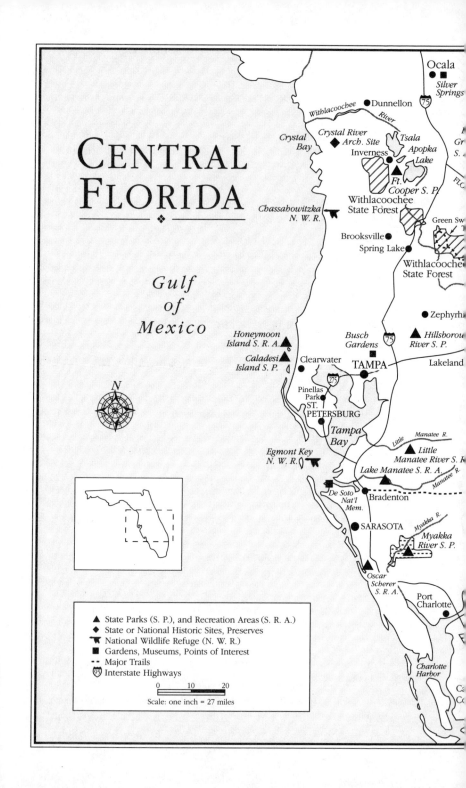

# CENTRAL FLORIDA

❖

Gulf
of
Mexico

N

Ocala
Silver
Springs

●Dunnellon
Withlacoochee River

Crystal
Bay

Crystal River
Arch. Site
Inverness

Tsala
Apopka
Lake

Gr
S.

Ft.
Cooper S. P.

FLO

Withlacoochee
State Forest

Chassahowitzka
N. W. R.

Brooksville●
Spring Lake●

Green Sw

Withlacooche
State Forest

●Zephyrhi

Honeymoon
Island S. R. A.▲

Busch
Gardens

▲Hillsborou
River S. P.

Caladesi▲
Island S. P.

Clearwater

TAMPA

Lakeland

Pinellas
Park●
ST.
PETERSBURG

Tampa
Bay

Little      Manatee R.

▲ Little
Manatee River S. R.

Egmont Key
N. W. R.

Lake Manatee S. R. A.        Manatee R.

De Soto
Nat'l
Mem.

Bradenton

●SARASOTA

Myakka R.

Myakka
River S. P.

Oscar
Scherer
S. R. A.

Port
Charlotte

Charlotte
Harbor

Ca
Co

▲ State Parks (S. P.), and Recreation Areas (S. R. A.)
◆ State or National Historic Sites, Preserves
🦅 National Wildlife Refuge (N. W. R.)
■ Gardens, Museums, Points of Interest
-- Major Trails
⑮ Interstate Highways

0        10        20

Scale: one inch = 27 miles

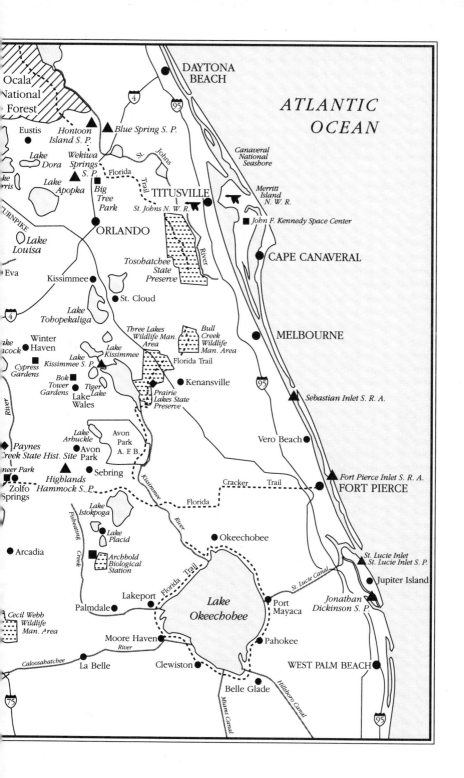

Europe," is delightfully manicured and has more Tiffany glass than can be found on New York's Fifth Avenue; and Kissimmee, the historic gateway to Brahma cattle country, is now the "gateway to Walt Disney World." The small cities of Titusville, Merritt Island, and Melbourne are only minutes from the crowds at the Kennedy Space Center. Vero Beach and Fort Pierce are huge marketplaces for citrus; Fort Pierce is also known for its cattle ranches. Sarasota, on the Gulf coast, is renowned for its Ringling Museum of Art, as winter home to the circus world, for its botanical gardens, and as the site of the state's first golf course (1886).

Once you get away from the crowds you will have choices of wide diversity. The federal government has preserved more than 25 miles of unspoiled shoreline in Canaveral National Seashore, and Merritt Island National Wildlife Refuge is home to some 200,000 birds in the peak season of wintertime. Hardly more than half an hour away is Tosohatchee State Reserve, where black bear and wild turkey roam freely in virgin forests. No place in the region provides more diversity for hikers, bikers, equestrians, and canoeists than Withlacoochee State Forest in the northwest corner of the region. Prairie-Lakes State Preserve is isolated, accessible only from remote CR 523 between Saint Cloud and Kenansville. Once there, as on sections of the Florida Trail that runs through it, you may not see humans for days, but wildlife surrounds you. You could easily spend a week at Myakka River State Park, the state's largest, with waterfowl and backcountry wild animals; at any of the state's twenty-five other parks, recreation areas, historic sites, and preserves in this region; or at one of the national wildlife refuges at Pelican Island, Saint Johns, Chassahowitzka, Pinellas, Egmont Key, Crystal River, and Passage Key. Across the peninsula from Bradenton to Fort Pierce is the Florida Cracker Trail, a backcountry highway horse trail. Other adventures in this region are hiking the Florida Trail through the Kissimmee River basin, fishing almost everywhere, bicycling in the lake country, and surfing at Sebastian Inlet. If you wish other remoteness, try wild Bull Creek Wildlife Management Area near Holopaw on US 192, and Archbold Biological Station, which is south of pleasant Lake Placid but so hidden it is not on a road map. Canoeists have 126 miles of somnolent, placid rivers.

## INDIAN RIVER

Indian River, a 135-mile saltwater estuary, is more of a lagoon system than a river. Teeming with marine life and dotted with hundreds of island wildfowl habitats, it varies in width from 5 miles near Merritt Island National Wildlife Refuge and the John F. Kennedy Space Center to 0.1 mile at Vero Beach. Except at the Merritt Island area, it is near the Atlantic Ocean between US 1 on the west and SR A1A on narrow barrier islands on the east. An Intracoastal Waterway route, it is favored for its fishing and water sports. In its waters is the Pelican Island NWR, the first wildlife refuge in the nation (1903), and many aquatic reserves, preserves, natural areas, and parks. Grown on its border areas is the internationally known Indian River citrus. A houseboat adventure with bicycles to reach the beach parks is an option for exploring the Indian River area, but the trip described here is chiefly on the SR A1A motor route to all the major natural beach areas, parks, wildlife refuges, and historic sites, with a challenging side trip to the remote Tosohatchee State Reserve.

*What to See and Do:* You can hike 25 miles of unspoiled beach in Canaveral National Seashore and 22 miles in Tosohatchees virgin forests of slash pine and cypress, and you can spend weeks biking, birding, sailing, and fishing in the ocean, surf, river, bay, and inlet. Water sports include skiing, sailing, boating, and boardsailing. Scuba diving and snorkeling are popular at Vero Beach and Jupiter Inlet, and Sebastian Inlet is considered Florida's finest area for surfing.

*Where to Begin:* If you are traveling south on I-95, take Exit 84 and turn east on SR 44 toward New Smyrna Beach. After 3.5 miles, turn right (south) on Mission Road for 1.7 miles to

Sugar Mill Ruins Travel Park, a full-service commercial camp-
ground, to organize your journey. The nearest airport is
Daytona Beach Regional, and the nearest Amtrak station is in
De Land on SR 44, west. (If traveling north on I-95 to reverse
the route of this trip, take Exit 61, SR 76 [Kanner Highway] east
to Stuart and SR 707 north on Indian River Drive to the
Savannas Campground. The nearest airport is West Palm
Beach International.)

*About the Adventures:* Your journey on the space coast,
part of central east coast, begins in the undisturbed 57,000-
acre Canaveral National Seashore between New Smyrna
Beach and the Kennedy Space Center. With 25 miles of beach,
sand dunes, and seashells, it is the largest undeveloped and
protected area of Florida's Atlantic coast. The ranger station is
at Apollo Beach on the north end; it and the Playalinda Beach
on the south end are accessible by highways, but the wild
central area, Klondike Beach, can be reached only by foot. To
reach the north entrance station from the Sugar Mill Ruins
Travel Park, drive east across the Indian River North causeway
and follow A1A 10 miles south. At the station area are a boat
launch to the Indian River Lagoon (also called Mosquito
Lagoon), a picnic area, and three short interpretive trails:
Eldora Hammock; Castle Windy at a midden; and Turtle
Mound, a 40-foot-high historic relic of Indian shellfish dinners.
Obtain a backcountry camping permit to canoe to designated
island campsites or hike to campsites on the beach. Surfing
and surf fishing (for pompano and scrappy bluefish) are
permitted anywhere on the seashore. Swimming at Canaveral
can be dangerous in rough surf and undertows and among the
Portuguese man-of-war and stinging jellyfish. Frequent and
violent thunderstorms occur here in the summertime, and
stormy high tides can leave you without a beach on which to
hike. You must pack all fresh water to your campsite. You may
wish to call ahead to the ranger about a period in late spring
through August when the park is closed to accommodate sea
turtles that come ashore at night to nest: the Atlantic green, the
loggerhead, the leatherback, and sometimes the hawksbill—

all endangered or threatened. The females arrive on high tide, use their hind flippers to dig a hole, and deposit, depending on species, ten to three hundred leathery white eggs about the size of Ping-Pong balls. Covered by sand and incubated by the sun, the eggs hatch within 60 days, unless a predator such as a raccoon discovers them. Each 2-ounce baby turtle uses a carnucle to open its shell, and collectively the babies break open the sand during nighttime, when they are protected from the sun's heat. Tiny and vulnerable in their risky race to the reef beds, they may fall prey to ghost crabs and fish, particularly sharks. From eggs to maturity, approximately one in ten thousand survives. At maturity, a green turtle, also called a black turtle, weighs between two hundred and six hundred pounds and has long flippers for marathon swimming. (For information on guided turtle watches, see *Jupiter Island*, Chapter 6.)

From New Smyrna Beach, drive south on US 1 to a full-service commercial campground, a central location from which to visit Merritt Island National Wildlife Refuge, Spaceport USA, and the Tosohatchee State Reserve. Campgrounds are North Gate Travel Trailer Park (no tents) 2 miles north of the junction with SR 46, and KOA–Cape Kennedy, 2 miles west on SR 46 (0.5 mile) west from I-95. Both are 5 miles north of Titusville. Or check the Space Center Campground in Bellwood, south of SR 405, the NASA Causeway.

To reach the visitor center of Merritt Island NWR from Titusville, drive 5 miles east on SR 406/402. The center has displays and descriptions of the island's wildlife habitats and offers information on the canoe and boat launches and on auto and foot trails. The center is open 8 A.M. to 4:30 P.M. weekdays and 9 A.M. to 5 P.M. weekends, closed Sundays from April through October and on holidays. One of the nation's most unique natural areas, the 140,000-acre refuge has a subtropical climate. Shaped by a million years of wind and waves, the barrier island has ridges, swales, and marshes that support eighteen endangered or threatened wildlife species, more than any other refuge in the nation. Sixty-five species of amphibians, 117 fishes, 25 mammals, and 310 birds live here in diverse habitats of freshwater impoundments, saltwater estuaries, brackish marshes, shallow water grasslands, hardwood hammocks, and pine flatwoods. The refuge and the seashore are on the Atlantic flyway, a major migration route for wildfowl that journey up to 6,000 miles from the Caribbean to Canada.

Archeological finds at mounds and shell middens indicate that Indians may have lived on the island as early as 7000 B.C. Although explored by the Spanish and the English, its inhospitable marshes and swarms of mosquitoes discouraged settlement. But in 1958, the relatively unpublicized area suddenly made news when the National Aeronautical and Space Administration (NASA) began operations at Cape Canaveral. In 1961, the area became significantly important when President John F. Kennedy expanded NASA's space exploration. For a buffer zone, NASA initially acquired 88,000 acres on Merritt Island in 1963; that was the beginning of the refuge, which has since become a modern example of how nature and technology can coexist. (However, the use of DDT for mosquito control in the 1940s began the extinction of the dusky seaside sparrow [*Ammospiza maritima nigrescens*], a nonmigratory songbird.)

To see a prime birding area in the refuge, explore 6-mile Black Point Wildlife Drive. From November through February you may find a concentration of birdlife, more than 200,000 at its peak: white pelicans, rails, soras, blue-winged teals, wigeons, shovelers, scaups, bald eagles, hawks, coots, gulls, terns, ibis, and egrets. In January, songbirds include tree swallows and yellow-rumped warblers. Every month has a rewarding display, but the summer months are stormy, hot, muggy, and buggy, which makes hiking less desirable. For a 5-mile foot trail off the Black Point auto route, begin at stop No. 8 and follow the loop of the Cruickshank Trail (named in honor of Allan D. Cruickshank, naturalist and influential leader in establishing the refuge). The open, grassy route will lead you through knot and spike grasses, sedges, willows, ferns, and black mangrove. In the winter you may see the hooded merganser, with its fan-shaped white crest, the wood stork, or the American kestrel. A volunteer staff of birders offers guided tours during the winter season each Thursday at 9 A.M. from November through March, leaving from the visitor center. Access to Black Point is 0.4 mile north on SR 406 from its juncture with SR 402 near the visitor center.

Another auto drive is the 4-mile Max Hoeck Wildlife Drive between Playalinda Beach and SR 3, along the railroad tracks, which parallels SR 402. Also on SR 402 are two foot trails: Old Hammock, an interpretive trace on ecology, and Palm Hammock, a partial boardwalk of 2 miles that winds through a hardwood forest. Both share a parking area, 1.2 miles east on SR 402 from the visitor center. While on SR 402, go to Playalinda Beach and take the 5-mile drive north beside the foredunes. At frequent intervals you will find parking with crossways to the beach and views south to space-shuttle pads B and A. At Eddy Creek is a boat launch access to the islands for sailing, fishing, and birding in the Indian River Lagoon.

As a side trip west of Merritt Island and Indian River, visit the Tosohatchee State Reserve. Access is on SR 50 (Orlando Road) 9.8 miles west of the junction with I-95 (Exit 79) to the community of Christmas. Turn left (south) on Taylor Creek Road, and after 2.8 miles, turn left again. The gates are open 8 A.M. to sundown, for a small fee per vehicle. At the ranger's office is a sign: "Huntin' and Fishin' Talked Here."

One of the interesting legends about the people of Tosohatchee regards the Indians who lived here and left their mounds between the Saint Johns River (the east boundary of the reserve) and Tosohatchee Creek. A group of warriors went east to attack a rival group on Merritt Island, but a dragon rose from the river to defend the islanders. Today a 20-ton concrete and steel dragon (the 1971 work of Tampa sculptor Lewis Vandercar) near the Eau Gallie Causeway guards Merritt Island and Cape Canaveral. A more recent story is of chewing gum tycoon William Wrigley, Jr., who in 1912 purchased the area that is now the reserve and built the Beehead Ranch

House (a well-preserved homesite of native woods) for his cowhands. Wrigley sold the property in the 1920s, and from 1930 to 1977 it belonged to the Tosohatchee Gun Club. Then the state purchased 28,000 acres, including Beehead Ranch House, with funds from the Environmentally Endangered Land Program. Since then, one of Wrigley's ranch hand ghosts unlocks the ranch house each morning, perplexing the ranger who has locked it the night before.

Hiking options at the reserve are to backpack and camp overnight on the 17-mile section of the Florida Trail that passes through the reserve, or on the 22.6 miles of loops and connecting trails. You will have the opportunity to see deer, turkey, gray fox, wild hog, raccoon, osprey, hawks, and songbirds. Beauty-berry, clematis, orchids, butterweed, butterwort, yellow pea, aster, and dwarf iris are prominent among the wildflowers. You may also see handfern, which grows on the cabbage palmetto. Two area forests are a 900-acre virgin cypress swamp, along Jim Creek, and a virgin slash pine stand near Beehand Ranch House, the largest tract in Florida, with some trees older than 250 years. The Florida Trail is blazed orange, and loop trails are white; because it is easy to become disoriented, a map from the ranger's station is essential. An excellent place for you to walk and study the flora and fauna is under a power line that runs through the reserve. In addition to hiking, you may ride your horse or go fishing. Cutting through the center of the reserve is the Martin Anderson Beeline Expressway; you will pass under it on the Florida Trail but avoid it on the loop trails north of it.

If you plan to hike the Florida Trail section, contact the ranger for reservations and information on designated sites for backpack camping. The north terminus is on SR 50, 0.1 mile east of the Christmas RV Park, and the south terminus is on SR 520, one mile west of the Saint Johns River bridge. If you hike from the south, you will follow a number of old forested dikes for the first 6 miles to SR 528, the Beeline Expressway. Cross under the bridge, unless the water level is too high and you have to cross the expressway. After joining one of the reverse loop trails, follow west and then north for 6.6 miles as the trail continues on an independent route from the Tosohatchee Creek.

On your return drive to the community of Christmas, visit the Fort Christmas Museum, a replica of an 1837 fort immortalizing the Seminole Wars and with artifacts of pioneer settlers. It is open daily except Mondays, 10 A.M. to 5 P.M., with access 2 miles north on SR 420 from SR 50.

To continue your journey south, return to Merritt Island for a visit to Spaceport USA at the Kennedy Space Center on SR 405, the NASA Parkway. The educational displays in the visitor center, of space art, spacecraft, shuttle models, and the five-building Gallery of Space Flight, are free to the public. The IMAX Theater and a bus trip to the space launch pads and the gigantic vehicle assembly building require small fees.

When leaving the Kennedy Space Center, drive east one mile to SR 3 and turn right (south) on a narrow peninsula between the Indian River and Banana River Aquatic Preserve. Highway 3, or Tropical Trail, is a scenic route among old homesteads and the rivers. After 33 miles, reach SR 518 at Eau Gallie Beach and rejoin A1A, south. (An alternate route, with options for pier fishing and surfing at Port Canaveral, and scuba diving and beach biking at Cocoa Beach, is SR 528/SR A1A east on Bennett Causeway from SR 3, 9.8 miles south of the NASA Parkway. Also at Cocoa Beach are water-sport shops and a waterway tour on the *Little Dixie River Queen*. If you are boardsailing and need equipment, rentals, or instructors, contact the Space Coast Sailboard Club, Rockledge, on the west bank of the Indian River on US 1. In Cocoa, by the Indian River, try the Brevard Hotel, inexpensive and family oriented, and Bernard's Surf, a restaurant with one hundred entrees. See *Information*.)

From Eau Gallie, drive south on SR A1A another 23.4 miles to Sebastian Inlet State Recreation Area (about halfway between Melbourne and Vero Beach), your next campground. You can make reservations in advance. The shaded, full-service campground overlooks the inlet from the south

*Sebastian Inlet at the Atlantic Ocean.* PHOTO BY Florida
Dept. of Commerce.

side, and on the north side you can enjoy what is considered
the best surfing area in the state. Snorkeling, scuba diving,
fishing, and boating are other adventures here. Popular
locations for fishing are the catwalks under the bridge, jetties,
and the inlet channel. The 643-acre park is about one mile
wide, between the Indian River Aquatic Reserve and the
Atlantic Ocean, with lagoons, coastal hammocks, and mangrove swamps; it is a habitat for about 200 species of birds,
including egrets, herons, terns, gulls, and ibis. The roseate
spoonbill may be seen here in the tidal flats, except in the
winter. For a reminder of this area's history, be sure to visit the
McLarty State Museum, the site of an old Spanish salvage camp
at the south edge of the park on SR A1A. In 1715 a fleet of
twelve Spanish ships with heavy cargoes of gold, silver, and
jewels from Mexico and Peru met a violent storm here. A
thousand passengers drowned, and the fifteen hundred who
made it to shore set up camps to salvage some of the treasure,
much of which was later pirated by the English. Since 1988,

Mel Fisher has had salvage rights to the underwater treasures. The museum exhibit covers the Spanish world of trade, the history of the Ais Indians, other shipwrecks in the area, and Fisher's recent discoveries.

In the Indian River, between here and Wabasso Beach, is the nearly 5,000-acre Pelican Island National Wildlife Refuge. President Theodore Roosevelt initially established the 3-acre island refuge in 1903 to protect the pelicans from plume hunters in response to urging from the Florida Audubon Society and the American Ornithologists Union. The Audubon Society had to defend the rookery again in 1918 when Florida fishermen invaded it and killed many young pelicans, claiming that the birds were eating millions of pounds of food fish. Since those early years, the refuge has been expanded to include other mangrove islands, wetlands, and bottomlands. Nesting species other than brown pelicans are white and wood ibis, the double-crested cormorant, egrets, and the Louisiana heron. They reach their peak nesting in April and May. Access is by boat only, and the nearest boat ramp is on SR 510, one mile west of SR A1A in Wabasso Beach Park. The Merritt Island NWR administers the refuge.

Your next park on SR A1A is Fort Pierce Inlet State Recreation Area, 24 miles south of McLarty State Museum. Along the way, after 13.3 miles, you will reach the SR 60 intersection in Vero Beach. Here, at Sexton Plaza by the beach, is Ocean Grill, a heritage seafood restaurant widely known for its coquilles Saint Jacques. Whether or not you stay overnight, you will find The Driftwood Inn overlooking the sea in Vero Beach to be one of the state's most unusual farragoes of architecture. Vero Beach is a major shipping center for Indian River citrus: succulent mandarins, navel oranges, tangerines, tangeloes, and pink grapefruit. Contact the local chamber of commerce for information on groves and process houses that welcome visitors.

Jack Island State Reserve is the first of three separate sections of the Fort Pierce Inlet State Recreation Area. You will see a road sign, right, directing you 0.3 mile to the 958-acre

Jack Island impoundment. Cross a footbridge to the island, where you can hike one-mile Marsh Rabbit Run Trail through dense mangrove and coastal hammocks to an observation tower. Thousands of egrets, herons, and ibis inhabit the island. Another 4-mile trail follows the island's perimeter dikes. Other areas of the park are Pepper Beach, farther south on the left, with its Saint Lucie Museum of Spanish gold salvage, and the 340-acre Fort Pierce Inlet, farther ahead. Recreational activities are picnicking, swimming, surfing, fishing, and hiking on the Coastal Hammock Trail.

When you approach the North Beach Causeway, you will see a small park for picnicking, fishing, and boating. Of special interest near the boat ramp is a cluster of mangroves usually covered with pelicans vying for the last available tree branches. After you cross the Indian River into Fort Pierce, turn left (south) one mile to CR 707. Follow CR 707 south 5.4 miles to The Savannas, a 550-acre city-county wilderness park near The Savannas State Preserve. Approach on CR 712, right (west). The park has a botanical garden, freshwater fishing, canoeing, hiking trails, and campgrounds that offer unimproved to full-service sites. The Saint Lucie Audubon Society has compiled a list (available at the entrance gate) of 125 bird species. If you watch carefully, you may see the Everglades kite, searching in the marsh for the pomaceous snail, its only food source.

For a relaxing day trip from The Savannas, make a 41-mile loop around Indian River on CR 707 and SR A1A. Drive back to Fort Pierce, turn right on SR A1A, and visit the Saint Lucie County Historical Museum at the end of the bridge. Open Wednesday through Saturday, 10 A.M. to 4 P.M., it has a prominent display of artifacts from Seminole Indian history. Follow A1A on Hutchinson Island through long sections of unspoiled dunes, forests, beaches, and posh parks and resorts. Near the end of the island is Gilbert's Bar House of Refuge. Built in 1875, it is the only remaining structure that was once a haven for shipwrecked sailors. After crossing the Indian River drawbridge, turn right on Indian River Drive for

Indian River drawbridge, turn right on Indian River Drive for your return to The Savannas. Along the route of exclusive properties you will see wading birds, wildflowers, palms, spreading banyans, Australian pines, and a wide range of architecture among historic mansions. (For an adventure south of Stuart, see *Jupiter Island*, Chapter 6.)

### Information

Counties: Volusia, Brevard, Indian River, Saint Lucie

Average Temperatures: January, 50.1°F (low), 69.8°F (high); August, 72.1°F (low), 88.4°F (high)

National Properties: Canaveral National Seashore, 2532 Garden St., Titusville, FL 32796, (904) 428-3384/(407) 267-1110; Merritt Island NWR (and Pelican Island NWR), P.O. Box 6504, Titusville, FL 32780, (407) 861-0667; NASA Kennedy Space Center's Spaceport USA, Kennedy Space Center, FL 32899, (407) 452-2121

State Properties: Fort Pierce Inlet Recreation Area, 905 Shorewinds Dr., Fort Pierce, FL 34949, (407) 468-3985; New Smyrna Sugar Mill Ruins State Historic Site, P.O. Box 861, New Smyrna Beach, FL 32170, (904) 424-2026; Sebastian Inlet State Recreation Area (and McLarty State Museum), 9700 South A1A, Melbourne Beach, FL 32951, (407) 984-4852; Tosohatchee State Reserve, 3365 Taylor Creek Rd., Christmas, FL 32709, (407) 568-5893

City and County Properties: Brevard Museum of History and Natural Science, 2201 Michigan Ave., Cocoa, FL 32926, (407) 632-1830; Saint Lucie County Historical Museum, 414 Seaway Dr., Fort Pierce, FL 34949, (407) 464-6635; The Savannas, 1400 Midway Rd., Fort Pierce, FL 33450, (407) 464-7855

Chambers of Commerce: Brevard County Tourist Development Council, 2235 N. Courtenay Pkwy., Merritt Island, FL 32953, (800) USA-1969; Cocoa Beach Area CC, 400 Fortenberry Rd., Merritt Island, FL 32952, (407) 459-2200; Melbourne–Palm Bay Area CC, 1005 E. Strawbridge Ave., Melbourne, FL 32901, (407) 724-5400; Saint Lucie County CC, P.O. Box 8209, Port St.

Lucie, FL 34985, (407) 335-4487; Sebastian River Area CC, 1302, US Highway 1, Sebastian, FL 32958, (407) 589-5969; New Smyrna Beach/Oak Hill/Edgewater CC, 115 Canal St., New Smyrna Beach, FL 32168, (904) 428-2449; Titusville CC, 2000 S. Washington Ave., Titusville, FL 32781, (407) 267-3036; Vero Beach–Indian River CC, 1216 21st St., Vero Beach, FL 32960, (407) 567-3491

Services and Amenities: *Commercial Campgrounds:* Cape Kennedy KOA, Titusville, (407) 269-7361; New Smyrna Beach KOA, Mission Rd., (904) 427-3581; Northgate Travel Trailer Park, Titusville, (407) 267-0144; Outdoor Resorts, Melbourne Beach, (407) 724-2600, or (800) 327-8550; Sugar Mill Ruins Travel Park, New Smyrna Beach, (904) 427-2284; Vero Beach KOA, (407) 589-5665; *Inns:* Brevard Hotel, 112 Riverside Dr., Cocoa, FL 32922, (407) 636-1411; The Driftwood Inn, 3150 Ocean Dr., Vero Beach, FL 32960, (407) 231-0550, or (800) 432-3166

*Beach-Bike Rentals:* (see Ron Jon's, below); *Boardsailing* (instructions, rentals, accommodations): Space Coast Sailboard Club, 2050 Rockledge Dr., Rockledge, FL 32955, (407) 632-3936; Calema Boardsailing, 362 Magnolia Ave., Merritt Island, FL 32952, (407) 453-3223; *Restaurants:* Bernard's Surf, 2 S. Atlantic Ave., Cocoa, FL 32922, (407) 783-2401; Ocean Grill, Sexton Plaza, Vero Beach, (407) 231-5409; The Strawberry Mansion, 1218 E. New Haven Ave., Melbourne, FL 32901, (407) 724-8627; *Scuba Diving and Snorkeling:* American Divers International, 691 N. Courtenay St., Merritt Island, FL 32952, (407) 453-0600; *Sight-Seeing Cruise of Indian River:* Gatesby's Dockside, 480 W. Cocoa Beach Causeway, Cocoa Beach, FL 32931, (407) 783-2380; *Surfing Equipment and Rentals:* Ron Jon's Surf Shop, 4151 N. Atlantic Ave., Cocoa Beach, FL 32931, (407) 784-1485; *Water Sports* (skiing, boardsailing, sailing, and boating): The Water Works, 1891 E. Merritt Island Causeway, Merritt Island, FL 32952, (407) 452-2007

## LAND OF LAKES

Among the topographical characteristics that make the heart-
land of Florida so appealing are its thousands of clear,
sparkling, natural lakes. Concentrated in the rolling hills of the
four adjoining counties of Polk, Osceola, Orange, and Lake,
these waters form Florida's lake country, also known as its
land of lakes, or its chain of lakes. On Florida's highlands, they
form the longest series of "genetically" related lakes in the
nation. Some large ones, over 200 acres each, are yet
undeveloped and unnamed. Others are known for the towns
and cities on their shorelines. Lake County, established in
1887 and named for its fourteen hundred lakes, has more than
202 square miles of lakes that are cyan and royal blue, azure,
pure (as at Lake Louisa), and with landscaped edges (as at
Lake Dora and Lake Harris). Sharing wide Lake Apopka with
Lake County, Orange County has such jewels as Turkey Lake
and Clear Lake in the city of Orlando. In Osceola County,
34,948-acre Lake Kissimmee, the largest in the four counties,
has not a town on its border. Other treasures are the
wilderness Lake Marian, Cypress Lake, with only a boat dock,
and the twin Tohopekaliga lakes between Kissimmee and
Saint Cloud. In Polk County, the large Lake Arbuckle has
hardly a house in sight; in contrast, Lake Howard is beautifully
encircled by Winter Haven, where the land of lakes title
began. In these waters Native Americans fished and canoed
more than 5,000 years ago. Today, anglers catch largemouth
bass, crappie, bream, and catfish there, and the smooth lake
surfaces entice sailboaters and skiers. Cutting through this
land of lakes, hills, forests, orange groves, and expanding
cities are crisscrossing highways that take you from Florida's
"coast to coast to coast," as the state's Department of Tourism
boasts.

*What to See and Do:* Even if you wanted only to fish in this
lake paradise, to canoe the placid, meandering rivers, to pedal
the 155-mile network of bicycle trails, to study flora and fauna
at the natural and developed gardens, and to hike the Florida

Trail along the Kissimmee River, you would need weeks to complete your adventures. But you and your family may also be inclined to see Florida's major man-made theme attractions—Sea World, Universal and MGM studios, Walt Disney World, Experimental Prototype Community of Tomorrow (EPCOT)—all less than an hour away from your favorite campground, motel, or hotel. Furthermore, if you are centrally located at Kissimmee, you are only 75 miles from Busch Gardens in Tampa, 71 miles from Daytona Beach, and 55 miles from the Kennedy Space Center. On no other trip to the natural Florida will you be so tempted to enter the diverse and spectacular world of science, culture, enchantment, and fantasy. (If you plan a trip to the Orlando area, I suggest buying a guidebook such as Frommer's *Dollarwise Guide to Orlando, Disney World and EPCOT* from your local bookstore before you go.)

*Where to Begin:* I have chosen Lake Kissimmee State Park campground, near Lake Wales, as your northern base, and Highlands Hammock State Park campground at Sebring as your southern base. Not far away from these parks are large commercial campgrounds, some with eight hundred campsites. Others are small county campgrounds, like Lake Arbuckle in Polk County, tucked away from the crowds. Hundreds of hotels and motels and some historic lodges and inns also await you. To reach Lake Kissimmee State Park, drive 4.5 miles east of Lake Wales on SR 60 (from the SR 60 and CR 17B junction), turn left on Camp Mack Road, and go 8.3 miles to the entrance, right. The nearest airport is Orlando International; Amtrak stops in Kissimmee, Winter Haven, and Sebring.

*About the Adventures:* If you arrive on I-4 from the north into Orlando, you might stop at two natural places of interest at the north edge of the city. Turn off at Exit 49 on SR 434 and go east 3 miles to turn left on CR 427. After 2 miles, turn right by a lookout tower to Big Tree Park. Here is the huge Senator, a 3,000-year-old cypress 126 feet high and 17.5 feet in diameter. To get to the other natural area, go west on SR 434. Go one mile beyond the I-4 exit and turn right on Wekiwa

Springs Road to 6,400-acre Wekiwa Springs State Park. Not only does this park have abundant wildlife and wildflowers, it has camping and cabins (that can be reserved); canoe rentals for 15 miles on the Wekiva River that junctions with the Saint Johns River; 13.5 miles of white-blazed hiking trails in pines and hardwoods; and 8.5 miles of day-use horseback trails. Once home to the Timucuan Indians, the word *Wekiwa* derives from *wakiva*, meaning "springs of water." Also here is another large tree, the nation's largest sand pine (*Pinus clausa*), more than 100 feet high. In addition, you will find a protected area of trees and flowers at Mead Botanical Gardens and Leu Gardens in Orlando. To reach them, continue south on I-4 from Exit 49 to Exit 43, Princeton Street, and go east.

However you approach Lake Kissimmee State Park, you may see a sign in Mount Dora, Apopka, Orlando, Kissimmee, or Haines City about the Orange Blossom Trail. Look no farther; this is not a hiking trail but the name of a section of historic US 441/92/17/SR 500/600 now clogged with vehicular traffic. If you wish for a scenic auto route through the lake country and orange groves, begin at the charming model village of Mount Dora and go south on as many back roads as possible. If you do not have a county map, the DeLorme *Florida Atlas and Gazetteer* will serve nicely. After the Winter Haven area, you can parallel US 27 on SR 17 all the way to Sebring. Inexpensive lodgings along the southern stretch are historic and amiable Hillcrest Lodge in Babson Park; Jacaranda Hotel, a sedate bastion of the past at Avon Park; and the patrician and spacious 1916 Kenilworth Lodge in Sebring.

Kissimmee (pronounced kis´-im-ee) means "heaven's place" in Calusa Indian language. When you visit the lake, you will find the name appropriate. Lake Kissimmee State Park is a pristine, 5,030-acre area of lakes, floodplain prairies, pine flatwoods, and live oak hammocks. It is almost surrounded by Lakes Kissimmee, Tiger, and Rosaline, and connected with creeks and canals. Sandhill cranes, deer, bald eagles, bobcats, and turkeys find this park a haven. A distinctive feature is its living history site, a reconstructed 1870s cow camp with lean "scrub cows," which, like Texas longhorns, are descendants of Spanish cattle from Andalusia. At the camp you will meet the "cowhand" or "cow hunter," the western cowboy's counterpart. He will describe roundups, brandings, and drives through frontier cattle country to ports on the Gulf for shipment to Cuba. Feigning no knowledge of any more recent history, he may mention his boss, Jacob Summerlin, Florida's first cattle king, beginning in the 1860s. You will find the whip cracker cow hunter at his shelter only on Saturdays, Sundays, and major holidays, 9:30 A.M. to 4:30 P.M.

Other features of the park are its loop backpacking trails—the 5.6-mile North Loop Trail and the 5.9-mile Buster Island Loop Trail—both connected with a short bridge. You will see bromeliads and Spanish moss on the oaks, pangola grass fields, orchids, and ferns. Near the campground are a nature trail, a picnic area, and superb views of Lake Kissimmee from an observation tower. Nearby is a boat ramp, which provides access to the 100-mile Kissimmee Waterway, north to the town of Kissimmee, or south on the Kissimmee River to Lake Okeechobee. A concessionaire at the park provides boat and canoe rentals and a 4-hour canoe-trail tour to Lake Rosalie.

When you boat on the Waterway south, the first lock and spillway you will come to are at the south end of Turkey Hammock (the SR 60 bridge). For the remaining 55 miles, follow the Waterway through five more locks and three weirs, where caution is essential. You can also go north about 26 miles to the Kissimmee Waterfront in the town of Kissimmee. This section has one lock and spillway at the south end of Lake Tohopekaliga. Do not attempt this fascinating, adventurous trip without a free map guide obtained from the South Florida Water Management District. (See *Information.*) You will also need to telephone the district office a day or two before you begin your trip for information on water elevation and what locks are open. Because seasonally fluctuating water levels alter the lake contour, your boat should not draw more than 3 feet.

The Waterway has a controversial history. In 1928 and

1947, hurricanes caused river flooding, drowning hundreds of residents and cattle on the nearby ranches. Locally, and at the state capital, pressure mounted to control flooding of the Kissimmee with channels. As a result, the U.S. Army Corps of Engineers began a 10-year canal construction period in 1961. Seven navigational locks measuring 30 by 90 feet each were deployed, and other canals were built to nearby lakes to drain 45,000 acres of wetlands. But it soon became apparent that transforming the serpentine river from Lake Kissimmee to Lake Okeechobee was an ecological mistake. The waterfowl population declined by 90 percent. Environmentalists, who had opposed the project from the beginning, pointed out that straightening the river left stagnant oxbows that plaited the marshes, and alien plants disturbed the ecosystem. By 1987 the state government had announced plans to begin restoring the river. Congress had approved limited funding to help with the costly change, something the U.S. Army Corps of Engineers initially refused to accept. Since then, Floridians and the Corps of Engineers appear to be changing their attitudes toward making the river natural again. "No one has ever attempted to restore to nature what a public works project took away, to re-create a river," said Governor Bob Martinez in January 1990. At present there are two rivers: the original, which is being restored in parts, and the canal locks, which control flooding. On your trip you will see this duality; you will also see wildfowl returning to join the ospreys that have conveniently adopted the navigational markers for their nests, and willows replacing wax myrtle.

Of two canoe routes suggested on this journey to central Florida, the longest is Peace River. Called Rio de la Paz ("river of peace") by the Spanish in 1844, it later became the "peace boundary" between the U.S. Army, west, and Indian Chief Billy Bowlegs of Seminole history, east, in 1842. Paynes Creek State Historic Site, at Bowling Green, now has a visitor center at the confluence of the creek and the Peace River where you can learn about the government and Indian conflict, the fort, and the trading center. The river flows about 130 miles from

Lake Hancock near Bartow to Charlotte Harbor on the Gulf. But the most scenic, unspoiled, and ideal section is the 20 miles from Pioneer Park in Zolfo Springs to Gardner. Some canoeists put in at Fort Meade Recreational Park and take out 57 miles later at the SR 70 bridge in Arcadia. The Peace is slow moving, serene, isolated, and narrow between some high banks, and it sometimes has wide pools. Its tiny islands and sandy beaches make excellent campsites. Spanish moss hangs from the cypress and oaks along its boundaries, and cabbage palms flirt with the tannin-colored waters. You are likely to see deer in the saw palmetto flats, otter cavorting at the tributaries, and alligators, turtles, and wading birds on the river slopes.

The other exciting canoe route is the 19-mile Rock Springs Run and Wekiva River, only a few miles north of Orlando. In contrast to the Peace River, it is spring fed with clear water; it is also more crowded with canoeists. Access to Rock Springs is 5 miles north of Apopka on CR 435 to Kelly Road. Turn right (east) and then immediately left on Camp Joy Road. The first 8 miles on the Rock Springs Run have narrow channels in spots and a sandy bottom with patches of water reeds and lily pads. It is shaded by tall hardwoods. From the confluence with the Wekiva River, it is one mile upstream to Wekiwa Springs State Park, which rents canoes and has a campground. The remainder of the route has five access points, the last at High Banks Road Landing on the Saint Johns River, 2.9 miles west of US 17/92 and the town of DeBary. To avoid crossing the Saint Johns River in heavy motorboat traffic, take out at Katie's Landing and Campground. Access to Katie's from I-4, Exit 51, is on SR 46, 5 miles west to Wekiva Park Drive, right (north).

For fishing enthusiasts, largemouth bass lakes are Griffin, Harris, Yale, and Louisa in Lake County; Butler, Conway, and Hart in Orange County; Tohopekaliga, East Tohopekaliga, and Kissimmee in Osceola County; Marion and Hancock in Polk County; and Istokpoga and June in Highlands County. The most common catches other than largemouth bass are crappie, bluegill, redear, sunshine bass, and catfish at Lake Louisa.

The best way to see the countryside slowly and smell the orange blossoms is to take all or part of the 155-mile bicycle Route H: Land of Lakes, divided into five sections. Reedy Creek (H-1) section is 19.3 miles. Its trailhead is at the Kissimmee Chamber of Commerce on Monument Street, where the Monument of States, a 70-foot pyramid of stone from every state, is located. The route follows the old Tampa Highway through the small town of Loughman toward Winter Haven. There are two campgrounds along the way. The Citrus County (H-2) section is about 40 miles long and skirts the city of Winter Haven. Major points of interest include a candy factory, the famous 223-acre Cypress Gardens, where plants flower year-round, and one of the largest aviary exhibits in the South. There are plenty of service areas along the route and at least two campgrounds near Winter Haven. For the next 50 miles you will pedal a segment, Lilliput (H-3), through citrus groves and pasturelands on rolling hills, ending at Lake Kissimmee State Park. The first of the entrancing points of interest on the route is Chalet Suzanne, a visionary, daedal, storybook-type, expensive country inn. Founded by Bertha Hinshaw in 1931, it remains in the Hinshaw family and is renowned for its food and hospitality. Next is Spook Hill, with its natural optical illusion, and then the site of the Black Hills Passion Play that runs from mid-February to mid-April ([813] 676-1495).

By this time you will have sighted the majestic Bok Tower on the highest hill in peninsular Florida. With a Gothic motif of pink and gray marble, it houses a fifty-three-bell carillon and is called the Singing Tower. During the day, music plays every half hour; at 3 P.M. the resident carillonneur plays a 45-minute recital. The tower and gardens were made possible by Edward W. Bok, editor and publisher, and designed by Frederick L. Omstead, Jr. The serene beauty of this 128-acre shrine of flowers and wildlife makes it a good stop for resting sore muscles and increasing peace of mind.

After Lake Kissimmee State Park, take the 30-mile Lakes-N-Hills (H-4) through rolling hills and pasturelands and by Lake Marion, with a side trip to Lake Hatchineha for home-style cooking and a cottage. The county roads are well maintained and have wide, grassy shoulders. The last section, Mole Hill (H-5), returns 27 miles to the town of Kissimmee. A side trip takes you to South Port Park on Lake Tohopekaliga at South Port Canal, which has camping facilities and supplies. Oaks and cypress border the lake, which is well known for its largemouth bass. After crossing the Reedy Creek Overlook into a natural swamp with wildlife you will see the "Mole Hill," a school sheltered by earth and entirely dependent on solar energy. (To order bicycle maps, see *Information.*)

Nearly 100 miles of hiking trails will help you explore Bull Creek Wildlife Management Area, Prairie–Lakes State Preserve and Three Lakes WMA, the Kissimmee River basin, and Lake Arbuckle in the Avon Park Air Force Base. The trails are described in order of their location, traveling south from US 192, east of Saint Cloud, to US 98, east of Sebring. The Florida Trail Association maintains all or parts of these hiking trails.

To reach the 17-mile Bull Creek Trail, drive 17 miles east of Saint Cloud on US 192 (3.2 miles east of Holopaw) and turn right (south) on unpaved Crabgrass Road. After 6 miles (less if the gate is locked and you must walk to the trailhead), follow the trail 0.8 mile to the divide and begin clockwise. In the forest you are likely to see deer, turkey, fox, armadillo, squirrel, snakes, and songbirds. Some areas may be wet during the summer rainy season. After following an old road through hardwoods and pines, you will arrive at a large strand of cabbage palms, where you turn south. At 3.5 miles, cross Yoke Branch in an area of cypress and hardwood swamp. Before arriving at a wilderness campsite after 5.5 miles, you will shift from scrub oaks and old Union Cypress railroad grades to hunting and fire roads. On the last 8 miles you will follow hunting roads, scrub oak and pine flatwoods, and seemingly endless saw palmetto. (Because the trail is a WMA route, it may be closed during hunting season; call the Game and Fresh Water Fish Commission Office, [904] 629-8162, to inquire.)

Access to the Prairie–Lakes State Preserve from Lake

Wales is 43.5 miles on SR 60 to the junction with US 441, where you go north 13.9 miles on US 441 to Kenansville and take CR 523 west, 9.4 miles, to the preserve. (The Florida Turnpike, which parallels CR 523, does not provide access.) The preserve is an 8,000-acre natural area with extensive marshlands, live oak hammocks, pine flatwoods, and dry prairies. The vast dry prairies have dense saw palmettoes with scattered cabbage palms, longleaf pines, and occasional marshes. On the trail you may see sandhill cranes with their nests in grass ponds, burrowing and barred owls, turkey, deer, armadillo, and many species of songbirds. Epiphytes grow on live oaks, and wildflowers include the grass pink orchid and blazing star. Near the lake areas—Kissimmee, Jackson, and Marion—are marshes that harbor otter, alligator, and diverse wildfowl. All plants and wildlife are protected by rangers, and hunting and the use of firearms are prohibited, a policy different from that of the adjoining Three Lakes WMA, which extends north and south of the preserve. Backpack camping is allowed at designated places in the preserve, and reservations are necessary.

Both of the loop trails from the Parker Hammock parking area at the center of the loops are easy to day hike. If the entrance gate is locked, walk in 0.1 mile and follow the trail right or left. On the northern loop, 5.5 miles, you may hear armadillos rustling in the saw palmettoes and see them scratching under the fence near the Three Lakes WMA. On the south loop, 5.7 miles, are scrub prairies, small marsh ponds, and hardwood hammocks, and a connector with the Florida Trail. A primitive campsite is on the west side of the loop. (If you follow the Florida Trail south, it is 11.4 miles to SR 60, 4.5 miles east of the Kissimmee River bridge. If you follow the Florida Trail north, go 0.6 mile on SR 523 west of the preserve entrance gate before leaving the highway, right, to parallel or follow Williams Road for 6 miles. The remaining 3.8 miles is through a wooded area to the WMA gate on US 441, 7.3 miles north of Kenansville. Backpack camping is not allowed in the WMA during hunting season.)

The Kissimmee River section of the Florida Trail is 30.1 miles between SR 60 on the west side of the Kissimmee River bridge (24 miles east of Lake Wales) and the north end of Bluff Hammock Road from US 98, east of Sebring. It parallels the river through one of the state's most inaccessible areas and weaves among hardwood hammocks, open levees with scattered wild orange trees, oak scrub, open prairies dotted with conical anthills, and saw palmettoes. At times it skirts close to the riverbanks and meets stiles at ranch fencing. It crosses damp and marshy areas that may require wading during the rainy season between June and September. As well as having a varied landscape and botanical world of trees, shrubs, flowers, and ferns, it is particularly historic. Now more history is being made as the state plans to restore the channelized river to its original course.

The trail follows a levee the first 1.8 miles before curving around the River Ranch Resort and past a marina at 4.3 miles. Camping is permitted at 10.6 miles at the Rattlesnake Hammock, near an old homestead, and at 12.1 miles, the site of the Kicco ghost town where you can still see the sidewalks. Built about 1820 by the Kissimmee Island Cattle Company, Kicco is near the river. About 1.5 miles after Kicco you will come to Tick Island Slough, which you can cross on a footbridge, west of the levee. Another campsite is at 15.5 miles, near the site of an old homestead in Orange Hammock. Two miles farther you will see a short, blue-blazed trail that leads to a ranch dipping vat where cattle were treated for bug bites. At 18.6 miles is Fort Kissimmee (1849–1856); here is the only access road to the backcountry on the Fort Kissimmee Road inside the Avon Park Air Force Base Bombing Range. When you arrive at 26.8 miles, the dike direction changes as you come to a junction with a blue-blazed trail to a campsite. For the remainder of the trail, follow a river dike to Lock No. 65B. Access here is Bluff Hammock Road, 5.5 miles out to US 98/ SR 700 at Lorida, 16 miles east of Sebring.

Access to the 15-mile Lake Arbuckle Trail loop is only through the gate of the Avon Park Air Force Base, the east end of CR 64, 9 miles from Avon Park. After entering, report to the Natural Resources Office for permission to hike, and check in and out of the base with the security patrol at Building No. 425. Call ahead to find out if hiking will be permitted when you are there; the trail is closed during military activity and during certain hunting dates. From the Natural Resources Office, drive north on Frostproof Road; after 1.1 miles, notice the Lake Arbuckle Nature Trail sign, left. The short trail goes through a maple grove with sensitive and royal ferns, cypress, and air plants, and onto a boardwalk pier among water lilies and cypress. The views of the lake and waterfowl at sunset are unforgettable. Continue on the road 1.4 miles to the trailhead at Willingham Campsite, where you will find parking, water, and restrooms. You can hike the national recreation trail in one day, or camp overnight halfway around the trail at a site with water. You will pass through a mixture of hardwoods and pines, and saw palmetto, and you may see ospreys, warblers, hawks, deer, armadillos, and cattle that wander on the land leased for ranching. If you follow the trail clockwise, you will cross a stream and, at 1.4 miles, pass the site of the old Fort Arbuckle. Soon after you cross the paved road at 3 miles you will enter a pine plantation. The campsite is at 9 miles. On the final miles you will follow old forest roads and pass through another pine plantation.

Highlands Hammock is one of four original state parks created in 1935. Four years earlier, Margaret S. Roebling had purchased the property "to make accessible and to conserve in their natural state the vegetation and all forms of animal life herein." As you stroll along the eight short nature trails, a total of 3.5 miles, you can easily appreciate the foresight and generosity of those citizens and the CCC that made this park possible. While staring at the tall live, laurel, and water oaks, you will also see the nation's champion sabal palm, 90 feet tall. As you cross Charley Bowlegs Creek on the Cypress Swamp Trail, imagine huge prehistoric butterflies and giant dragonflies with 3-foot wingspans. Among the park's diverse plant life in swamps, pine and scrubby flatwoods, bayheads, and marshes are 60 species of native ferns; among the fauna are 177 species of birds. Some of the hawks, woodpeckers, flycatchers, herons, and wood warblers seem to know this park belongs to them; they ignore human visitors. A full-service campground allows reservations; other facilities are a restaurant, a grocery store, a picnic area, a day-use horse trail, and a paved loop bicycle trail. Access is on SR 634, 3.5 miles from US 27 in Sebring.

Some day trips can be planned from Highlands Hammock. It is 22.5 miles northeast to Lake Arbuckle Trail; 24.5 miles east to the south end of the Kissimmee River section of the Florida Trail; 21 miles east to a ramp for fishing in Lake Istokpoga, and 26 miles south to the Archbold Biological Station. Access to the latter is on US 27 to the SR 70 junction, where you turn right (west), go one mile, and turn left on the Old Station Road (before the railroad crossing).

You will find the station a valuable contribution to the study of Florida's natural environment. Here also is little Lake Annie, the southernmost lake in the Land of Lakes ridge. The Archbold Biological Station's primary function is to conduct research on vertebrate, invertebrate, plant, and aquatic ecology, with the principal focus on central Florida. Facilities include administrative offices, laboratories, libraries, greenhouses, dormitories, and other housing, and research supplies and equipment for field and lab research are also available. Founded in 1941 by Richard Archbold (1907–1976), the station is supported by Archbold Expeditions, a private nonprofit organization that explored world biology between 1929 and 1940. Major portions of the extensive collections are now housed in the American Museum of Natural History in New York City. Archbold was able to concentrate on Florida's biology after John A. Roebling contributed the station property. With the addition of 3,200 acres, the station now has 4,300 acres of xeric woodlands, flatwoods, swales, and bay forests.

There are six major terrestrial habitats in the station; the sugar sand Archbold Nature Trail takes you into the sand hill and pine scrub habitats. If you walk quietly, you may see typical scrub wildlife such as brown thrashers, towhees, armadillos, lizards, and gopher tortoises. Also look for scrub flowers among the scrub oak and hickory, saw palmetto, cactus, and scrub pawpaw. There are gopher apples (*Lycania michauxii*), silk bay (*Persea humilis*) that smells like bay leaves, and the sticky tarflower (*Befaria racemosa*). These and 367 other vascular plants are only some of the 2,673 plant and animal species recorded on station property. Station staff welcome your questions about their research center. If you would like a tour or use of the libraries, call for advance planning.

### Information

Counties: Lake, Orange, Osceola, Polk, Highlands

Average Temperatures: January, 52.0°F (low), 73.7°F (high); August, 73.3°F (low), 91.0°F (high)

National Properties: Avon Park Air Force Base, Avon Park, FL 33825, (813) 453-4119/4195

State Properties: General Van Fleet State Trail and Withlacoochee State Trail (described in the next section) have the same address as Lake Louisa State Park, but a different telephone number (904) 394-2280. Highlands Hammock State Park, 5931 Hammock Rd., Sebring, FL 33872, (813) 385-0011; Lake Griffin State Recreation Area, 103 Hwy. 441/27, Fruitland Park, FL 32731, (904) 787-7402; Lake Kissimmee State Park, 14248 Camp Mack Rd., Lake Wales, FL 33853, (813) 696-1112; Lake Louisa State Park, 12549 State Park Dr., Clermont, FL 32711, (904) 394-3969; Paynes Creek State Historic Site, P.O. Box 547, Bowling Green, FL 33834, (813) 375-4717; Rock Springs Run State Reserve, Rte. 1, Box 365D, Sorrento, FL 32776, (904) 383-3311; Prairie–Lakes State Preserve, P.O. Box 220, Kenansville, FL 32739, (407) 436-1626; South Florida Water Management District, (3301 Gun Club Rd.), P.O. Box

24680, West Palm Beach, FL 33416, (407) 686-8800, or (800) 432-2045 in Florida; Wekiwa Springs State Park, 1800 Wekiwa Circle, Apopka, FL 32712, (407) 884-2009

County and City Parks: Big Tree Park, Seminole County Parks and Recreation, Longwood, FL 32750, (407) 323-2500; Lake Arbuckle Park, Polk County Commissioners, Bartow, FL 33830, (813) 533-1161; Pioneer Park, Box 326, Zolfo Springs, FL 33890, (813) 735-0330; Southport Park, 2001 Southport Rd., Kissimmee, FL 32714, (407) 348-5822

Gardens, Museums, and Research Centers: Archbold Biological Station, P.O. Box 2057, Lake Placid, FL 33852, (813) 465-2571; Bok Tower Gardens, P.O. Box 3810, Lake Wales, FL 33859, (813) 676-1408; Central Florida Railroad Museum, 101 S. Boyd St., Winter Garden, FL 32787, (407) 656-8749; Cypress Gardens, 2641 South Lake Summit Dr., Cypress Gardens, FL 33884, (813) 324-2111, or (800) 282-2123 in state or (800) 237-4826 out of state; Florida Citrus Tower, US 27, Clermont, FL 34711, (904) 394-8585; Lake Wales Museum, 325 S. Scenic Hwy., Lake Wales, FL 33859, (813) 676-5443; Monument of the States, Monument St., Lake Front Park, Kissimmee, FL 32741, (407) 847-3174; Slocum Water Gardens, 1101 Cypress Gardens, Winter Haven, FL 33880, (813) 293-7151

Chambers of Commerce: Avon Park CC, 28 East Main St., Avon Park, FL 33825, (813) 453-3350; Bartow CC, P.O. Box 956, Bartow, FL 33820, (813) 533-7125; Fort Meade CC, P.O. Box 91, Fort Meade, FL 33841, (813) 285-8253; Greater Orlando CC, P.O. Box 1234, Orlando, FL 32802, (407) 425-1234; Greater Sebring CC, 309 S. Circle, Sebring, FL 33870, (813) 385-8448; Haines City CC, P.O. Box 986, Haines City, FL 33845, (813) 422-3751; Kissimmee-Osceola County CC, 1425 East Vine St., Kissimmee, FL 34744, (407) 847-3174; Lakeland Area CC, 35 Lake Morton Dr., Lakeland, FL 33801, (813) 688-8551; Lake Wales Area CC, 340 W. Central Ave., Lake Wales, FL 33859-0191, (813) 676-3445; Winter Haven Area CC, P.O. Box 1420, Winter Haven, FL 33882, (813) 293-2138; Winter Park CC, 150 N. New York Ave., Winter Park, FL 32790, (407) 644-8281

Services and Amenities: *Commercial Campgrounds* (near

the Florida Trail; otherwise, contact the chambers of commerce): Outdoor Resorts River Ranch (Kissimmee River; no tents), 24700 Hwy. 60 E, Lake Wales, FL 33853, (800) 282-7935 in state, or (800) 654-8575 out of state; *Lodging* (inns and hotels with restaurants): Chalet Suzanne, P.O. Box AC, Lake Wales, FL 33859, (813) 676-6011; Hillcrest Lodge, P.O. Box 67, Babson Park, FL 33827, (813) 638-1712; Jacaranda Hotel, 19 E. Main St., Avon Park, FL 33825, (813) 453-2211; Kenilworth Lodge, 836 SE Lakeview Dr., Sebring, FL 33870, (813) 385-0111
   *Bicycle Maps:* State Bicycle Program, (904) 488-7950; *Boat and Canoe Rentals:* Boat Rentals, 4266 Vine St., Kissimmee, FL 32741, (407) 845-3672; Canoe Outpost (Peace River), Rte. 7, Box 301, Arcadia, FL 33821, (813) 494-1215; Florida Pack and Paddle, 1922 Hammerlin Ave., Orlando, FL 32803, (407) 645-5068; Katie's Wekiva River Landing, 190 Katie's Cove, Sanford, FL 32771, (407) 322-4470

## WITHLACOOCHEE STATE FOREST

The Indians called it *Withlacoochee* ("crooked river"), a 138-mile twisting river that snakes out of the Green Swamp aquifer south of the town of Clermont and empties into the Withlacoochee Bay in the Gulf of Mexico. Unconnected with the Withlacoochee North, whose headwaters are in Georgia, Withlacoochee South flows through two of the five separate tracts that make up the 113,431 acres of Withlacoochee State Forest. Little Withlacoochee River begins in a swamp near the isolated community of Bay Lake and joins the main river near Ridge Manor North. Wildlife is diverse and plentiful in a patchwork of lakes, sinks, ridges, swamps, and flatwoods. Campgrounds, from primitive to full service, are scattered throughout the forest, and boat access is at intervals on the long river. Diverse trails are a specialty of the forest. Only a few miles from the forest are other exciting places: a manatee sanctuary, wildlife refuges, springs, state archeological and historic sites, and the De Soto auto trail. Less than an hour away are the cities of Ocala, north, and Tampa, south.

*What to See and Do:* Because of the large acreage and varied adventures, you will find you could stay a month in Withlacoochee State Forest and still not do everything available. To get an introduction, take advantage of any of the three backpacking loop trails, a total of 92 miles, or the Green Swamp section of the Florida Trail, another 19 miles through the Devil's Creek Swamp; two horse trails, 24 miles each; a 2,600-acre motorcycle-ATV area with trails in phosphate pits; and many miles of backcountry forest roads. Or paddle a day in the forest section of the Withlacoochee River Canoe Trail, which is a total of 84 miles. For bicyclists, the 120-mile Withlacoochee Meander Trail covers three counties and passes through the forest. Fishing, camping, and birding are other activities, and near the forest you can scuba dive at natural springs, boat and fish in the Tsala Apopka Lake, and explore historical sites. Also passing through the forest from Tribly north to Citrus Springs is the 47-mile paved Withlacoochee State Trail for hikers and bikers. There is a mountain bike trail in Flying Eagle Ranch near the forest and Floral City.

*Where to Begin:* When deciding on activities, visit the forest headquarters for information on permits, fees, hunting seasons, and maps. Located 0.5 mile north of US 41 (Broad Street) from CR 476, the headquarters is about halfway between Floral City and Brooksville. The nearest airports are Municipal in Ocala and International in Tampa.

*About the Adventures:* In 1958 the state purchased three large and two small tracts from the federal government, planning for them a multiple-use program of resource management and public recreation areas, much as in a national forest. The largest tract, Richloam, east of Lacoochee and Dade City, has 49,200 acres; Citrus, south of Inverness, has 42,531 acres; and Croom, east of Brooksville, has 20,470 acres. The 1,230-acre headquarters tract was formerly a CCC camp; it and the 110-acre Colonel Robins Recreation Area, both on US 41, are the other two tracts. The topography ranges from sandy xeric soil with limestone rocks in the northwest tracts to fertile damp soil and swamps in the southeast tracts. Both the river and the forest are in the northern half of the Southwest Florida Management District, which covers the physiographic Brooksville Ridge that traps the slow-moving Withlacoochee River and its tributaries in a profusion of prairie lakes. The result is a haven for reptiles, waterfowl, and fishes.

The large tracts are wildlife management areas with only recreational areas exempt from hunting. During legal seasons, hunters are allowed to kill deer, squirrel, quail, rabbit, opossum, coyote, skunk, armadillo, turkey, and migratory game birds: dove, duck, coot, and woodcock. Before you traipse into the woods, it is wise to know the seasons and to have the "Regulations Summary and Area Map" in hand. It is also wise to have the forest comprehensive map, separate tract maps, and special interests maps. The tract map may prevent you from becoming lost whenever you take a shortcut on any of the loop trails. For example, the Citrus and Croom tract maps show numbered forest roads that make a checkerboard pattern for every square mile.

The longest forest foot trail is the 46.7-mile Citrus Hiking Trail. As you will see from the forest map, you can enter from CR 491, CR 480, or CR 581. I suggest that you enter on the Holder Mine Road, off CR 581, 2.5 miles south of Inverness. After 2 miles you will be at Holder Mine Recreation Area, which has a campground, water, and restrooms. The trailhead, on the west side of the campground, is a blue-blazed 0.9-mile connector route to the orange-blazed main trail. Turn right on the 6.7-mile Loop A, your shortest, to help you decide if you wish to take longer loops. Along the trail, and on others in the forest, the blue-blazed trails are spurs, or cross trails, the double blue-band tree markers are horse trails, and the white-banded tree markers are for campsite zones. On the outer rim, camping zones are at Perryman Place, at 12.2 miles; FR 15, at 16.7 miles; and FR 13, at 26 miles. Another camping area is Mutual Mine Recreation Area, but to get there you must take a 1.5-mile spur off the main trail at 32.8 miles.

You will see forests of dense pine, others clearcut for timber, and some of new growth. A few of the timber roads have been seeded, forming grassy areas for soft side walks for bird-watching. Butterflies, particularly the yellow and orange sulphur, are prevalent. Wildlife you might see are some of the two thousand deer that roam this tract, fox squirrels dropping pinecone scales over your head, and soaring red-tailed hawks looking for field mice. Plant life changes; you may see pond, sand, and longleaf pines or scattered dogwoods and sparkle-berry among pines, oaks, and maples. Common wildflowers are black root, golden aster, dollar-weed, palafoxia, light lavender deer tongue, and purple blazing star.

In the Croom tract, the 22.3-mile Croom Hiking Trail has three loops with two cross trails and with two spur trails to Silver Lake Recreation Area. The sandy hills and vegetation are much the same as in the Citrus tract; the two major distinctions are man-made. One is the 2,600-acre Croom Motorcycle Area, where only two-wheel cycles and ATVs are allowed. The other facility is the Silver Lake Recreation Area, which has three campgrounds, all by the Withlacoochee River. Silver Lake has a boat dock and some electric service campsites, but noise carries from I-75 to it. The other campgrounds, Crooked River and Cypress Glen, both farther upstream, are more tranquil. Access to Silver Lake from I-75, Exit 61, is on US 98 east one mile, a turn left (north) on Rital Croom Road for 3.2 miles, and then a turn right. (The road continues downstream to connect with forest roads and trails and to exit at Nobleton after 6 miles.) Near the old railroad intersection in Croom (south of Nobleton on Croom–Nobleton Road) is a blue-blazed cross-hiking trail which connects "Loop B" of the Croom Hiking Trail (from the west) to the paved rails-to-trails Withlacoochee State Trail. (The latter trail is maintained under the supervision of the Florida State Parks system.)

Access to the Croom Hiking Trail trailhead from US 41 (1.4 miles north of Brooksville) is on CR 480, Croom Road, east 5.3 miles to the parking area near the Tucker Fire Tower. If hiking north, descend into a hardwood forest; after 0.2 mile you come to a junction with a 2.9-mile blue-blazed cross trail that divides Loop A and Loop B. Ahead is a camping zone, followed by sandy hills and an undulating route. At 7.3 miles you will come to a junction with a blue-blazed cross trail that leads to the Silver Lake campgrounds. After passing Twin Pond, begin to track northward for a return to FR 6 and the parking area.

On the north side of the river is 6.8-mile Hog Island Trail, a linear route that begins at Hog Island Recreation Area, follows upstream parallel to the river, and leads under I-75 to the River Junction boat dock. Access to Hog Island from I-75, Exit 62, is north on CR 476B for 0.5 mile to a forest road, west. Access to River Junction is south from Exit 62, 2.5 miles and under I-75.

Passing through the Croom tract of the forest is the paved 47-mile rails-to-trails Withlacoochee State Trail. The railroad right-of-way was purchased by the state in 1989 and is under the supervision of the state's Division of Recreation and Parks. A cooperative effort by the state forest and park systems, county and local governments, and citizens' groups have made this appealing trail possible. It connects with 29.1 miles of hiking trails of the Croom Hiking Trail and upstream trails to Silver Lake Recreation Area. Access to its south trailhead is on the south side of CR 575 at the west side junction with US 98/SR 700 (near US 301 junction). Access to the north trailhead is off US 41 on North Citrus Springs Boulevard in Citrus Springs. There are signs to follow to the parking area on Magenta Drive. Along the trail, from south to north, are connections with Silver Lake Recreation Area and camp-ground, Istachatta-Nobleton Park, Fort Cooper State Park, and Wallace Brooks and Whispering Pines Park (both city parks in Inverness). On its route north the trail parallels the west side of the Withlacoochee River to Istachatta; it criss-crosses CR 39 to Floral City where it parallels US 41/SR 45 to the east to Fort Cooper State Park and Inverness. It then parallels the west side of US 41/SR 45 for the remainder of the route. Scenic beauty includes hardwood and pine forests, streams, lakes, marshes, agricultural and cattle fields, historic areas, and municipal commercial areas. (See *Information* for trail management contact.)

The 25.3 Richloam Hiking Trail, orange blazed like the other major trails, is more remote than the Citrus or Croom trails. Its single loop is intersected by enough forest roads that you can make at least six shortcuts to return to the point of origin. Plant communities along the Richloam are in low, rich soil with many cypress ponds in the northwestern part of the loop and in flatwoods near the Withlacoochee River. Titi, saw palmettoes, cypress, gums, bays, pines, oaks, and cabbage palms are commonplace. The trail is wet during the summer season. More snakes, particularly cottonmouths, and feral hogs are in this tract. Deer, turkeys, raccoons, rabbits, armadillos, wild ponies, and cattle frequent the trail. Less likely to be seen are skunks, bald eagles, bobcats, and indigo snakes.

One of the more interesting creatures of this wildlife-rich area is the humble raccoon. These highly intelligent creatures have adapted to many environments, but are particularly suited to aquatic habitats and are commonly seen in Central Florida. They will hunt and scavenge on the forest floor and at streamside, and are not averse to taking a farmyard chicken. They are almost completely nocturnal. In the frontier era, these creatures were much hunted for their hide.

To reach the trailhead from Ridge Manor at the junction of US 301/98 and SR 50, go east 4.6 miles on SR 50 and turn right on narrow Clay Sink Road. After 0.6 mile park at the Richloam Fire Tower, where there is a forest-approved water faucet, the only potable water on the trail. Follow a 0.2-mile blue-blazed trail to the main loop and turn right if you are hiking clockwise. You will pass the edges of many lakes, in which frogs are croaking, and arrive at camping zones at 6.3 miles and 13.4 miles. At 18.3 miles is another camping zone and a junction with a 0.8-mile spur trail to Megs Hole. (From Megs Hole the 19.3-mile Green Swamp section of the Florida Trail goes southeast to a terminus at Rock Ridge Road. Access to this remote area is 10 miles from US 98 at Providence

Church, north of Providence, or 6 miles west from SR 33 at Eva. This trail is exceptionally isolated, pristine, hydric, and filled with wildlife; it is also the only trail that crosses the Withlacoochee River. If you venture off the Green Swamp Trail, you run a grave risk of being lost. Advance planning, with information from the Florida Trail headquarters, is advised.) When you continue on the Richloam Hiking Trail, you will be near the Withlacoochee River at 21 miles, and within one mile there are two blue-blazed side trails to campsites. After crossing a creek, you will return to your point of origin on an old jeep road. The Florida Trail Association maintains this trail, as it does the Citrus and Croom trails. Two day-use nature trails are worth hiking near the forest headquarters. One, the 2.5-mile McKetchan Lake Trail loop, begins at the forest main offices. A canopy of oaks and magnolias draped with Spanish moss covers it, and egrets and herons flock at the lake's edge. The other trail, the 3.2-mile Colonel Robins Trail, is a loop 3 miles south of the forest headquarters on US 41. Blazed in orange, it passes through a hardwood and longleaf–sand pine forest.

The 120-mile Route G: Withlacoochee Meander bicycle route, offers diverse options for cyclists. The suggested starting point is outside the forest at Crystal River State Archaeological Site (referred to as Yulee Ruins [G-1] on the state bicycle map). Access is from US 19/98, north of Crystal River on State Park Road. Allow time at the site to visit the Indian temple, burial (at least 450 sites), and refuse mounds that were occupied continuously from about 200 B.C. to the fifteenth century. Of major significance is the stelae ceremonial stone, an indication that these Indians made direct contact with the Yucatán cultures. On this 25-mile section, your first stop is at the Crystal River Pier to watch catches of fresh seafood arrive from the Gulf. Another 7 miles on US 98 brings you to an underwater observatory to view thousands of tropical and semitropical fish at Homosassa Springs. Take a break here for a tropical jungle cruise, or hike the nature trails through immaculate gardens. Nearby, on a short spur of SR

490, you can pedal to the 5,000-acre Yulee Sugar Mill Ruins, a state historic site. David Levy Yulee, the state's first U.S. Senator, began operations there in 1845. (Levy County is named in his honor.) The mill operated for about 13 years as a major supplier of sugar products to the Confederate Army during the Civil War.

From here, follow east, 5.5 miles, on CR 490A to CR 491; at this junction is a primitive campsite, Perryman Place, in the Citrus tract of the Withlacoochee State Forest. After another 9 miles your route section becomes Chinsegut (G-2), an Eskimo word for "spirit of lost things." Out of the forest on CR 581, pedal 4.6 miles south to Lake Lindsey Country Store, an excellent place for a soda pop, and to a junction with SR 476. Follow SR 476 east 1.7 miles to US 41, where your route turns south (north 0.5 mile is the forest headquarters), past another grocery store, to Colonel Robins Nature Trail, near the junction of CR 581. Your next 4 miles are to Brooksville, where you take a backcountry road, CR 485, for 7 miles to US 98/SR 50. From here, pedal east 9 miles before turning north on US 301.

The River Crossing (G-3) section is a 40-mile erratic route that takes you to Bushnell, to Nobleton, back to forest headquarters, north to Floral City, and finally to Inverness. You will find commercial campgrounds along the way. Near Bushnell, after you have left US 301 and turned on SR 476, you will reach Dade Battlefield State Historic Site. Passing through scenic hill country, you will come to Nobleton, where you will find groceries, a campground, and the Canoe Outpost at the Withlacoochee River. You could make a diversion here and take a river trip for 1 to 8 days, completely outfitted and with shuttle service by the outpost staff. The bicycle route takes CR 480 from Floral City west to CR 581 to approach Inverness, but you could stay on US 41 en route to Inverness and visit Fort Cooper. Access is on CR 39, the Old Floral City Road, north. The 704-acre park has clear Lake Holathlikala, with borders of forest and wildlife, and a nature trail to the old Fort Cooper. After Fort Cooper, you will come to services and commercial campgrounds in Inverness. Your last 22 miles, Fort Cooper (G-

4), are on US 41 to Hernando, and through the countryside of CR 486 to Crystal River.

If you plan to canoe parts or all of the 84-mile Withlacoochee River Canoe Trail, check in advance with forest headquarters or with the Nobleton Canoe Outpost about the river level. In dry weather, when the water is low, you may encounter stumps, logs, and thick water hyacinth jams that require portage. Liveries are infrequent on the river, but there are enough take-out points to provide access for supplies and food. You will pass through areas of expanding human development and other areas still like a wilderness. Between SR 48 and SR 44 of the watery Grand Prairie and Tsala Apopka Lake you will see abundant waterfowl. Alligators, minks, otters, hawks, frogs, and snakes are less frequent. The last recommended take-out is at Dunnellon, where the river becomes Lake Rousseau.

The first put-in is at Caulter Hammock Recreation Area in the Richloam tract of the Withlacoochee State Forest. Access is from Lacoochee, east on SR 575; immediately across the river take the Coit Road south for 2.5 miles. Paddle west for the first 6 miles, then north 13 miles to a take-out at Silver Lake Recreation Area in the Croom tract of the forest. Other take-outs precede Silver Lake, twice at US 98 bridges. Campsites and access points are at Silver Lake, a wide, beautiful area. (For access, see the Croom tract section, above.) On the east side of the river near Silver Lake is a take-out at River Junction Recreation Area near the confluence of the Little Withlacoochee River. Farther downstream, under the I-75 bridge, another take-out is at Hog Island Recreation Area.

The SR 476 bridge is near the Nobleton Outpost (where you may have planned your canoe adventure and arranged for shuttle service). North of the bridge the river divides: the left channel runs closer to the highway. At the campground in Nobleton you can rest and resupply for the remaining 55 miles. Farther downstream, after another 9 miles, is CR 48, the beginning point of your 15-mile journey through the swamps of Tsala Apopka Lake and Jumper Creek. About 10 miles after

CR 48 is Bonnet Lake, with a commercial campground at the northwest end. About 1.5 miles north of Bonnet Lake is Shell Island, habitat for oaks and wild orange trees. State property, the area called The Wanderings, is surrounded by swamp water. Upon approaching SR 44, use the Ruff Wysong Dam and Navigation Lock, operated by the Southwest Florida Water Management District. For the next 15 miles, between SR 44 and SR 200, at Stokes Ferry, the river becomes deeper and there are fewer lakes, but channels increase in the Gum Slough. In the final 15 miles, from SR 200 to Dunnellon, the river widens and passes more housing developments.

Before you leave the state forest area, visit four prominent natural places. Two—Crystal River NWR and the Chassahowitzka NWR—are about 7 miles west of the Citrus tract off US 19/98. Access is on King's Bay Drive, Paradise Road, and SR 44, west. The third is the 29-mile General Van Fleet State Trail. Its north trailhead at Mabel is near the northeast edge of the Richloam tract, 13 miles east on SR 50 from its junction with US 301/SR 35 at Ridge Manor. The fourth prominent place, Hillsborough River State Park, is about 21 miles south of the Richloam tract, on US 301. Crystal River NWR is in Kings Bay adjacent to the town of Crystal River. West Indian manatees congregate here more than anywhere else in the state. In this warm-water refuge, endangered manatees are protected in thirty natural springs of a constant 72 degrees Fahrenheit. In a space of nine islands and coves, this 33-acre national wildlife refuge was established in 1983 as the result of efforts by The Nature Conservancy and the citizens of Citrus County to protect the manatee. The U.S. Fish and Wildlife Service restricts motorboat passage in the area to prevent injury to the manatees. You are most likely to see them from January though March. You can rent scuba diving and snorkeling equipment at the dive shops located at the end of Kings Bay Drive and Paradise Road in Crystal River. Other wildlife you will see are herons, cormorants, and ring-necked ducks. Fishing offers bass, alligator gar, and mullet.

At Homosassa Springs, 9 miles south of Crystal River, is the

*West Indian manatee, Crystal River.* PHOTO BY Florida
Dept. of Commerce.

Yulee Sugar Mill Ruins. (See description in the bicycle route,
above.) You will find excellent campgrounds on Hall River
Road and Fish Bowl Drive. Another 4.3 miles south on US 19/
98 is the Chassahowitzka NWR headquarters. Here is a nature
trail, but the major access to its preserved beauty of springs,
islands, and swamps is 2 miles south at the junction of CR 480,
Miss Maggie Drive. Turn west on CR 480, and after 1.7 miles
you will arrive at the picturesque Lake Chassahowitzka
Campground, with full service, an ideal place to rent a boat
or canoe and explore the river and its tributaries. The staff at
Chassahowitzka can also provide shuttle service.

Florida's straightest long trail is the 29-mile General Van
Fleet State Trail, a rails-to-trails scenic route which was
opened and dedicated in 1992 by the Florida Department of
Natural Resources and with assistance from the Friends of the
Green Swamp, Inc. The trail passes through three counties:
Sumter (5 miles), Lake (12 miles), and Polk (12 miles). The
state purchased the 100-foot right-of-way in 1990. On this

multi-purpose trail for equestrians, hikers, and bicyclists, all motor vehicle traffic is prohibited. There are plans to provide trail sections for the physically disabled. Shelters have been constructed (and more are planned) for hikers, and so have visitor centers at Polk City (the southernmost terminus), Bay Lake (the north central), and Mabel (the northern trailhead on SR 50). The trail is routinely patrolled by park rangers and law enforcement officers.

The only curve in the trail is 5 miles north from Polk City and it is hardly noticeable. Wild and scenic, this sunny trail has swamps, blackwater streams and rivers, floodplains, and pine and hardwood forests. Access at Polk City is on the north side of SR 33 at the CR 655 junction. (Southeast on SR 559, it is 2 miles to I-4, exit 21.) Bay Lake access is off SR 33, 5.5 miles on Erie Lake Road (and 9 miles south on CR 565 from SR 50 at Mascotte). The north trailhead at Mabel on SR 50 is 5 miles west of Mascotte. Park administration (District 5) is the same for Withlacoochee State Trail and Lake Louisa. (See *Information.*)

Twenty-one miles south of the Richloam tract, on US 301, are Hillsborough River State Park and Fort Foster. Along the way, where US 301 and SR 39 separate at the south edge of Zephyrhills, is a sheltered display marker of the De Soto Trail, the route taken north by the Spanish explorer in 1539. Another 6.2 miles south on US 301 is the park, developed by the CCC in 1936. Flowing through the park is Hillsborough River, which has rapids over limestone, high banks, hardwoods, and silent waters through cypress swamps. Park facilities include a full-service campground, a youth camp, a boat dock, picnic tables, and hiking trails. Before you go for a walk, request a list of the park's wildlife from the ranger. From the trailhead parking area, make a loop on the River Nature Trail, then cross the river on a suspension bridge to take the Baynard Nature Trail loop that connects with the 3.2-mile backpacking trail to a sequestered primitive campsite. Along these trails you may hear owls in the daytime and anoles and skinks rustling lightly in the leaves. At the boat dock you can rent a canoe for downstream passage to serene habitats for otter, alligator, and chicken turtles. The most dramatic experience in the park is a visit to Fort Foster (open Friday through Sunday and holidays). Be sure to read the historic site brochure; the soldiers reenact fort life of 1837.

For an excellent day trip from Hillsborough River State Park, visit other nearby state parks and nature centers in the Tampa-Clearwater area. One major wildlife display, only 15 miles from Hillsborough, is the 300-acre Busch Gardens in north Tampa. The gardens have one of the nation's largest natural habitats for 3,600 free-roaming birds, mammals, and reptiles. Access from US 301/SR 41 to the gardens is west on SR 580 (Busch Blvd.).

Another 30 miles west from the gardens are two state parks with beautiful, cream-colored beaches: Honeymoon Island and Caladesi Island. Honeymoon Island is now both a preserve for 208 species of wild plants and one of the foremost south Florida virgin slash pine forests. Access to the island park from Busch Gardens is west on SR 580, which joins SR 584 in Oldsmar, and then SR 586 in Harbor Palms to the Honeymoon Island causeway. Access to the undisturbed Caladesi Island is by ferry from the dock on Honeymoon Island or from Dunedin on the mainland. Caladesi's nature trail and boardwalk protect its dunes. Both islands are crowded in the summertime.

The most recent attraction to illustrate the natural environment is the Florida Aquarium, which opened in 1995. It has more than 4,300 native plants and animals representing 550 Florida species. Magnificent exhibits include springs, wetlands, bays, beaches, reefs, and offshore currents. Admission rates are moderate, and there are special rates for groups. The aquarium is located within the Garrison Seaport Center near Tampa's downtown waterfront. Access from Busch Gardens is west to I-275, where you drive south on I-275 to the Ashley Street exit. Follow Ashley Street to Jackson Street, turn left, then right on Kennedy Blvd. to a right turn on Channelside Drive. Look for the aquarium on the left.

While the state park system has a strong program in

converting abandoned railroad right-of-ways to multiple use trails (see above and chapters 2, 3, and 4), counties and cities are also developing similar projects. An example of a county and municipal effort is the 47-mile Pinellas Trail, which runs through a metropolitan environment from St. Petersburg north to Tarpon Springs. The trail was constructed in sections; the first to open was from Seminole (near Park Boulevard) to Largo in 1990. Sections which followed are from Largo to Palm Harbor, Palm Harbor to Tarpon Springs, St. Petersburg to Seminole, and Tarpon Springs to Oldsmar. The 15-foot-wide asphalt route is skillfully designed with painted traffic lines for walking and bicycling/skating. Pedestrians and the physically handicapped have the right-of-way on the trail. No motorized vehicles or horses are allowed. This remarkable trail passes through historic districts, shady sections of live oaks and city parks, picnic areas, commercial malls, and business areas, and alongside tidal streams and lakes. For a detailed map of the trail's route contact the Pinellas County Park Department listed ahead in *Information*.

### *Information:*

Counties: Citrus, Sumter, Hernando, Pasco, Polk, Hillsborough, Pinellas

Average Temperatures: January, 52.7°F (low), 73.1°F (high); August, 73.7°F (low), 90.1°F (high)

National Properties: Chassahowitzka NWR and Crystal River NWR, P.O. Box 4139, Homosassa Springs, FL 32647, (904) 382-2201

State Properties: Withlacoochee State Forest, 15023 Broad St., Brooksville, FL 33512, (904) 754-6777; Withlacoochee State Trail, 12549 State Park Dr., Clermont, FL 32711, (904) 394-2280; Caladesi Island State Park, Causeway Blvd., Dunedin, FL 34698, (813) 469-5918; Crystal River State Archaeological Site, 3400 N. Museum Point, Crystal River, FL 32629, (904) 795-3817; Dade Battlefield State Historic Site, P.O. Box 938, Bushnell, FL 33513, (904) 793-4781; Fort Cooper State Park,

3100 S. Old Floral City Rd., Inverness, FL 32650, (904) 726-0315; Hillsborough River State Park, 15402 US 301 N., Thonotosassa, FL 33592, (813) 986-1020; Honeymoon Island State Recreation Area, Causeway Blvd., Dunedin, FL 34698, (813) 469-5942; Lake Louisa State Park, 12549 State Park Dr., Clermont, FL 32711, (904) 394-3969; Yulee Sugar Mill Ruins State Historic Site, same as Crystal River State Archaeological Site, above

Other Parks and Gardens: Busch Gardens, 3000 E. Busch Blvd., Tampa, FL 33674, (813) 987-5171/5082; Homosassa Springs Park, 9225 W. Fish Bowl Dr., Homosassa Springs, FL 32647, (904) 628-2311; The Florida Aquarium, 701 Channelside Drive, Tampa, FL 33602, (813) 273-4041 (group sales, 4020)

The Pinellas Trail: Contact Pinellas County Park Department, 631 Chestnut St., Clearwater, FL 34616, (813) 464-3347

Chambers of Commerce: Citrus County CC, 208 W. Main St., Inverness, FL 34450, (904) 726-2801; Crystal River CC, 28 N. US 19, Crystal River, FL 34428, (904) 795-3149; Greater Clearwater CC, P.O. Box 2457, Clearwater, FL 34617, (813) 461-0011; Greater Dunedin CC, 301 Main St., Dunedin, FL 34698, (813) 733-3197; Greater Tampa CC, P.O. Box 420, Tampa, FL 33601, (813) 228-7777; Greater Hernando County CC, 101 E. Fort Dade Ave., Brooksville, FL 34601, (904) 683-3700; Riverview CC, P.O. Box 18, Riverview, FL 33569, (813) 677-2604; Homosassa Springs Area CC, P.O. Box 709, Homosassa Springs, FL 34447, (904) 628-2666

Services and Amenities: *Commercial Campgrounds:* Chassahowitzka River Campground, 8600 Miss Maggie Dr., Homosassa Springs, FL 32646, (904) 382-2200; Clover Leaf Forest Campground, 910 US 41 N., Brooksville, FL 33512, (904) 796-8016; Duval's Campground, Nobleton, FL 33554, (904) 793-5179; Oaks Campground, Rte. 3, Box 164, Bushnell, FL 33513, (904) 793-7117; Shawnee Trail Campground, Boy Scout Rd., Inverness, FL 32650, (904) 344-3372; Turtle Creek Campground, P.O. Box 4079, Homosassa Springs, FL 32647, (904) 628-2928

*Bicycle Maps:* State Bicycle Program, (904) 488-7950; *Boat*

*and Canoe Rentals:* Nobleton Canoe Outpost, P.O. Box 188, Nobleton, FL 33554, (904) 696-4343; *Canoe Maps:* Division of Parks and Recreation, (904) 487-4784; *Equestrian Club:* Croom Trail Horsemen, 25492 Mondon Hill Rd., Brooksville, FL 34601, (904) 796-6423

## FLORIDA CRACKER TRAIL

The 150-mile Florida Cracker Trail is the state's longest equestrian trail. Straight across the peninsula from Bradenton to Fort Pierce, it mainly follows state and county roads through expansive ranchlands, farms, and forests. It crosses the Manatee, Myakka, Peace, and Kissimmee rivers, touches the north edge of Lake Istokpoga, and passes through the small towns of Zolfo Springs, Spring Lake, and Lorida. Designated a historic trail by the state legislature in 1986, the route is marked by signs showing a horseman on a Pony Express–type steed. In cooperation with the Department of Transportation and county governments, the Florida Cracker Trail Association provides public programs and projects on or near the trail, as well as private activities of interest to equestrians and the cattle industry.

*What to See and Do:* Each year, beginning in 1988, the Florida Cracker Trail Association sponsors a distinctive trail ride for a week in late April and early May. Complete with chuck wagons and sanitary facilities, the equine entourage camps each night at a different host ranch or public park where riders partake in rodeos, barbecues, entertainment, campfires, and nostalgic cowhand folklore. Advance registration is necessary, and all riders must be experienced.

*Where to Begin:* The ride begins at the Schroeder-Manatee Ranch, 2.7 miles east of I-75 (Exit 42) in Bradenton on SR 64. (For riders who plan to arrive by airplane and rent horses and carriers, Sarasota-Bradenton Airport is nearest, 12 miles southwest off I-75 at Exit 40.)

*About the Adventure:* The idea for the Florida Cracker Trail (FCT) is credited to Marvin Kahn of Sebring, but the concept for a cross-Florida ride came from the cattle families and cattle industry. Association members talk ardently about the history of Cracker culture, but they also say the organization has a mission "to promote, maintain, and enhance the cultural beauty of the FCT." Whether you drive this route by auto any day of the year or take the 8-day ride in the springtime, you will be pleasantly astonished at its lack of traffic and commercialization.

The ride usually begins on a Saturday at 9 A.M. when riders begin arriving at the Schroeder-Manatee Ranch to sign in and complete plans to ride out the next morning. A kick-off barbecue dinner is part of the evening program. The riders, under the supervision of a trail boss, head out each morning at 7 A.M., take a 2-hour lunch break at noon at a host ranch, and are in the saddle again from 2 P.M. to 5 P.M., completing about 20 miles daily. Mainly primitive camping at selected host ranches is closed to the public, but camping at public parks or fairgrounds is open to the public. Public evenings may have rodeos, music festivals, and other events. Meals are served from the chuck wagons, and road patrol cars provide safety escorts.

With the option to ride any number of days or the entire distance, begin your preparation by becoming a member of the association and complete forms for registration, food packet, and liability waiver. You will receive a rider camp list that will tell you what to bring and what you must have in a horse-grooming box and in your truck for the horse. You must have a healthy horse (not a stallion) or mule experienced in multiple riding days. It must have tested negative for equine infectious anemia within the past 12 months. Of course you should also be healthy, with appropriate allergy tests. While on the trail, you must stay with the group and be responsible for the care and feeding of your horse. Other rules forbid firearms and pets and prohibit riding bareback or doubleback.

On the first day you will follow SR 64 east on slightly rolling sandhills by the 556-acre Lake Manatee State Recreation Area to a private ranch near Myakka Head. En route are marshes, woodlands of oaks, and sand pine scrub with saw palmetto. Speckled perch, shellcracker, and sunshine bass swim in the Manatee River you cross. The second day you will enter Hardee County and have lunch near Ona. The countryside is 55 percent ranchland, with sections of vegetable crops, dairy farms, and citrus groves. Your campsite is at Pioneer Park in Zolfo Springs. Pioneer Park is beside the Peace River, a river claimed by Creek Indian Chief Secoffe after the U.S. government pushed his tribe out of Georgia. His son, legendary Billy Bowlegs, fought to save this area, and it seemed that peace had come in 1839 when the U.S. government signed a treaty agreeing that white settlers would claim the west side of the river and the Creeks (also called Seminoles) would have the east side. Eleven years later white settlers broke the treaty, and fighting continued until 1858 when Chief Bowlegs signed a truce for exile to Oklahoma. Nearly 100 years later, in 1954, a citizens group in Wauchula invited Chief Bowlegs' grandson, Billy III, and members of his tribe to visit the Peace River and Wauchula, the land of their heritage.

In Pioneer Park is the William Henry Hart cabin of 1879, the Bryant blacksmith shop, and a heritage locomotive. A nearby marker honors Bone Mizelle, who the *Miami Herald* labeled "the Will Rogers of the Cattle Rustlers." Near the locomotive is the Cracker Trail Museum, usually open Thursday through Sunday, or by advance reservations or on special occasions. The museum has exhibits on the history of the early Indians, Florida Crackers, and branding irons, and history books such as *Florida Cowman* and *Peace River Pioneers.*

On the third day you will see a countryside of ranches, farms, orange groves, and open prairies, some with flowing wells. Your campsite is likely to be near the border of Hardee and Highlands counties. The next day you will come to the intersection of CR 635, from which Highlands Hammock State

Park is only 4 miles north. Although Highlands County large citrus groves, you will see them only near Red Bea Lake, after you leave SR 66 and begin US 98 south of Sebring. At Arbuckle Creek the *Cracker Trail Queen* takes visitors at the Florida Cracker Trail fish camp to Winding Waters Recreation Park. After crossing Arbuckle Creek, you are likely to camp at the Lorida Rodeo Ground in Lorida, with entertainment and dinner open to the public.

Two thirds of the fifth-day ride is on US 98, where traffic is greater than on previous days. You will parallel the Seaboard Coast Line for 9 miles before curving more eastward to Fort Bassinger (established by Gen. Zachary Taylor in 1838), near the Kissimmee River bridge and spillway. You will see forest, farm, rangeland, and vegetable crops. Near the entrance to CR 68 you will pass through the Chandler Slough, then follow a bridge over Taylor Creek a few miles later.

On your sixth day the countryside changes remarkably. For example, US 441 and CR 68 are flat and straight. You will also see more citrus groves as you near the Fort Pierce area. You will camp on a private ranch or at the public fairgrounds. The next day is the Cracker Riders Day celebration in Fort Pierce, which may include such activities as parades, barbecues, and rodeos.

If you are seeing this part of Florida by auto, make a loop returning from Fort Pierce to Bradenton on SR 70, a south route that parallels the Florida Cracker Trail road system. You will see similar Cracker countryside, and pass through the historic towns of Okeechobee and Arcadia. Arcadia has a historic district (1886–1930) of 374 buildings in 58 blocks. Two notable structures are the De Soto County Courthouse and the Railroad Depot Museum. Exceptionally tall, slender palms grace the old railroad sides. In Bradenton are a number of historic places of special interest regarding the De Soto Trail and south Florida. The De Soto National Memorial Park recalls sixteenth-century history, with park staff recreating in dress and conversation from December through April the lives of the Spanish and early Indians. The visitor center also has route *n*

n about the De Soto Trail, which origi-
r the park is part of a celebration of the
e Soto, sponsored by the Hernando de
at Shaw's Point. The event is usually the
of April.) Access to the park from I-75
is west on SR 64 to 75th Street West. Along the way on SR 64,
near 15th Street East, are Manatee Village Historical Park and
South Florida Museum at 10th Street West. The museum has
life-size dioramas of Indian and other state history. Other
historic areas are the Braden Castle Park historic district (1850,
1924–1929), with 206 structures, and the Palmetto historic
district (1890–1930), with 208 significant buildings, located on
the north side of the Manatee River by SR 45. Nearby, east on
US 301, is the Gamble Plantation State Historic Site (1845-1850),
the oldest restored plantation home on Florida's west coast.

### Information

Counties: Manatee, Hardee, Highlands, Okeechobee, Saint
Lucie

Average Temperatures: January, 51.5°F (low), 72.5°F
(high); August, 73.4°F (low), 89.8°F (high)

National Properties: De Soto National Memorial Park, 75th
St., NW, Bradenton, FL 33529, (813) 792-0458

State Properties: Gamble Plantation State Historic Site,
3708 Patten Ave., Ellenton, FL 34222, (813) 723-4536; Lake
Manatee State Recreation Area, 20007 SR 64, Bradenton, FL
34202, (813) 741-8042

City and County Properties: Braden Castle, #1 Office Dr.,
Bradenton, FL 34208, (813) 746-7700; Pioneer Park, Zolfo
Springs, FL 33890, (813) 735-0330/0550; South Florida Mu-
seum, 201 Tenth St. W., Bradenton, FL 34205, (813) 746-4131

Historical Organizations: Hernando de Soto Historical
Society, Spanish Manor House, 910 Third Ave. W., Bradenton,
FL 34205, (813) 747-1998

Chambers of Commerce: De Soto County CC, 16 S. Volusia
Ave., Arcadia, FL 33821, (813) 494-4033; Greater Sebring CC,

319 West Center Ave., Sebring, FL 33870, (813) 385-6350 or (800) 255-1711; Hardee County CC, P.O. Box 683, Wauchula, FL 33873, (813) 773-6967; Manatee CC, 222 Tenth St. W., Bradenton, FL 34205, (813) 748-3411; Saint Lucie County CC, P.O. Box 8209, Port St. Lucie, FL 34985, (407) 335-4487; Saint Petersburg Area CC, P.O. Box 1371, Saint Petersburg, FL 33731, (813) 821-4069

Services and Amenities: *Information on ranches, horse stables and carriers, and campgrounds:* The Florida Cracker Trail Association, 5301 Oakland Rd., Sebring, FL 33870, (813) 385-6136/5101, or 471-0001

## MYAKKA RIVER STATE PARK

Florida's largest state park, 28,875-acre Myakka River, is distinctive for its diversity, protection, and accessibility for wildlife observation. Known for its 300 species of wading and forest birds, it is also home to an incredible variety of mammals, reptiles, fishes, and amphibians. Its flora, in spacious marshes, hardwood hammocks, pine flatwoods, palm and palmetto prairies, and floodplains, offers opportunities for extensive botanical study. To observe this marvelous world of plants and animals, use some of the 39 miles of hiking trails and some of the many backcountry road and water routes. For your convenience, a concessionaire provides guided wildlife and nature tours every day, except Tuesday, by boat or tram; an interpretive center helps you understand wildlife and plant communities; and concessionaires sell supplies and books about nature. If you have only a few days to visit a Florida state park, make Myakka your choice.

*What to See and Do:* You can spend many hours watching the wildlife from boats, on trails, or from the observation deck. Because the area is a sanctuary, many of the birds and mammals ignore your presence. Whether bird-watching, camping in the full-service campground, fishing and boating in the lakes, horseback riding, bicycling, or hiking and backpacking, you will feel rewarded for your stay.

*Where to Begin:* From I-75, Exit 37, drive east 9 miles on SR 72 to the park entrance, left. An eastern approach is 27 miles from Arcadia on SR 72. A north entrance on CR 780 (7 miles from SR 70 at Verna) is open only on weekends and holidays, ·8 A.M. to 5 P.M. The nearest airport is Sarasota-Bradenton, 25 miles west.

*About the Adventures:* Not only is the park Florida's largest, it is one of the state's oldest, with the first acquisition in 1936. Two years earlier the sons of Mrs. Potter Palmer had donated a substantial tract (from a 1910 working ranch) to the state as a memorial to their mother, and in 1935 the CCC developed sections for public recreational use. Other contributions and state purchases followed. Flowing through the park on its way to Charlotte Harbor, the Myakka River forms the Upper and Lower Myakka lakes. Other notable water areas are the Deer Prairie Slough and flowing wells in the park's eastern panhandle. Occasionally the park is closed during a wet season when high water innundates the entrance road and camping area for a few days. The area is natural, except for a single paved road, a few rustic cabins with double beds and fireplaces, a campground, an interpretive center, a picnic area, and a boat basin. One natural attraction is the 7,500-acre wilderness that is undisturbed by roads or humans. (Ask park officials for information on park policies for a limited visit in the wilderness by foot or boat travel.) Park rangers can take you on guided walks for nature study and bird-watching, or you can rent a bicycle or take an educational wildlife tour for a fee. Campground reservations are accepted in advance. Horseback riders must bring their own horses; there are no overnight stables. Three equestrian loops, a total of 15 miles, are combined and accessible from SR 72, east of the main gate.

On a typical lake tour your guide not only will describe the wildlife you see and hear, but will answer questions about migratory birds and the park's underwater world. Binoculars are recommended for these tours. From the dock you will notice a few tall trees with sun-bleached limbs, the roosting home of nearly two hundred red-headed turkey vultures and black vultures. You may be close enough to notice the bare, featherless red head of the turkey vulture. It has a 6-foot wingspan and can soar motionless, in contrast to the bare, gray-headed black vulture, which has a shorter tail and flaps 5-foot wings more frequently. Closer to you are little blue herons, white until the age of three. They carefully lift their green legs to avoid splashing the water while constantly searching for food. White ibis, with their turned-down bills, gaze at the shallow water, and kingfishers noisily swoop to catch minnows. Out on low limbs are anhingas (also called "snake birds") with wings outspread to dry. Not far away are great blue herons, with 6-foot wings, standing quietly among water hyacinths. A great delicacy for these large herons are water snakes. Snowy egrets fly by as pied-billed grebes dive and swim underwater for food. At least twelve species of ducks are here in the wintertime. Some are the blue-winged and green-winged teal, American wigeon, ring-necked duck, American coot, northern shoveler, and common pintail. The great egret (also called the American egret), the largest of the egret species, is pure white with a yellow bill and long black legs. Near the edge of the lake in the marsh are sandhill cranes 4 feet tall and with red crowns. Mates for life, pairs usually band together; a third adult following is likely an offspring that has not acquired a mate or that has lost one. By the time you turn at the northern end of the lake, you may have seen ospreys, red-shouldered hawks, and double-crested cormorants. Land-based tree swallows may dart about in lake coves looking for insects among the water lilies, buttonbush, and coastal willows. And while you watch the birds, the "lord of the lake" may be watching you: the American alligator glides through the hydrilla and grasses, with barely more than its nostrils and eyes above the water.

Before you begin your adventure on the Myakka River Hiking Trail, you may wish to become acquainted with the plant life of the park. The Hammock Nature Trail and the Tram Safari provide introductions. The nature trail is a short loop on the right side of the road after you cross the Myakka River from the park entrance. Here, on the bromeliads, you will see "water pots," water trapped in the cuplike bases of the leaves for use in dry seasons; each base is a minihabitat for small tree frogs and insects. There are pines, oaks, palms, and saw palmettoes, tree serpent ferns, maiden cane, and spartina. The tram route follows backcountry roads, where the guide discusses forest succession, wildlife habitats, flowers, and epiphytic plants.

Access to the parking area for the Myakka River Hiking Trail is on Park Drive, 0.3 mile beyond the lake observation deck. The trail is a combination of four loops, with primitive campsites in each loop, and three cross trails. Maintained by members of the Florida Trail Association, the 33.3-mile main perimeter trail has white blazes; blue marks the 5.5 miles of cross and side trails. If you backpack camp, you must register and get a permit for a designated campsite. Maximum user limit is twelve. At or near the campsites are pitcher-pump-equipped wells. Park officials recommend that you boil or chemically treat all water, including pump water, for drinking or food preparation.

After you hike the 0.2-mile access trail you will reach the first loop, Bea Island Loop. If you follow it clockwise, you will reach Bea Island Cross Trail at 5 miles. One mile west on the cross trail is a campsite and a spur trail to the historic site of a cattle dip vat, reminiscent of those early years in the twentieth century when the area was cattle country. Twice a month the cattle were corralled and channeled through the solution here as treatment for ticks and biting flies. If you continue clockwise you will find another vat site near the campsite in East Loop at 12.5 miles. At 6.7 miles is the 0.8-mile Bobcat Cross Trail between Honore Loop and Deer Prairie Loop, and at 10.1 miles is the 1.5-mile Slough Cross Trail that connects the Deer Prairie Loop and the East Loop. Other notable points on the trails are old railroad grades, power-line crossings, and horse-trail crossings.

On the trails are wide sections of pine flatwoods with strong slash pine up to 40 feet high. "Ecological burns" have at places prevented hardwoods from smothering the pines. Prairie areas have broom sedge and dog fennel, and on many of the hardwoods, particularly the live oaks, are resurrection ferns, a polypody that can appear dead for up to 8 years in dry seasons. Among the bromeliades are the quill leaf, wild pine, and Spanish moss. Both red basket and gray lichen add color combinations to the hardwoods. Other plant life you will notice are cabbage palm, saw palmetto, thorny water locust, and swamp willow (whose new leaves come out in December).

From the beginning you will notice where feral hogs, a menace to the park, are rooting. With a destructive diet and no natural enemies, twenty-five hundred of them proliferate in the park. They dig up and eat almost everything except large tree roots. Snakes, salamanders, lizards, rodents, turtle eggs, frogs, young birds, worms, grubs, and other small animals make up at least one fourth of their diet. In eating nuts, acorns, and berries, they deprive other forest animals of food. Tubular roots of rare orchids are a delicacy to them. Feral hogs usually disappear before you arrive to see them, but if you go quietly you can hear the grunts of the adults or the squealing of the piglets. They are commonly infected with brucellosis, an infectious disease that can be transmitted to humans through the soil or water. The resulting undulent fever, also called Malta fever or melitensis fever, is treated with antibiotics.

Turkeys and deer are abundant in the park, and raccoons are common campsite visitors. You may come upon twenty-five to fifty turkeys wandering as a flock to gobble insects exposed by hogs. If you hear their clucking it is possible to sneak near and follow them for a better view. They will watch you closely, but will ascend in a roaring flight only if you approach too closely or alarm them. You may also see deer, especially a fawn watching curiously as you approach, which use the trail. And do not be surprised if you see an otter at the Deer Prairie Slough, or raccoons that do not follow nocturnal habits. Although bobcats may watch you, you are not likely to see them. You may, however, see armadillos that, instead of sleeping in their burrows in the daytime, are out exploring and feeding. The females have four babies, no more or less, always all male or all female.

A side trip is west 17 miles on SR 72 to Sarasota, frequently referred to as Florida's cultural capital, the "Palm Beach of West Florida," "Home of the Greatest Show on Earth," and the "cradle of golf" (because the first course in the state was laid out here in 1886). The mainland part of the city is known for its performing arts centers, its art districts, its gardens, and such places as the Asolo Theater, with its interior decor of 1798 Asolo, Italy, at the Ringling Museums. Sarasota Bay is famous for its fishing, marinas, and water sports. (See *Information*.) Although the 35 miles of once-natural island beaches are now developed with condominiums, resorts, and elegant homes, Sarasota still has small public parks, such as at the southern tip of Lido Beach. Of special importance to naturalists is the Marie Selby Botanical Gardens near the bay, with its outstanding displays of orchids, bromeliads, tropical trees, and rare flowers. Access is by 811 South Palm Avenue, off US 41. Of marine interest is the Mote Marine Science Center at 1600 City Island Park, with its aquarium displays of marine life from the Gulf area. At the south edge of the city on US 41, 2 miles south of Osprey, is Oscar Scherer State Recreation Area, a 460-acre natural environment. Through the pine forests flows beautiful tidal South Creek. The area is habitat for ospreys, hawks, herons, owls, jays, thrushes, vireoes, and warblers. More than three hundred species of fauna have been identified here. The park has a full-service campground, and reservations can be made in advance. There is a boat dock for canoeists.

### Information

Counties: Sarasota, Manatee
Average Temperatures: January, 52.6°F (low), 73.2°F (high); August, 73.7°F (low), 89.8°F (high)
State Properties: Myakka River State Park, 13207 SR 72, Sarasota, FL 34241, (813) 361-6511; Oscar Scherer State

Recreation Area, 1843 S. Tamiami Trail, Osprey, FL 34229, (813) 483-5956

Gardens, Science Center, and Museums: Marie Selby Botanical Gardens, 811 S. Palm Ave., Sarasota, FL 34236, (813) 366-5730; Mote Marine Science Center, 1600 City Island Park, Sarasota, FL 33577, (813) 388-2451; Ringling Museums (located 0.5 mile south of the Sarasota-Bradenton Airport on US 41), P.O. Box 1838, Sarasota, FL 33578, (813) 355-5101

Chambers of Commerce: Sarasota CC, 1819 Main St., Suite 240, Sarasota, FL 34236, (813) 955-2508; Sarasota Convention and Visitor's Bureau, 655 N. Tamiami Trail, Sarasota, FL 34236, (813) 957-1877 or (800) 522-9799; Siesta Key CC, 5263 Ocean Blvd., Siesta Key, FL 34242, (813) 349-3800

Services and Amenities: *Bicycling:* Bicycle Center, 3551 Webber St., Sarasota, FL 34239, (813) 924-2228, and 2610 Cortes Rd. W., Bradenton, FL 34207, (813) 756-5480; *Boating and Sailing:* O'Leary Sarasota Sailing School, Island Park, Bayfront, (813) 953-7505; Marina Plaza, Sarasota, (813) 366-6659; *Canoeing:* Canoe Outpost, Rte. 2, Box 330–J, Sarasota, FL 33582, (813) 371-3820, or (904) 454-2900; *Horseback Riding:* Myakka Valley Campground and Stables (7.5 miles east of I-75 on SR 72), 7220 Myakka Valley Trail, Sarasota, FL 34241, (813) 924-8435

# 6

## SOUTH REGION AND THE KEYS

South Florida includes part of the moderately populated "Treasure Coast" (from Sebastian south to Juno Beach), all the densely populated "Gold Coast" (from North Palm Beach south to North Miami Beach), the megalopolis of Miami, and the Biscayne Bay reefs on the eastern seaboard. Its "Shell Coast" (from Charlotte Harbor to Marco Island) is on the Gulf of Mexico. On the north is Lake Okeechobee, the state's largest lake, with "sugar land," home of the nation's largest sugarcane company, on its southern rim. At the end of the Florida peninsula is Everglades National Park, with its bays, islands, capes, alligators, and crocodiles. South of Florida Bay is a tropical 100-mile east-west string of coral and oolite islands, the Florida Keys, connected to Key West with forty-seven ocean bridges. In the center of the region are Big Cypress Seminole and Miccosukee Indian reservations, two of the state's four. West of the reservations is Big Cypress Swamp, which has the state's largest natural concentration of royal palms, and east is the Everglades' upper drainage system. East-west through the center are highways I-75 (Alligator Alley) and US 41 (Tamiami Trail). The north-south Florida Turnpike and I-95 run parallel near the Atlantic shore.

Topographically, the entire region is flat, below 25 feet in elevation, with a 50-foot exception at Immokalee Rise, southwest of Lake Okeechobee. Two major physiographic features in the region are 488,000-acre Lake Okeechobee and the Everglades. Instead of having many lakes and rivers and rolling hills as in the central and north regions, the more tropical south has vast marshes, sloughs, swamps, prairies, and flatwoods. The only long river, the Caloosahatchee, became a 75-mile canal in 1882. The Kissimmee River originates in central Florida and flows south. There are a number of shorter rivers, most of which flow from the Everglades to the Gulf. Emptying into the Atlantic Ocean are the Miami and the New rivers, and into the Gulf are Shark, Harney, Broad, Lostmans, Turner, and Chatham rivers. Two major sloughs are Shark River and Taylor. The region is wet, with an annual rainfall of about 55 inches, 70 percent between May and October. Easily flooded by excessive rainfall and parched by droughts, the region has had a controversial water-management program since 1881 when Hamilton Disston began the first full-scale drainage project. Since then, a massive levee has been built around Lake Okeechobee and five major canals have been cut through the Everglades' natural drainage system. In addition to a wet surface, the area has two prominent subterranean aquifers: Chokoloskee, beneath Big Cypress Swamp, and Biscayne, beneath the Everglades and the Atlantic coast from West Palm Beach south. They can store a huge mass of water in porous limestone thousands of feet deep. As a result, well fields can yield 2,000 gallons of fresh water per minute.

Natural communities of pine flatwoods and saw palmetto prairies are found mainly in Hendry, Lee, Palm Beach, and Collier counties. They are adaptable for ranchland, timber, and agriculture. In Palm Beach County, 97 percent of the farmland is devoted to vegetable crops, with the center in Belle Glade; Hendry County, with its rich mucklands, is the state's leading producer and refiner of sugarcane and also has rangelands and timber forests. Collier and Lee counties are similar, except that they do not produce sugarcane; the town of Immokalee, which straddles the border between the two counties, is their major center for vegetable crops. Cabbage palm hammocks are most prominent on the west and east side of Lake Okeechobee but are found scattered throughout the flatlands. From Lake Okeechobee south to Florida Bay are the famous Everglades marshes, sloughs, and tree islands, with

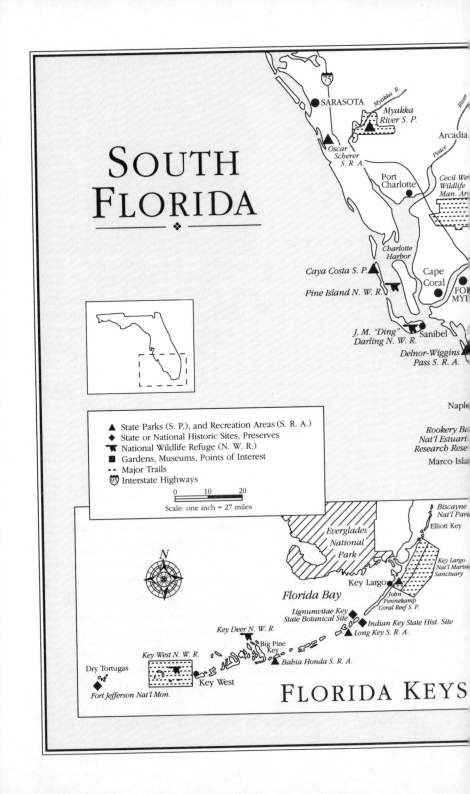

# SOUTH FLORIDA

SARASOTA

*Myakka R.*

*Myakka River S. P.*

Arcadia

*Peace*

*River*

Oscar
Scherer
S. R. A.

Port
Charlotte

Cecil We
Wildlife
Man. Ar

*Charlotte
Harbor*

Caya Costa S. P.

Cape
Coral

FO
MYI

Pine Island N. W. R.

J. M. "Ding"
Darling N. W. R.

Sanibel

Delnor-Wiggins
Pass S. R. A.

- ▲ State Parks (S. P.), and Recreation Areas (S. R. A.)
- ◆ State or National Historic Sites, Preserves
- ⊀ National Wildlife Refuge (N. W. R.)
- ■ Gardens, Museums, Points of Interest
- -- Major Trails
- Ⓘ Interstate Highways

0    10    20

Scale: one inch = 27 miles

Naple

Rookery Ba
Nat'l Estuari
Research Rese

Marco Isla

*Biscayne
Nat'l Par*
Elliott Key

*Everglades
National
Park*

Key Largo
Nat'l Marin
Sanctuary

N

Key Largo

*Florida Bay*

John
Pennekamp
Coral Reef S. P.

Lignumvitae Key
State Botanical Site

Indian Key State Hist. Site

Key Deer N. W. R.

Long Key S. R. A.

Big Pine
Key

Key West N. W. R.

Bahia Honda S. R. A.

Dry Tortugas

Key West

*Fort Jefferson Nat'l Mon.*

# FLORIDA KEYS

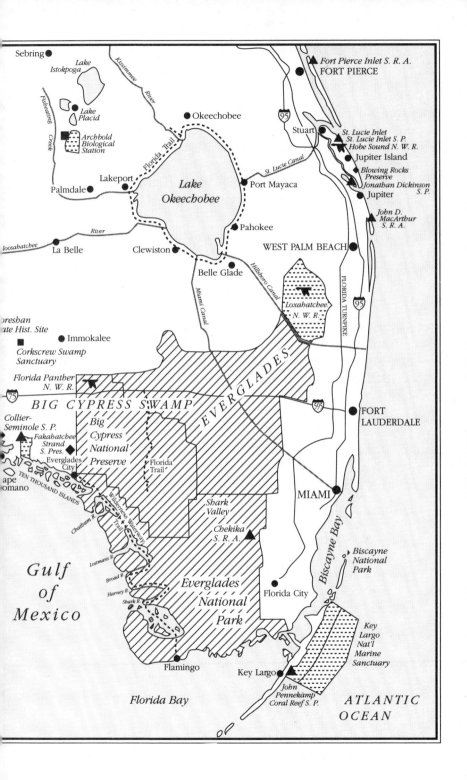

their red bay, willow, and saw grass waving to the horizon like a river of grass. Big Cypress Swamp, in Collier County, has prairie marshes and cypress-swamp forests with coco plum, air plants, and saw grass. Mangrove swamps and coastal marshes line the entire western and southern coasts.

Natives in the region lived on islands, near the mouths of streams and inlets, and at Lake Okeechobee. On the Atlantic coast, from Pompano Beach south to Cape Sabe in the Everglades, were the Tequesta, and on the west coast and the Florida Keys and at Lake Okeechobee were the tall and powerful Calusa. They, like other Florida aborigines, became extinct within 250 years of the first Spanish incursions in the early 1500s. Current Florida Indians, collectively called Seminoles, represent two linguistic and four political groups.

South Florida developed nearly 300 years after the first European settlement at Saint Augustine in north Florida. The first settlement in the south was at Key West (1822), Florida's largest city in the early 1880s. The towns of Fort Myers and Fort Lauderdale began as U.S. government forts in the Second Seminole War (1835–1842). Palm Beach was settled in 1861 and later, with the arrival of Henry M. Flagler's East Coast Railroad and his construction of the Royal Poinciana Hotel, became an opulent resort in the late 1890s. Flagler's railroad reached Miami in 1896; then he did the unthinkable by completing the Overseas Railroad to Key West in 1912. Today, Greater Miami and its twenty-six municipalities is a cultural aggregation and a center for international commerce, tourism, industry, arts, and agriculture; it is the nation's gateway to Latin America. Less feverish in pace than Miami and the Gold Coast are the small resort cities of Naples (1887) and Fort Myers (1850) on the Gulf coast. Elegant, charming, quiet, and refined, they are a classic as Naples' name implies.

Among the natural areas of the region, none is more enchanting and significant than Everglades National Park, a park like no other in the world. You could plan a 100-mile canoe trip on the park's backwater bays and inlets or visit some of the region's eleven national wildlife refuges (half of the entire state), experiencing close up the waterfowl on Sanibel Island and the toy deer on Big Pine Key. Do not overlook the excitement of west coast shelling, and be sure to hike at least some of the 38 miles of the Florida Trail through Big Cypress National Preserve. In Biscayne National Park and Pennekamp Coral Reef State Park you can scuba dive to see a fantastic display of colorful tropical marine life, and on Lignumvitae and Indian keys you will see banded tree snails, golden orb spiders, and sisal agave. Corkscrew Swamp Sanctuary offers a long boardwalk to one of the nation's largest and oldest stands of bald cypress, where you can see butterfly orchids on tree trunks. When you arrive at the west coast's Cayo Costa for the sunsets, or at Blowing Rocks on Jupiter Island by the Atlantic for sunrises, you may wonder if any place in Florida could have more Paul Gauguin colors.

## JUPITER ISLAND

On Florida's "Treasure Coast," between Saint Lucie Inlet at Port Salerno and Jupiter Inlet to the south, is Jupiter Island, a thin, 16-mile strip of beach, estuaries, and dune forests. A combination of Hobe Sound National Wildlife Refuge, Saint Lucie Inlet State Park, Blowing Rocks Preserve, public beaches, and private residences, it is the only barrier island between here and Biscayne Bay to the south to be so well protected from further urban development. On its west side the Intracoastal Waterway runs through the lakes and sounds that separate it from the mainland. On the beach are the rare beach star plant and sea turtle tracks. Ghost crabs forage at the tide-mark, and cliffs are sculpted by the ocean surf. Near the island in 1696, Jonathan Dickinson and his family from Pennsylvania survived shipwreck and Indian capture. A state park on the mainland is named in honor of him and his adventures. Flowing through the park is Loxahatchee River, a water route to more history at the site of reclusive Trapper Nelson.

*What to See and Do:* Take a day hike on Jupiter Island or a 9.3-mile backpacking-camping trip to the junglelike Kitching

Creek in Jonathan Dickinson State Park. Canoeing and other types of boating are options on the Loxahatchee River, and fishing is popular in the sounds and ocean. Take a side trip to turtle watch, or canoe into the Everglades' Loxahatchee NWR.

*Where to Begin:* Jonathan Dickinson State Park is 12.2 miles south of Port Salerno on SR A1A and 4 miles north of Jupiter-Tequesta on US 1/SR A1A. The nearest access from I-95, Exit 60, is on SR 708, Bridge Road, east. The Palm Beach International Airport is 20 miles south.

*About the Adventures:* Choose Jonathan Dickinson State Park as your base campground. Schedule at least 2 days to hike all the trails and canoe the Loxahatchee River, and another full day to explore Jupiter Island. The 10,328-acre park has sand pine scrub, pine flatwoods, mangrove thickets, cypress strands, river swamps, and the Loxahatchee River, which flows through its southern boundary. With such diverse topography, it is not surprising that more than 600 species of vascular plants, many species of reptiles and mammals, and at least 150 species of birds inhabit the area. To get an overview of the park, begin by hiking the Hobe Mountain Trail to the observation tower. From here you can see all the park, Hobe Sound, Jupiter Island, and sunrises over the Atlantic Ocean. At the base of the tower is sand pine scrub, the largest forest of its kind on the southeast coast.

The park was logged in 1900 and 1940 and was a CCC camp in the 1930s. The state acquired it in 1947 and named it for Jonathan Dickinson, a Pennsylvania Quaker who, with his wife, infant child, and others, survived a shipwreck of the *Reformation* on Jupiter Island in 1696. They were captured by a band of Indians, were released, and walked 225 miles to Saint Augustine on their way home to Philadelphia. Dickinson's description of his journey in *God's Protecting Providence* revealed much about the Florida Indians and the flora and fauna in the late seventeenth century.

In addition to full-service camping (with advance reservations accepted), the park offers boating, canoeing, birding, bicycling, and hiking. An overnight campsite for the 9.3-mile

Hiking Trail provides exposure to the nocturnal wildlife in the dense growth of Kitching Creek. Maintained by the Florida Trail Association, the trail sometimes has wet areas that require wading. With temperatures as high as 95 degrees Fahrenheit in midday summer, you may wish to hike between December and April, the most comfortable time. Two drinking-water pumps are provided, but the one halfway along the trail may not be functioning. You should boil or chemically treat the water before drinking it. Park rangers recommend that you take a portable stove and contact the ranger for reservations, a trail map, and information about the designated campsite. The east terminus of the white-blazed Hiking Trail is at the north side of the park entrance station. You will soon be in a scrub pine forest, where you are likely to see towhees, scrub jays, and gopher tortoises. After 2 miles you will cross the Old Dixie Highway (formerly US 1) and the Florida East Coast Railway. Soon thereafter the forest becomes slash pine, cabbage palm, willow, maple, and wax myrtle. At about 5.7 miles you will enter a pine flatwood with an understory of saw palmetto, gallberry, and fetterbush. When you cross a wooden bridge over Kitching Creek at 7.8 miles, notice a cypress strand mixed with popash. From here, among deer and otter, you parallel the creek to reach the campsite. If you hear a rustle in the leaves during the night, it is likely to be a fox, opossum, or raccoon.

At the park's picnic area and Loxahatchee River boat ramp, you can hike three short trails. The Wilson Creek Trail and the Kitching Creek Trail form double loops with a combination of cypress and maple wetlands and pine flatwoods. Expect to hear the drumming of woodpeckers—flicker, pileated, downy, red-bellied, all common to the park—or the clear call of the bobwhite. On the Kitching Creek Trail loop, which received its name from the Walter Kitching family, who began in 1886 to ferry supplies from Titusville to the pioneer settlers, are ferns, dancing-lady orchids, swamp mermaids, white tarflowers, and other wildflowers. Shorter than the other trails is the Loxahatchee River Trail, which passes through communities of pine and mangrove from the parking area to the river. If you are at the river near dusk, you will likely see raccoons making their way to feed on crustacea and frogs at the river's edge.

Access is by boat (rentals are available) to Trapper Nelson's Interpretive Site on the Loxahatchee River. A guided tour is more informative, and easier, on the thirty-passenger *Loxahatchee Queen* that departs daily except Monday and Tuesday. A unique feature of the site is a nature sanctuary that Trapper Nelson developed around his cabin during his 38 years as the "wild man of the Loxahatchee."

On your route to Jupiter Island, take US 1/SR A1A north 2 miles to the Hobe Sound NWR Nature Center and Museum. Information available here will acquaint you with the refuge and the short Sand Pine Scrub Nature Trail on the west side of Hobe Sound. A brochure explains how controlled burning of undergrowth in the sand pine forests is necessary for its regeneration. Established in 1969, the refuge began with 229 acres donated by Jupiter Island residents. Additional donations have enlarged the refuge to its present 968 acres. From here, travel north 2.5 miles to SR 708 and turn right on Bridge Road to SR 707. Take a left on the island and pass through the refuge on the left and by luxurious private homes on the right until you arrive at the parking area. A major management effort of the refuge is to protect the beach nesting area of the leatherback, green, and loggerhead sea turtles that may produce a combined total of 100,000 hatchlings in a favorable year. Other wildlife in the refuge are pelicans, ospreys, deer, raccoons, foxes, bobcats, doves, bald eagles, songbirds, and wading- and shorebirds.

In planning, consider taking a picnic lunch and canteens of water on your hike north to the end of the island. After 2.5 miles you leave the refuge and enter Saint Lucie Inlet State Park, where for another 2.5 miles you hike to the jetty at the inlet. Both the refuge and the park allow beach usage during daylight only. In the park are a ranger station, a restroom, and a picnic shelter. Drinking water may not be available. Park vegetation includes wild lime, paradise tree, live oak, coco plum, and sea grape. If you smell an odor of skunk, it is likely to be the white stopper bush. A 0.6-mile boardwalk trail wanders from the beach to the ranger station and dock at the Intracoastal Waterway; from this dock you can visit the park by boat. Charters are available from the many marinas in Port Salerno, about 3.5 miles from the park. Call the ranger to learn if public transportation is available.

From the refuge boundary on SR 707 you can drive south on the island for 6.5 miles among residential mansions and landscaped gardens to a parking area for the Blowing Rocks Preserve, a 113-acre tract protected by The Nature Conservancy, made possible by a group of island residents when the refuge was established. Dramatically different from the smooth Florida beaches, this one-mile Anastasia limestone outcropping, formed by millions of years of marine sediment cementation, is the largest on the Atlantic coast. Endless wave action has since carved fissures and solution holes in it. During storms, seawater is forced up and through apertures, causing high, geyserlike white plumes. Also in the preserve are diverse plant communities: oceanfront dunes, coastal strands, interior mangrove wetlands, and tropical coastal hammocks. Of the 120 plant species, 2 are rare: the endangered beach star (*Remirea maritima*) and the threatened beach creeper (*Ernodea litoralis*). Other flowers are goldenrods, dune sunflowers, and purple railroad vines. As at the other beaches described in this trip, the sea turtles use the smooth areas of the preserve for nesting. Brown pelicans often skim the ocean breakers in search of baitfish.

Recreational fishing for redfish, mangrove snapper, black drum, pinfish, snook, spotted sea trout, flounder, and pompano is popular in the area. To launch your boat, find a charter service, or to rent a boat, contact the local chamber of commerce or the Florida Marine Institute in Saint Petersburg and ask for the "Recreational Fishing Site Access Map" for Martin County. It lists about sixty-five marine locations and facilities, the largest concentrations being at Port Salerno and

Stuart. In addition, you can get a saltwater fishing update from Sebastian Inlet south to Hillsboro Inlet titled "Where They're Biting" from the Jupiter-Tequesta Chamber of Commerce, or sailfishing information from the Stuart Sailfish Club. (See *Information.*)

To learn the history of the Jupiter Island area, visit the Loxahatchee Historical Society Museum at 305 North US 1 (south from Jonathan Dickinson State Park). Exhibits show the shaping of nature by history; shipwrecks; and Indian history, including that of the Jaega and Ais tribes. The museum is open daily, except Mondays; call about its limited hours. Each Sunday from 12 noon to 3 P.M. the museum provides tours to Jupiter Inlet Lighthouse, a 105-foot-tall brick structure built between 1855 and 1859. Access in Jupiter is the first right (Captain Armour's Way) (east) on SR 707 from its junction with US 1. The lighthouse and another historic place, the Jupiter Inlet Historic and Archaeological Site, are listed in the National Register of Historic Places. Access to the archeological site is on the south side of the inlet, off SR A1A on Dubois Road. The Indian mounds of shell vary in height from 3 to 20 feet and are evidence of human occupation of the area as early as 500 B.C. The Harry Dubois home, a pioneer dwelling (1898), sits on top of an Indian midden. The Loxahatchee Historical Society conducts tours each Sunday from noon to 3 P.M.

One way to see Hobe and Jupiter sounds, on the west side of Jupiter Island, is to take a tour on the *Jupiter Queen*, which runs daily except Monday and Thursday. On the trip you will be able to view the resplendent homes and natural areas along the Intracoastal Waterway. The tour ferry is docked at the Southern Star Restaurant, 1106 Yarborough Street, in Jupiter. Another restaurant, Harpoon Louie's, with seafood specials, is next door to the berth of the *Jupiter Queen*. All are easy to locate from the junction of US 1 and SR A1A, the south end of the Loxahatchee River bridge. For old-fashioned home cooking anytime, try the Lighthouse Restaurant, open 24 hours, at 1500 North US 1, north of the bridge.

Four side trips are worthy of your time on this trip or en

route to your next adventure: north to the Saint Lucie Lock and Dam of the Saint Lucie Canal; south for a turtle watch at Juno Beach; to the John D. MacArthur State Recreation Area; and to Loxahatchee NWR. Access to the lock and dam from Dickinson Park is north on US 1 to SR 722. Turn left and left again on SR 76. After the I-95 intersection (Exit 61), take the first right off SR 76 to the south side of the canal. For the canal's north side, continue on SR 76 0.5 mile and take SR 76A. Turn at the first right after crossing the canal. The Saint Lucie Canal is part of the 144-mile Okeechobee Waterway, the only water route across the width of Florida. Its western terminus is in the San Carlos Bay of Cape Coral–Fort Myers. With a powerboat, register for the journey and stay overnight at the camp-grounds, which accept reservations, along the canal. On the canal, pass through Lake Okeechobee, small historic villages like La Belle and Alva, the city of Fort Myers, and on to Sanibel Island on the Gulf coast. En route, fish for largemouth bass, bream, crappie, and catfish, and relax at the campsites at locks like Moore Haven, Ortona, and Franklin. There are many access points to the waterway at highway crossings. For planning information, contact the Office of Waterway Navigation of the U. S. Army Corps of Engineers in Jacksonville and ask for the "Okeechobee Waterway Map," which lists recreation facilities and regulations. (See *Information*.)

From Dickinson Park, drive south on SR A1A 9 miles to the Marine Life Center of Juno Beach. Established by Eleanor N. Fletcher, the museum emphasizes the history and protection of sea turtles, raises and tags hatchlings, and conducts guided turtle watches between June 1 and July 15, the height of nesting season. The museum is open daily, except Sunday and Monday, 10 A.M. to 3 P.M. Sea turtles are protected by U.S. government laws. In Florida, report on the status of sea turtles and about human damage to the turtles and their nests on the Department of Natural Resources' toll-free Resource Alert Line, (800) 342-1821.

When you go on a turtle watch, choose a guide, like those at the museum, who has been trained and who has state permits to remove the eggs and raise the hatchlings for a better chance of survival. (Other turtle watches are conducted in Georgia by the Caretta Research Project, described in Chapter 7.) Very little is known about how young sea turtles survive in the open ocean. Some speculate that they ride the currents, such as the Gulf Stream, where clumps of seaweed provide food and shelter from sharks. Only the adult female comes ashore to dig a 12-inch-deep nest with her hind flippers and lay her eggs in it. During the hour or less it takes to lay approximately one hundred eggs, the sea turtle must shed tears to keep her eyes wet so she can see. After she covers the eggs with sand, she returns to the sea, never to know if the eggs hatch. Florida's most common sea turtle is the logger-head, whose diet is crabs, shrimp, jellyfish, and sea plants. Unlike other turtles, the green turtle, which eats only sea plants, returns to nest at the same beach each year. The largest of the sea turtles, the leatherback, is less common on the shores of Florida and Georgia. It feeds mainly on jellyfish, may grow as large as 1,300 pounds, and travels as far as 3,000 miles from its nesting place. To learn more about the five classes of sea turtles found in Florida (green, hawksbill, ridley, leather-back, and loggerhead), and to find out how you can help in their survival, contact the marine turtle coordinator, Depart-ment of Natural Resources in Tallahassee. (See *Information*.)

Five miles south on A1A from Juno Beach (or 5 miles east on SR 786 from Exit 57 of I-95) is John D. MacArthur State Recreation Area. The 225-acre state park is a fine example of how state government and local citizens can preserve a special subtropical coastal habitat for wild plants and animals. In addition to its barrier island and reef outcroppings, the recreation area includes Lake Worth Cove, a lagoon, and Munyon Island. Dr. Munyon popularized the island, once a lush resort, with his health nostrum in the early 1900s. On the marsh and mud flats you can observe wading birds, and on the shore are pelicans, sandpipers, terns, and herons. From May through August you may see the tracks of sea turtles. You may also notice sea lavender (*Tournefortia gnaphalodes*), a marine shrub, and bay cedar (*Suriana maritima*), found only in central and south coastal areas of Florida. For nearly 2 miles you can snorkel in the shallow waters, swim, fish, and collect shells. Indian middens on the island indicate that it has long been a favorite place for humans and wildlife.

At this point you are close to Palm Beach and can visit the fifty-five-room Henry Morrison Flagler Museum, a marble palace on Coconut Row. Founding partner of Standard Oil, head of the East Coast Railroad, and developer of the Gold Coast, Flagler had much influence on the economic development of Florida. At the museum you will find much about the vast Flagler enterprises and those influences. Open Tuesday through Saturday, 10 A.M. to 5 P.M., and Sunday, 1 to 5 P.M., the museum charges admission. (Write for information about the anniversary open house the first Saturday of each February.) Access from MacArthur Park is south on SR A1A, the first right after you cross the Flagler Memorial Bridge.

The northernmost protected area of the Everglades is the 220-square-mile Arthur R. Marshall Loxahatchee NWR. Between Lake Okeechobee and the Atlantic Ocean, it is directly west of Boynton Beach. If you are traveling from Palm Beach, go west 2.5 miles on SR 704 (Okeechobee Boulevard) to I-95, Exit 52, and take I-95 south 12 miles to SR 804 (Boynton Boulevard). Go west on SR 804 for 8 miles to US 441 and turn left. After 1.9 miles on US 441, turn right to the refuge visitor center. The refuge is intended to maintain an optimum habitat for wildlife and at the same time provide recreational activities and environmental education for the public. Camping is not allowed, but refuge staff can arrange for guides to take you on a night prowl. Guides also lead birding tours, swamp strolls, and photography walks. These activities begin at the visitor center, where you can also get essential information for exploring on your own. You will have a choice of two short walking trails—the Cypress Boardwalk Trail and the Marsh Nature Trail—and see a variety of ferns (sword, shield, leather, swamp), buttonbush, cypress, primrose willow, spider lily, and orchids. If you hear a piglike grunt, it could be either an alligator or the large, olive black pig frog; a high-pitched whistle is probably a fulvous whistling duck, one of 253 bird species in the refuge. The bouncing black-and-yellow striped butterfly you see on the pickerel weed is the zebra longwing.

Also at Loxahatchee is a 5.5-mile canoe loop into the Everglades. (Refuge boat rentals are not available.) A dock is near the visitor center. Or enter the refuge at Twentymile Bend Recreation Area on US 98/441, west of West Palm Beach, where US 98 and US 441 divide. The dock there, used mainly for fishing, is at the first left after you cross the canal bridge, going west. Because of low water, the area may be closed during dry seasons. Call the visitor center for charter information. A good commercial campground in the area is Pine Lake Camp Resort, on SR 704 (Okeechobee Boulevard) one mile west of the Florida Turnpike (Exit 40) and also west of I-95 (Exit 52), and 16.9 miles north from the visitor center via US 441 and SR 7 and east on SR 704.

### *Information*

Counties: Martin, Palm Beach

Average Temperatures: January, 67°F (low), 77.2°F (high); August, 76°F (low), 88.6°F (high)

National Properties: Hobe Sound NWR, 13640 SE Federal Hwy., Hobe Sound, FL 33455, (407) 546-6141; Loxahatchee NWR, Rte. 1, Box 278, Boynton Beach, FL 33437, (407) 734-8303; Okeechobee Waterway, U.S. Army Corps of Engineers, 400 W. Bay St., Jacksonville, FL 32202, (904) 791-1133

State Properties: Dept. of Natural Resources, 3900 Commonwealth Blvd., Marjory Stoneham Douglas Bldg., Tallahassee, FL 32303, (904) 488-1554; Jonathan Dickinson State Park, 16450 SE Federal Hwy., Hobe Sound, FL 33455, (407) 546-2771; John D. MacArthur Beach State Park, 10900 SR 703, North Palm Beach, FL 33408, (407) 627-6097; Saint Lucie State Preserve, c/o Jonathan Dickinson State Park, Hobe Sound, FL 33455, (407) 744-7603

Private Properties (open to the public): Blowing Rocks Preserve, P.O. Box 3795, Tequesta, FL 33469, (407) 575-2297

Museums and Nature Centers: Butterfly World, 3600 W. Sample Rd., Coconut Creek (near Boynton Beach), FL 33073, (305) 977-4400; Marine Life Center of Juno Beach, 1200 US 1, Juno Beach, FL 33408, (407) 627-8280; Henry Morrison Flagler Museum, Box 969, Palm Beach, FL 33480, (407) 655-2833; Loxahatchee Historical Society Museum (also Jupiter Lighthouse and Dubois Home), 805 N. US 1, Jupiter, FL 33477, (407) 747-6639

Organizations: Loxahatchee National History Association, P.O. Box 2737, Delray Beach, FL 33447; The Nature Conservancy, 1353 Palmetto Ave., Winter Park, FL 32789, (407) 628-5887

Chambers of Commerce: Jupiter-Tequesta CC, 800 N, US 1, Jupiter, FL 33477, (407) 746-7111; Palm Beaches CC, 401 N. Flagler Dr., West Palm Beach, FL 33401, (407) 833-3711; Stuart-Martin County CC, 1650 S. Kanner Highway, Stuart, FL 34994, (407) 287-1088

Services and Amenities: *Commercial Campgrounds:* Pine Lake Resort (no tents), 1700 Okeechobee Blvd., West Palm Beach, FL 33411, (407) 686-0714; West Jupiter Campground, 17801 N. 130th Ave., Jupiter, FL 33478, (407) 746-6073 (in Jupiter, take SR 706 to 130th Ave. 4.5 miles west of I-95, Exit 59)

*Bicycle Rentals:* Palm Beach Bicycle Trail Shop, 105 N. County Rd., Palm Beach, FL 33480, (407) 659-4583; *Boat Rentals and Charter Services:* Sailfish Marina, 3565 S. Saint Lucie Blvd., Port Salerno, FL 33492, (407) 283-1122; *Fishing:* Blue Heron Fishing Fleet, West Palm Beach, (407) 844-3573; Stuart Sailfish Club, P.O. Box 2005, Stuart, FL 33495, (407) 286-9373; "Where They're Biting," 17967 S. Federal Hwy., Tequesta, FL 33499, (407) 575-9918; *Recreational Fishing Maps:* Florida Marine Research Institute, 100 Eighth Ave., SE, Saint Petersburg, FL 33701, (813) 896-8626; *Restaurants:* Harpoon Louie's, 105 US 1/A1A, Jupiter, FL 33477, (407) 744-1300; Lighthouse Restaurant, 1500 N. US 1, Jupiter, FL 33477, (407) 746-4811; *Sailing:* Singer Island Sailboat Rentals, Blue Heron Blvd., Riviera Beach, FL 33404, (407) 848-BOAT; *Scuba and Snorkel-*

*ing Rentals:* Force E, 155 E. Blue Heron Blvd., Riviera Beach,
FL 33404, (407) 845-2333; *Sight-Seeing Cruise: Manatee Queen,*
1000 N. US 1, Jupiter, FL 33477, (407) 744-2191

## LAKE OKEECHOBEE

The Seminole Indians called it *oki* ("water") *chobi* ("big") long
after the aboriginal Calusa Indians had told Spaniards of the
big waters they called *Mayaimi.* In 1823 English explorer
Charles Vignoles described the remote, difficult-to-locate
body of water as Lake Mayaco, "which like the fountain of
youth has never yet been found." In 1837 Col. Zachary Taylor
learned from a captured Seminole of the lake's location, but
he arrived on a U.S. government mission to capture or kill the
Seminoles, not to fish and explore the natural resources of the
488,000-acre lake. That became the goal of private entrepreneurs, like Hamilton Disston in 1881 and frontiersmen who
followed in the 1890s: Cracker cowmen, hunters, trappers,
fishermen, and farmers. Shallow, with a central depth of 14
feet, the lake is more symmetrical than elongated—about 30
miles west to east and 35 miles north to south. Islands dot its
west and south waters, and miles of marsh and grass are
segmented on the west side. After disastrous hurricanes in
1926 and 1928, a 34-foot-high dike was constructed around
the lake to control flooding, a development that changed the
ecosystem. Outside the lake, sugarland replaced muckland,
and custard apple groves and marinas replaced banks of
moonvines. But many features have not changed; coots,
cooters, curlews, 'coons, and acres of 'gators still inhabit the
area. Wood storks still come fishing, and catfish barbels are
just as long. Some older citizens say the "chizzy-wink" insects
never allowed the dike to make a difference in their bites. And
Lake Okeechobee is still one of the best places in the world
to go freshwater fishing for largemouth bass and speckled
perch.

*What to See and Do:* This is the right place to be if you are
an angler. You will find marinas with boat ramps, slips, boat

sales, rentals, repairs, equipment, supplies, and guides for your successful fishing pleasure. You can take an airboat or canoe into isolated sections of the lake and adjoining rivers inaccessible to regular powerboats, or canoe on Fisheating Creek near US 27. If you are hiking, a 100-mile section of the Florida Trail circles the lake. Or you can visit a museum, like the Lawrence E. Will Museum in Belle Glade and the Cypress Knee Museum in Palmdale, and the Okeechobee Battlefield.

*Where to Begin:* Start this fishing or hiking adventure at any of twenty or more access points around the lake. Zachary Taylor Camping Resort on US 441, southeast in the town of Okeechobee, is a good north-side access area. It is situated at Taylor Creek near the Taylor Creek Access Area. On the south side, try Belle Glade Marina Campground on Torry Island, SR 717. A few of the many other possibilities are, clockwise from the north: Pahokee Marina and Campground, US 441; Crooked Hook Campground, Lake Harbor, US 27; La Master's Recreation Village, Moore Haven, off of First Street, in town; Buckhead Ridge Marina, SR 78, one mile west of Kissimmee River; and Okee-Tantie Recreation Area, SR 78, 5 miles west from the town of Okeechobee. These and other campgrounds may request reservations, particularly during the fall and winter season. Amtrak stops in the town of Okeechobee, and Palm Beach International Airport is about 50 miles from Pahokee and Belle Glade.

*About the Adventures:* If you plan in advance, call one or all of the five chambers of commerce—for the towns of Okeechobee, Pahokee, Belle Glade, Clewiston, and Moore Haven—for information on facilities that fit your plans and budget. Acquire two maps: "Welcome to Waterway Okeechobee," by the U.S. Army Corps of Engineers in Jacksonville (free by mail or at lake parks and marinas), and "Lake Okeechobee Fishing Map and Sportsman's Guide," provided by the Map Maker in Belle Glade. The latter has lake depth charts, island and canal locations, and helpful advertising of supplies and marinas. It is available for a small charge at the chambers of commerce, marinas, and local stores. (See

*Information*.) If you need a navigational map, ask for "Nautical Chart 11428" at the marinas.

After you arrive at a base camp, visit the Lawrence E. Will Museum at 530 South Main Street in Belle Glade. There you will find exhibits and displays of local pioneer history, and artifacts of the Calusa and Seminole Indians. Other information will provide you with an excellent introduction to the lake's history. The museum and library are open daily, except Sundays, 9 A.M. to 5 P.M. While you are driving, also consider getting better acquainted with the lake area by visiting nearby towns and the countryside. In the Belle Glade area alone, approximately 380,000 acres of sugarcane are planted in the "black gold" soil, formerly wet muckland. Locals also raise beef cattle, rice, and more than thirty winter vegetable crops. Clewiston, "America's Sweetest Town," west of Belle Glade, is the nation's leading producer and refining center for sugar. At the small town of Moore Haven, west from Clewiston, is the Corps of Engineers lock and dam for the coast-to-coast Okeechobee Waterway. The operations area is open daily for observation. Although Glades County is sparsely populated, the area produces high volumes of sugarcane, cattle, winter vegetables, and citrus. (Historically, Moore Haven is significant for having the state's first female town or city mayor, Marian Horwitz, in 1917.) If you drive north on SR 78, you will see many species of birds at the swampland of Fisheating Creek, and at the junction with SR 721 you could drive through the Brighton Seminole Indian Reservation. If you stay on SR 78 you will see parts of the largest palmetto forest in the state. At the northernmost end of the lake is the town of Okeechobee, "the Speckled Perch Capital of the World." It celebrates its title with an annual festival the third week in March. Between Taylor Creek and Nubbins Slough on US 98/441 is the site of the Battle of Okeechobee. Here in 1837 Colonel Taylor and his troop of 960 men advanced through the mud and saw grass to fight the Seminole leader, Coacoochee, and his 380 warriors. Colonel Taylor claimed victory, but his strategy cost him 27 dead and 112 wounded men, compared to 12 dead

Indians. Information about the battle is available at the museum of the Okeechobee County Historical Park on US 98, north. It is open Friday, Saturday, and Sunday afternoons. Completing the loop around the lake, you will pass through the small town of Pahokee, where you will find a park and a 125-foot observation pier that offer you the best views of the lake.

The first known human inhabitants of the lake area were the Calusa Indians. Archeologists have examined a series of mounds of the Glades period, 300 B.C. to A.D. 1600. Considered one of the finest examples of ceremonial earthwork in south Florida, Big Mound City is on private property about 10 miles east of Canal Point; another mound complex is in Fort Center, about 5 miles inland on Fisheating Creek from Lake Okeechobee; still another is Chosen Mounds, between Belle Glade and the lake, near the old Democrat River. One of the earliest reports on the Calusa and their villages in the lake area was from a Spanish youth, Escalente de Fontaneda, who was captured from a shipwreck by the Calusa in 1545. After his release 17 years later he wrote about the Calusa and their reference to *Mayaimi* (Lake Okeechobee).

Seminole Indians moved to the area in the eighteenth century and remained until the U.S. military either killed them in battle or paid bounty hunters to find them and relocate them in Oklahoma. Because the area was wet and easily flooded, white settlers did not move in until the last of the nineteenth century. A few hunters and fishermen came as early as the 1850s after word spread about the lake and General Taylor's Battle of Okeechobee in 1837. One hunter, Andrew P. Canova, said that he saw "turtles that paved the ground" on Observation Island. The first white settler at what is now the town of Okeechobee was Peter Raulerson in 1896 who built himself a log cabin by Taylor Creek and raised cattle. Lawrence E. Will and four other men were the first white settlers in the saw grass glades 4 miles south of the lake in 1913. They and the farmers who followed were proud of their land, as illustrated in a humorous parade tattoo chanted when Belle Glade was incorporated in 1928:

> I'm from old Lake Okeechobee
> Where they raise gators
> Beans and pertaters
> Catfish and termaters
> Prohibition haters.
> Custard apple, moonvine,
> Catfish moonshine
> All the time.

Lake Okeechobee, the second largest freshwater lake in the conterminous states, is in the middle of Florida's longest surface water flow. It is central to the concern and controversy of the twenty-first-century water-control projects of south Florida. From the north, as far as the Orlando area, the waters of the Kissimmee River and its tributaries drain into the lake. Some of the other natural sources on the north side of the lake are Popash and Nubbins sloughs and Taylor and Henry creeks. On the lake's west side, water sources are Indian Prairie and Harney Pond canals and Fisheating Creek. Rainfall, about 50 inches annually, is the lake's other source. Water from the lake flows southeast through the West Palm Beach, Hillsboro, North New River, and Miami canals. It also flows out the Caloosahatchee Canal on the west side and the Saint Lucie Canal on the east, particularly when the lake holds excess water. Before the canals were built, Lake Okeechobee drained slowly into the upper and lower Everglades, and sometimes flooded southeast Florida. An ancient sea shaped like a gargantuan saucer, it has been at the mercy of both floods from the Kissimmee Valley and storm winds. In 1928, hurricane winds first flooded the lake's north edge; then, as the eye of the hurricane passed and the winds changed direction, the south edge flooded, causing great loss of life.

The first artificial drainage of the immense water system began in 1881 when Hamilton Disston purchased 4 million acres of land from the state. Heir to the Keystone, Saw, Tool and File Works of Philadelphia, he invested in land south of

Orlando to 25 miles within the Everglades south of Lake Okeechobee, west to much of the Caloosahatchee River, and east almost to the Atlantic Ocean. He aimed to drain the wetlands, connect the lakes and rivers, and provide a coast-to-coast waterway from Fort Myers on the Gulf to Jacksonville on the Atlantic. Within 2 years he had cut canals between lakes in the Kissimmee River headwaters, making a radical change that lowered the lake levels as much as 8 feet. He straightened and dredged the Kissimmee River and contracted dredge crews from New Orleans to connect the Caloosahatchee River through Lake Hicpochee to Lake Okeechobee. This accomplishment made steamboat traffic possible from Fort Myers to the cattle town of Kissimmee, a number of years before the railroad arrived.

Among his other drainage plans, Disston intended to dredge a 70-mile channel from Lake Okeechobee to the headwaters of the Shark River in what is now Everglades National Park. Crew engineers started at Lake Okeechobee's south end, near Ritta Island, and followed the small Ritta River. After about 12 miles, the dredge hit limestone and the effort temporarily ceased. (Later the first 8 miles of this canal became part of the Miami Canal, which was directed southeast to the Miami River rather than into the heart of the Glades.) The national economic depression of 1893 and Disston's death 3 years later ended the ambitious plans of the Disston Land Company. Disston's family, never supportive of his development schemes for central Florida, allowed his vast properties, some of which were not so wet, to be sold for a fraction of their value.

But what Disston had not accomplished with private funds the state began to finance by 1913. To oversee the continued drainage of the wetlands, the state legislature, under the governorship of Napoleon B. Broward in 1907, created the Everglades Drainage District, a regional agency. With public funds the state constructed six major canals, a number of smaller water routes, sixteen locks and dams, and 440 miles of levees. During 1923–1925 the state built a 6-foot-high retaining levee around the south side of the lake, from Bacom Point to west of Moore Haven, to protect the farm settlements from floods like those of 1922 and 1924. In September 1926 a hurricane melted the muck and sand levee like sugar and drowned 243 inhabitants at Moore Haven. The state patched up the dike. Two years later, almost to the day, another powerful hurricane funneled the water into South Bay, breached the dike, and drowned approximately 2,000 residents and Bahamian sugarcane workers. Because of these disasters, the state created the Okeechobee Drainage District in 1929, and President Herbert Hoover and Congress had the U.S. Army Corps of Engineers build a 34-foot-high levee. Known as the Hoover Dike, it was constructed of rock, marl, and soil. Finally completed in 1971, it has since undergone additional reinforcement.

During the 1930s and half of the 1940s, droughts lowered water levels throughout the Kissimmee River–Lake Okeechobee–Everglades water flow. As a result, salt water began to intrude on the fresh water of the Miami River, other metropolitan shoreline areas, and the southern borders of the Biscayne Aquifer. Another hurricane and floods in 1947 shifted the water level to yet one more extreme, thus prompting Congress in 1948 to create the Central and Southern Florida Flood Control Project. In addition, the state created a control project. Among other things, it made Lake Okeechobee a significant water-storage area, where water was back-pumped if necessary into the lake.

This and other projects to control flood and drought affected Everglades National Park waters adversely. From 1954 to 1971 Congress authorized the Army Corps of Engineers to channelize the Kissimmee River from a shallow, crooked, 90-mile-long water source to a deeper 50-mile route. Five water impoundments with locks and stabilization systems were constructed. No sooner had it been completed than evidence showed that altering the natural flow of water had altered wildlife habitats and changed water quality. Attention was again focused on water management when the state's worst drought on record occurred in 1970–1971. The trophic change of Lake Okeechobee was severe enough to create public concern and a demand for investigations. By the late 1980s water was flowing in the original sections of the Kissimmee River and the channel.

Since the 1950s the federal and state governments have established conferences, plans, and projects to jointly control and utilize Lake Okeechobee waters. In 1976 the Central and Southern Florida Flood Control Project became South Florida Water Management District (SFWMD), the current administrative title. The district covers sixteen counties—all of the Kissimmee Valley and the south Florida region. Its jurisdiction is over 40 percent of the state's population and 30 percent of the state's land acreage. It must manage fresh water for cities, cattle farms, dairies, sugarcane farms, thirty-eight varieties of vegetable farm, fruit groves, and Everglades National Park. At Lake Okeechobee the Army Corps of Engineers operates and maintains the navigational locks and other primary structures around the lake, while the SFWMD operates and maintains secondary structures and pump stations.

The lake has a varied ecosystem of phytoplankton species, some of which are imports to the United States and others commonplace in a merger of middle and subtropical lakes. On the west side of the lake are large sections of marsh, grass, and hydrilla, with the largest concentration of marsh on the southwest corner. Water lilies flourish at some fringes of the grassy areas, and aquatic white-flowering duck potato and arrowhead are closer to shore. Growing on the west side banks of the dike are miles of naturalized Australian pine, Brazilian pepper, and punk tree. Because of their fast growth they require annual clearance from the base of the dike. Deer, raccoon, and wild turkey are resident inhabitants of the west side. Flocks of coots with white beaks and gallinules with red beaks, all nodding their heads while swimming, are prominent in the wet grassy areas. Egrets, herons, ibis, wood storks, anhingas, and limpkins are also on the water edges. In the spring and summer the swallow-tailed kite is prevalent, and in the summer migrant shorebirds—ducks, rails, and terns—are plentiful in the winter vegetable fields near Belle Glade; in winter large flocks of black and turkey vultures fly over the main dike and adjoining canal levees. Alligators, turtles, frogs, and snakes are among the reptiles and amphibians. The lake is well known for its largemouth bass and speckled perch, and other fish inhabit it as well. Other bass are the Suwannee, redeye, spotted, shoal, striped, white, sunshine, and butterfly peacock. Additionally, chain pickerel, bluegill, shellcracker, warmouth, sunfish (redbreast, redear, and spotted), and American shad live in the lake. The alligator gar is the largest fish there, and catfish (channel, white, and brown bullhead) are most commonly caught by commercial fishermen.

If you are a newcomer to fishing in the lake, you can receive information on lake weather conditions, game fish bag limits, prime fishing times, and equipment requirements from any local marina. The cost of an annual or week-long fishing license is moderate for residents and nonresidents. In addition to pleasure fishing, which takes in more than 1 million pounds annually, commercial fishing brings in more than 5 million pounds from the lake annually. Temperatures are moderate in the winter, with a few mornings in the 30s. You and each member of your craft will need to have a life jacket, and your boat must be equipped with a horn, throw cushion, signal device, paddle, and on boats 16 feet or longer, a fire extinguisher. All crafts must also have stern and bow lights, an anchor, and anchor rope. Local fishermen say the best time for fishing for largemouth bass is from February through May; for speckled perch (black crappie), November through March; for sunshine bass, November through March; and for bream (bluegill), May through September. If you wish to canoe in some of the marsh areas, ask at the marinas about rentals and appropriate route maps.

You can hike sections of the 110-mile loop Florida National Scenic Trail along the rim of Hoover Dike, or a complete loop that may take a week or more. (Or try a 9-mile spur trail that follows the canal rim of Nubbin Slough at its lake junction near the town of Okeechobee northwest to Cemetery Road.) If you wish to hike the entire distance, first request the maps listed in *Information*; they are your best guides to the lake, places, and services along the way. Chambers of commerce can offer you other details. In addition, the Florida Trail Association shows the route around the lake on county maps in its guide. Think about going in the dry season, usually between December and April, and call ahead to reserve a base campground. The nearest campgrounds on the trail are Zachary Taylor Camping Resort at the southeast edge of the town of Okeechobee; J and S Fish Camp, southeast of the town of Okeechobee; Pahokee Marina and Campground in Pahokee; Belle Glade Marina Campground on Torry Island; Angler's Marina and Campground in Clewiston; Uncle Joe's Fish Camp between Clewiston and Moore Haven; Moore Haven Recreation Village in Moore Haven's Aruba Camp Resort in Lakeport; and Okee-Tantie Recreation Area southwest of the town of Okeechobee. Other area campgrounds are listed in *Information*. Be sure you can leave your car or van safely at the campground parking area while you are gone, and if you hike only part of the trail and use a shuttle, arrange for the same security. You will need full hiking gear, a portable stove (open fires are not allowed on the dike), insect repellent, and sun protection. Dike campsites must be outside the boundaries of the locks, water gates, and pump stations, and should be as inconspicuous as possible on the lakeshore side. Although a permit is not required to hike the dike, it would be wise to inform personnel at your base campground of your itinerary. Except at access points where there are campgrounds, parks, or stores, there is no drinking water, so carry your own or plan to chemically treat or boil the lake water.

A good place to begin is the east side of Taylor Creek bridge, where you can organize your schedule at the Zachary Taylor Camping Resort close to stores and restaurants. Begin clockwise, south, following the access road by the lock to the dike, and turn left. After 2.4 miles, cross Nubbin Slough, the area of the Battle of Okeechobee described earlier in this chapter. You will notice a highway access and a 9-mile Florida Trail spur trail to your left. Continue on the dike another 3.4 miles and cross Henry Creek, where there is another access to the highway. From here it is 6.5 miles to Chancy Bay; here is a lock and pumping station S-135, one of nine around the lake. (The principal function of the pumps is to divert excess water from the drainage areas into Lake Okeechobee for storage and later use in dry periods.) A short access road here leads to the J and S Fish Camp (campsites, showers, a snack bar, and drinking water) on US 98/441.

From Chancy Bay to Port Mayaca the dike is an almost straight 7.5 miles. The distance seems less monotonous if you watch the egrets, herons, ibis, hawks, blue- and green-winged teals, wood ducks, and gallinules that frequent the lakeshore and canal side. It is not unusual to see armadillos and raccoons in the early morning. Wildflowers, such as morning glory, cassia, and pencil flower, blend with the thick grasses. From your lofty route you will also notice how isolated you are from others, though highway traffic is to your left and fishing boats are to your right. You have a clear view of the lake's horizon and private homes between you and the highway. By now you are aware of exposure to the sun, wind, and rain.

When you arrive at Port Mayaca lock, follow the access road to US 98/441 and cross the high bridge (under which passes the Saint Lucie Canal, part of Florida's only all-water route from the Atlantic to the Gulf). After crossing the bridge, descend and go under it at a junction with SR 76. Here is a store, Trading Post (canned groceries and drinking water), and, across the road, a county-maintained, sheltered picnic area. You have now hiked 20.6 miles.

To return to the dike, follow the paved access road south. East of the lake are expansive sugarcane fields extending to the horizon and a few citrus groves. Burning of excess sugarcane fodder sends billowing smoke up to color the rain clouds tan. On the lakeside the 7- to 10-foot-deep water is deeper than elsewhere on the lake's edge. After 4.7 miles you will pass a grassy access to the highway at Sand Cut, where you will notice family vegetable gardens and palm, orange, and banana trees. You will also pass another public-use access road at Canal Point (West Palm Beach Canal) after 3.9 miles. When you reach Pahokee public recreation area (showers, a laundry room, campsites, and drinking water), you will have hiked a total of 33 miles. Pahokee is an excellent place for you to camp by the lakeside and observe the lake at sunset from an observation pier. Two blocks east in town is a restaurant, drugstore, and grocery store.

Three miles from Pahokee you will observe Palm Beach County Glades Airport on the mainland, and Kreamer Island across Pelican Bay in the lake. Rardin Park, an access point to SR 715, is 3 miles ahead; it has sheltered picnic tables and drinking water in a shady grove of trees. Hike another 3.8 miles and turn right to cross the Torry Island bridge and reach Slim's Fish Camp, left. Near Slim's is Belle Glade Park and Recreation Area (a campground, showers, and laundry facilities). Request a short ferry to the other side of the gauging station of the Hillsboro and North New River canals. (Call Slim's before you start your hike to determine if someone at the marina can ferry you across. If Slim's cannot assist, ask a camper to drive you toward Belle Glade and back on the other side of the canal, a trip of about 10 miles.) After ferrying across to a rocky beach, you will soon turn west; from here it is 7.6 miles to Lake Harbor lock. On the way you will see the South Bay Park access area from US 27 to the lakeside of the levee.

On your immediate left is noisy four-lane US 27, and beyond it sugarcane fields stretch as far as you can see. On your right is the Rim Canal, an alternate route of the Okeechobee Waterway and a connector between the Saint Lucie Canal and the Caloosahatchee River Canal. On the lake you will see marshy islands, the largest of which is Grassy Island; Australian pine obstruct complete views. Arrive at the Miami Canal and Pumping Station in the community of Lake Harbor, called Ritta until 1931. Historically, this was the site of one of the first pioneer settlements on the lake's south side. In a landscape of palms is John H. Stretch Memorial Park (picnic tables, drinking water, and restrooms) on the west side of the canal. At this point you have accumulated 49.6 miles on your journey.

Soon you will see water and marshes on both sides of the dike as you approach Clewiston, the largest town along the trail route. When you leave the dike you will notice the South Florida Office of the U.S. Army Corps of Engineers, Jacksonville District. After crossing the canal bridge on US 27 (Sugarland Highway) you will see Donnelly's restaurant. Nearby is a grocery and drugstore. Return to the dike on the west side of Industrial Canal and pass Angler's Marina (a campground, showers, and drinking water). You have hiked 9 miles from Lake Harbor.

Ahead, the scenery changes. You will see thick vegetation of punk tree, popash, moonflower, and Brazilian pepper at the base of the levee, right, and asters in the thick grasses of the dike. Five miles from Clewiston you will be at Uncle Joe's Fish Camp, a serene place in a grassy field where you can camp, take a shower, and hear stories about Uncle Joe's Trail in the marshes. From here to SR 78 is a peaceful hike. You cannot see the lake because of marshes and trees, and the graveled treadway can twist an ankle, but views of the black-soil farmland on the dike's south side make this section of the trail worthwhile. There are honeybee hives on the dike slopes. Scarlet morning glory, puncture weed, and yellow Mexican poppy bloom among the dike grasses. When you reach the Moore Haven lock and Caloosahatchee River Canal, leave the dike on a stabilizing access road that connects to a paved road. Then turn west on US 27 and cross the canal bridge. At the corner of First Street is small, friendly, Moore Haven restaurant, and at your return to the dike on the west side of the lock is Moore Haven Recreation Village (sheltered picnic tables, a campground, and showers).

On the dike the treadway is gravel and the views south are across ranchlands, which replace the sugarcane fields for the remainder of the hike. After 3.6 miles the trail begins to parallel SR 78. This continues 2.7 miles to the junction with SR 78. (The dike across the road is a dead end.) Turn north on SR 78 and follow the highway 3 miles, across four bridges and through Curry Island marshlands. At the third bridge, cross Fisheating Creek. Immediately after the fourth bridge and wayside park, leave SR 78 in Lakeport and return to the dike rim, eastward. (Ahead, on SR 78, about 0.2 mile, are a grocery store and Aruba Camp Resort, with showers, a restaurant, and a laundry room.) You have now hiked 82.3 miles.

Continue on the dike and pass the marshes of Fisheating Bay. If you camp near the marshes at the base of the dike, you will be serenaded by frogs, insects, whippoorwills, and owls. Raccoon also inhabit the area. At Harney Pond Canal and access is Beck's grocery and snack bar. Nearby is also a laundry, restaurant, and bait and tackle store. Leave the highway and begin an 8.1-mile stretch of the trail to Indian Prairie Canal with a canal on the left and Australian pine on the right. Look for the rare snail kite, which has adopted the marshy side of the lake. Flocks of blackbirds and egrets fly back and forth across your path between the canal and the marshes. At 94.4 miles, cross the SR 78 bridge at Indian Prairie Canal and return to the lake. What you will see is a straight 5.8-mile trail. West of the dike are beautiful ranchlands and palm groves, and east of the dike are the marshlands.

Cross the Buckhead Ridge lock, and at 104.1 miles cross the Kissimmee River bridge to Okee-Tantie Recreation Area (a campground, a store, showers, and a restaurant). For the remaining miles of the loop you are likely to see an increase in waterfowl and rookeries of great blue heron in the dead Australian pines. Moonflowers blanket the understory. Soon you will have unobstructed views of the lake. When you pass the Bicentennial Park (sheltered picnic tables and a fishing pier) you will hear and see flocks of coots. From this access road is the intersection of SR 78 and US 98/441, and stores at the south edge of the town of Okeechobee. Arrive at the Taylor Creek pump station and take the access road to US 98/

441 and Zachary Taylor Camping Resort. You have completed a 110.9-mile journey around Florida's largest lake.

If you hike the spur trail that extends north from Nubbin Slough, follow the levee (the canal is L-63) on the west side one mile and turn left. (The Florida Trail Association requests that you have a membership card to protect you from trespass.) The canal parallels a railroad for 2.5 miles, crosses it and SR 710, and at 5.1 miles crosses SR 70. Take care to not disturb any gates, fences, or cattle. You will see meadowlarks, vultures, hawks, and other birds through an open area of scattered palm, cypress, and wax myrtle. After you ascend the west bank from US 70, follow the channel rim to Taylor Creek and complete the trail at Cemetery Road. Access to the north terminus from SR 70 and US 98/441 in downtown Okeechobee is by going north 2.6 miles on US 441 and turning right at the Okeechobee Missionary Baptist Church. After 0.1 mile on Cemetery Road, look for a locked gate, right, and an orange blaze.

For a backcountry adventure, a canoe trip on Fisheating Creek has long been popular with naturalists. The creek weaves through a dense forest of cypress, oaks, and orchids, birds and wildlife. For a number of years the Lykes Brothers provided tour guides, but the Fisheating Creek Campground and the tours are now restricted. Instead you can arrange canoe service from the adjoining Palmdale Campground in Palmdale. Access is on US 27, 0.8 mile north from the junction of SR 29 at Tom Gaskins Cypress Knee Museum. Take a few hours at the museum if you wish to see all the exhibits of natural sculpture, visit the craft shop, and take a walk on the boardwalk trail into the swamp of black gum, cypress, palms, and ferns. Palmdale is 17 miles from Moore Haven, west on US 27.

### *Information*

Counties: Okeechobee, Martin, Palm Beach, Hendry, Glades

Average Temperatures: January, 55.8°F (low), 81.1°F (high); August, 70.6°F (low), 91.3°F (high)

National Properties: Brighton Seminole Indian Reservation, Okeechobee, FL 33474; Okeechobee Waterway, US Army Corps of Engineers, 400 W. Bay St., Jacksonville, FL 32202, (904) 791-1133

Museums: Cypress Knee Museum, Palmdale, FL 33944, (813) 675-2951; Lawrence E. Will Museum, 530 S. Main St., Belle Glade, FL 33430, (407) 996-3453; Okeechobee County Historical Park, US 98 and NW 18th St., Okeechobee, FL 34974, (813) 763-6464

Chambers of Commerce: Belle Glade CC, 540 S. Main St., Belle Glade, FL 33430, (407) 996-2745; Clewiston CC, P.O. Box 275, Clewiston, FL 33440, (813) 983-7979; Glades County CC, P.O. Box 490, Moore Haven, FL 33471, (813) 946-0440; Okeechobee County CC, 55 S. Parrott Ave., Okeechobee, FL 34974, (813) 763-6464; Pahokee CC, 115 E. Main St., Pahokee, FL 33476, (407) 942-5579

Services and Amenities: *City, County, and Commercial Campgrounds:* Angler's Marina and Campground, 910 Okeechobee Blvd., Clewiston, FL 33440, (813) 983-2128/7330; Aruba Camp Resort, Rte. 2, Box 11B, Lakeport, FL 33471, (813) 946-1324; Belle Glade Marina Campground, 110 .SW Ave. East, Belle Glade, FL 33430, (407) 996-6322; Buckhead Ridge Marina, Rte. 4, Box 670, Okeechobee, FL 34974, (813) 763-2826/8998; Crooked Hook Campground, P.O. Box 56, Lake Harbor, FL 33459, (813) 983-7112; J and S Fish Camp, Rte. 1, Box 1340, Okeechobee, FL 34974, (407) 597-9938; KOA–Clewiston/Lake Okeechobee, Clewiston, FL 33440, (813) 983-7078; Moore Haven Recreation Village, P.O. Box 1064, Moore Haven, FL 33471, (813) 946-2181, (800) 445-7407; Okee-Tanti Recreation Area, SR 78 West, Okeechobee, FL 34974, (813) 763-2622/8632; Pahokee Marina and Campground, P.O. Box 929, Pahokee, FL 33476, (407) 924-7832; Palmdale Campground (at Fisheating Creek on US 27), P.O. Box 298, Palmdale, FL 33944, (813) 675-1852; Slim's Fish Camp, P.O. Box 250, Belle Glade, FL 33430, (407) 996-3844; Zachary Taylor Camping Resort, 2995 US 441, SE, Okeechobee, FL 34974, (813) 763-3377; Uncle Joe's Fish Camp,

Rte. 3, Box 221, Moore Haven, FL 33471, (813) 983-9421/4818

*Airboat Guides:* Captain Tom, 200 SR 78, Okeechobee, FL 34974, (813) 763-2700; *Boat and Canoe Rentals:* contact chambers of commerce; *Fishing Guides:* contact chambers of commerce; *Maps:* Okeechobee Waterway, US Army Corps of Engineers, 400 W. Bay St., Jacksonville, FL 32202, (904) 791-1133; The Map Maker, P.O. Box 407, Belle Glade, FL 33430, (407) 996-3462; Recreation Guide to Lake Okeechobee, South Florida Water Management District, P.O. Box 24680, West Palm Beach, FL 33416, (407) 686-8000; *Restaurants:* Donnelly's, 842 E. Sugarland Hwy., Clewiston, FL 33440, (813) 983-8119; Moore Haven Restaurant, US 27 and First St., Moore Haven, FL 33471, (813) 946-2929

## BIG CYPRESS SWAMP

In a 2,400-square-mile section of subtropical Florida, limestone bedrock under sand, peat, and marl supports a unique ecosystem of prairies, cypress strands, pinelands, and hardwood hammocks: This is Big Cypress National Preserve. Flat and wet most of the year, except in winter, the limitless sweeps of saw grass and dwarf cypress are filled with air plants, orchids, butterflies, birds, and aquatic life. They and the largest forest of royal palm in Fakahatchee Strand State Preserve are part of a larger domain, the Big Cypress Swamp. The preserve, established in 1974, has only two major roads, I-75 in the northern half, and US 41 in the southern half, both east-west in the center of south Florida. Its most distinguishable water veins are sloughs—Gum, Lostmans, Dixons—through which fresh water moves slowly to the Gulf. Bordered by the even more remote Everglades on the east and south, the preserve is best explored from its foot trails and infinite water routes.

*What to See and Do:* The most challenging adventure is backpacking the 38-mile section of the Florida National Scenic Trail that snakes from the preserve's southernmost terminus on CR 94 to I-75 north. Each day of your hike you will see wildlife (perhaps the rare snail kite or a more common giant water bug) and a wide range of plants. You can also follow a backcountry road on a swamp buggy, or a water route on an airboat, with permits. Hunting, fishing, and frogging are allowed with appropriate licenses. In addition you can visit the Miccosukee Indian villages and roadside parks on US 41 (the Tamiami Trail), and the Fakahatchee Strand State Preserve in the western part of the Big Cypress Swamp.

*Where to Begin:* For information, first go to the park headquarters on US 41, 2.7 miles east of Carnestown (and 1.6 miles west of Ochopee) at the SR 29 junction. The Oasis Ranger Station is 18.5 miles east of park headquarters and 17.4 miles west of the Miccosukee Indian Reservation (near Sharks Valley). When you hike overnight on the Florida Trail, it is recommended that you leave your car at the Oasis Ranger Station and arrange for a shuttle from the trail's south or north terminus. The nearest airports to the park headquarters are Miami International, 70 miles east, and Naples Municipal, 34 miles west.

*About the Adventures:* Without Florida's commercial ambitions in 1968 to build a colossal jetport and super-city at the western edge of the Everglades, the public might have been slower to rally for federal protection of Big Cypress Swamp. Public outcry resulted in the abandonment of the jetport plans and the beginning of an unusual role for the National Park Service. Instead of adding the area to Everglades National Park, whose boundary was only 7 miles southeast of the jetport site, Congress created the Big Cypress Swamp National Preserve in 1974. The 570,00-acre preserve includes 40 percent of the larger Big Cypress Swamp, which covers half the width of south-central Florida. The category of preserve allows for more liberal restrictions than in a park: Hunting could continue; private landowners could retain their homes, hunting lodges, and remote airstrips; off-road vehicles with permits could roam the saw grass (even churn the Florida Trail in crossing it, but not follow it); oil and gas sources could be explored; and cattle grazing could continue—all things that might be permitted in a national forest but not in a national park. But in the compromise, however unsatisfactory to both commercial developers and environmental leaders, ecosystems of the Everglades and the Big Cypress Swamp were protected. The jetport dream has boiled down to a single 2-mile airstrip at the Fifty Mile Bend on US 41 that commercial air pilots use for instrument training. The airfield is closed to the public, and white ibis fly over the tarmac in sweeping multisquadrons more frequently than airplanes.

Frontiersmen timbered much of the preserve in the 1930s and 1940s when they went deep into the swamp for the tall bald cypress with flared bases. Of the 600- to 700-year-old trees, only a few remain. The name of the swamp developed not from the size of these big trees, but from the tremendous expanse of cypress wetlands. Other cypress varieties, such as dwarf pond, cover nearly one third of the preserve in two types of growth: trees of the same height in immensely wide, wet, flat strands; and trees that vary in height and form dome-shaped groves. The dome shape is a result of water pockets in which the tallest trees grow in the center where the water is deepest. The trees shed their needlelike leaves in the winter, creating a ghostly gray landscape. Marl prairies and flat pinelands are the other most common ecosystems. Saw grass is common in the prairies, and slash pine grows above saw palmetto on earth that is usually not flooded. In some low sandy peat bogs are popashes, and a few higher bogs have stately royal palm and lustrous gumbo-limbo. Hardwood hammocks are sparse, with the larger ones in the northern half of the preserve. This diverse world of grasses and sedges, shrubs and trees, and wet and dry ground is home to the nearly extinct Florida panther. (See *Wildlife*, Chapter 1.)

The south boundary of the preserve is at Everglades National Park, a section mainly of mangrove swamps into which flow Turner River, New River, and many sloughs. On the east is the Everglades, whose water flow is critical to the park south of US 41, a river of grass and a wildlife management area. To the northeast is more state property and the Florida State Miccosukee Indian Reservation, and north is the Big Cypress Seminole Indian Reservation. The west boundary parallels SR 29, a straight south-north highway between the preserve and the Fakahatchee Strand State Preserve. Through the north of the preserve is toll I-75 (SR 84, Alligator Alley). A number of overpasses on I-75 allow water and wildlife—particularly the endangered Florida panther—to pass freely. Cutting through the south from Naples to Miami is US 41 (the Tamiami Trail) built in 1928. On US 41 you will see more of the diverse preserve with easier access than elsewhere. Along it are scattered craft and service stores at Indian villages, Indian guides for airboat tours into preserve waters, small roadside parks, and a number of entrances for primitive camping, fishing, or wildlife watching. The highway has two lanes heavily traveled and slick when wet, and speed laws are consistently violated. Billboards mar the natural beauty but make useful perches for some birds, like anhingas that dry their wings on the signs that say "Beer Worm." Signs also warn of panther crossings, but drivers do not slow down and the big cats cannot read. Because their curiosity attracts them to automobile lights, the animals are in more danger after dark; at the same time, birders and night wildlife watchers must pay attention more to traffic than to their cameras.

On the north side of the highway is a canal where you are likely to see plenty of waterfowl: black-crowned night-herons; great blue, little blue, green-backed, and tricolor herons; snowy, cattle, and great egrets; bitterns; anhingas; wood storks; white ibis; limpkins; and also warblers, sparrows, hawks, and many others. You are most likely to see the endangered snail kite (*Rostrhamus sociabilis*) in winter on this highway, a few miles west of and at the Miccosukee village and restaurant. The kite's survival depends on its food source of apple snails. While in flight, the gray brown bird snatches the snail with its talons and ascends (like a kite, hence its name) to perch on the top of a nearby marsh willow. It uses its sharp, curved beak to extract the snail from its shell. Unlike its look-alike, the marsh hawk, which primarily eats rodents, the kite chooses only apple snails. In dry seasons, raccoons and other wildlife also eat the snails. When airboats depress or tilt the marsh grass, the apple snails are more exposed for predators, further endangering the snail kite. While looking at the birds along US 41, you will see alligators and turtles, and possibly snakes, river otters, and frogs.

Fast travelers on US 41 may miss two roads worth exploring. The westernmost graded dirt SR 839 (Turner River Road), 4 miles east of park headquarters at H. P. Williams Roadside Park, goes straight north 22 miles on the left side of Turner River Canal. It is passable during all seasons but may be dusty in winter and muddy in summer. From this quiet road you can watch wildlife, mainly waterfowl, in areas of cypress, grassy prairies, and pinelands. The road ends at Bear Island, a primitive campground. The other backroad to explore is the 23-mile CR 94 (Loop Road) between Monroe Station, 4 miles west of Oasis Ranger Station, and Forty Mile Bend, 15 miles east of the station; CR 94 is paved for the first 8 miles, from Forty Mile Bend to a small settlement called Pinecrest. Here is the Everglades–Big Cypress Loop Road Interpretive Center in the Tamarind Hammock. Groups use the center, open to the public, primarily for educational sessions about the preserve. The remainder of the road can be exceptionally rough and flooded in the rainy season and is not well suited for low passenger cars. The Florida National Scenic Trail has its southernmost terminus on this road.

Other good places from which to watch wildlife are the junction of SR 839 at the Turner River Canal and H. P. Williams Roadside Park (a picnic area 4 miles east of park headquarters) and Kirby Storter Roadside Park (a picnic area and boardwalk nature trail, from which you may see a playful otter sliding over the logs) 11.4 miles east of park headquarters. Primitive camping without a fee is permitted at the following locations east of park headquarters: Ochopee, 2.8 miles, right; Burns Lake, 6 miles, left; Monument Lake, 13.5 miles, left; and Midway, 21.3 miles, right (2.7 miles east of Oasis Ranger

Station). In addition you can camp at a number of unmaintained turn-offs on the south side of the highway if you remain out of sight of the highway. There are also two fine full-service campgrounds near the Big Cypress Swamp area. Nearest is a private facility, Barren River Marina and Campground, on the river side as you enter Everglades City on SR 29. The campground also has cottages and other housing. Collier-Seminole State Park is the public campground on US 41, 15.4 miles west of the SR 29 junction at Carnestown and 15 miles east of Naples. Either would be a good base camp for your journeys into Big Cypress Swamp and the western part of Everglades National Park.

Hiking all or part of the 38-mile Florida National Scenic Trail can be the highlight of your explorations in the preserve. The trail is orange blazed, except for blue-blazed alternate routes north of the Oasis Ranger Station. There are four designated campsites, each with a hand-lever well pump, but depending on your schedule you may have to use whatever dry place and water source you can find. If possible, arrange a vehicle shuttle to the south terminus on CR 94, and have your vehicle parked at the Oasis Ranger Station if you plan to camp overnight on the first 8.3 miles. This arrangement would also allow you to make a loop on the north section of the trail rather than use another shuttle at I-75. Overnight parking at either CR 94 or I-75 is at your own risk. The best time to hike is between January and April, during the dry season, when there are fewer bugs and the hunting season is over. March is the driest month. In some years rainfall exceeds the average 55–60 inches, causing rainwater absorption in the porous limestone later in winter. Regardless of the season, prepare to face some wet spots, particularly near the north section of the preserve, and realize in advance that you will get your feet wet occasionally. Most backpackers agree that taking a second pair of hiking boots and plenty of dry socks is wise. To minimize the discomfort of mosquitoes and other biting insects, wear light, long trousers, long-sleeve shirts, and a cap; use an insect repellent; and sleep in a tent. On some windy days and at dry places, mosquitoes are surprisingly absent in the swamp. Other articles to bring are a compass, a preserve map, and, if you desire detail, USGS topo maps of Monroe Station NE and Immokalee 4 SE and NE. Take a portable stove for food preparation and trash bags to pack out what you pack in. Also note that being in a swamp does not necessarily mean drinking water will be easily accessible. Pumps will probably need to be primed. To accomplish this, use the container at the base of the pump, which former campers should have left filled with water. Pour the water in the plunger opening at the top of the pump and begin pumping after it settles. Be sure to leave water for the next camper. (If no container with water is there on your arrival, later inform the park ranger or contact the Florida Trail Association. You might also take at least a one-gallon plastic container, with a screw top, filled with fresh water in case of such a problem.) If water is not available at the wells, you will need to find another source and chemically treat or boil the water. Although you do not need a permit to hike the trail, you should inform park headquarters or the staff at the ranger station of your overnight plans. For the record it would help the Florida Trail Association if you would sign the register at the west side of the parking lot, near the telephone booth, at the Oasis Ranger Station.

To begin at the southern terminus, go east 15.4 miles from the Oasis Ranger Station (or 21.5 miles west from the US 41 and SR 997 junction at Sweetwater) to Forty Mile Bend at the Indian Trail Baptist Church and junction with CR 94. Follow CR 94 (Loop Road) for 15 miles, of which the first 8 miles are paved. The other 7 miles are on a narrow, rocky road filled with potholes. Exit on US 41 at Monroe Station. Look for an orange blaze and a sign (which may have been vandalized) on the right. Off-road vehicles are not allowed within this section. Here the treadway is a combination of soft loam, marl, and hard, ragged limestone. In the winter you will see glade lobelias (a common, strongly zygomorphic, lavender flower), horned bladderworts, and patches of bayberry and willows. Grass is above your knees through long stretches of dwarf pond cypress. Quill-leaf, wild pine, and other epiphytes look like ruffled birds clinging to cypress for as far as you can see. For the first 3 miles on the trail, follow an old tram road (Sawmill Road) rough with limestone. Leave the old road, left, at a campsite and well, and go north 2 miles to a grassy lake area at Roberts Lake Strand. Turn left (west), but after 0.8 mile turn sharply right onto a less distinctive route. Now go straight north for the final 2.5 miles of this section. Along the way you will notice wildflowers and many wildlife trails that crisscross the Florida Trail. Exit at US 41, across the road from the Oasis Ranger Station.

Continue on the Florida Trail at the west corner of the parking lot of the ranger station and follow through an open area for 0.5 mile. On your left is a swamp area usually filled with a wide range of aquatic life and from which white ibis noisily swoop skyward to the treetops at the slightest disturbance. Here you may notice the first indication that the trail has been damaged by crisscrossing swamp buggies. Soon you are in the forest with dense saw palmetto, and the trail is more distinctive. Because hikers use this section more than the south section, you will notice an increase in footprints and signs of effort to jump or go around water and mud holes. A blue-blazed trail forks left 2.9 miles from the highway. (This alternate route of 9.5 miles is 1.6 miles shorter than the main trail. It can be used as part of a scenic loop.) Continue right on the orange-blazed trail that leads, after 4 miles, to Seven-Mile Camp, a natural area among slash pine and saw palmetto where you will find a well pump.

By this point you will have seen or heard a variety of the preserve's plant, aquatic, and terrestial wildlife. In the water pockets are crayfish, tiny crustacea, giant water bugs, red water mites, water scorpions, turtles, fisher spiders, and damselflies. In some of the sloughs are glass shrimp and gambusia. Deep in the swamp you may hear, see, or at least notice evidence of marsh rabbits, anoles, deer, foxes, pileated woodpeckers, barred owls, wood ducks, frogs, otters, turkeys, raccoons, and alligators. Black bears have a tendency to investigate campsites; even if you do not see one you may see the tracks. It is extremely unlikely you will see the paw prints of the Florida panther. Snakes reported seen on the trail are the Florida king, green, and peninsula ribbon snakes. Rarely are hikers bitten, but poisonous snakes—the dusty pigmy rattlesnake, which often bites with the slightest provocation, and the cottonmouth, identified by its light tan or creamy white scales on the mouth edges—are along the route. Recently, preserve personnel report, eastern diamondback rattlers have been seen. The dry season usually draws many animals to alligator holes, pools formed when alligators clear the peat and vegetation from limestone depressions. Here the classical food chain is evident, with the alligator getting the last meal. (See *Everglades National Park*, this Chapter.) Birds make considerable noise, and some make startling sounds, such as the wail of the limpkin and the scream of the red-shouldered hawk. These and other birds will not let you forget that you are a visitor to their world.

From Seven-Mile Camp, about 0.1 mile farther, a 2.3-mile blue-blazed connector trail, left, leads to the alternate blue-blazed trail. After another 3 northeasterly miles the main trail comes to another campsite and well. From here you soon turn north, and after another 4 miles you reach the north end of the alternate trail. From here you can continue north on the main trail 2.7 miles to another campsite, or continue 13 miles beyond that to I-75, or return on the blue-blazed alternate trail for a loop total of 26.4 miles. If you continue to I-75, you will see signs of off-road vehicle usage, pass through hardwood hammocks and cabbage palm groves, and enter the wettest parts of the entire trail in the Bamboo Strand. (The access to I-75 has been fenced, so hikers may not have passage in this part of the Florida Trail. Hikers should make an inquiry of the trail's condition and exit to I-75 from the Oasis Ranger Station on US 41 before planning a hike through.) At the north terminus on I-75 you are 0.3 mile east of milepost 38, and 0.7 mile west of milepost 39.

*Florida panther, Big Cypress Swamp.* PHOTO BY Florida
Game and Fresh Water Fish Commission.

Before you leave the preserve, take a side trip to the
57,850-acre Fakahatchee Strand State Preserve. Entrance is at
Copeland, 2.5 miles north on SR 29 from its junction with US
41 at Carnestown. Drive northwest on W. J. Janes Scenic Drive
and stop after 3 miles at the preserve headquarters office,
right. The preserve is known for its habitat of black bear, fox
squirrel, and Florida panther. Because the Florida panther
feeds on deer, more of the endangered cats live in the
Fakahatchee and the Florida Panther NWR north of I-75 than
in Big Cypress National Preserve, where hunters are allowed
to kill the deer. Wildlife you are likely to see are hawks,
warblers, owls, woodpeckers, deer, and raccoons. Some
ornithologists also claim to have seen the rare short-tailed
hawk near the entrance of the preserve. Plant life is similar to
that of Big Cypress National Preserve except that the
Fakahatchee has little pineland. On the west boundary is a
streak of hardwood hammocks, and about 7 miles in from the

road is one of the forest's prides, Florida's largest and oldest stand of royal palm. You will see other tall royal palms from the road and can explore the old gated tram roads. After 5.5 miles you approach private property at a canal. Beyond is a testimony to what greed and disregard for natural resources can produce; you might wonder if the miles of abandoned streets and canals will someday become the super-city of western Big Cypress Swamp that was halted at the jetport.

### *Information*

Counties: Collier, Dade, Monroe

Average Temperatures: January, 56°F (low), 76°F (high); August, 75°F (low), 90°F (high)

National Properties: Big Cypress National Preserve, Star Rte., Box 110, Ochopee, FL 33943, (813) 695-2000/262-1066; Florida Panther National Wildlife Refuge, 2629 S. Horseshoe Dr., Naples, FL 33942, (813) 643-2636; Loop Road Interpretive Center, (813) 695-4111; Oasis Ranger Station, (813) 695-4111

State Properties: Collier-Seminole State Park, Rte. 4, Box 848, Naples, FL 33962, (813) 394-3397; Fakahatchee Strand State Preserve, P.O. Box 548, Copeland, FL 33926, (813) 695-4593

Chamber of Commerce: Everglades Area CC, P.O. Box 130, Everglades City, FL 33929, (813) 695-3941

Services and Amenities: *Commercial Campground:* Barren River Marina and Campground, P.O. Box 116, Everglades City, FL 33929, (813) 695-3591/3331

*Adventure Tours:* All Florida Adventure Tours (including Big Cypress Swamp and Corkscrew Swamp Sanctuary), 11137 N. Kendall Dr., D105, Miami, FL 33176, (305) 270-0219; Miccosukee Indian Village and Airboat Riders, US 41, P.O. Box 440021, Miami, FL 33144, (305) 223-8380/8388; Wooten's Air Boat Tours, Ochopee, FL 33943, (813) 695-2781; *Restaurant:* Miccosukee Restaurant, US 41, (305) 233-8380; *Trail Information:* Florida Trail Association, P.O. Box 13708, Gainesville, FL 32604, (904) 378-8823, or (800) 343-1882 in Florida

## THE SHELL COAST

Southwest Florida, the "Shell Coast," first seen by Spaniard Ponce de León in 1512 and explored by him in 1521, has more islands than any other region in the state. One group of red mangrove islands, between Marco Island and Everglades National Park, is called Ten Thousand Islands. Other thousands cluster, large and miniscule, among bays, rivers, and lakes, and south to Florida Bay. Major barrier isles with white sand beaches stretch from Gasparilla Island in Charlotte Harbor south to Marco Island near Cape Romano. Boca Grande Pass at Gasparilla Island is known as the "tarpon capital of the world"; Cayo Costa, North Captiva, Captiva, and Sanibel islands are known for their island preservation and four hundred species of shells; and Pine Island, the largest bay island, and Mound Key are among the islands once inhabited by the now-extinct Calusa Indians, a tall, fierce tribe whose poison arrows killed Ponce de León. On the mainland is the wide Caloosahatchee River, which harbors endangered manatees and empties into San Carlos Bay between Cape Coral and Fort Myers, the "City of Palms." A few miles east of Bonito Springs is the priceless Corkscrew Swamp Sanctuary; east of Marco Island is another natural treasure, Collier-Seminole State Park and Wilderness Preserve; and between Marco Island and Naples is the National Estuarine Sanctuary.

*What to See and Do:* The Shell Coast's wildlife refuges, sanctuaries, preserves, parks, and nature centers are all features worth visiting. Journeys may range from short visits to wildlife centers and indoor museums to overnight adventures with backpacks on land trails or to canoe trips. Adventures hiking, fishing, canoeing, sailing, other types of boating, birding, bicycling, and shelling may take weeks to complete. There are uncrowded beaches, such as Cayo Costa State Preserve, an unspoiled area for shelling, hiking, and beachcombing. There are wilderness camping and backpacking on the same trail with black bears in the Collier-Seminole State Park, and a canoe trip that independently and adventurously takes you to the most secret of islands.

*Where to Begin:* Choose a base camp before finalizing plans for your adventures to the islands and the mainland backcountry. Among the twenty-plus full-service commercial campgrounds, two are suggested for their central secluded locations, and two public park campgrounds are recommended for the same reasons. Woodsmoke Camping Resort is at Estero (at the southern edge of Fort Myers), and Koreshan State Historic Site Campground is 2 miles farther south. Both are off the west side of US 41, accessible from I-75, Exit 19, west on Corkscrew Road. The other campgrounds, farther south, are peaceful Naples KOA, in a tropical setting off the west side of SR 951 and south from its junction with US 41 near Belle Meade, and a campground among royal palms at Collier-Seminole State Park, 8 miles farther south on US 41. The nearest airport is Southwest Florida Regional 10 miles south of Fort Myers and 25 miles north of Naples.

*About the Adventures:* If you camp at Estero, your first journeys could be to the Webb Wildlife Management Area to look for red-cockaded woodpecker colonies, and an unforgettable swamp-buggy trip into Telegraph Swamp in Babcock Wilderness. Drive north on I-75 to Exit 27 and Tucker Grade. Turn right, and after 0.4 mile you will see the C. M. Webb WMA office, left. The 65,343-acre preserve offers options for boating (gasoline motors prohibited), fishing for largemouth bass, and camping near elongated Webb Lake. Hunting and frogging are also allowed with appropriate licenses. Or watch for red-cockaded woodpeckers, deer, coyotes, armadillos, and white-winged doves from either of two roads, Oilwell Grade or Tram Grade, both near the office but north of Tucker Grade. From here drive 12.5 miles east on Tucker Grade, a straight back road, to SR 31. (Inquire at the WMA office about road conditions.) At SR 31 you are at the Babcock Crescent Ranch, but enter only where the sign welcomes you to Babcock Wilderness Adventures. The gate will be locked except during tour hours (usually from 8 A.M. to 5 P.M.). Reservations and admission fee are required; group rates can be arranged. (See

*Information.*) The adventure is on the private 90,000-acre Babcock ranch, purchased for forestry development in 1914. Your tour guide will drive a custom-built swamp buggy and show you wildlife, wild plants, and a Cracker cowmen ranch house. Also a part of the trip will be colorful stories about the rugged backcountry and its early settlers. As you advance deeper into the swamps and oak hammocks, you are close to swamp lilies (*Crinum americanum*), climbing aster, and fire flag. The guide maneuvers the large but remarkably quiet vehicle through the water and prairies, where you may see paper hornet, otter, bear, alligator, deer, fox, and wild turkey. It is not unusual to see a rattlesnake, but your high observation seat will offer security as you watch the guide leave the buggy to demonstrate his skill and become better acquainted with the long, fat reptile. The closest wildlife to you may be the yellow cabbage and yellow dogface butterflies and the Isabella moths, whose favorite trees seem to be the tupelo and willows. Before you leave the ranch you may see armadillos and wild hogs, and the trip would not be complete without touching some of the horses or cattle.

After you leave the ranch, follow SR 31 south 8 miles and take a scenic drive east on CR 78 to La Belle. Along the 25-mile route are a number of historic sites where you can get a feel for the life-style of early Florida settlements. After the first 5 miles, stop at the W. D. Franklin Lock and Dam, right, on the Caloosahatchee River (part of the Okeechobee Waterway, the only cross-state canal route), where you will find a public campground, launching ramp, and picnic area. About 1.5 miles beyond the lock you will cross Fichter Creek bridge. If you look closely, a few yards left after the Fichter Creek Road, you will see state property signs. Here is an undeveloped natural area among trees, grasses, and wildflowers, and a Brazilian pepper–arched jeep road.

Continue now on CR 78, and stop at the pioneer town of Alva and visit its century-old country store and museum. Your next stop is at the junction of CR 78 and 78A (5.7 miles west of La Belle) at the Turnstile Bridge. The bridge is one of only a few such types, partly operated by hand, left in the state. Across the Caloosahatchee River is Fort Denaud, the site of an outpost used by U.S. troops in the Second Seminole War to protect settlers from the Indians. When you reach the junction with SR 29 in La Belle, turn right, cross the bridge to Barron Park, and take a rest. In La Belle the Swamp Cabbage Festival is held the last weekend in February. Since 1967 the festival has highlighted pioneer life with parades, rodeos, arts and crafts, and delicacies of hearts of palm from the state tree, the cabbage palmetto (*Sabal palmetto*). La Belle is named for Laura, Lee, and Belle, the three daughters of pioneer leader and Confederate cattleman Capt. Francis A. Hendry, for whom the county is named. One of the largest oaks you will see in southwest Florida is at the historic clock-tower courthouse. The La Belle area was once the site of seasonal religious rites by the Calusa Indians, whose last known descendants emigrated to the Bahamas in the 1760s. In the 1820s the Seminole Indians who had migrated from north Florida settled in the area.

Return to Fort Myers on SR 80, and in your approach to Orange River canal and I-75 stop at the Florida Power and Light power plant to watch the manatees that come in for warmer water in the winter months. According to some reports, as many as two hundred of the endangered mammals have been seen here in the plant's water discharge. Park on the south side of SR 80.

On your trip to Pine Island, your fastest route from Estero is to go north on I-75, cross the Caloosahatchee River bridge, and take Exit 26 to SR 78, Pine Island Road, west. On your route you will cross the Matlacha Pass Aquatic Preserve causeway to Little Pine Island, then to Pine Island and a junction with CR 767 (Stringfellow Road). Turn right (north), and after 4 miles turn left (west), to Pineland. From Pineland Marina you can launch your own boat, rent a boat, or arrange for a guide to take you across Pine Island Sound to explore the barrier islands and sound islands. Or, you can choose to take the *Tropic Star* cruise boat to stay for a day or overnight.

Bay Services operates the boat, and the staff will assist you in plans for lodging at inns, cabins, and campsites and for activities such as bird-watching. The usual departure from Pineland is at 9:30 A.M. with a return at 4:00 P.M. Call in advance to inquire about weather, necessary reservations, and fishing conditions. Bay Services can also arrange for water taxi service to Boca Grande Pass and Port Boca Grande at the south tip of Gasparilla Island, where you can see at the historic lighthouse and assistant keeper's quarters (1890).

Johnson Shoals, on the north tip of Cayo Costa (a large undeveloped barrier island), is a splendid unspoiled area for shelling. At Cayo Costa State Park, south of the shoals, is another good place for finding whelks, coquinas, lucinas, scallops, olives, cockles, and the more unique murices, spiny jewel boxes, tulips, and nautiluses. Here, as on other islands in the area, shelling is best in the winter or after a storm. Cayo Costa has clean beaches, mangrove swamps, live oaks, and palms, and you may see colorful frigate birds and rookeries of brown pelicans. On Cabbage Key, a popular island for tourists, there is a restaurant papered with dollar bills and with worldwide autographs on the walls and ceiling. The key's modern history began in 1938 when mystery novelist and playwright Mary Roberts Rinehart built a retreat there. Now you can arrange for lunch or dinner, stay at the Cabbage Key Inn near the Intracoastal Waterway, and hike the short nature trails.

Historic Pine Island, famous for its bald eagles, has its own worthwhile places for you to visit. Near the marina at Pineland is the site of a major pre-Columbian Indian religious center, thought to be one of the largest and oldest villages of the Calusa Indians. Mounds that form a complex of pyramids and other elevations are believed to have been significant for religious purposes. A large canal excavation by the Indians connected the site with Matlacha on the eastern shore of the island. Archeologist Frank Cushing began excavating in 1895. Private homes are now on top of some of the mounds. A drive among the avocado groves and lush forests will take you 3 miles north on CR 767 to Bokeelia, where the Crab Shack, an informal old house with exceptional views of Charlotte Harbor, can offer you home-cooked seafood. Nearby, the Bokeelia Seaport Pier provides excellent fishing.

As you head south on CR 767 to Saint James City you will come to Demere Key in Pine Island Sound. The key has several high mounds on a flat, truncated temple pyramid, parts of which were made with conch shells by the Calusa between A.D. 800 and A.D. 1700; this is one of the best examples of the remains of a Calusa settlement in the Shell Coast area. It is on private property but is accessible by boat or on a narrow causeway, 1.5 miles south of the junction with SR 78. Another privately owned island on the National Register of Historic Places, like Demere Key, is Josslyn Island, halfway between Demere and the Pineland Marina. Deep channels divide Josslyn's central plaza mounds. In Saint James City are fine seafood restaurants with the same home-style service as at Bokeelia. At the end of CR 767 you can see terns, gulls, ducks, and many species of shorebirds. If you did not see the Sandy Hook Crab House at Matlacha on the way in, look for it on your way out. The Crab House serves good food and displays natural nautical artifacts.

Your next island journey is to Sanibel and Captiva islands, a pair of barrier islands united at a narrow pass by the Turner bridge. Geographically, the islands are about 5,000 years old; they may have once been a single island. Gulf tides and currents rolled and swept thousands of tons of seashells to help form the island of Sanibel, developed from an east-west sandbar. In time, vegetation developed in the silt, and freshwater pools and sloughs became part of the topography. Calusa Indians lived on the island as early as A.D. 600 and were there when the Spanish first saw the islands in the early sixteenth century. According to one theory, the Spanish originally named the island Santa Isabella, which later became Sanibel. The adjoining island, Captiva, may have developed its sobriquet from the pirate Jose Gaspar, who held women captive on the island.

White explorers, fishermen, and farmers began to settle on Sanibel and Captiva in the mid to late 1800s. But not until 1963 did a 3-mile connector bridge from the mainland west of Fort Myers begin to significantly increase tourism to Sanibel Island. As a result, the community incorporated and established strict zoning laws. Sanibel is world famous for its environmental planning and controlled development. Its citizens have been successful at preserving half the island as a natural resource, and more acres are targeted for protection. One of its nonprofit organizations dedicated to protecting the island's environment, the Sanibel-Captiva Conservation Foundation (SCCF), works to keep the islands "natural, beautiful, uncluttered and ecologically sound" for present and future generations. Not only does Sanibel take care of its property and people, it has a compassionate organization to care for its wildlife, Care and Rehabilitation of Wildlife (CROW), which serves as a hospital for approximately seven hundred wild animals that are injured or sick annually. Sanibel is sophisticated and clean, its offices, shops, and residences artfully designed; it is a model for accommodating people, palms, and pelicans.

On such a small island, it is surprising to find so many options for adventure: birding, fishing, boating, canoeing, shelling, crabbing, shrimping, hiking, and bicycling. If you participated in only a third of the available activities you would be there for weeks. Other adventurers already on the islands will share their experiences with you. Naturalist Mark "Bird" Westall is ready to guide you into the mangroves, mud flats, forests, and animal habitats, and to historic sites. For fishing and shelling, ask for Bob Sabatino, or other guides at the marinas. Another contact is Scott Martell, award-winning reporter, environmentalist, and author of *Island Journeys*. You may also call the shelling guides listed in the *Islander*, a first-class newspaper. Or read the *Sanibel Shell Guide*, by Maggie Greenberg and Nancy Olds, for assistance. Elinore Dermer is an excellent source for information about Sanibel's history, lighthouse, early stores, and life before the causeway. The chamber of commerce also has plenty of information to make your adventure a success. (See *Information*.)

If you are camping at Estero, go north 8 miles on US 41 and turn left (west), on SR 865 (Gladiolus Drive). After one mile turn left on CR 869 (Summerlin Road) and follow it to SR 867 and the Sanibel Causeway. After you cross the toll bridge and arrive in Sanibel, look to the right and stop at the chamber of commerce at 1159 Causeway Boulevard. Ask for a map of the island that shows the location of all businesses, accommodations, and shops. Plan to visit the Jay Norwood "Ding" Darling National Wildlife Refuge early in the morning, late in the afternoon, or at low tide, when the waterfowl are most likely to be out in numbers. Turn right (north) from the junction of Causeway Boulevard and Periwinkle, and after 5.2 miles (including the changes to Palm Ridge Road and Sanibel-Captiva Road), watch for the sign of the preserve, right. Park at the visitor center to become oriented to the refuge topography and facilities.

The refuge is named in memory of Jay Norwood Darling, one of the pioneer leaders of the conservation movement. He had a winter home on Captiva Island in the 1930s and was largely responsible for the establishment of the 5,014-acre Sanibel National Wildlife Refuge in 1945. The refuge was renamed in his honor in 1967 and formally dedicated in 1978. In 1923 and 1942 Darling won the Pulitzer Prize for his evocative political cartoons in the *New York Herald Tribune*, where his signature was Ding. His greatest legacy is in the millions of acres of endangered wildlife habitats that have been preserved as part of the National Wildlife Refuge System, which he played a leading role in establishing. He also initiated the Migratory Bird Hunting Stamp ("Duck Stamp") in 1934, whose proceeds have helped purchase 186 national wildlife refuges, and designed the familiar blue flying Canada goose sign that you see at refuges across the nation. During President Franklin D. Roosevelt's administration Darling was the chief of the U.S. Bureau of Biological Survey, a forerunner of the U.S. Fish and Wildlife Service.

*Spoonbel*

The refuge has 291 species of birds and more than 50 species of reptiles and amphibians. From March through May you will see painted buntings and red-eyed vireos, and from December through February blue-winged teal, pintails, and red-breasted mergansers. Year-round are the egrets, herons, ospreys, and brown pelicans. The refuge has canoe rentals and two canoe trails, three hiking trails, and a number of picnic areas. Fishing is allowed, but a license is necessary for freshwater fishing. Crabbing is restricted to dip net only, and feeding of wildlife is prohibited.

From the refuge visitor center you can hike the 4-mile South Dike Trail or take the 5-mile auto drive. Near the causeways you will notice white ibis and other wading birds in the mud flats. With them are the Louisiana heron, distinguishable by the stripe down its neck as if it were formally dressed. Two species of egrets, snowy and great, are among the wading birds. One way to distinguish the snowy is by its yellow feet ("golden slippers") and black legs. The great egret, larger than the snowy, also has black legs. The largest wading bird is the great blue heron, easily identifiable with its white head and gray blue plumage. Another wading bird, less frequently seen than the egrets and herons, is the roseate spoonbill. Mostly bright pink, it has a white neck and orange tail and swings its head from side to side when feeding, using its bill like a spoon to feed on aquatic insects, small snails, and shrimp. During breeding season, both the male and female shoulder feathers change to crimson. Wintering primarily in the Everglades, roseate spoonbills are most likely to be seen here from April to September. One permanent inhabitant of the refuge is the brown pelican, which you will see posing on a post, floating serenely in the water, or diving for fish. A large bird, it has a 7-foot wingspan. It prefers a saltwater habitat and nests in large groups on small undeveloped coastal islands. Monogamous, brown pelicans mate and stay together for a lifetime. Other wildlife on this route are hawks, moorhens, raccoons, ospreys, and tiny yellow-throated warblers that sing all day. Near the end of the drive is Shell Mound Trail, an interpretive short loop over Calusa Indian mounds. White stopper (*Eugenia axillaris*), which smells like skunk, ball moss (*Tillandsia necrvata*), and twisted air plant (*Tillandsia circinata*) are distinctive plants on the trail.

Outside this part of the refuge is Bailey Tract, where a foot trail leads to alligators and other wildlife. It meanders for 2 miles near small lakes and the Sanibel River. Access is on Tarpon Bay Road, a street you crossed on your way from Causeway Boulevard to the refuge visitor center. The refuge's two canoe trails are the 2-mile Commodore Creek and the Buck Key. Access to the former is at a canoe rental dock at the north end of Tarpon Bay Road. Featured on this route is wildlife among the red mangroves. Access for the Buck Key Canoe Trail, a 4-mile canoe trip in red mangroves is at the canoe rental dock on the east side of Captiva Island, about 1.5 miles beyond the Turner bridge.

Between Tarpon Bay Road and the entrance to the refuge is Sanibel-Captiva Nature Center, supported by the Sanibel-Captiva Conservation Foundation. The foundation, founded in 1967, 7 years before Sanibel became a city, is committed to protecting the island's environment. At the center are live and informative displays, a native plant nursery, and 4 miles of loop and cross trails. If you begin counterclockwise, follow the Sabal Palm Trail to an alligator hole and continue on the Upper Ridge Trail, the Wildflower Trail, and the West River Trail. Along the way expect to see the gopher tortoise en route to its trailside burrow. At the Sanibel River overlook and observation tower you may see ospreys and other birds. Return on the East River Trail Loop by another river overlook to resting benches on the trail. You can study a wide range of plant life on the trails, including ferns (Boston, goldfoot, blechum, shoestring, and leather), the brilliant yellowtop herb (*Flaveria linearis*), and the gray nickle bean (*Caesalpinia crista*), a spiny legume. Buckthorn (*Bumelia celastriana*) grows in a grove between the West River Trail and the Upper Ridge Trail. Other plants include climbing hemp, sea purslane, Indian tobacco, snowberry, and necklace pod.

Shelling is synonymous with Sanibel. Plan some time to develop the famous "Sanibel stoop" while looking for mollusks, but adhere to the city ordinance that limits you to taking two live shells per species per person. You should easily find bivalves such as scallops, turkey wings, lucinas, cockles, and angle wings. Among the univalves you will find are alphabet cones, fighting conches, tree tulips, junonicas, lion's paws, olives, and lightning whelks. You may also find sand dollars and sea fans. Secure a map from the chamber of commerce that will show beach public parking, restricted areas, and restrooms. One restricted area is in the Darling Wildlife Refuge, where no shells can be collected. You can have a guide help you choose a location and explain the mollusks, one of the oldest and largest groups of animals in the world. Failing to collect what you wish, you can always visit the dozen or more shell shops on the island. And you can visit the popular Shell Factory 4 miles north of Fort Myers on US 41; it has a wide collection of shells from around the world. The Sanibel Shell Fair is held the first weekend in March.

If you did not go to Cabbage Key from Pineland Marina, you can go there from 'Tween Waters Marina at Captiva. The journey is on *Island Queen II*, a charming old Navy patrol boat familiar to the porpoises that playfully follow the craft. The cruise leaves at 10 A.M. and returns about 3 P.M., allowing you 2 hours at Cabbage Key for lunch and to walk on the nature trail. The sponsor, Island Seafood, also offers other island journeys for moderate fees. Before you leave the islands take a leisurely 15- or more mile bicycle trip on the bicycle trails to places of history and interest like the Island Historical Museum on Dunlop Road, near City Hall. The museum is open 10 A.M. to 4 P.M. Thursdays and Saturdays. Farther east, at the end of Periwinkle Road, is the Sanibel Lighthouse, an active landmark since 1884. The Care and Rehabilitation of Wildlife on Sanibel-Captiva Road, near the Sanibel Elementary School, welcomes your visit. If interested in exploring the area by power- or sailboat, contact the Boat House on North Yachtsman Drive. Windsurfing boards are available at The Windsurfers

Works, 1554 Periwinkle Way. Saltwater fishing expeditions can be planned from any of the island marinas. With all the exercise from your trips, you will fast become hungry. Inquire at the chamber of commerce about restaurants to fit your budget (but do not expect neon-flashing fast-food shrines). For someplace unique, try Mucky Duck on Andy Rosse Lane on Captiva Island.

On the mainland is Corkscrew Swamp Sanctuary, a prominent and popular natural area for your next journey. From your campground at Estero, take US 41 south 10.8 miles to CR 846, David C. Brown Highway, and follow it east 18.9 miles to CR 849. Turn left (north) and go 1.6 miles to the sanctuary. (If you prefer to follow I-75 south from Estero to CR 846, Exits 19 and 17, do not follow Corkscrew Road east at Exit 19. The road does not go to the sanctuary.) Owned and operated by the National Audubon Society, the 11,000-acre wilderness contains the nation's largest stand of virgin bald cypress. Some of the trees, up to 130 feet high and 8 feet in diameter, are estimated to be 700 years old. Efforts to protect the cypress began as early as 1912 when the society employed a seasonal guard to defend the wood storks, great egrets, and other waterfowl from plume hunters. In 1954 the Corkscrew Cypress Rookery Association, a coalition of fourteen organizations managed by the National Audubon Society, was formed to protect 6,000 acres. In 1968 the rest of the acreage was purchased to better preserve the integrity of the sanctuary. Yet residential development nearby remains a threat, specifically to the wood stork.

At the visitor center is a guide booklet that will help on the self-guided 1.7-mile boardwalk. A slow, quiet walk will enable you to see many of the more than seven hundred species of flora, birds, amphibians, reptiles, and mammals in the sanctuary. Your first encounter of the preserve is through slash pine and saw palmetto. Soon the boardwalk will cross a wet prairie—too wet for pines and not wet enough for cypress. Once into the cypress stand you will see a variety of epiphytes—nonparasitic air plants securing moisture from the rain or dew in air pockets. Particularly noticeable are the yellow catopsis (*Catopsis berteroniana*) and the blue-flowered, stiff-leaved wild pine (*Tillandsia fasciculata*). There is a spicy, sweet smell of forest moisture and decay. Gracing the swamp's rich floral base are swamp ferns: Boston, strap, and the largest of them, the leather (*Acrostichum danaeafolium*). By the time you arrive at an observation platform, you may wonder why few mosquitoes bother you here; it's because nature has its own method of control with the minnowry gambusia, or mosquito fish, which feeds on mosquito larvae. A long stay at the platform will make you feel kinship with the sanctuary; birds and other animals are ever present. You may see an anole change its color to match a tree and the five-lined skink run near your feet, or hear the squirrel tree frog croak mildly in comparison to the loud grunts of the pig frog (*Rana grylio*). On your route you will cross small lettuce lakes where water lettuce, floating on the surface, appears like a tufted thick green carpet. A log slanted from the water may be a perch for a red-bellied turtle, or it may parallel a stationary alligator. Before you complete the walk you may see a wood stork, whose nest is high in the cypress. Identify it in flight by its bald head and its wide white wings edged in black. Although you will not see all thirty species of wild orchids, you will see the clamshell orchid attached to the custard apple tree and the yellow-flowering cowhorn orchid leaning from a cypress.

Closer to the campgrounds in Estero are a drive to the Nature Center and Planetarium of Lee County and to the Edison Winter Home and Botanical Gardens, and a canoe trip to Mound Key via the Estero River. To get to the nature center, drive north 13 miles on I-75 from Corkscrew Road to SR 884 (Colonial Boulevard), Exit 22, and go west 0.5 mile to CR 865 (Ortiz Avenue), right. After 0.2 mile enter the center at 3450 Ortiz Avenue. Open daily, the 105-acre pine and cypress forest has two nature trails—Pine Loop and Cypress Loop—on which you will see rusty lyonia, epiphytes, Florida holly, Carolina willow, and swamp flag. Of 60 species of birds, you

*Banyan tree, Thomas A. Edison home, Fort Myers.*
PHOTO BY Allen de Hart.

can expect to see or hear Carolina wren and blue-gray gnatcatcher. Also spend some time in the museum, the Audubon aviary, Seminole village, Iona House, and Avian Garden. From here to the Thomas Alva Edison home, continue north 2 miles on Ortiz Avenue to SR 82 (Anderson Avenue), turn left (west), and drive to SR 867 (McGregor Boulevard). Turn left (south) and, after a few blocks, look for 2350 McGregor Boulevard. Turn left to a parking area. A tour of the home, chemical laboratory, and museum gives you an appreciation of the inventive genius of Edison. Wintering here for nearly 50 years, he became a master horticulturist, experimenting with thousands of plants. One of the most impressive is the banyan tree. A gift from rubber tycoon Harvey Firestone, the 2-inch-diameter tree was planted in 1925. Dropping its aerial roots as it spread, the tree grew to its current perimeter of more than 300 feet. Edison discovered that carbonized bamboo fibers made the light bulb practical, and he produced rubber from goldenrod, a widespread perennial herb. Tours, requiring an admission fee, are given every 30 minutes, daily, 9 A.M. to 4 P.M. If you have not seen the hundreds of royal palms, a landscaping project initiated by Edison on McGregor Boulevard, take this drive before you leave Fort Myers. Also, you may find the Fort Myers Historical Museum of interest. Its exhibits cover local history from 1200 B.C. to the present, Indian artifacts, and Spanish shipwrecks. It is a few blocks northeast of the Edison home at 2300 Pea Peck Street in the old Atlantic Coastline Railroad Depot.

If you choose the Koreshan State Historic Site for your campground, a tour of the park (if you have not already taken one) is worth your curiosity. In 1895 Cyrus Reed Teed, a religious visionary, brought a celibate communal group from Chicago and established a pioneer settlement called Estero. The settlers built twenty buildings, including a school, and created a botanical garden of trees and shrubs. The sect used scientific and economic theories to support and explain the universe. Near the buildings is a river trail to the campground, on which fern, moss, palm, pine, and spicebush grow. At Koreshan you can make arrangements with a park ranger to canoe or motorboat the Estero River to Mound Key State Archaeological Site in Estero Bay. En route, on the 4.5 miles to Mound Key, you will see ospreys, ibis, herons, oystercatchers, pelicans, and perhaps an alligator. The 100-acre uninhabited island is like a tropical jungle with mangroves, guava, gumbo-limbo, strangler fig, and the showy blue-flowered jacaranda. Archeologists believe that the man-made canal and large oval mound were in the capital town of the Calusa. From such a mound the Calusa chief could see all vessels approaching the island. They also believe that Spanish explorer Pedro Menéndez de Avilés visited here in 1565. If you take this fascinating journey on your own, be sure to get information from the ranger about tides and the access point for docking.

Next, journey south on I-75 to The Conservancy Nature Center in Naples and choose another campground. If you go to the campground first (Naples KOA or Collier-Seminole State Park), drive back northwest to Naples. If you visit the nature center on your way, leave I-75 at Exit 16, SR 896 (Pine Ridge Road), west to North Naples. After 3.5 miles, turn left (south) on SR 851 (Goodette-Frank Road). Go 3.2 miles and turn left on 14th Street to 1450 Merrihue Drive. The center, and another near the Isle of Capri, are managed by The Conservancy, an organization begun in the mid-1960s that has created a consortium of hundreds of area leaders and volunteers seeking "constructive solutions to problems of balancing growth with environmental concerns." Bordering a tidal lagoon, the 13.5-acre center has a wildlife museum, an animal rehabilitation clinic (similar to CROW on Sanibel), an environmental education building for teaching and research in a natural science laboratory, and an auditorium for meetings and symposia on environmental issues. The center is free of charge Monday through Saturday October through April and Monday through Friday May through September.

The Conservancy's other center, Briggs Nature Center, is located 13.3 miles south. From the Naples center, go south on CR 851 and US 41 for 9.5 miles to SR 951. Turn right and follow SR 951 for 2.7 miles, then turn right (west) on Shell Island Road for one mile. A 6,000-acre sanctuary, the center serves as an educational facility for the adjoining 8,400-acre Rookery Bay National Estuarine Research Reserve, which was designated in 1978. (The reserve is part of the 32,000-acre Rookery Bay Aquatic Preserve.) Dedicated in 1982, the center has a 0.5-mile boardwalk that leads to an observation deck for viewing wildlife. Along the trail are lichens, wildflowers, birds, and reptiles. Some of the plant life you will see are blue porterweed (*Stachytarpheta jamaicensis*), a glabrous tropical herb, and purple edible coco plum (*Chrysobalanus icaco*). Some of the other plants are white indigo berry, marlberry, satinleaf, and bay cedar. On the sand banks along the boardwalk you are likely to see a gopher tortoise. The center offers a 2-hour trip to explore the adjoining Rookery Bay, and 4- to 6-hour canoe trips on the local rivers and creeks, all for moderate fees. Because some of the excursions are seasonal, an advance call is recommended.

Naples offers other nature activities: fishing, birding, boating, sailing, shelling, and beachcombing for shark teeth. The teeth are different shades of color, representing extinct sea creatures over eons of time. First settling here in 1887, Naples' pioneers found shelling and "teething" pleasurable pastimes; they had 40 miles of unspoiled beach on the Shell Coast. The pastime is no less desirable today if you can be the first to some of the more remote beaches—like Barefoot Beach State Preserve and Delnor-Wiggins Pass Recreation Area—after a major storm. Or try a 3-mile strip between Vanderbilt Beach Estates and North Naples, or the most remote area between Gordon Pass and Little Marco Pass. The resort city of Naples, also the seat of government for Collier County, has long been described as elegant, refined, quiet, classic, "a blue-chip community with an entrepreneurial climate." To get a sense of its history and rich development, visit the Collier County Museum on US 41 (3301 East), which emphasizes everything from Calusa Indian history to modern vacation retreat culture. It is open Monday through Friday. One of the oldest structures in the city is the Seaboard Coastal Line Railroad Depot at 1056 Fifth Avenue, South. Built in 1926, it is now a community art center and railroad museum. Another historic place is Palm Cottage at 137 12th Street, South. It was built in 1890 and is one of the few houses made of tabby, a primitive form of cement, in the state.

From Naples it is 15 miles southeast on US 41 to Collier-Seminole State Park. The park's 6,423 acres are at the northwest edge of the Everglades National Park mangrove swamps and the southwest edge of Big Cypress Swamp. It is a meeting place of land and sea, of fresh and salt waters, of tropical- and temperate-zone vegetation. The conditions provide for a great diversity of plant and animal life: 40 species of trees, 44 species of mammals and reptiles, and 117 species of birds. The park also has a 4,700-acre nearly impenetrable wilderness preserve in a mangrove swamp of tidal creeks, bays, and the Blackwater River.

On the upland portion of the park are tropical hammocks

of gumbo-limbo, Jamaica dogwood, catclaw, mastic, and strangler fig, trees frequently seen in the Caribbean Islands and the Yucatán Peninsula of Mexico. One of the hammocks' most beautiful trees is the royal palm, which may grow to a height of more than 100 feet. The park is one of three sites in Florida where it grows naturally in significant numbers. Like most tropical forests, the hammocks are characterized by a large number of epiphytic plants. Between the tropical hammocks and the mangrove swamps is a transition area called a marl prairie, which is flooded by high tides and dominated by tall grasses. A variety of wading birds live here, and northern harriers (marsh hawks) soaring low in search of marsh rabbits and rice rats are common in the winter. Small mammals are the common prey of the bobcat, which prowls the marsh. Other birds to look for in the park are red-bellied woodpeckers and pine warblers.

Human history of the park began with the Calusa Indians nearly 2,000 years ago. More recent Indians, the Seminoles in the nineteenth century, fled the area to escape U.S. government troops. Some of the final campaigns of the Second Seminole War were conducted near the park, and a replica of a blockhouse used by the troops has been erected near the park's campground. By the 1920s a white pioneer developer, Barron Collier, owned at least 1 million acres of land in southwest Florida. In a royal palm section of the present-day park, he set aside 150 acres he hoped would become the Lincoln-Lee National Park. The U.S. government rejected his offer first because of the small acreage, and again later even after he gave adequate land. The county, which bears his name, accepted it, but later, in 1944, turned it over to the state of Florida. It is a park of great beauty and delightful outdoor-activity options: boating, canoeing, fishing (ramp, dock, and canoe rentals available), nature study, camping, and back-packing.

If you plan to take the 13.5-mile canoe trail, report at 8 A.M. at the park entrance office and registration. (There is a rental fee, and reservations cannot be made in advance.) You will receive paddles and seat cushions or life jackets, and you must return on your final day one hour before sunset (5 P.M. in January, for example), after which park officials send out a search patrol. You will also receive a map, which may need extra markings from the ranger. You will need a day pack with drinking water, food for lunch, a flashlight, a pocketknife, a compass, a first-aid kit, sun screen, insect repellent (and a "Shoo Bug Jacket," if you have one, to protect you from mosquitoes), the map, and above-knee waders if you hope to keep your feet dry. If you stay overnight in the mangrove forest, take the usual backpacking gear. Pack everything in a waterproof bag that can be properly tied to the canoe.

When you reach nautical marker No. 56, turn right. At marker No. 47, begin your loop by steering right. (To the left is Blackwater River, your return route.) Soon you will be at Mud Bay. If it is low tide, you will see hundreds of wading birds, such as sandpipers, plovers, white ibis, egrets, and herons. Use your waders or go barefoot while pulling the canoe through the knee-deep muck. Be sure to follow the arrows and go south around Mud Bay's major island.

After about 3.5 miles you will arrive at the small campsite, right, called Grocery Place (from an old homestead trading post last used in 1935 and accessible only by boat). Your nocturnal companions may be raccoons, anoles, Florida cricket frogs, and the ever-present mosquitoes.

Once into Palm Bay you are approaching the Ten Thousand Islands area and will need to hug the left side of the bay. Turn east after you reach the south tip of the mangrove forest. At low tide you may need to get out and pull the canoe across oyster bars. (Waders or tennis shoes are necessary.) Bobbing colorful balls in the bay are not buoys; they are location markers for lobster traps set by commercial harvesters. Other seafood here is mangrove snapper, redfish, and snook. For the next mile you will face many look-alike mangrove islands. It is important to stay left and cross the oyster bars when necessary. If at this point the tide is coming in you will not see the oysters, and the strong water flow will require strenuous paddling. Look for marker No. 13, a day beacon in the Blackwater River channel, and keep left. Stay in the channel watching for the higher numbered markers as you paddle north. Waterfowl perch on the mangrove roots, and osprey dip to catch small fish. Gradually the river narrows and becomes more silent and cloistered by the mangrove forest. At day beacon No. 47 you have completed your loop; turn right for an easy and quiet return.

To hike the remote 7-mile Hiking Trail, register at the ranger's office and secure a map and a key to open the gate at the trail's parking area. The distance is 0.7 mile east on US 41 from the park entrance. Take with you a day pack with drinking water and insect repellent, and wear shoes that you do not mind getting wet. If you plan to stay overnight at the primitive campsite, take regular backpacking gear and drinking water. Pets and firearms are prohibited. Follow the short 0.1-mile blue-blazed trail that connects with the white-blazed trail (maintained by the Florida Trail Association). If you go counterclockwise you will pass through a pine forest with open areas of grasses, cabbage palm, and wildflowers. Among the flowers are swamp lilies, hat pins, bog buttons, ten-petal sabatia (*Sabatia dodecandra*), and ladies' tresses. You may also see zebra and ruddy orange dagger wing butterflies. The dagger wing is unique because when it folds its wings together it is perfectly camouflaged as a dead leaf. By the time you cross a park service road you will be aware that black bears also use the trail. More evidence near the campsite might include signs of chewing and droppings. A watery route through a cypress swamp follows, and then you will need to wade through two small drainages with alligators in them to complete the loop.

### Information

Counties: Charlotte, Hendry, Lee, Collier
Average Temperatures: January, 52.8°F (low), 77.6°F (high); August, 72.3°F (low), 91.8°F (high)

National Properties: Caloosahatchee River Canal, U.S. Army Corps of Engineers, 400 W. Bay St., Jacksonville, FL 32202, (904) 791-1133; J. N. "Ding" Darling NWR, 1 Wildlife Dr., Sanibel, FL 33957, (813) 472-1100 ·

State Properties: Cayo Costa State Island Preserve, P.O. Box 1150, Boca Grande, FL 33921, (813) 964-0375; Collier-Seminole State Park, Rte. 4, Box 848, Naples, FL 33962, (813) 394-3397; Delnor-Wiggins Pass State Recreation Area, 11100 Gulf Shore Dr., North Naples, FL 33963, (813) 597-6196; Gasparilla Island State Recreation Area, P.O. Box 1150, Boca Grande, FL 33921, (813) 964-0375; Koreshan State Historic Site, P.O. Box 7, Estero, FL 33928, (813) 922-0311; Webb WMA, South Region Office, Florida Game and Fresh Water Fish Commission, 3900 Drane Field Rd., Lakeland, FL 33803, (813) 644-9577

Other Properties: Cabbage Key, c/o P.O. Box 200, Pine Island, FL 33945, (813) 283-2278; Collier County Museum, 3301 Tamiami Trail, E., Naples, FL 33962, (813) 774-8476; Corkscrew Swamp Sanctuary, Rte. 6, Box 1875A, Naples, FL 33964, (813) 657-3771; Edison Winter Home and Gardens, 2350 McGregor Blvd., Fort Myers, FL 33901, (813) 334-7419; Fort Myers Historical Museum, 2300 Peck St., Fort Myers, FL 33901, (813) 332-5955; Nature Center and Planetarium of Lee County, 3840 Ortiz Blvd., Fort Myers, FL 33905, (813) 275-3435; The Conservancy, 1450 Merrihue Dr., Naples, FL 33942, (813) 262-0304/6771, and Briggs, (813) 775-8569

Organizations: Care and Rehabilitation of Wildlife, P.O. Box 150, Sanibel, FL 33957, (813) 472-3644; Sanibel-Captiva Shell Club, P.O. Box 355, Sanibel, FL 33957, (813) 472-4709; Sanibel-Captiva Conservation Foundation, 333 Sanibel-Captiva Rd., Sanibel, FL 33957, (813) 472-2329; Southwest Florida Land Preservation Trust, P.O. Box 2721, Naples, FL 33939, (813) 261-4007; The Conservancy, see Other Properties

Chambers of Commerce: Bonita Springs CC, P.O. Box 1240, Bonita Springs, FL 33959, (813) 992-2943; Boca Grande CC, Box 704, Boca Grande, FL 33921, (813) 964-0568; Greater Fort Myers CC, P.O. Box 9289, Fort Myers, FL 33901, (813) 332-

3624; Pine Island CC, P.O. Box 525, Matlacha, FL 33909, (813) 283-0888; La Belle CC, P.O. Box 456, La Belle, FL 33935, (813) 675-0125; Marco Island Area CC, P.O. Box 913, Marco Island, FL 33969, (813) 394-7549; Naples Area CC, 3620 Tamiami Trail N., Naples, FL 33940, (813) 262-6141; North Fort Myers CC, 3405 Hancock Bridge Pkwy., North Fort Myers, FL 33903, (813) 997-9111; Sanibel-Captiva Islands CC, P.O. Box 166, Sanibel, FL 33957, (813) 472-1080

Services and Amenities: *Accommodations (inns, motels, hotels):* contact the chambers of commerce; *Commercial Campgrounds:* Naples KOA, 1700 Barefoot William Rd., Naples, FL 33962, (813) 774-5455; Woodsmoke Camping Resort, 19251 US 41 SE, Fort Myers, FL 33908, (813) 267-3456; contact chambers of commerce for other campgrounds

*Adventure Guides:* Adventure Sailing Escape, Royal Palm Tours, 6296 Corporate Ct., B–201, Fort Myers, FL 33907, (813) 489-0344; Babcock Wilderness Adventures, Star Rte. A, Box 66, Punta Gorda, FL 33982, (813) 639-4488; Marco Aviation, P.O. Box 286, Marco Island, FL 33969, (813) 394-5233; Sanibel Outdoor Experiences, 910 Fitzhugh St., S. Sanibel, FL 33957, (813) 472-2995; Scott Martell, 2340 Periwinkle Way, S. Sanibel, FL 33957, (813) 472-5185; Mark "Bird" Westall, Sanibel, FL 33957, (813) 472-5218; *Bicycling:* Fun Rentals, 4th St., Boca Grande, FL 33921, (813) 964-2070; Jim's Bike Rentals, 11534 Andy Rossi Ln., Captiva, FL 33924, (813) 472-1296; Trikes and Bikes, 3234 Fowler St., Fort Myers, FL 33907, (813) 936-4301; Finnimore's Cycle Shop, 1223 Periwinkle Way, Sanibel, FL 33957, (813) 472-5577; Pop's Bicycles, 4265 Bonita Beach Rd., Bonita Springs, FL 33923, (813) 947-4442; *Boating (guides, rentals, and services):* Pineland Marina, P.O. Box 13, Pineland, FL 33945, (813) 283-0080; Port-O-Call, Marina of Naples, 550 Port-O-Call Way, Naples, FL 33942, (813) 774-0479; *Canoeing:* Boat House, Sanibel Marina, 634 N. Yachtsman Dr., Sanibel, FL 33957, (813) 472-2531; Lakes Park, Fort Myers, FL 33908, (813) 481-7946; Tarpon Bay Marina, Sanibel, FL 33957, (813) 472-8900; *Cruise Boats: Island Queen II,* 'Tween Waters, P.O. Box 249, Captiva, FL 33924, (813) 472-5161; Kingfisher Cruise

Lines, Fishermen's Village, Punta Gorda, FL 33982, (813) 639-0969; *Tropic Star*, P.O. Box 569, Bokeelia, FL 33922, (813) 283-0015; Vacations Afloat, 1104 N. Collier Blvd., Marco Island, FL 33969, (813) 642-7772; *Fishing:* contact the chambers of commerce for lists of marinas and guides for saltwater fishing; *Restaurants:* The Crab Shack, Main St., Bokeelia, FL 33922, (813) 283-2466; Mucky Duck, Andy Rossi Ln., Captiva, FL 33924, (813) 472-3434; Sandy Hook Crab House, Pine Island Rd., Matlacha, FL 33909, (813) 283-0113; Cabbage Key Inn, Cabbage Key, P.O. Box 200, Pineland, FL 33945, (813) 283-2278; contact the chambers of commerce for lists of restaurants; *Sailing:* Boat House, Sanibel, FL 33957, (813) 472-2531; Marco Island Sea Excursions, Marco Island, FL 33969, (813) 642-6400; Wheel and Keel, Fort Myers Beach, FL 33931, (813) 463-5363; *Shelling:* contact the chambers of commerce for list of guides; *Windsurfing:* Windsurfing Works, 1554 Periwinkle Way, Sanibel, FL 33957, (813) 472-0123

## EVERGLADES NATIONAL PARK

The contrast is astonishing. You leave the noise of greater Miami, pass through open, rich vegetable farms with twitching plumes of irrigation, and cross a canal into thick pines and oaks that tower and arch. There is a feeling of cloister, like entering a sanctuary. You are in the 1.5-million-acre Everglades National Park, the world's largest freshwater marsh. Described by writer Jack de Golia as "broodingly beautiful, deceptively serene," its expanse of saw grass, hammocks, and mangrove swamps sweeps the horizons. The glades' earliest name appeared on English maps in the eighteenth century when surveyor Gerard de Brahm mapped the area as "River Glades," *glades* meaning an open space surrounded by woods. River became "Ever" on later English maps, and in 1823 the Turner map used "Everglades" for the first time.

Established in 1947, the park encompasses only 12 percent of the Florida Everglades, an enormous wetlands system that originates in the Kissimmee Valley of central Florida and slowly seeps to the state's southernmost bays. Without this sheet of shallow water its diverse wildlife would perish. The Calusa Indians named the area *Pa-hay-okee,* meaning "grassy water," and conservationist Marjory Stoneman Douglas called it "the sea of grass," a vast area "never wholly known." The Everglades' haunting serenity, subtlety, and complexity entice newcomers and veteran naturalists to enter again and again to explore its nearly 225 miles of water and land trails and learn more about its intricate and delicate web of life.

The Everglades and Biscayne national parks were in the vortex of Hurricane Andrew August 24, 1992. Roaring winds in excess of 164 m.p.h. mangled the human and natural communities. Reports indicate it to be the nation's most costly hurricane (one damage estimate put the total as high as $70 billion). The region's loss of life, the displacement of nearly 250,000 of its residents, and its commercial districts left in ruins will show the hurricane's effects for many years. Many homes vanished, leaving neighbors searching for each other and leaving signs noting location or status. One example was Homestead's favorite bed and breakfast home, Grandma Newton's, where the strongly built heart pine house splintered and blew away. Grandma survived with a few others in a low cement shed. Later a neighbor's shattered wall had a large hand-painted sign that said "Grandma is O.K."

Much of the island foliage in Biscayne Bay was uprooted or all its leaves stripped away; more than 70,000 acres of mangroves in the Everglades were leveled. Mangrove rookeries received damage in the Everglades, and in Biscayne Bay more than 50 percent of the sponges were lost, but manatee populations and the crocodile nesting beaches escaped unharmed. Visitors to the natural areas will find them recovering by themselves. There is also an enormous recovery of the human spirit as well as the rebuilding of homes and businesses. Impacted plant life shows new buds and green foliage. All the major facilities and services in the parks have been restored.

*What to See and Do:* If you want to keep your feet dry, get an introductory glimpse of the park by driving the 38 miles from the headquarters at the eastern entrance to Flamingo, or take a 14-mile tram tour at Shark Valley off US 41. You can hike most of the 60 miles of land trails, some paved or with boardwalks and dry enough for bicycles where allowed. You can also stay dry on boat tours into back bays or on Florida Bay to Cape Sable.

But to become more acquainted with the park in all its intensity and complexity, you must begin on the 65 miles of short canoe trails, some overnight routes on which you are likely to get your feet wet. Park rangers also lead watery hikes into the saw grass. The ultimate backcountry water trail is the 100-mile Wilderness Waterway from Everglades City to Flamingo through a myriad of mangrove swamps, bays, lakes, and rivers to campsites on islands, beaches, and park-made chickees (10-by-12-foot platforms constructed on stilts in bays where there is no high ground, each with a roof and catwalk to a chemical toilet). You can camp at two campgrounds in the park or stay in an air-conditioned lodge or cabin at Flamingo. On the trails are orchids, lilies, cypress, mahogany, flocks of snowy egrets and white ibis, deer, alligators, tree snails, otters, and snakes. In addition to hiking and canoeing, you can go bicycling, fishing, sailing, oystering, crabbing, and birding.

*Where to Begin:* Stop first at the new park headquarters, which stand on the same site as the one destroyed by Hurricane Andrew in 1992. At the junction of US 1 and West Palm Drive in Florida City, follow the signs west on West Palm Drive (SR 9336, SR 27 on some maps). Turn left at Tower Road (at the Robert Is Here fruit stand) and reach the park entrance after 9 miles. The nearest major airport is Miami International, about 45 miles northeast of the park. The western entrance to the park is at the south end of SR 29 in Everglades City, 4.5 miles south of its junction with US 41. The Shark Valley visitor center is on US 41, 40 miles northwest from Florida City, about halfway between the main headquarters and the ranger station in Everglades City. A fourth park contact is the ranger station in Key Largo, 38 miles from the main headquarters and between mile markers 99 and 98.

*About the Adventures:* The park's western boundary is near Everglades City in the Ten Thousand Islands, and its southern border is Florida Bay between the mainland and the north Florida Keys. On the east side, the park is within a few miles of Florida City, north to Sweetwater and facing a canal grid of vegetable farms west of SR 997. Its north edge, US 41 and the Everglades Wildlife Management Area, extends from near the junction of SR 997 west to near the Forty Mile Bend and adjoinment to Big Cypress National Preserve. Flowing south through the park's center is Shark Valley Slough, part of a 50-mile-wide sheet of water that moves slowly, about a quarter-mile daily, and is an average of 6 inches in depth. Another major slough is Taylor Slough, which runs more easterly and is particularly prominent at Royal Palm. Other defined water flows in the western coastal area are Turner River, Lostmans River, Chatham River, Huston River, Rodgers River, Broad River, Harney River, Shark River, and Avocado Creek. Near the main entrance, to the west, is Long Pine Key, with dry, higher elevation between Shark Valley Slough and Taylor Slough.

The Everglades has a solid limestone bedrock, estimated to be 100,000 years old, frequently visible in the freshwater interior. Shallow water veils the limestone during the summer wet season, but its jagged and torn forms show white and dry in the winter. In some places, alligators seek deep solution holes in the bedrock to use for winter water storage. In other areas, marl or peat accumulates on top of the limestone. During the wet season, from May to late November, the climate is tropical and humid. Torrents of rain fall almost every day from cottony thunderheads billowing in from the Gulf. Average rainfall is about 60 inches, ranging from 100 inches in excessive years to 30 inches or less in drought years. Although porous limestone can absorb water like a sponge, water evaporates in the hot sun faster than it seeps into the Biscayne Aquifer.

Plants of the glades grow in mud, peat, humus, marl, and limestone, in salt and fresh water, and on the piney ridges. Pine groves are the highest, rockiest, and driest plant communities at an elevation of only 6 or 7 feet above mean sea level. The mud-banks-and-seaweed community is the lowest in Florida Bay; its low tide, shallow water, and mud attracts wading birds such as the great white heron and the reddish egret. At the western edge of the bay, Cape Sable has shelly grit beaches, low-growing grasses, and salt-tolerant plants. Gulls, egrets, pelicans, and sandpipers leave their footprints here with those of raccoons and with the tell-tale furrow of the loggerhead turtle. The mangrove swamps, the most dense of which is the red mangrove, are transition zones between salt and fresh waters. The only way to explore this tangled wilderness is by canoe, a subject covered in the pages ahead.

Plants in the hardwood hammock grow above the water level, free of saline waters and protected from freshwater floods. Hurricanes, droughts, and fires have destroyed many of the prime hammocks; one of the finest (but severely damaged by Hurricane Andrew in 1992) is the Royal Palm Hammock near the entrance of the park. Here are palm, oak, gumbo-limbo, bustic, pond apple, and woody vines. Only a few miles away is the glades' best example of a pineland, tall slash pine in Long Pine Key. The most common and prominent plant of the glades is saw grass (*Cladium jamaicense*), which has blades with sharp-toothed edges. A member of the sedge family, saw grass remains green except in the driest of winters. Invertebrates find food among its roots, and small fish find protection. You may look across miles of the saw grass and see on the horizon a dome-shaped cluster of trees, usually pond cypress shaped by the concave depth of the water pocket in which they grow. On them and in the dimness of hardwood hammocks grow the air plants—epiphytic ferns, vines, and orchids—seen throughout the park. Altogether, the park has 1,000 varieties of plants and 120 species of trees.

The Everglades is well known for its 350 species of birds,

admired for their beauty and used as a food source by the Indians and the Europeans who followed. Although you will see many species and perhaps some of the large flocks, nearly one hundred of the total—seven of which are endangered—are so rarely seen that you would need to go birding for weeks. Four species—red-cockaded and ivory-billed woodpeckers, the brown-headed nuthatch, and the eastern bluebird—no longer inhabit the park. Another one hundred species are so uncommon that you would need to know specific seasonal habits in order to see them. Since 1930, human developments and alterations in the natural water flow have reduced the population of wading birds by nearly 90 percent. Nevertheless, you will be well rewarded in seeing many of the more common species, such as egrets, herons, ibis, bitterns, and limpkins.

Of the forty species of mammals in the park, you will most frequently see raccoon, opossum, and deer, the latter as often in the watery saw grass as elsewhere. You may also see a marsh rabbit, bobcat, bottle-nosed dolphin, manatee, gray fox, or river otter. You are not likely to see black bear or the endangered Florida panther. The more than fifty species of reptiles include twenty-six species of snakes, of which the cottonmouth moccasin, dusty pygmy rattlesnake, eastern diamondback, and eastern coral snake are poisonous. Endangered are the eastern indigo snake, the American crocodile, and three turtle species—green, hawksbill, and loggerhead.

The alligators' engineering skills are useful to other animal life during the dry season. Incredibly aware of what the dry season will mean, alligators prepare a pool, called "a 'gator hole," in the muck and vegetation of a limestone solution hole. Using their snouts and feet they create an oasis in a barren area for two purposes: as a waterbed and as a source of food. The alligators make a weekly meal mainly of the spotted gar and soft-shelled turtles, and sometimes a raccoon (who comes to visit for snails and frogs). Other meals for the alligators may also include a snowy egret or a white ibis that comes to dine on the smaller fish and crayfish. Each year alligators push up the sediment to form large circular mounds, from which willows and larger vegetation grow. After a few years the 'gator hole resembles a huge donut hole.

You will see alligators, still king of the park, at your first stop at Royal Palm Hammock. Because the hammock has water year-round, you will not see any 'gator holes at this site. Here, too, are eighteen species of amphibians, the majority of them frogs. Expect to hear them more than see them. One eel-shaped amphibian, the Everglades dwarf siren (*Pseudobranchus striatus*, subspecies *belli*), is found only in the Everglades. Snook, bonefish, grouper, mackerel, tarpon, snapper, pompano, mullet, and largemouth bass are plentiful. These and other fish, oysters, clams, and crabs were part of the food supply for the area's first known human inhabitants, the Calusa Indians.

Some archeologists estimate that the Calusa were in the glades as early as 450 B.C., and certainly by A.D. 700. Mounds, pottery shards, and shell carvings indicate home bases from Cape Sable north to the Shark, Chatham, and Turner rivers and to Marco Island, and from Charlotte Harbor inland to Lake Okeechobee. The Calusa were at the glades when the Spanish arrived in the sixteenth century. Originally the Spanish believed that the Calusa had an interior city of culture and wealth, but they never explored the mystery of the glades or saw what they called the "Lake of the Holy Spirit." The Seminole Indians hid here temporarily and survived for most of the early nineteenth century in some of the most remote bays and hammocks. In 1857, a year before the end of the Third Seminole War, Capt. John Parkhill began the last battle against the glade Indians north of Chokoloskee. Captain Parkhill was slain and his troops returned to Chokoloskee without further pursuing the Indians. A few family settlements remained in the glades until 1947 when the establishment of Everglades National Park required that they move to a reservation north of the park boundary. Today they have stores and a museum on US 41, and some serve as skillful guides on airboats into Big Cypress National Preserve.

White explorers circulated reports in the midnineteenth century that the glades' interior harbored large leeches, writhing serpents, and screaming sabor-toothed tigers—all near mysterious vats of quicksand. But in 1840 Lt. Col. William Harney and ninety-two men in canoes crossed the glades from the Miami River to the Gulf in search of the Indians responsible for the Indian Key massacre in August of that year. In the 1870s serious organized explorations began to investigate the feasibility of a telegraph and railroad line to Cape Sable, and in 1883 the *New Orleans Times Democrat* sponsored an expedition from Lake Okeechobee to Shark River for a possible telegraph cable route. In 1887 *Harper's* magazine published an article by Daniel Bellou, who was a team member of the *Times Democrat,* which described sleepless nights with noisy alligators and owls, biting insects and leeches. Bellou complained that the flesh of ducks and curlews was "wormy, soft, and unfit to eat." About 2 years later, Lt. Hugh L. Willoughby wrote a "hair-raising story," *Across the Everglades,* about his scientific expedition. As if to encourage tourism, A. W. Dimock in 1907 wrote a contrasting story to that of Bellou. Dimock and his party were the first known explorers to use a powerboat with the canoes across the glades from Ten Thousand Islands to the little village of Miami. In his story, published in *Harper's,* he wrote that "one meets delay in the Everglades, but not danger. The water is pure and sweet and food plentiful enough. Limpkins taste like young turkey." Instead of finding quicksand, he said, his feet "sank but little in the soft ground." By 1922 a dirt road had been completed from Florida City to Flamingo, making the glades more accessible for exploration, except in rainy weather when the muddy road was impassable. You will begin your adventures into the glades on this route, partly changed and completely paved since then.

    If you are a first-time park visitor and plan to stay for a few days or more, make advance plans. Write or call ahead for free trail maps, special-interest brochures like "Birds of the Everglades National Park" (or mammals, or butterflies, or reptiles and amphibians), tour schedules, and information on ranger-led trips. Also request a copy of the "Sales Catalog of

Publications and Related Products." As starters, I recommend *Everglades—The Story Behind the Scenery* and *Everglades Wildguide*. If you plan to take the 100-mile canoe trip, choose the *Guide to the Wilderness Waterway of the ENP*, by William Truesdell, and appropriate nautical charts. Also consider the season and weather conditions during your visit to the park. Summer is terribly buggy, with numerous mosquitoes, horseflies, yellow flies, and other biting insects, and with thick humidity and frequent thunderstorms. Late summer and early fall is hurricane season, a time when you will not want to be isolated. The cooler season, December to April, is the best period weather-wise, but it is also the park's most crowded season. Advance reservations for the Flamingo Lodge are advisable during this season; if you are staying at either of the park's three campgrounds—Lone Pine Key, Flamingo, and Chekika—space is available on a first-come-first-served basis. Rates at the Flamingo Lodge are much reduced in the summer. Bring with you casual, comfortable clothes: long pants, long-sleeve shirts, a cap, tennis shoes, and hiking shoes (bring an old pair to use when you traipse through the watery saw grass). If you have binoculars, this is a good time to use them. Regardless of the season, you will find mosquitoes; the park does not spray them en masse because they are part of the park's wildlife food chain. Personal use of repellents, including permethrin, can be effective for most people. Green Ban, a natural oil repellent, and Avon bath oils are also helpful. A "Shoo Bug Jacket" may be your best choice. (See *Information.*)

While planning what to do on your trip, keep in mind the things that are not done. First, advertised airboats and swamp buggies do not go into the park but tour Everglades areas such as Big Cypress National Preserve and the state wildlife management area. Only park service personnel or research scientists use these craft, when necessary, in the park. It is illegal to remove any animal, plant, coral, driftwood, or Indian artifact from the park. The feeding of wildlife is also prohibited (so you will need to resist the temptation to bribe an animal closer to you). All camping must be at designated camp-grounds and water-trail campsites. Waterskiing is prohibited to prevent disturbing aquatic and nesting birds. The use and possession of spear guns and spear poles for fishing gear is forbidden. Dip nets, cast nets, landing nets, and hook and line are acceptable under state and federal laws. Oysters and blue crabs can be harvested for personal use. There are guidelines for legal length and possession limits for recreational fishing; request a list from the park before you go. In the warm, calm water of Florida Bay are spiny lobster nurseries; taking the lobster is illegal, but shrimp may be taken by a dip net no wider than 3 feet, or by a cast net up to 12 feet. None of the seafood you harvest can be sold; commercial fishing is also forbidden in park waters. A few park islands, beaches, and bays are closed year-round to protect rookeries and endan-gered wildlife populations. Currently closed areas are all keys and beaches in Florida Bay except North Nest Key, Little Rabbit Key, and Carl Ross Key—all campsites. (A permit and map are necessary to use them.) All the back bays in northeast Florida Bay, home to the endangered American crocodile, are also closed to the public. Of the Ten Thousand Islands, only Pavilian Key is closed, and there you may land on the north-ernmost sand spit. Swimming in the park is discouraged. Alligators inhabit freshwater ponds, mud is thick in mangrove areas, and sharks and barracuda live in saltwater marshes and in the open sea.

After you leave the main visitor center of the park headquarters on the road to Flamingo, stop to pay an entrance fee. After another mile, turn left to the Royal Palm Hammock and visitor center. You may see as many photographers as birds and alligators; the 0.5-mile Anhinga Trail is probably the park's most visited trail for seeing wildlife. Wildlife can always be seen here because the Taylor Slough provides fresh water in all seasons. Alligators sun on trail banks, nuzzle through marsh grasses, and may decide to cross the trail in front of you. Purple gallinules share space with egrets, herons, and moor-hens. From the boardwalk you can see an anhinga dive to

*Shell orchid, Everglades National Park.* PHOTO BY Florida
Dept. of Commerce.

spear a fish, ascend to a tree limb, flip the fish, and swallow it whole. Then the anhinga, lacking natural body oils, spreads its wings to dry. Another trail at Royal Palm is the 0.3-mile Gumbo Limbo Trail, where most of the royal palms were destroyed by Hurricane Andrew. In this tropical jungle there are 160 plant species, including gumbo-limbo, pigeon plum, wild coffee, air plants, orchids, and ferns.

Your next stop is Long Pine Key, 4 miles farther on the main road. Here is a campground (no hookups or showers) in a tall slash pine forest. Branching from it is the 7-mile (one-way) Long Pine Trail that extends west from the campground entrance to the main road near Pine Glades Lake. Unless you plan to backtrack, you will need a shuttle. You can also acquire a backcountry camping permit. On this trail you almost forget you are in a watery park. The treadway is dry in winter and on old roads; it is easy to follow under towering pines that sough in the breeze. Forming an understory are saw palmetto and the fragrant marlberry (*Ardisia escallonioides*) above the grasses. Other plants you will see are coco plum, sweet acacia, dahoon, and satin leaf. The campground has two other trails; a 3.6-mile loop and a 5-mile loop, both beginning at gate No. 3 at the entrance to the campground. Go east, and after 0.7 mile turn right to take the 3.6-mile trail. It goes south through the pines to gate No. 2A at Research Center Road. Follow the road right, pass the Boy Scout camp, and turn right off the road at gate No. 2B. After 0.5 mile you will have returned to the campground. The 5-mile loop begins at the same point as the 3.6-mile trail but goes 1.5 miles past the shorter trail's ending point to Research Center Road and a right turn. Research Center Road, which goes to the South Florida Research Center and the Daniel Beard Center, is a good bicycle route, as are some of the gated backcountry dirt roads.

Two miles farther on the main road, look to the right for a sign of the 0.4-mile Pineland Trail. In a fire-sculpted pine forest, the starchy Florida arrowroot, or coontie (*Zamia pumila*) grows in exposed limestone. Six miles ahead on the main road, right, is Pa-hay-okee Overlook. From the observation deck you have a typical view of an apparently endless sea of beard, muhly, and saw grasses among the cypress heads. To assist in explaining the natural history of the glades, the trail has interpretive signs. After another 7 miles on the main road you will come to a side road, right, that leads through a marl prairie to Mahogany Hammock. A short boardwalk trail enters the hammock of large, glossy-leaved, tropical mahogany. One of the mahogany trees (*Swietenia mahagoni*) is listed as the national champion in height and spread. The fury of both Hurricane Donna in 1960 and Hurricane Andrew in 1992 reshaped the hammock, but the nation's largest mahogany survived them both. In wet seasons, the colorful, cone-shaped liguus tree snails become active and you may see them browsing on the tree trunks. Do not be surprised to hear a barred owl making calls in the daytime.

During the next 8.7 miles on the highway you will pass Paurotis Pond, named for the rare paurotis palms, and canoe trail entrances. At the 5.2-mile loop Nine Mile Pond Canoe Trail the route goes through shallow freshwater muck with scattered mangrove islands, and at the 2-mile loop Noble Hammock Canoe Trail you will find creeks and small ponds lined with mangroves. The 5.5-mile (one-way) Hells Bay Canoe Trail can be an overnight canoe trip northwest to creeks and ponds in a mangrove swamp. It leads to a campsite at Lard Can and remote chickees at Pearl Bay and Hells Bay.

On the highway at West Lake are 7.7-mile (one-way) West Lake Canoe Trail, a boat dock, restrooms, and a short boardwalk trail. The canoe trail follows the south side of the lake into a series of small lakes and mangrove creeks to a backcountry campsite at Garfield Bight in Florida Bay. On the West Lake Boardwalk Trail you can be close to the four species of mangroves that form a tight mixture of roots and limbs. Just beyond West Lake is Snake Bight Trail, left from the highway. This 1.6-mile (one-way) road trail is through a tropical hardwood hammock of air plants and climbing cacti, with the haunting noises of frogs and birds coming from an old canal that parallels the trail. Your footing is assured here on the trail used by the concession tour bus. At the trail's end is a boardwalk, from which you can get a spectacular view of the mud flats in Florida Bay at low tide. After 1.6 miles on the main road, you will notice Mrazek Pond, left. Stop here for close-up views of the waterfowl, including the beautiful roseate spoonbill, most frequently seen in the winter.

Coot Bay Pond, right, is another excellent place for photographing birds, and 0.7 mile ahead on the main road is the trailhead for 2.6-mile (one-way) Rowdy Bend Trail. Thick with overhanging boughs and dense, weedy treadway, the trail snakes through a buttonwood forest en route to Snake Bight Trail. Mosquitoes discourage you from hiking this trail, or the 1.8-mile (one-way) Christian Point Trail, left, 0.9 mile ahead. Within a few yards of Christian Point, on the opposite side of the road, is a passable dirt road alongside Buttonwood Canal to the Bear Lake foot trail. At its trailhead is also a canoe portage route between Buttonwood Canal and Homestead Canal to Bear Lake. A hike on the 1.2-mile Bear Lake Trail leads through mixed mangroves and hardwoods to a fine fishing spot near the cross water of Bear Lake and the canal. Back on the main road you are immediately at the Flamingo visitor center and ranger station.

In the nineteenth century Flamingo was a fishing village approached only by boat. West of Flamingo is an old road, now a wilderness area, which extends to a campsite at Clubhouse Beach. Named the Coastal Prairie Trail, it leads 7.5 miles (one way) through a buttonwood forest with grasses, sedges, fig, and poisonwood. In the summertime the route is wet and buggy. The last trail in the Flamingo area is the 0.5-mile Eco Pond Trail on the north side of the Flamingo Campground.

Two of the most popular canoeing adventures on the lakes and bays near Flamingo are a day-trip loop on the 8.4-mile Mud Lake Canoe Trail, and a camping round-trip on the 30.8-mile Bear Lake Canoe Trail. (If you have your own canoe, you can shorten the round-trip distance by 4 miles on either trail by driving to the end of Buttonwood Canal Road, which parallels the canoe route to Homestead Canal dock.) Both trails begin at the Flamingo dock, follow the wide Button-wood Canal 2 miles to narrow Homestead Canal, and connect with 300 feet of portage. After 1.2 miles under a canopy of hardwoods you will arrive at the north edge of Bear Lake. Bear Lake Canoe Trail continues straight, west, on Homestead Canal, and Mud Lake Canoe Trail turns right into a narrow channel.

On the Bear Lake Canoe Trail you will paddle through dense mangrove and buttonwood environments, marshlands, and lakes. In the winter months you will see thousands of heron, snowy egret, white ibis, wigeon, coot, and other wading and floating birds. Trail marker numbers serve as guidance. At marker No. 6 is Fox Lakes; at marker No. 8 is the entrance to Gator Lake; between markers No. 10 and 11 is Gator Lake campsite (8.4 miles from the dock in Flamingo); between markers No. 14 and 16 the canal is shallow with deep, sticky mud, and it may be impassable during the dry season of January to April; Raulerson's Marsh campsite is at marker No. 17; a turn south on East Cape Canal is at marker No. 18 (11.8 miles from the dock in Flamingo); and at marker No. 21 is a portage of 20 feet across an earthen dam. After arriving at Florida Bay, turn right and paddle 1.1 miles in the open shallow sea to the East Cape campsite to complete a 15.4-mile trip. The beauty of the changing Gulf water colors at sunset and sunrise makes paddling to this beach well worthwhile.

From Homestead Canal at Bear Lake, the Mud Lake Canoe Trail goes north a few yards through a channel to Mud Lake. Coot and ibis are plentiful on the lake's north side, and tarpon flash their silver sides near your canoe. At the northeast end of the lake, look for a narrow channel through dense mangrove. Soon you are in the open waters of Coot Bay, where you turn right (east). After 0.5 mile along the bay's edge, turn right at Coast Guard marker No. 2, and return 2.8 miles on the Buttonwood Canal to Flamingo.

The Flamingo Lodge Marina and Outpost Resort is the authorized concessionaire for this part of the park. It runs a 102-room motel with 16 kitchen-equipped cottages, a restaurant, a gift shop, and a full-service marina with skiffs, canoes, and houseboats for rent; bait; tackle; fuel for boats and cars; groceries; and camping supplies. All services have seasonal hours; call with questions. The usual busy schedule is from November 1 to April 30, when all services are available on regular daily hours. In addition, the concessionaire offers an interpretive backcountry cruise on the *Bald Eagle* to Whitewater Bay; a Florida Bay cruise on the *Pelican* to see mangrove islands and wading birds; a wilderness tram tour on the Snake Bight Trail; a sailing cruise on the *Nomad* to Cape Sable for exploring; a sailing tour on the schooner *Windfall* to explore Florida Bay; a bird-watching tour on the *Osprey* with a camping shuttle; and other services. Make reservations in advance. The campground west of the motel has drinking water, picnic tables, grills, tent and trailer pads, restrooms, and cold showers (but no hookups). Fees are charged in the winter season. A ranger station, a park museum, and a post office are in Flamingo. Despite the area's name, do not expect to see any flamingos at Flamingo, for they have never been common here.

Another Everglades National Park campground is Chekika Campground (Chekika State Recreation Area until the early 1990s), a quiet 640-acre tropical hardwood hammock and wetland for camping, fishing, hiking, and swimming. A major feature is a large artesian spring. Access to the campground is 11 miles north of Homestead on Krome Avenue (SR 997) to a turn west on Richmond Road. (See Biscayne National Park section later in this chapter.)

Another park visitor center is Shark Valley on US 41 (the Tamiami Trail, between Miami and Fort Myers). The highlight here is a ride on the concessionaire's open-sided bus (November through March) on a 14-mile loop into the geographical heart of the glades. Halfway along the route is a tall observation tower, which is noted as having the best panoramic view in the park of grasses, cypress heads, and prairies. From here you can also see birds, alligators, and turtles. (The tram and observation tower may be closed during stormy weather or high water. Call in advance.) Flowing south under the vegetation is the clear and slow fresh water of the Shark Valley Slough. The tram route doubles as a bicycle route (rentals at the visitor center). Near the visitor center is a 0.3-mile foot trail, the Bobcat Boardwalk Trail, which winds through islands of willow, coco plum, wax myrtle, and leather ferns (the largest fern species in North America). Adjoining the trail is short Otter Cove Trail, an interpretive path to limestone holes and underground water spots. Shark Valley does not have sharks, but Shark River, 30 miles south, does.

The westernmost ranger station is at Everglades City, 92 miles west from the main headquarters and 35 miles southeast of Naples (off US 41). Neither the town of Everglades City nor nearby Chokoloskee Island are park property, but both are significant in glades history. A good introduction to the Ten Thousand Islands is a boat tour by the concessionaire. Ospreys and bottle-nosed dolphins are prominent on the route, and the narrator may point out other wildlife common to the bays and islands. One of the most historic sites in Everglades City is the Rod and Gun Club, whose original structure was built by William S. Allen, the first permanent settler, in 1883. By 1928 Chicago millionaire Barron Collier had bought the Allen mansion, established a bank, railroad station, theater, and store, and, on some of his 1.3 million acres of southwest Florida, planted a grandiose vegetable patch he called "Everglades City." Collier first dreamed of and later led the campaign for the Tamiami Trail Highway across the state. At the time, he offered the U.S. government a large chunk of land for a national park—but the government rejected it. Instead, 6,423 acres became the Collier-Seminole State Park. When he transformed the Allen house into a luxurious club, it brought jobs to the community. He brought chefs from Europe to serve his distinguished guests: actors, writers, royal families, executives, and four U.S. presidents. Burl Ives, Christopher Plummer, and Gypsy Rose Lee stayed here during the 1958 filming of *Wind Across the Everglades*. A genuine curio, the movie is about a game warden's efforts to protect wildlife from poachers. After Hurricane Donna damaged the resort in 1960, it fell on less glittering times. In 1973 fire destroyed the motel section of the resort. But you can still get good service and food here and soak up some history from those who remember the chronometers, lures, rods, and tarpon mounted on the cypress walls. Another place in town is the Glade Haven Marina and Campground, which has less history but just as much friendly service for campers and apartment renters.

Everglades City is the western terminus of the 100-mile Wilderness Waterway Trail. Overnight campsites are provided on the beach, in the forest, and at single or double chickees. Maximum capacity at each chickee is six persons, and ground sites may have space for as many as twenty persons. Overnights allowed at the campsites range from 1 to 7, depending on location. Required permits are free and can be picked up at the ranger station at Everglades City or in Flamingo no more than 24 hours in advance. Campsites are allocated on the principle of first come, first served. Between Everglades City and Flamingo are fourteen campsites either on the main trail or no more than 3 miles off it. (There are at least twenty other beach and ground or chickee sites farther away from the main route.) From Everglades City, the route is marked by diamond-shaped brown-and-white signs numbered from 130 to 1 at Oyster Bay and maintained by the park. From Oyster Bay to Flamingo the route is marked by circled numbers from 48 to 1 by the U.S. Coast Guard. All nautical charts show the locations of markers, making it easy to determine your direction. Two sections of the route require special attention: the narrow Alligator Creek, 26 miles after you leave Everglades City, and the "Nightmare" between markers 25 and 12, where it is impossible to navigate at low tide (an alternative unmarked Gulf route may be necessary).

While canoeing, with the brackish water and sunny sky, you will see island after island of mangroves, bays, mud flats, wide and narrow rivers, and, occasionally, hardwood hammocks and beaches. The route follows a transition area of fresh and salt water, with a few exceptions when the bay or river is farther east and more isolated from the Gulf waters. In the water, which is usually shallow and rarely deeper than 7 feet, are many species of fish (tarpon, striped mullet, redfish, snook, killifish, anchovy), about ten species of sharks, bottle-nosed dolphins, and alligators. Turtles, snails, and frogs are commonplace, and with them are the microscopic crustacean called copepod. Oyster beds and spawning beds of crabs and shrimp are also common. Raccoons seem to know that where there are people there is food. And you will certainly see birds. Among the aerial birds are the black skimmer, fish crow, and royal tern, which you may see feeding on mud flats. Wading birds, which primarily eat fish, snails, and insects, may be seen in shallow waters. The most conspicuous of them are snowy egrets, herons, and white ibis. Anhingas, brown pelicans, coots, and moorhens float and dive for fish and eat mollusks, and some of the smaller birds, such as the spotted sandpiper and the king rail, probe for mollusks in the mud flats. You will see ospreys and the red-shouldered hawk (and possibly a bald eagle), all birds of prey.

For advance information, contact the ranger station and ask for current material on the tidal schedule and fishing and motorboat regulations, and the "Backcountry Trip Planner." The planner lists all campsites and their capacities, facilities and fire policy, the distance between each campsite, and safety precautions. You will also need National Oceanic and Atmospheric Administration (NOAA) nautical maps: Lostmans River to Wiggins Pass (No. 11430), Shark River to Lostmans River (No. 11432), and EPN Whitewater Bay (No. 11433). The latter is also on a multicolor chart with descriptions of all canoe and land trails in the Flamingo and Whitewater Bay area. Unlike the NOAA map, the chart shows access routes to some of the more remote campsites and chickees from Whitewater Bay. Order these charts and maps from the park's main office. Ask for a free copy of the "Sales Catalog of Publications and Related Products." If you wish to have more detail, try the *Guide to the Wilderness Waterway of the ENP*, by William Truesdell.

When planning your trip, think about how many days you have, how many people in your party, and whether you will paddle only or use part or full motor power. If you plan to only paddle, allow 7 to 10 days for the main route and perhaps a few side trips. If you plan to use some motor power, choose an 18-foot-long square-stern canoe with a 5- or 6-horsepower engine and cut your time in half or more. If you want to use only a powerboat, you can make the trip easily in one day. Any use of motor power requires that you check with the ranger about Coast Guard regulations.

Plan to have at least one companion in your party; two canoes and four paddlers make a good balance. Be certain that at least one person in your group is an experienced canoeist and camper; the Everglades backcountry is not a place for the entire party to learn by chance. Someone in your group should have knowledge of first aid and how to use a first-aid kit. (Ideally, you would also have along a sailor with the nautical knowledge of maps and tides to guide you through the "Nightmare.") Transport all food and fresh water, and allow for emergency rations in the event you become delayed. (Your nearest large food markets are in Naples for Everglades City and Florida City for Flamingo.) Allow one half to one gallon of water per person per day, and use heavy plastic 3- or 5-gallon jugs. A superior quality cooler with block ice can keep food chilled for at least 3 days. Do not leave your food and water where raccoons can tear them open; the bandits can be persistent and clever. To prepare your food, use a portable stove or charcoal. If you plan to supplement your menu with oysters, do not expect to find them of commercial quality. Unless you know something about the fish and baits needed to catch them, it is easier to purchase enough for dinner from a passing experienced fisherman.

If you do not have your own canoes, you can rent at either Everglades City or Flamingo. If you rent a powerboat, also get enough fuel, spare parts, and a repair kit. At Everglades City, canoe rentals and canoe shuttle can be arranged with Everglades National Boat Tours, or arrange for canoe rental, canoe shuttle, and transportation of you and your gear with North American Canoe Tours–Everglades Outpost. North American Canoe Tours can provide a professional guide. A guided tour will about triple your cost, but you will not have to worry about maps, directions, getting lost, and food and its preparation. Another advantage is that a guide will know the human and natural history of the backcountry.

The best season to go is between November and the end on March when the weather is coolest and driest. Rain, storms, and wind are less of a problem then. If you encounter high winds, try to avoid paddling against the wind and the incoming tide. Usually the winds pick up about 9 A.M. and begin to calm about 5 P.M. If you have problems, flag a fishing boat (which is likely to have a CB radio) or wait for the park ranger who patrols the trail route. On your list of items to take, include soft-framed backpack and duffel bag, food and water, insect repellent, an insect net or cover such as a "Shoo Bug Jacket," a sun hat, sun screen, sunglasses, a life jacket, an extra paddle, clothes, comfort items, a tent, a sleeping bag, a tarp, a compass, a stove, a flashlight with extra batteries, heavy-duty trash bags, a knife, a rope, towels, toilet paper (in case it is absent at the chemical toilets), and a lantern (darkness comes about 5:30 P.M. during mid-winter). Optional items may include a camera, binoculars, and guidebooks, such as *Birds of the Everglades Identification Guide*, by Art Weber, or *Florida Birds*, by James Tucker. After all these preparations are complete, pick up your backcountry permit and file your float plan at the ranger station. Because the park service does not initiate a search and rescue if you do not complete your trip on the day you indicated, you should also leave your schedule with a relative or other trusted person who can notify the ranger station if your arrival is overdue.

Starting at the Everglades City ranger station dock in Chokoloskee Bay, paddle southeast 0.5 mile to marker 130 and choose one of two routes around Chokoloskee Island. If you choose the route closest to shore, pass under the causeway bridge by frequent oyster bars to the mouth of Turner River at marker 129. Two thousand years ago Calusa Indians navigated this river to their upstream settlements and to a large community on Chokoloskee Island, opposite the river's mouth. Later the Cherokee gave the island its current name, meaning "old house." Beginning with the John Weeks family, white settlers moved to the island in the early 1870s, and by 1900 C. S. "Ted" Smallwood and his father owned the 144-acre island. Smallwood cultivated groves of avocado (alligator pear), banana, and guava and built a trading post and dock in 1906. A few years later the post became a board-and-batten store, which is now listed in the National Register of Historic Places. Accused multiple murderer Ed Watson was shot at Smallwood's dock by Luke Short and others in self-defense in 1910.

After the first 5.9 miles you will reach the Lopez River, followed by the Lopez River campsite 3 miles farther. By now you will have noticed the mangrove trees common to the transition zone of fresh and salt water. On the trail you will pass through the largest concentration of mangrove swamps in the Western Hemisphere and see four species. Each species has its own specialized environmental requirement at different locations, but you may see them mixed where the water and soil are favorable. The thick red mangrove (*Rhizophora mangle*), the most common, grows in the deepest waters and mud flats and has aerial arching roots. What look like bean pods hanging from the limbs are actually young plants that fall from the tree to start new life in the mud or drift away to another mud flat. In contrast, the buttonwood (*Conocarpus erectus*) grows just above the high-tide line. The black mangrove (*Avicennia germinans*) usually grows at levels exposed at low tide but covered at high tide. Its dense asparagus-shaped roots sticking up from the mud and fragrant white flowers are easily recognized. The white mangrove (*Languncularia racemosa*) does not have a specific root system and prefers higher ground. It can be recognized from the two small lumps at the base of its oval leaves, which serve as salt glands used to secrete excess salt. Fallen mangrove leaves provide nutrients essential to the food chain of the fish and other aquatic life.

It is 9.5 miles from the Lopez River campsite through Sunday, Oyster, Huston, and Last Huston bays to marker 99 at Chatham River. In Huston Bay you will pass a small island with a cabin at marker 107; this is the last inholding of the park, and the park service has arranged to remove the building. At Chatham River, paddle right for 1.5 miles to the Watson Place campsite. (Another option would be to continue on the route to marker 97 and turn left for a 2-mile side trip to double Sweetwater chickees.) The Watson camp is named after Edward J. "Ed" Watson, who lived here in a two-story clapboard white house from the 1890s until his death in 1910. On his farm he grew sugarcane and vegetables, and from a boat house and dock he transported the products to market at Key West and as far as Tampa. For his farm labor he chose drifters, criminals, and workers of dubious character. Neighbors on other islands knew that there were killings among the workers, and Watson apparently had killed some of his workers to avoid paying them. After a triple murder on Watson's property in 1910, neighbors confronted him at Smallwood's dock. Watson pulled a gun, but it misfired and neighbors fired at him as he reached for his six-shooter. Neighbors later found more than fifty graves on his property. The property had infrequent renters or owners, and the park service razed the house after Hurricane Donna damaged it in 1960.

After leaving marker 97, pass through Chevelier Bay, and at marker 87 arrive at Possum Key. The small key has a long history of human habitation; it was an early favorite of settlers who came to cultivate its high, fertile soil. Jean Chevelier, a French eccentric and naturalist, lived here from the 1880s until his death in 1895. In his botanical garden were avocado, banana, and guava. Other settlers followed; one of the best known was the hermit Arthur Leslie Darwin, who claimed distant blood ties to Charles Darwin. Darwin built himself an almost hurricane-proof cabin and stayed from the 1930s until 1971.

Passage through Cannon Bay is among small mangrove islands. At marker 81 you enter Tarpon Bay, a lake connected to larger Alligator Bay by Alligator Creek. Tarpon Bay received its name from the acrobatic, heavy-bodied, bony-mouthed everyman's game fish. Not only will you find this species in the bays through which you pass, it is also prominent in Florida's coastal waters and along the Gulf coast at such places as Charlotte Harbor. In 1911 A. W. Dimock and his party of canoeists published their story of catching tarpon in the rivers and bays of this route in *Outing* magazine. He described how a hooked tarpon towed his canoe for a quarter of a mile in Broad River before it "seemed to leap at me with wide-open jaws." Called the silver king, tarpons hunt other fish, shrimp, and crabs, feeding more at nighttime than in the daytime. Do not be surprised to see them leap into the air in a blaze of silver during moonlit nights. Experienced anglers suggest that a newcomer to tarpon fishing employ a guide for a first encounter with this ingenuous fighter. Other fish along the route are mullet, redfish, snapper, barracuda, grouper, and sea trout.

Alligator Creek, from markers 77 to 75, is narrow, crooked, shallow, and arbored with low mangrove, as is Plate Creek, ahead, between markers 68 and 67. The tidal flow here is unique; if it is with you on the creek, it will be against you when you exit into Alligator Bay. Fresh water in this area makes it suitable for a mixture of ferns, grasses, palms, and mangroves. After 5.5 miles from Darwin's Place, you will arrive at Plate Creek Bay chickee, one of the most beautiful bay areas on your trip, between markers 65 and 63. One mile farther is Lostmans Five Bay and Lostmans Five Bay campsite, east of marker 60. There are a number of legends about the name Lostmans: One is that five soldiers suspected as deserters were abandoned here; another is that three sailors were lost here after skipping ship in Key West; still another claims that it is a corruption of the last name of Surg. Gen. Thomas Lawson, who in 1838 led 240 men from Fort Denaud to Cape Sable in search of Seminole Indians.

At Onion Key, between markers 58 and 56, notice a national park service patrol cabin in a once-busy development community destroyed in the 1926 hurricane. The cabin is off-limits to visitors. (From marker 52 it is 5.5 miles southwest on unmarked Lostmans River to the South Lostmans campsite at the south tip of Lostmans Key in the Gulf.) You will pass around a series of islands between markers 52 and 42, where you enter Big Lostmans Bay, the recipient of numerous freshwater streams that enter from Big Cypress National Preserve. (At marker 38 is Lostmans Creek, a side route to Rocky Creek, Rocky Creek Bay, and Willy Willy campsite, 2 miles from the marker. The remote campsite is in a freshwater area and hardwood hammock with limestone in the creek and shade trees of gumbo-limbo, cabbage palm, and pigeon plum.)

From marker 32 it is one mile west to the Rogers River Bay double chickee on the north side of the bay. From marker 32 it is 3 miles to marker 26 in Broad River Bay, from which a side route, east, goes 3 miles to Camp Lonesome. (Camp Lonesome has cabbage palm, gumbo-limbo, mangrove, banana, and sea grape vegetation.) From marker 26 turn west on Broad River (toward the Gulf) and paddle nearly 6.5 miles before you see Broad River campsite on the left, only a few yards before you reach marker 25. Here is the last campsite before you enter the "Nightmare," an 8.5-mile narrow, crooked, mosquito-infested, tightly arbored mangrove swamp. One canoeist, Bob Brueckner, who paddled in a team of five through the "Nightmare" in January 1988, described "mosquitoes and gnats that swarmed in the murkiness and wanted to feast upon our bug-bitten hides." Crawling on the latticework of mangrove roots are small crabs, and underneath the roots are snails. You hear the wings of ibis flutter overhead. The route is passable only at high tide; otherwise you must detour 2 miles west on Broad River to the Gulf, turn south 5 miles to Harney River, and paddle 4 miles inland on Harney River to Harney River chickee and marker 12.

Harney River is named for Lt. Col. William Harney, a

member of a U.S. Army expedition to hunt down Chekika, a Seminole Indian leader responsible for a massacre of settlers. The Army team found and killed Chekika, then, en route to the Gulf, took a wrong turn and stumbled on the river that now bears Harney's name.

After leaving Harney River chickee at marker 12, turn right at marker 11 and stay on the Harney River to marker 9, a distance of 5.5 miles from the chickee. Here you have a choice of taking a 4-mile (one-way) side trip that turns left to Canepatch campsite through Tarpon Bay or staying on the main route by turning right on Shark River for 4.5 miles to Shark River chickee at marker 6. (If you go to Canepatch you will observe an increase in fresh water and wildfowl. You will also see a variety of wild orange, lime, banana, and guava trees. Upstream on Squawk Creek and Rookery Branch are rookeries that may be posted during nesting season.)

Shark River is wide and deep with tall mangroves and an exceptionally good stream for fishing. It has more than forty species of primarily saltwater fish—tarpon, snook, sea trout, and snapper—including lemon and blacktip sharks in shallow areas, and hammerheads in deeper water. Rangers say these are among about one dozen shark species known to be in the park's coastal waters. At marker 6, the Shark River divides, with the main channel continuing right. Stay straight on Little Shark River to Shark River chickee at the confluence of a small stream. You are now 21 miles from your destination in Flamingo. Turn off Little Shark River at marker 5, left, and follow Shark Cutoff to Oyster Bay. Paddle straight southeast and left of the largest islands in the bay to look for marker 2. About 500 yards ahead is the U.S. Coast Guard channel marker 48. (To the right the Coast Guard markers lead 6 miles to the Gulf; as you continue ahead to Flamingo, markers go from 48 to 1.)

From marker 48, go one mile to the Oyster Bay double chickee. Access is right to U.S. Coast Guard marker 50; then turn left (south). From here it is 18 miles on the main route through Whitewater Bay. (With an early start and good weather, and without a strong headwind, you could make the distance to Flamingo in one day.) If your float plans include one or more of the chickees on the east or west side of Whitewater Bay, make an effort to stay at your planned site. From Oyster Bay to Joe River chickee is 4 miles; from Joe River chickee to South Joe chickee is 6 miles; and from South Joe chickee it is 6 miles east to the main route at U.S. Coast Guard marker 10. Enter Tarpon Creek into Coot Bay, and at marker 2 begin the final 2.7 miles to Flamingo on Buttonwood Canal.

When you touch the tender Everglades, listen for its cry for help in healing wounds that have bled for nearly 100 years. "It is on life-support, like a patient with an IV drip, hanging on the end of the line," says Joe Podger, a leader in Friends of the Everglades, a public interest group formed in the 1960s by environmentalists and centenarian Marjory Stoneman Douglas, "the First Lady of the Everglades." "It may be the first national park we lose," stated a CBS–TV reporter in February 1990. Robert Chandler, who became the park's superintendent in 1989, responded to printed media headlines ("Everglades on the Brink of Ecosystem Collapse," "Mercury Found in Everglades Bass," "Agricultural Drainage Judged Everglades' Worst Enemy") by saying "There is nothing that holds a candle to the Everglades in terms of needs. It's beyond threats; it's really in serious trouble."

The wounds to the glades have never gone unnoticed by Floridians. From the 1920s, when Ernest F. Coe led the Everglades National Park Association, to David M. Fairchild, Stephen T. Mather, John K. Small, John Pennekamp, the State Federation of Women's Clubs, and Florida Governor Bob Graham, who began a Save Our Everglades initiative in 1983, the crusade continues. In April 1990 John Lancaster of the *Washington Post* reported that "engineers hope to restore what they've wrecked." Today the U.S. Army Corps of Engineers, in a project with the South Florida Water Management District, is under orders to modify the water infrastructure. Perhaps in the twenty-first century Florida's environmental troubadours, Dale and Linda Crider, will have their prognosis "Foreverglades."

### Information

Counties: Collier, Dade, Monroe

Average Temperatures: January, 68°F (low), 80.7°F (high); August, 81.5°F (low), 91.5°F (high)

National Properties: Everglades National Park, 4001 SR 9336, Homestead, FL 33034, (305) 242-7700 (Main Visitor Center) or (305) 247-1216 for bookstore of the Florida National Parks and Monument Association; Everglades City Ranger Station and Visitor Center, (813) 695-3311; Chekika Campground, (305) 251-0371; Flamingo Ranger Station and Visitor Center, (813) 695-2945 and Lodge (305) 253-2241 or (800) 600-3813; Key Largo Ranger Station, (305) 852-5119; Shark Valley Visitor Center, (305) 221-8776; Shark Valley Tram Tour, (305) 221-8455; Emergencies, 24 hours, (305) 247-7272; Resource Management, Backcountry Office, (305) 245-1381

State Agencies: South Florida Water Management District, 3301 Gun Club Rd. (P.O. Box 24680), West Palm Beach, FL 33416, (407) 686-8800, or (800) 432-2045 inside Florida.

Chambers of Commerce: Greater Homestead–Florida City CC, 43 North Krome Ave., Homestead, FL 33034, (305) 247-2332; Everglades Area CC, P.O. Box 130, Everglades City, FL 33929, (813) 695-3941

Services and Amenities: *Commercial Campgrounds:* Glades Haven Campground, 800 S.E. Copeland, Everglades City, FL 33929, (813) 695-2746; *Campgrounds near the eastern entrance to the park:* see *Information* Biscayne National Park; *Inns:* The Rod and Gun Club, 200 Riverside Dr., Everglades City, FL 33929, (813) 695-2101

*Airboat Tours:* Miccosukee Indian Village (US 41), P.O. Box 440021, Miami, FL 33143, (305) 223-8380, Ext. 347; *Bicycle Rentals:* Flamingo Lodge, Marina and Outpost Resort, Box 428, Flamingo, FL 33034, (305) 253-2241; Shark Valley Visitor Center, (305) 221-8776; *Boat Docks, Boats, Canoes, and Houseboat Rentals:* see Flamingo Lodge, above; Everglades National Park Boat Tours, Box 119, Everglades City, FL 33929,

(813) 695-2591; Majestic Everglades Excursions, P.O. Box 241, Everglades City, FL 33929, (813) 695-2777; North American Canoe Tours/Everglades Outpost, Box 5038, Everglades City, FL 33929, (813) 695-4666; *Guides and Tours:* see Boat Rentals, above. (North American Canoe Tours has rental equipment, canoes, kayaks, and shuttle car service to and from Flamingo. Also provided are four- to seven-day guided tours with all food and equipment on the Wilderness Waterway Trail. Majestic Everglades Excursions offers two daily private day trips of about 4 hours in the 10,000 Islands: at 8:45 a.m. and 1:45 p.m. These are available from October 1 through May, but there are no operations in the month of September.) *Insect Protection:* Shoo Bug Jacket, Cole Outdoor Products of America, 801 P St., Lincoln, NE 68508; *Maps:* NOAA Nautical Charts, Distribution Division N/CG33, 6501 Lafayette Ave., Riverdale, MD 20737

## BISCAYNE NATIONAL PARK

Biscayne National Park, established as a national monument in 1968, was designated a national park in 1980. With 181,500 acres, of which 96 percent are aquatic, it is the nation's largest marine park. It is located in Biscayne Bay from Miami south to Key Largo National Marine Sanctuary. A subtropical paradise for wildlife, it has a mainland shoreline of mangroves, a translucent bay, living coral reefs, 250 species of fish, and thirty-three unspoiled islands. Seven-mile Elliott Key, the largest of the islands, is a forest of gumbo-limbo, mahogany, Jamaica dogwood, and strangler fig. The park is rich in history, with facts and legends about pirates, alien smugglers, bootleggers, fortune hunters, millionaires, angry developers who opposed the preserve designation, and shipwrecks at Soldier Key, Long Reef, and Fowery Rocks.

*What to See and Do:* Scuba diving, boating, canoeing, camping, and hiking are the primary activities of this adventure. More coral reef here and at Pennekamp park is accessible than anywhere else in Florida. Canoeing is near the mainland, but you can motorboat out to the Keys and beyond. Hiking is on a 7-mile trail on Elliott Key. Fairchild Tropical Garden is on the mainland, only a few miles from the park.

*Where to Begin:* In Homestead, at the junction of US 1 and Lucy Street (SE 8th Street), turn east on Lucy Street, which becomes North Canal Drive (SW 328th Street), and go 9 miles to park headquarters at Conway Point. If you come from the Florida Turnpike, turn south on Tallahassee Road (SW 137th Avenue) to North Canal Drive and then left. The Miami International Airport is 35 miles north.

*About the Adventures:* The park's keys, shoals, and lagoons are northernmost of the Florida Keys, reachable only by boat. The north boundary is less than one mile from Cape Florida State Park and Key Biscayne, and the south boundary adjoins Card Sound, John Pennekamp Coral Reef State Park, and Key Largo Coral Reef Marine Sanctuary. The waters are exceptionally clear, cleansed by the Atlantic Ocean, the bay, keys, and reefs. Within Biscayne Bay the water depth is no more than 12 feet. High humidity, abundant sunshine, hot, wet summers, and warm winters give the park a subtropical climate. Mosquitoes and other biting insects are least aggressive from January to April.

Your stay in the park can be divided into three major locations: on top of the water, underwater at the reefs, and on the Keys. Preparations for all of these can begin at park headquarters with the Biscayne Aqua-Center, the park's only official concessionaire. The center will provide instructions or give you information about where you can be trained (Pirate's Cove Dive Center in Homestead, for example). Above water, the center can take you on the glass-bottom *Reef Rover* past sponge harvesters and Adams Key to view the marine life at the coral reefs. Reservations are required for all trips. (The bobbing of the boat sometimes causes seasickness; if you are susceptible, take medication before your trip.) If you scuba dive you will see many species of fish, including friendly

French and angelfish, blue parrot fish, neon gobies, and copper sweepers. You may also swim by sea urchins, sea fans, sponges, coral, and green moray eels.

Additionally, the center's captains can shuttle you 10 miles to Boca Chita Key, an island with Mark C. Honeywell's ornamental lighthouse, restrooms, and picnic/campground facilities; to Adams Key, a day-use island that has a nature trail and picnic area; and to Elliott Key Visitor Center (in the middle of Elliott Key) with its marine displays and the only beach in the park. Here you can be left to camp (with picnic tables, drinking water, restrooms, and shower) and to explore the 7-mile Elliott Key Trail. The trail generally follows an old road through gumbo-limbo, willow, Jamaica dogwood, satinleaf, devil's potato, and vines. At another island, Sands Key, the captain will leave you for backcountry camping (no facilities). Free permits are available for all camping areas; you must carry all provisions in and all trash out. All of the facilities and most of the vegetation on the barrier islands was destroyed or damaged by Hurricane Andrew in 1992. Contact the park service for information about restored facilities.

Closer to the mainland, you can rent a canoe to explore the mangrove shoreline creeks, all within 2 miles of park headquarters. Only the Arsenicker Keys (south of park headquarters) are off-limits, because they are wildfowl nesting grounds. Gentle breezes and shallow water can make your canoe trip in the bay a pleasant experience. If unsure how far out in the bay you can canoe, discuss your plans with a park ranger.

Exploration of the park is more flexible with a powerboat or sailboat. The two mainland boat docks are Homestead Bayfront Park, near Conway Point, and Black Point Park Marina, at the east end of Coconut Palm Drive, 5 miles north of the Bayfront Park. At Black Point you can rent fully equipped runabouts or open fishing boats. You must acquire a free permit from the park headquarters at Conway Point to camp at designated sites. Also, consult the ranger about park regulations and necessary navigational maps. Bay fish include sea trout, Spanish mackerel, snapper, and grouper. A license is not required, but other regulations, on size, number, and season, do apply. Crabbing is allowed, but lobsters are protected in the bay.

To visit other points of interest near the park, begin at the junction of West Palm Drive and Krome Avenue (SR 997) in Forest City. West, 1.5 miles, is the famous Robert Is Here fruit stand with its locally grown tropical fruits. North on Krome Avenue, within 1.6 miles, are the State Farmers Market and the Florida Pioneer Museum, a national historic site, left. After another 4.4 miles north on Krome Avenue, turn left on Coconut Palm Drive to the Redland Fruit and Spice Park. In order to reach the Chekika Campground, a quiet campground and a large artesian spring in the Everglades, go 5 miles farther north on Krome Avenue and turn left on Richmond Drive. In order to reach the Metrozoo, noted for its cageless animals that roam over 280 acres, turn east on Eureka Street (one mile before the Richmond Drive turn off of Krome Street) and go 4 miles; turn left on Lindgren Avenue, go 2 miles, and turn right on Coral Reef Drive to the Metrozoo entrance, right (west of the Florida Turnpike). In order to visit the Fairchild Tropical Garden, continue east from the Metrozoo on Coral Reef Drive (which is also Southwest 152nd Street) to its junction with Old Cutler Road. Turn left and then go 4 miles to the entrance, right. The nation's largest and one of the world's most distinguished tropical gardens was severely damaged by Hurricane Andrew in 1992, particularly the 500 species of palms in the Montgomery Palmetum and Bailey Palm Glade. Costly but immediate action was taken to use support scaffolding to restore palms and cycads that had a chance of survival. The 83-acre botanical garden, dedicated in 1938, has more than 2 miles of trails that can be traversed by walking or by tram. Dotted with lakes, there special gardens of flowering trees and vines, ornamental shrubs, aroids, bromeliads, ficus, sedges, and mangroves. There are also a rare plant house, museum, bookstore, library, and research labs. The garden is open daily with an admission charge. One access from US 1 in South Miami is on SW 42nd Ave., 1.5 miles to Old Cutler Road. Turn right and continue south for 2.1 miles to the garden entrance on the left.

### *Information*

County: Dade

Average Temperatures: January, 63°F (low), 74°F (high); August, 78°F (low), 88°F (high)

National Properties: Biscayne National Park, P.O. Box 1369, Homestead, FL 33090, (305) 230-7275 (located at Conway Point Visitor Center, east end of North Canal Dr. [S.W. 328th St.])

Other Properties: Fairchild Tropical Garden, 10901 Old Cutler Rd., Miami, FL 33156, (305) 667-1651; Florida Pioneer Museum, 826 N. Krome Ave., Florida City, FL 33034, (305) 246-9431; Fruit and Spice Park, 24801 S.W. 187th Ave., Homestead, FL 33031, (305) 247-5727; Miami Metrozoo, 12400 S.W. 152nd St., Miami, FL 33177, (305) 251-0400; Robert Is Here Fruit Stand, 19200 Palm Dr., (S.W. 344th St.), Homestead, FL 33039, (305) 246-1592

Chambers of Commerce: Greater Homestead–Florida City CC, 43 N. Krome Ave., Homestead, FL 33034, (305) 247-2332; Greater South Dade/South Miami/Kendall CC, 6410 S.W. 80th St., Miami, FL 33143, (305) 661-1621; Miami-Dade CC, 9190 Biscayne Blvd., Miami, FL 33138, (305) 751-8648

Services and Amenities: *Commercial Campgrounds:* Southern Comfort Campground (one block east of US 1 on Palm Dr., in Florida City), (305) 248-6909; Aquarius Park (no tents), 451 S.E. 8th St., Homestead, FL 33030, (305) 248-9383; Miami South KOA (from junction of US 1 and S.W. 216th St., 4.7 miles west on S.W. 216th St., then turn north 0.2 mile on 162nd Ave.), (305) 233-5300

*Boat Docks, Power- and Sailboat Rentals:* Black Point Marina, (305) 258-4092; Club Biscayne Boat Rentals, (305) 258-1477; *Boating, Glass-Bottom Boats, Reef Scuba–Snorkeling Trips, Canoe Rentals:* Biscayne National Underwater Park,

Inc., (a concessionaire of Biscayne National Park), P.O. Box 1270, Homestead, FL 33090, (305) 230-1100; *Swimming, Marina:* Homestead Bayfront Park (a Dade County park adjoining Biscayne National Park), P.O. Box 900444, Homestead, FL 23090 (305) 230-3033/3034

## THE FLORIDA KEYS

Florida's southernmost archipelago is the Florida Keys, hundreds of low tropical islets, some now forming from spider-legged red mangrove thickets and others the product of ancient coral and oolite limestone. With the Florida Bay and the Gulf of Mexico to the north and the Florida Straits of the Atlantic Ocean to the south, the waters are ever-changing hues. Varying with the sun and the storm, they can be as blue as the kissing chromis and the parrot fish or as green as jade sea fans. Underwater in a living coral reef are crustacea, sponges, anemones, octopi, cardinal soldierfish, and purple creole wrasses. Roseate spoonbills and great white herons flock to their rookeries, candy-striped tree snails climb in dark hammocks, and lignum vitaes bloom blue as they have for centuries. But modern engineering has changed forty-two of these islands, connecting them by the Overseas Highway, whose precursor was the Overseas Railroad, from Key Largo to Key West. This historic route is your passageway to the preserved natural areas: John Pennekamp Coral Reef State Park, the only one of its kind in the world; Lignumvitae Key State Botanical Site; Indian Key Historic Site; Long Key and Bahia Honda state parks; and Key Deer National Wildlife Refuge, the habitat of the endangered delicate key deer. Beyond Key West is the Dry Tortugas, where you can travel by seaplane to Garden Key, near North America's only nesting ground of the sooty tern.

*What to See and Do:* Options on this journey are camping, hiking, birding, scuba diving, snorkeling, sailing, motorboating, fishing, and shelling.

*Where to Begin:* From Homestead, take US 1 south (or ride a Greyhound bus) all the way to Key West. Beginning at Key Largo, the highway distance is marked every mile. Airports are at Marathon and Key West.

*About the Adventures:* When you arrive in the town of Key Largo, on a 30-mile island of the same name, you sense a Florida different from the other Floridas you know. This difference is first apparent when you cross Cross Key, part of the Everglades' roaming range of the nation's only crocodile (*Crocodylus acutus*). The fewer than three hundred endangered reptiles deliberately hide here, and their habitats are closed to the public. You can see other wildlife, however, such as ospreys, which engineer their nests on high power-line columns and show off by making high dives for fish in the bay. The highway itself is also different: At one time it rated as "the eighth wonder of the world," a 127-mile Overseas Railroad from Homestead to Key West, constructed by thousands of strong men, hundreds who died in the process, with a price tag of $28 million to Henry M. Flagler, founder of the Florida East Coast Railroad. Started in 1906 and finished in 1912, the graceful track of steel over viaducts of imported German cement connected Key West to far-away New York City and Standard Oil, the source of Flagler's money. The first year of construction, called a "web-footed job all the way," a hurricane drowned 130 men. But the intrepid Flagler said "go ahead," and in 1909 another hurricane washed away 40 miles of track and embankment. Again, the dreamer said "go ahead." Finally, on January 22, 1912, the *Extension Special* left Miami with Flagler in his own luxurious car, the "Rambler" (built in 1886 and now at the Flagler Museum in Palm Beach), and with four passenger cars filled with dignitaries and news reporters. Key West celebrated with a 3-day fiesta, at which schoolchildren sang songs of welcome and threw roses in the pathway of the partially blind Flagler. Tears streamed by his silver mustache. He died 16 months later, at the age of 84, and the railroad that went to sea died at sea 23 years later in a horrifying Labor Day hurricane.

The road to Key West, the Overseas Highway (completed in 1938), is superimposed on the same historic route, with few diversions. The railroad's mile markers (MM) have been retained, and you will see the small green-and-white signs beginning at 110 at Lake Surprise and ending in Key West. Many years ago explorers and settlers grouped the keys into upper, middle, and lower divisions, with Key West having sufficient distinction to be an island unto itself. The Upper Keys are from Key Largo through the Matecumbe Keys, the Middle Keys extend to Bahia Honda, and the Lower Keys include everything in the southwestern 36 miles, except for Key West. Key Largo was known as Rock Harbor until a citizens' and postal decree changed its name in 1952 to cash in on the 1948 film *Key Largo*. The film's director, John Huston, made a few shots inside the Carribean Club, but Humphrey Bogart and Lauren Bacall remained on their California sets.

From Key Largo to Tavernier you will find a number of dive centers that offer instruction, rentals, and tour guides for exploring the nine main diving sites in the 178-square-mile John Pennekamp Coral Reef State Park (MM 102.5). Additionally, the Coral Reef Park Company, a park concessionaire, provides scuba and snorkeling instruction, boats and equipment rentals, guides, and daily trips on the glass-bottomed *Discovery*. Through the glass you are likely to see a variety of sponges and corals, reef tenants such as the yellow-striped grunt and the black double-collared porkfish. (If the water is choppy and you have a tendency for seasickness, take preventive medication before you go.) Diving is the best way to see many of the 650 varieties of colorful tropical fish, blue-eyed squid, octopi, purple sea fans, orange sponges, coral shrimp, spiny lobsters, and 40 species of corals—including star, pillar, staghorn, and stone flower. Otherwise, snorkeling is a must if you want to familiarize yourself with the marine world of the reef. For visibility, summer months are best. Whatever your choice, you need either experience or a guide, because the reef is about 5 miles out to sea and the shoals and coral outcroppings can be hazardous. The park reef is only a section of the Florida Straits that parallel the Keys all the way to Key West. All coral is protected by law.

On the park's land section are a visitor center (where you should go first for information and orientation) and a full-service campground (make reservations in advance). Wild Tamarind Trail, a tropical hardwood hammock, and Mangrove Swamp Trail acquaint you with the park's vegetation. There are also a swimming area and a sailboat and canoe rental dock in the serene Key Largo Sound. Adjoining the park, east, is the Key Largo National Marine Sanctuary, where you can dive and snorkel (without a fee) to see fish, sea turtles, dolphins, and marine invertebrates. More recently protected is the Key Largo Hammock State Botanical Site, with limited access arranged through the park manager. Key Largo has a number of commercial campgrounds, motels, and restaurants. To assist you in deciding where to eat and where to stay (if not camping) from Key Largo to Key West, consult *The Florida Keys* by Joy Williams.

For 40 miles between Lake Surprise and Long Key, the Everglades National Park boundary and the Intrastate Waterway parallel US 1, about 4 miles out in the Florida Bay. The bay is a vast area of uninhabited islands where you can see egrets, herons, pelicans, plovers, and, possibly, an American bald eagle and a roseate spoonbill. Information is available at the park's Key Largo ranger station (MM 99–98). Less than 10 miles into the bay is North Nest Key, an isolated island campsite that requires advance reservations for an overnight trip. Rental boats are available in Key Largo and at the Tavernier Creek Marina (MM 90.5). You will probably be required to take a compass, a nautical map chart, and safety equipment, and be prepared for squalls or rough water.

Islamorada (MM 82), which the Spanish named when they saw beaches of purple at a distance from the janthina shells in the springtime, is on Upper Matecumbe Key. It has a history of tragedy. Shipwrecked sailors were killed or enslaved here by the Calusa Indians, and the worst hurricane in the Keys' history drowned half of its one thousand people in 1935. Only the locomotive Old 447, an evacuation train, was left on the tracks when a 17-foot-high tidal wave battered the island. It was the end of what critics had called "Flagler's Folly." A monument (MM 81.5) at Islamorada Methodist Church honors those who died in the storm. Today the town is promoted as "the sport-fishing capital of the world" and "the culinary capital of the Keys." It has a number of marinas and fishing tournaments.

At the west end of Islamorada (MM 79) are a parking area and dock, northside, where you can get a boat to Lignumvitae State Botanical Site, north, and Indian Key Historic Site, south, under the US 1 bridge. Although you can rent a boat at Bud 'n' Mary's Marina (MM 80), you will miss valuable information unless you take the trip with a state guide on a passenger ferry. Advance reservations at Long Key State Recreation Area (11 miles farther west) are necessary, unless by chance someone fails to show. Guided tours may not run on Tuesday or Wednesday; check in advance for the schedule.

Indian Key, like Islamorada, has a history of human tragedy. Shipwrecked sailors met the same fate here as on the Matecumbe Keys, and in 1840 Seminole Indians raided and destroyed a flourishing settlement. Among those slain was Dr. Henry Perrine, botanist and physician, who had befriended the Seminoles by treating their sick. In 1825 Capt. Jacob Housman, an enterprising wealthy salvager of reef-wrecked ships, left Key West to avoid paying taxes and obeying salvage laws. On dry, rocky, 11-acre Indian Key he established a model settlement. Soil was shipped in for his short tree-lined streets, and wharves, homes, warehouses, a post office, and the Tropical Hotel were built. In the process, Captain Housman persuaded the state legislature to designate his island the seat of Dade County. Supported by Captain Housman, Dr. Perrine and his family settled here to research tropical plants and to establish nurseries in the Matecumbes. Among Housman's visitors were ornithologist John J. Audubon and his assistant, background artist George Lehman, who came for a week in 1832. They were rowed to Sandy Key and other islands in

Florida Bay, and from this trip Audubon added the great white heron, roseate tern, reddish egret, and double-breasted cormorant to his research list. He also reported spotting the quail dove, rarely seen. Your park interpretive guide will not only describe the history of the island as you relax on the observation deck, but explain the plant life, including Dr. Perrine's favorite sisal agave, and the life-style of the golden orb spider and the white butterflies that migrate in May.

Even if you have only a miniscule interest in botany, you must go to Lignumvitae Key, a 332-acre "primeval past" owned and preserved by William J. Matheson from 1919 to 1953, devoutly managed by Capt. Abner Sweeting and his son Hugh, and saved by The Nature Conservancy in 1970 until the state could purchase it that same year. A state guide walks with you on the trail through Florida's most tropical hardwood forest. The lignum vitae (*Guaiacum sanctum*), one of the featured forest trees, has a holy history. Revered as a tree in the Garden of Eden, honored in the Renaissance as "the tree of life" for health and immortality, claimed to be the source of the Holy Grail, and called "holywood" in the Bahamas, the lignum vitae is prominent here in the largest stand in the United States. The tree blooms in late March and early April and has yellow fruit with red skin. One lignum vitae on the trail is estimated to be 1,500 years old. Some of the other known plants on the key are black ironwood (which is hard to saw and weighs 86 pounds per cubic foot); pigeon plum (a source of pectin); poisonwood (under which you should not pass in the rain, because rainwater carries the poison); quick stick tree (stick a piece of it in the ground and it grows); mahogany (whose seeds are as large as goose eggs); and white stopper bush. Torchwood blossoms contain citrus, a favorite of the butterflies, and the Jamaica dogwood is a favorite for the coloful Florida banded tree snails. If you see an animal the size of a squirrel running up a tree, look closer; it may by a Key Largo wood rat.

At Long Key State Recreation Area (MM 67.5) you will find both human and natural history. Here a hurricane in 1906 swept to death a large quarterboat full of Overseas Railroad workers, and another in 1935 destroyed Flagler's famous Long Key Fishing Club for the rich and famous. Zane Grey, who first visited here in 1913, explored, fished, and wrote some of his books—including *Code of the West*—at Long Key. The park has a full-service campground and special sheltered tent decks with exceptional views of the iridescent ocean and colorful sunrises. Interpretive nature trails such as the Golden Orb Trail lead you through dense tropical hammocks to an observation tower and to the beach, where you can wade and snorkel far out on the flats with plenty of shorebirds to keep you company. At MM 50 is the Museum of Natural History of the Florida Keys. In a 63.5-acre preserve there is a Tropical Nature Trail and a rare virgin palm hammock. The museum is open daily from 9 A.M. to 5 P.M.

You will find one of your most spectacular views, and your highest from the road (65 feet), when you cross over Moser Channel (MM 43.5) on the Sevenmile Bridge (completed in 1982) on your way to Bahia Honda State Recreation Area (MM 37.2). (*Bahia*, pronounced bay-uh, *Honda* means "deep bay.") The park has the Keys' finest swimming beach, fishing and boating docks, and a full-service campground. Cabins are also available for rent. Near Sandspur Beach is a nature trail that enters a coastal hammock and brings you to a tidal lagoon, where you can see rare dwarf morning glory, silver palm, spiny catesbaea, and yellow satinwood trees. White-crowned pigeons, reddish egrets, and brown pelicans seem accustomed to the beach crowds. The campground is the only public one in the Lower Keys; make reservations in advance. At Ramrod Key (MM 27) you can engage the Reef Divers to take you about 7 miles out to Looe Key, a national marine sanctuary, which some divers consider the Keys' most beautiful.

An endangered species, the trusting and friendly key deer (*Odocoileus virginianus clavium*), may walk out in front of your car in the Key Deer National Wildlife Refuge. Fewer than 50 of the species in the 1940s proliferated to nearly 400 in the

1970s, but now the estimate is back down to about 250. It took the nationally syndicated cartoons of J. N. "Ding" Darling and a concerned nation to persuade Congress finally to create the refuge in 1954. Environmentalist Jack C. Watson (1913–1982), more than any other individual, devoted his efforts to creating the refuge and making certain that poachers and land prospectors did not exterminate the species. Today the greatest threats are automobile collisions (sixty or more each year) and loss of habitat on Big Pine Key and No Name Key. The animals, which are rarely more than 75 pounds and are less than a yard tall, are "too cute for their own good," according to an Associated Press report.

Access to the refuge from US 1 is at the junction of Key Deer Boulevard (MM 31 and CR 940). Drive 1.5 miles and turn left on Watson Boulevard to the refuge headquarters. After another 1.6 miles you will come to a parking area, left, and the Watson Wildlife Trail. The loop walk of less than one mile will orient you to the harsh environment that provides the toy deer with their drinking water and vegetable diet. The deer use small sinkholes in the oolite limestone as drinking fountains. The vegetation is different from that in surrounding dry areas. Plumy brake fern, saw and sabal palmetto, wax myrtle, buttonwood, satinleaf, sweet acacia, and slash pine are on the trail. Two palms, the thatch and the silver, offer fruit for the deer and the birds. The best times to see the deer are early in the morning and late in the day. Whatever your proximity and good intention, do not feed them.

Before you leave the refuge, follow the Blue Hole Road (about 0.3 mile from the trail) and park at the end. Walk into the Watson Hammock, where you will see huge mahogany, torchwood, strangler fig, and guava. The area is also good for birding, except in the winter, and you may see the unusual light-yellow raccoon here. Guides will help you explore the unrestricted waters and islands of the national wildlife refuges—Great White Heron, Key Deer, and Key West. One is biologist Stan Becker. (See *Information.*)

Key West is the state's most southern, sunny, and

imperturable city. With its epithets many, its "island of bones" a mystery, and its history magical, it is the end of the road but not the end of your adventure. In a city 2 miles wide and 5 miles long, you can walk and bicycle to gardens of frangipani, sapodilla, and jacaranda; forts; museums; beaches; harbors; graveyards; and other historic sites. Claimed by the fierce Calusa centuries ago, rejected by Ponce de León in 1513, named Key West by the English in the 1700s, and sold for $2,000 by Spaniard Juan Salas to John Simonton from Mobile, Alabama, in 1821, it was declared of interest to the U.S. Navy when Lt. Matthew Perry raised the first U.S. flag there in 1822. Seven years later William Whithead surveyed the town and counted three hundred pioneer settlers. In spite of yellow fever, mosquitoes, hurricanes, pirates, pillagers, and dubious transients, Key West was here to stay. Or was it? Fires nearly destroyed it in 1859 and 1866, and in 1934 the town was bankrupt and starving. The state recommended that all the citizens abandon the island and relocate on the mainland, away from Flagler's railroad, which had nothing to carry and was going "nowhere for nobody" during the Great Depression. The next year the railroad was gone, with 42 miles of track and fill washed away.

But Key West survived and endured. It remembered its days of glory in the 1880s when it had been Florida's largest city and the nation's wealthiest per capita. After the Overseas Highway was completed, Julius Stone arrived with his skills for tourism, and World War II made it the "Singapore of the West," a city fast becoming a vacation mecca. Key West, said writers and critics, was "self-indulgent," "bohemian," "alien," "full of contrasts," "crazy but elegant," "intolerably tolerant," "Truman's retreat," and "Pulitzer paradise." "A fine country," wrote Ernest Hemingway; "umbilically extravagant," said poet Richard Eberhart.

The first place to visit is the chamber of commerce at 402 Wall Street, where you will receive information on the wide variety of lodgings (from sleeping-bag housing to luxury hotels); it is best to know in advance what type you would prefer and how much you can spend. Ask for an accommodation directory, information on bicycle and boat rentals, and guides to the reefs. The two commercial campgrounds in Key West are Boyd's Key West and Jabour's Trailer Court. The winter season, when lodging is most expensive, is usually from mid-December into April. The 190-block historical district is the state's largest concentration of wooden buildings and bed-and-breakfast homes. Some of these famous structures are the Audubon House, the Hemingway House, and the house of Joseph Porter, Key West's first native-born physician. The city's cosmopolitan architecture represents a period in its history when English settlers from the Grand Bahamas (whose descendants are known as Conchs) constructed gingerbread houses, Cubans brought Spanish culture, and Americans from the eastern seaboard brought New England and Southern styles. Other historic areas to explore are Mallory Square, Key West Lighthouse at 938 Whitehead Street, Wrecker Museum on 322 Duval Street, and the Fort Taylor State Scenic Park at the southwest tip of the island. A trapezoidal fort of granite, brick, and slate, Fort Taylor was begun in 1845, took 21 years to complete, and was unique for its desalination plant. In 1973 it was designated a National Historical Landmark. Sunsets, which Audubon called "a blaze of refulgent glory," are honored events in Key West. One of the best views is from Fort Taylor. Tank Island does not interfere there as it can at Mallory Square, the site of the major evening ritual to watch the sunsets.

No other key compares with Garden Key, the last outpost, the "Gibraltar of the Gulf"—Fort Jefferson National Park. Ponce de León, who discovered Garden Key in 1513, named it and six others Los Tortugas ("the turtles") after the many turtles he saw. The name was later changed to Dry Tortugas because fresh water did not exist on the islands. The keys were a nest for pirates and slave traders until the early nineteenth century, changing only when the United States became interested in the island's strategic value in the 1820s. In 1845 the federal government began plans for a large fort at

Garden Key, and a year later Lt. Horatio Wright arrived to supervise the construction of a hexagonal monolith covering most of the island's 16 acres. During the Civil War it served as a prison for slaves, criminals, and deserters, among them three Lincoln assassination conspirators and Dr. Samuel Mudd, whose only crime had been to set John Wilkes Booth's fractured leg. (After nearly 4 years, Dr. Mudd was pardoned.) The huge fort was never completed, nor were any of its 140 guns ever fired. In 1935 it became a national park, Florida's "slumbering giant."

You can travel the 70 miles from Key West by boat, taking 8 hours or more, or by seaplane in 30 minutes. From the low-altitude flight you can see a desert under a sea of glass, a myriad marine life, and the changing colors of the water: blue, dark green, black, silver, and yellow. Views of the Marquesas atoll and the wreckage site of the Spanish galleon *Atocha*, which sank in 1622 and became famous with Mel Fisher's treasure find in 1985, are also better from the plane than from the boat. If you go by boat, however, you can see the coral reefs and marine world of tropical fish up close. Seaplane outfitters, such as Key West Seaplane Service, can take you to Garden Key for a few hours or for a few days. Access to the service at Murray's Marina on Stock Island is from US 1 (MM 5 and 4.2) on Junior College Road. You must take all drinking water, food, and gear with you and bring all trash out. Before you go, call the park service and ask for information on restrictions, fishing, charter boats, and air taxi operators. Because seaplane service limits your luggage to about 40–50 pounds, you must wisely consider your needs for overnight tenting (up to 14 consecutive days). You can snorkel, swim, and explore the fort. A ranger is on duty. Bush Key, which is nearby, is closed between May and September to protect thousands of sooty terns during nesting. Other birds frequenting Bush Key are brown and blue-faced boobies, roseate terns, brown noddies, and large gliding frigate birds. A night on Garden Key can be mesmerizing and a treat for the senses. While here, you can observe Florida's combined interests of preserving its historic sites and protecting its natural environment.

## Information:

County: Monroe

Average Temperatures: January, 67.7°F (low), 78.7°F (high); August, 79.6°F (low), 91.1°F (high)

National Properties: Everglades National Park (Key Largo), 98710 Overseas Hwy., Key Largo, FL 33037, (305) 852-5119; Dry Tortugas National Park (formerly Fort Jefferson National Monument), 4001 State Road 9336, Homestead, FL 33034, (305) 242-7700; Key Deer NWR, P.O. Box 510, Big Pine Key, FL 33043, (305) 872-2239; Key Largo National Marine Sanctuary, 300 Ocean Dr., Key Largo, FL 33037, (305) 451-1644

State Properties: Bahia Honda State Recreation Area, Rte. 1, Box 782, Big Pine Key, FL 33043, (305) 872-2353; Fort Zachary Taylor State Historic Site, P.O. Box 289, Key Wêst, FL 33041, (305) 292-6713; Indian Key Historic Site and Lignumvitae Key State Botanical Site, P.O. Box 1052, Islamorada, FL 33036, (305) 664-4815; John Pennekamp Coral Reef State Park, P.O. Box 487, Key Largo, FL 33037, (305) 451-1202; Key Largo Hammock State Botanical Site, same address as Pennekamp; Long Key State Recreation Area, P.O. Box 776, Long Key, FL 33001, (305) 664-4815

Other Properties: Audubon House and Gardens, 205 Whitehead St., Key West, FL 33040, (305) 294-2116; Lighthouse Maritime Museum, 938 Whitehead St., Key West, FL 33040, (305) 294-0012; Museum of Natural History of the Florida Keys, Bayside MM 50, Marathon, FL 33050, (305) 743-9100; Wreckers Museum, 322 Duval St., Key West, FL 33040, (305) 294-9502

Chambers of Commerce: Florida Keys Visitors Bureau, 416 Fleming St., Key West, FL 33040, 800-FLA-KEYS (covers all the Keys); Islamorada CC, P.O. Box 915, Islamorada, FL 33036, (305) 664-4503 or (800) 322-5397; Key Largo CC, 105950 Overseas Hwy., Key Largo, FL 33037, (305) 451-1414 or (800) 822-1088; Key West CC, 402 Wall St., Key West, FL

33040, (305) 294-2587; Lower Keys CC, P.O. Box 430511, Big Pine Key, FL 33043, (305) 872-2411 or (800) 872-3722

Services and Amenities: The Keys offer far too many services to all be listed here. Check with the Florida Keys Visitors Bureau, listed above. A few examples are: *Commercial Campgrounds:* Calusa Camp Resort (MM 101.5), 325 Calusa Rd., Key Largo, FL 33037, (305) 451-0232; American Outdoors (MM 97.5), Rte. 1, Box 38A, Key Largo, FL 33037, (305) 852-8054; Fiesta Key KOA Resort (MM 70), Long Key, FL 33001, (305) 664-4922; Sugarloaf Key KOA (MM 20), Rte. 2, Box 680, Summerland Key, FL 33042, (305) 745-3549; Boyd's Key West Campground (MM 5), 6401 Maloney Ave., Stock Island, FL 33040, (305) 294-1465; Jabour's Trailer Court, 223 Elizabeth St., Key West, FL 33040, (305) 294-5723

*Bicycle Rentals:* Key West Bicycle Rentals, 601 Truman Ave., Key West, FL 33040, (305) 296-3344; *Boating, Boat Rentals, Sailing, Water Sports:* Tavernier Creek Marina, P.O. Box 6, Tavernier, FL 33070, (305) 852-5854; Bud 'n' Mary's, P.O. Box 628, Islamorada, FL 33036, (305) 664-2461; Stan Becker, P.O. Box 62, Big Pine Key, FL 33043, (305) 872-2620; Club Nautico, 717–C Eisenhower Dr., Key West, FL 33040, (305) 294-2225; *Diving, Snorkeling, and Allied Water Sports:* American Diving Headquarters (MM 106), P.O. Box 1250, Key Largo, FL 33037, (305) 451-0037, (800) 634-8464; Reef Divers (MM 27), Ramrod Key, FL 33042, (305) 872-2215; Reef Raiders Dive Shop (MM 4.5), Stock Island, FL 33040, (305) 294-0660; *Seaplane and Water Transportation to Dry Tortugas:* Key West Seaplane Service, 5603 Jr. College Rd., Key West, FL 33040, (305) 294-6978; Sea 'n Sail Excursions, Lands End Marina, 274 Margaret St., Key West FL 33040, (305) 294-7280

# 7

## GEORGIA SEA ISLANDS
## AND OKEFENOKEE SWAMP

Georgia's 100-mile Atlantic coastline, from South Carolina south to Florida, is composed of a significant chain of barrier sea islands that Spanish explorers of the 1500s called "golden isles." The islands are in seven major groups, separated by tidal river inlets that create a remarkable and distinctive estuary system. Each grouping has younger islands with beaches and older upland islands on the west, with salt marshes in between. The eastern and western islands of each group were formed in two different geological periods. During the Pleistocene epoch, 35,000 to 40,000 years ago, the sea level was about 6 feet higher than it is now and the western islands were the beaches. Also during this period, the last great ice sheet froze enough sea water for the ocean to recede nearly 400 feet, placing the shoreline about 70 to 80 miles eastward on the continental shelf. A subsequent remelting of the Earth's ice returned the ocean to its former level, causing new islands to be formed about 18,000 years ago. During the Holocene period, about 5,000 years ago, more new barrier islands were formed, mainly the ones you see with the beaches today. Even now, tidal currents and storms constantly buffet the islands, changing the shape of the newer islands and making it likely that, within a human generation, you will be able to see new shoals visited by pelicans, gulls, and terns. For example, Williamson Island, located south of Tybee Island, did not exist in 1957, but in 20 years it grew to nearly 250 acres, with sandbars and dunes, grasses, and sea oats. Because barrier islands have a tendency to move, this island may shift westward to join Petit Chou Island, or it may disappear entirely after a major storm.

In your journeys you may notice that a number of the islands have a drumstick shape, with the north ends being wider. This shape is caused by the inlet tidal currents temporarily deflecting the southward-moving shoreline currents. When the currents swing back to the shore, they cause sand erosion that widens the shoals. In this manner, tidal energy across a low continental shelf has formed the islands. Two main currents produce normal waves: the Gulf Stream, which flows south to north about 4 miles per hour, 100 miles off the coast at the edge of the continental shelf; and the shoreline current, which flows in opposite directions close to shore. Reefs are rare off the Georgia coast, but Gray's Reef on a limestone outcrop about 17 miles from Sapelo Island is prominent. Plant and animal life at the reef, dependent on clear water for sunlight, would be destroyed if the water became cloudy from pollutants, and the government is watching to see that this does not happen. (See *Appendix* for list of Georgia threatened and endangered wildlife.)

Located along a concave coastline, the islands are in an oceanographic section called the Georgia Bight between Cape Hatteras in North Carolina and Cape Canaveral in Florida. When the tides approach the Atlantic coastline, they first hit the northern shores of the bight with a 2- to 3-foot tide, but the wave energy is deflected southward. Without a shoreline, the waves fall over each other in a rush to the islands, as toward the end of a giant funnel, to cause faster and higher tides that range from 6 to 9 feet. Here, more than anywhere in the Carolinas or in Florida, boaters must have a tide schedule to be safe.

The barrier ecosystems are ocean beach, salt marsh, forest, and freshwater sloughs, all similar to those of north Florida. The Georgia coast's distinctive salt marshes, which cover about 0.5 million acres, make up one third of all Atlantic seaboard salt marshes. In the levee and low marshes, smooth cordgrass (*Spartina alterniflora*) is dense, and animal life is active. Mud fiddler crabs, oysters, mussels, periwinkle snails, mud snails, and coffee-bean snails are prominent. Among the fiddler crabs, the brackish-water fiddler (*Uca minax*) is larger than other species. It can be recognized by its white pincers and red dots on the pincer joints. At the high marsh and marsh border, where there is saltwort (*Batis maritima*), needlerush (*Juncus roemerianus*), and yellow-flowering sea oxeye (*Borrichia fruitescens*), you will notice fiddler and wharf crabs, a clear sign of lower water salinity. (See *Appendix* for list of Georgia endangered flora.) Farther inland, at shallow tidal fringes of cabbage palm, yaupon, and wax myrtle, are nurseries of young marine species such as shrimp, crab, flounder, and menhaden. The maritime forests of hardwoods and loblolly and slash pines are easy to see from the few roads that penetrate the estuaries or cross to the islands, but some causeways and boats will suddenly take you into cordgrass over your head. Some of the most expansive salt marshes can be seen from Sapelo Island, Fort Pulaski National Monument by the Savannah River, and the Marine Extension Center on Skidaway Island. The Sapelo Island area also has excellent estuaries and superb beach dunes. On Little Saint Simons, Cumberland, Wassaw, and Blackbeard islands are examples of freshwater ponds. Sounds unspoiled by dredging or commercial development are near Ossabaw and Saint Catherines islands, and the most natural maritime forests are in Wassaw Island National Wildlife Refuge and the Cumberland Island National Seashore.

Georgia's coastal rivers are high organic blackwater (Satilla is an example), high sediment alluvial (such as the Altamaha), and tidewater (Jerico is this kind). A number of coastal rivers, particularly the Altamaha, Ogeechee, and Satilla, run through wilderness areas featuring forests of cypress, tupelo, bay, oak, and magnolia as they approach saltwater inlets. All the rivers flow southeastward to the ocean, except for Saint Marys, which first flows south, then north, and finally eastward to the coast. From north to south, the islands are Tybee and Wassaw, between the Savannah and Ogeechee

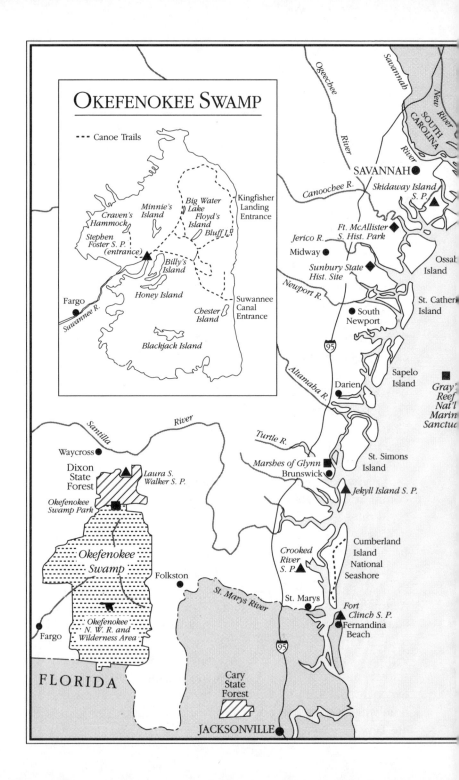

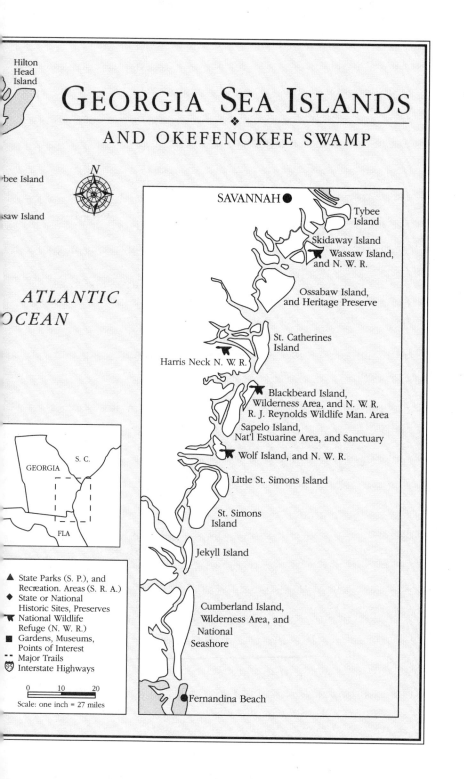

# GEORGIA SEA ISLANDS

## AND OKEFENOKEE SWAMP

Hilton
Head
Island

*bee Island

*saw Island

*N*

*ATLANTIC
OCEAN*

SAVANNAH ●

Tybee
Island

Skidaway Island

Wassaw Island,
and N. W. R.

Ossabaw Island,
and Heritage Preserve

St. Catherines
Island

Harris Neck N. W. R.

Blackbeard Island,
Wilderness Area, and N. W. R.
R. J. Reynolds Wildlife Man. Area
Sapelo Island,
Nat'l Estuarine Area, and Sanctuary

Wolf Island, and N. W. R.

Little St. Simons Island

St. Simons
Island

Jekyll Island

Cumberland Island,
Wilderness Area, and
National
Seashore

Fernandina Beach

S. C.

GEORGIA

FLA

▲ State Parks (S. P.), and
  Recreation. Areas (S. R. A.)
◆ State or National
  Historic Sites, Preserves
🦅 National Wildlife
  Refuge (N. W. R.)
■ Gardens, Museums,
  Points of Interest
-- Major Trails
🛣 Interstate Highways

0    10    20

Scale: one inch = 27 miles

rivers; Ossabaw, between the Ogeechee and Jerico rivers; Saint Catherines, between the Jerico and Sapelo rivers; Blackbeard and Sapelo, between the Sapelo and Altamaha rivers; Little Saint Simons, Sea, and Saint Simons, between the Altamaha and Turtle rivers; Jekyll, between the Turtle and Satilla rivers; and Cumberland, between the Satilla and Saint Marys rivers.

One of the appealing characteristics of the chain of barrier islands is that they are largely undeveloped. Other than the islands of Tybee, Saint Simons, Sea, and Jekyll, which have access roads, the natural environment is protected in national wildlife refuges and monuments, wildlife management areas, estuarian sanctuaries, state parks, forests, and historic sites, much to the credit of the state of Georgia and private citizens groups such as The Georgia Conservancy. Two islands, Jekyll and Cumberland, have characteristically different protection. The state of Georgia in 1947 purchased Jekyll, once a private resort of the Jekyll Island Club, formed in 1886 by sixty millionaires, including J. P. Morgan, William Rockefeller, Joseph Pulitzer, R. T. Crane, and Edwin Gould. Under the Jekyll Island Authority, high condominiums have not been allowed on the island; instead, a populated resort blends with the natural quality of the island. Most of Cumberland Island is now Cumberland Island National Seashore, owned by the federal government since 1972. The largest of Georgia's golden isles, it has unspoiled beaches, dunes, marshes, and freshwater lakes accessible only by boat. Bridge access is prohibited, and further development of the few private inholdings is forbidden. Complementing this world of sea islands and vast marshes are the circuitous rivers, equally free of human habitation in long sections.

Historians claim that the thousands of acres of wetlands, dense foliage, extreme tides, and marsh have discouraged long-term human habitation of the sea islands. But the islands and riverbanks are rich in Indian history, folklore, and stories of explorers and pirates, Spanish missions, pioneer farmers, slaves, wealthy developers, and recluses, all who have attempted to claim and tame the wilderness. That heritage and the islands' remoteness will make your journey a first-class adventure. Alluring and subtropical, the islands have been home to the Paleo, Guale, Creek, and other Indians, who found abundant fish in the estuaries, deer and turkey in the island hammocks, and shellfish on the shores. Shell middens, some as high as 15 feet, dot the Indians' favorite islands: Saint Catherines, for example, the capital of the Guale Indians. To convert the Indians, the Spanish set up a chain of Catholic missions on some of the islands beginning in 1565, and they lasted a century before English raiders pushed them and the Indians farther south. The English constructed Fort King George in the early 1700s to guard the main channel of the Altamaha River, and in 1736 Gen. James Oglethorpe built Fort Frederica on Saint Simons Island to defend the fledgling Georgia colony against the Spanish and French. The U.S. Navy acquired Blackbeard Island, a national wildlife refuge since 1940, in 1800 as a source of live oak for shipbuilding, but between 1830 and 1900 the island housed a yellow fever quarantine hospital. All you will see of its services under the National Board of Health is a brick oven, probably used to create a sulphur gas disinfectant. Farther south, on Cumberland Island, you will see the remains of the second Dungeness, a magnificent mansion of Thomas Carnegie and family in the 1880s, now covered with vines and other vegetation. Feral horses and wild turkeys freely roam within the shadows of the crumbling brick walls.

Unrelated to the barrier islands is the more than 700-square-mile Okefenokee Swamp, one of the world's largest and most famous swamps. Officially established in 1937 as the Okefenokee National Wildlife Refuge, it has since become a preserved wilderness area largely in three Georgia counties, with 4,000 acres in Baker County, Florida. An enormous bog of dark brown clear water inside a saucer-shaped depression, the swamp is between 100 and 128 feet above sea level. Once a great lake, it has been the site of many named and unnamed islands, habitats for Indians, explorers, lumberjacks, hermits, and imaginary objects of fear. Hundreds of small lakes, particularly in the center and northeast, dot the landscape where dense, moss-draped cypress hammocks and wet prairies cover black peat bogs. *Okefenokee*, an Indian word, means "land of the trembling earth," describing the quaking layers of peat that shift on the swamp's sandy foundation. Heralded to the world in documentaries, fiction, and motion pictures, it is both a retreat shrouded in mystery, as portrayed in 20th Century Fox's *Swamp Water* and Warner Brothers' *Black Fury*, and a vibrant, pulsating showcase of life and science. About 50 miles inland and west from Cumberland Island, the swamp's low Trail Ridge runs in a north-south direction. The ridge deflects and directs the slowly moving swampwater southwestward to the famous Suwannee River, which flows through Florida to the Gulf of Mexico. The waters east of the low ridge create the Saint Marys River, which flows into the Atlantic Ocean. The swamp has an outstanding display of wildlife: alligator, otter, raccoon, black bear, cottonmouth, deer, thirty-four species of fish, and two hundred species of birds, including the elegant sandhill crane. Wildflowers are profuse, with acres of red chokeberry, orchids, golden club, and pink-veined pitcher plant.

The Okefenokee may have been formed 800,000 years ago as part of the Atlantic Ocean during the early Pleistocene epoch. Humans are believed to have inhabited the area as early as 2000 B.C. Indian mounds indicate that communities were established at least 2,500 years ago. Creeks, Timucuans, and Seminoles were the most recent inhabitants, with Seminoles there as late as the nineteenth century. White settlers lived on the northern border of the swamp in the late eighteenth century. In 1891 Capt. Harry Jackson of the Suwannee Canal Company acquired 238,120 acres from the state to be drained for logging and agricultural purposes. After building 13 miles of canals over 6 years, the project went bankrupt and was abandoned. The next attempt at commercial exploitation of the swamp's interior was by the Charles Hebard Lumber Company of Philadelphia. After purchasing the Suwannee Canal Company land, and more acreage, that company harvested more than 431 million board feet of timber, mainly cypress, between 1909 and 1927. During this period J. L. Sweat of the Georgia legislature led a campaign to preserve the swamp, a foundation effort that led to establishment of the national wildlife refuge in 1937.

To protect this watery wonderland, only three access points are allowed for boat passage into the interior. The Okefenokee Swamp Park at the north edge of the swamp can be entered by highway, but it does not have a boat entrance that joins the other routes. Camping, limited to one night at each campsite, is allowed at designated wooden platforms along the network of 107 miles of canoe trails. Reservations by telephone are required and can be accepted up to 2 months in advance.

To supplement your exploration of the sea islands and the Okefenokee Swamp and enrich your adventures in coastal Georgia, you might want to visit the area's other attractions. Of primary interest is the Bartram Trail, an auto route that follows the explorations of William Bartram during his first visit in 1765 and a subsequent 4-year visit beginning in 1773. The Bartram Trail Society has traced his research in Georgia and made a map of the area from Tybee Island to Cumberland Island along parts of what is now US 17 and to villages such as Springfield, Sunbury, Midway, Cox, Fort Barrington, Darien, Brunswick, and Kingsland. In his *Travels*, Bartram described a rare flowering tree that was later named *Franklinia alatamaha* (in honor of his friend Benjamin Franklin and the Altamaha River). Last seen in the wilds in 1803, the plant has survived from the seeds that Bartram took back to Pennsylvania for propagation. If you are interested in his travels in Georgia and Florida, contact the Bartram Trail Society. (See *Information, Georgia Sea Islands,* this Chapter.)

Another regional activity is paddling the streams of the coastal plain. The rivers most recommended are the Savannah and a tributary, Brier Creek; Ogeechee and a tributary, Canoochee; Altamaha and its tributaries, Ohoopee, Oconee,

Little Ocmulgee, and Ocmulgee; Satilla; and Saint Marys. Detailed descriptions of highlights and scenery, accesses, months runnable, and maps are included in *Southern Georgia Canoeing,* by Bob Sehlinger and Don Otey. Suggested trips on the coastal rivers and a list of charter services, boat ramps, fish camps, marinas, and canoe outfitters for the rivers and barrier islands are in *A Guide to the Georgia Coast,* by The Georgia Conservancy.

In the narrative ahead, the sea islands and the Okefenokee are described separately because of the different preparations needed and facilities available. All locations featured in this chapter can be reached by motor vehicle or by boat within 2 or 3 hours from either the Savannah Municipal Airport in Georgia or the Jacksonville International Airport in Florida.

## GEORGIA SEA ISLANDS

For thousands of years the Georgia sea islands have been forming and changing. Sandbars in the beginning, they became grassy as waves and wind formed berms and dunes that rose high enough to become wave shelters and develop into shrub zones and, eventually, climax forests. In time, new sandbars and new islands formed, with tidal creeks and salt marshes between new and old islands to serve as water and storm barriers to the mainland. This profile interests both natural scientists and curious visitors. The diversity of the islands and coastline have attracted such naturalists as William Bartram, John Muir, Alexander Wilson, Mark Catesby, and John James Audubon. Indians have lived on some of the islands, drinking from the freshwater pools and feeding on the wildlife, particularly fish and shellfish. They and the Spanish and French who tried to establish land claims abandoned the golden isles when the English constructed powerful forts in the mid-eighteenth century. English plantations soon produced rice, indigo, and sea island cotton. Imported African slaves, like their neighbors on Hilton Head Island in South Carolina, later acquired land and created a Gullah culture and dialect unique to America. Today the Georgia Sea Island Singers, a folk group, tours in honor of its heritage. Only a few remaining descendants own their cherished land. Wealthy Americans who purchased entire or large parts of islands in the nineteenth century protected them from large-scale commercial development. Little Saint Simons Island, open to the public since 1976, is the last family-owned barrier island.

*What to See and Do:* You will see many species of land and marine wildlife, particularly birds, on every island: shore- and wading birds, loggerhead turtles, mollusks, alligators, deer, and raccoons. Equally intriguing is the plant life: salt cedar, salt grass, saltwort, fireweed, sea rocket, and yellow lotus. You can hike miles and miles on the beaches and old roads in the forests and visit historic churches, cemeteries, museums, and mansions. The saline marsh and beach breeze will stimulate your appetite and give you reason to visit the fishing village restaurants. Boating, including canoeing; deep-sea diving; and fishing for mackerel, redfish, and speckled trout are other activities.

*Where to Begin:* The routes to the islands are described from I-95 and US 17 from South Carolina to Florida. To locate campgrounds, boat docks, and sites of interest, see the head of each feature. The Savannah Municipal Airport is 5 miles east from either GA 21, Exit 19, or US 80, Exit 18.

*About the Adventures:* In preparing for your personal safety and comfort, consider the weather, tides, the season and temperature, your physical health, your boating experience, and the length of your trip. If you plan to operate your own boat without a guide, secure nautical maps and a tidal schedule, and let someone at the marina know where you are going and when you expect to return. If you are unfamiliar with the waters, inquire at the marinas about tides and other conditions in the inlets and sounds. Take sun protection and a strong insect repellent. Mosquitoes, sand gnats, midges, deerflies, ticks, and chiggers are common. Take a day pack with plenty of drinking water in canteens and a first-aid kit. Storms and sudden changes of weather may drastically change the temperature, and remember that the temperature can drop below freezing in the wintertime. Extra clothing is essential in case you should fall into the water or mud. Be watchful for rattlesnakes in the higher and drier forests and for the cottonmouth in freshwater rivers and sloughs. Do not feed the wildlife, and do not wade or swim in any backwater areas, which alligators inhabit.

If you are driving south on I-95, make plans to spend most of one day at the Savannah National Wildlife Refuge. Access is from Exit 5, I-95, at Hardeeville, South Carolina. Drive south 8 miles on US 17 to the refuge entrance. (Camping is not allowed in the refuge, but you can stay at the full-service Stoney Crest Plantation Campground near Pritchardville. Access from US 17, the route you took from Hardeeville, is 3 miles east on SC 170 and 2 miles east on SC 46.) The 26,580-acre Savannah NWR, one of seven in the Georgia Coastal Complex, is in both South Carolina and Georgia, divided by the Savannah River. Four of the other six—Wassaw Island, Harris Neck, Blackbeard Island, and Wolf Island—are in Georgia, and the other two—Pinckney Island and Tybee Island—are in South Carolina. At the Savannah National Wildlife Refuge you will see freshwater marshes, tidal waters, and hardwood swamps. You will also notice the former rice fields of the colonial period that have since been impounded for waterfowl management. Each year some twenty thousand migratory ducks, representing more than twelve species, winter here from November through February. Wood ducks, purple gallinules, and king rails are regular nesters. Bird-watching for the more than two hundred species is best from October through April, and alligators are noticeable from March through October. Fishing is permitted from March 15 to October 25. You have a choice of walking or driving a 6-mile loop, the Laurel Hill Wildlife Drive, from the parking lot. After 1.1 mile you will come to the Cistern Trail, a short loop through live oak, cabbage palmetto, hackberry, and mulberry. From here you will pass dikes where egrets, herons, pintails, and ring-necked ducks pay little attention to you.

After arriving in Georgia you may wish to group your activities in two sections. The first would include the 50 miles from Savannah to Darien, with base camps at Skidaway Island State Park, Fort McAllister Historic Park, or Darien Island Harbor Campground. Plan the second 50 miles from Darien to Saint Marys while at the Jekyll Island Campground or from Crooked River State Park near Saint Marys.

At parks where fees are charged, there is a 20 percent discount for senior citizens and a 25 percent discount for disabled Georgia military veterans.

To reach Skidaway Island State Park from I-95, Exit 16, go east 10.5 miles on SR 204, which becomes Abercorn Street. Turn right on Montgomery Cross Road, and after 1.5 miles turn right on Whitfield Avenue. Go 1.9 miles and take Diamond Causeway, left, to the park, left. Skidaway is a captivating island, formed thousands of years before Wassaw Island, farther east of the marshes. To acquaint yourself with Skidaway, walk the Sandpiper Trail to see spike grass, salt meadow hay, salt flats, salt marshes, and oak and palmetto hammocks. The park has a picnic area, a sheltered observation deck, campsites for tents and RVs, interpretive programs, and a swimming pool. A public boat ramp is at the Skidaway Narrows bridge, part of the Intracoastal Waterway.

Only 4.5 miles east of the park, on McWhorter Drive, is the University of Georgia Marine Extension Center and Skidaway Institute of Oceanography, once part of the Modena Plantation. Located on a bluff of the Skidaway River, the 680-acre campus has an aquarium for fish and other marine organisms. There are exhibits of Gray's Reef and archeological displays that represent 12,000 years of area history. The center offers group educational programs, from an hour to a week, which can be reserved, to study the barrier islands, marine life, and marshlands. A field trip to Wassaw Island NWR can be included. Reservations for these programs should be made well in advance. (A "Recreational Guide to Offshore Georgia," with a map with buoy locations for Gray's Reef, is available here. For more about the reef, see the description for Sapelo Island, located 17 miles west of the reef.)

Another worthwhile educational center is Wormsloe Historic Site. To access from Skidaway Park, return on Diamond Causeway 2.8 miles to Ferguson Avenue. Make a right turn and go 2.3 miles to Skidaway Road; turn right and, after 0.4 mile, look for the stone archway entrance, right. The Georgia Department of Natural Resources now maintains the plantation, owned for nearly 200 years beginning in 1733 by the Noble Jones family. A unique one-mile nature trail has posted reproduced paintings by eighteenth-century naturalist Mark Catesby. The site has a museum, a picnic area, and tours. A small fee is charged.

The nearest public site for launching a boat trip to Wassaw NWR from Skidaway Island State Park is at the public dock at Skidaway Narrows on the Diamond Causeway. The nearest commercial marina is 2 miles east of the park off McWhorter Drive through the third gate of The Landings Harbor. Other marinas are Isle of Hope Marina, one mile east of the Wormsloe Historic Site, and Water Taxi (which can arrange chartered passage) on Palmetto Street on Wilmington Island, off US 80, between the city of Savannah and Tybee Island. Wassaw NWR, composed of Wassaw and Little Wassaw islands, has retained its primitive character, more so than most of the other barrier islands. Added to the Georgia Coastal Complex NWR system in 1968, it was a gift from The Nature Conservancy, which had acquired it from the descendants of George Parsons, owner since 1866. Open to the public only during daylight hours, the refuge has 10,050 acres that include 7 miles of beaches, rolling dunes, an expansive salt marsh, and forests of slash pine with dark green glossy needles and of live oak with green blankets of resurrection fern. The refuge has 20 miles of old dirt roads for bird-watching and viewing wildlife. Egret and heron rookeries are here, and flocks of migratory birds are common in the spring and fall. In the spring and summer you will notice tracks of loggerhead turtles that come ashore during the night to lay their eggs in the sand.

The Caretta Research Project of the Savannah Science

Museum has conducted volunteer research on the logger-heads in a special study since 1972 in association with the U.S. Fish and Wildlife Service and the Wassaw Island Trust. If you are interested in participating, apply to the museum. (See *Information*.) Notice on the beach that the entrance to the 180-acre Wassaw Island Trust is closed to the public, but the beach road is open. Plan for a full day on this alluring island, and consider fishing and exploring in the tidal creeks on the north and south side of the refuge.

Other highlights of the Savannah area are the city's historic district, Fort Pulaski National Monument, the Savannah Science Museum, and Oatland Island Education Center. Savannah (1733) was founded by Englishman James E. Oglethorpe, who drew the rectilinear street crossings at right angles, creating squares for parks studded with palms and other semitropical trees. The city was at the center of action during the Revolutionary War but was blockaded during the Civil War. Unlike Atlanta and Columbia, it was not burned when Gen. William T. Sherman's troops arrived in 1864. Known for its charm and beauty, "the hostess city of the South" has a number of firsts: It is the United States' first planned city; Eli Whitney invented the cotton gin here in 1793 during a visit to the home of Gen. Nathanael Greene at Grove Plantation; the first steamship, the SS *Savannah,* crossed the Atlantic from here to Liverpool in 1819; Juliette Gordon Low (1860–1927) founded the Girl Scouts of America here; and in 1966 the Department of the Interior designated 2.2 square miles a National Historic Landmark District, the largest in the nation. Prominent are restorations of Classic Revival, Regency, Colonial, and Victorian architecture. For a city map and information on sight-seeing tours, visit the Savannah Visitor Center on West Broad Street, near the east end of I-16. A few of the many special places on your tour are the Riverfront Plaza and River Street, the Cotton and Naval Store Exchange, the Girl Scout National Center, the Trustees' Gardens, Madison Square, the Ships of the Sea Museum, Factors' Walk, Pulaski Square, and the King-Tisdell Cottage.

The Savannah Science Museum at 4405 Paulsen Street has live and natural science exhibits of 185 reptiles and amphibians, a rock and mineral collection, and pressed Georgia plants representing more than two thousand species. A small admission fee is usually charged, but the museum is open free the second Sunday of each month. The museum also sponsors the Caretta Research Project for the study of loggerhead sea turtles (*Caretta caretta*) on the barrier islands. The project is similar to another study on the Cumberland Island National Seashore.

To reach the 175-acre Oatland Island Education Center from the waterfront, downtown Savannah, go east on President Street Extension, which becomes Islands Expressway. After crossing the Wilmington River bridge, go 0.7 mile and turn right onto Barley Drive. Follow Barley Drive to 711 Sandtown Road and enter the second gate. The unusual center, a joint service of the city and Chatham County, presents interpretive programs, special events, and demonstrations for the public school system. Open to the public Monday through Friday, it houses live mammals, alligators, owls, and eagles in a natural maritime forest. On the second Saturday of each month from October through May, guided tours and special demonstrations are given chiefly for the public. The center is also The Georgia Conservancy's coastal headquarters.

From the Oatland Center, continue east on Islands Expressway, which joins US 80/SR 26, and go 8.5 miles to the 5,615-acre Fort Pulaski National Monument, left. Established in 1924 the historical fort has been restored to its midnineteenth century appearance. Surrounded by a moat, the castlelike structure with catacombs provides a memorable setting in which to illustrate the Confederate soldiers' efforts to guard the Savannah River during the Civil War. A museum, exhibits, and demonstrations add to the perspective. The fort is named for Revolutionary War hero Count Casimir Pulaski, who lost his life in the British Siege of Savannah. The historic dike at the fort was originally surveyed by Robert E. Lee, whose first assignment after graduation from West Point was here. The fort is also important for its view of the salt marshes. Walks on the three short trails—Island Trail, Nature Trail, and Dike System Circuit Walk—provide an encounter with the salt marsh, plants, and wildlife. Fishing and boating are allowed in the park. Among the special events at the fort is Pulaski Day each October 11.

For your next adventure, return to US 17 and go south to cross the Ogeechee River bridge to Richmond Hill. Turn east on SR 144, and after 10 miles, including the SR 144 Spur, you will be at Fort McAllister State Historical Park. The park is a combination of historic Fort McAllister and an adjacent full-service campground (Richmond Hill) on Savage Island. The fort has a museum, exhibits, and trails through the earthworks and fortifications. Oaks, pines, and palmettoes, located on the bank of the Ogeechee River, are part of the landscape. The fort was the southernmost guard for Savannah during the Civil War; it fell to General Sherman's troops in face-to-face combat in December 1864. Reenactments of some of the fort's defenses are scheduled the last weekend of July and the first weekend of December. Henry Ford commenced restoration after he bought the fort in the 1930s, and the Georgia Historic Commission completed it after the International Paper Company purchased it from Ford. The paper company donated it to the state in 1958. Campsites are spacious and shady in a combination of pines and hardwoods. Raccoons have been known to make nocturnal visits and climb your van or RV and peer into the windows. Campsites can be reserved. A boat dock at the campground allows for boating and crabbing.

Southeast of Fort McAllister and across the marshes is 11,800-acre Ossabaw Island Heritage Preserve. Managed by the Georgia Department of Natural Resources, its interior is not open to the public without permission. The isolated 9.5 miles of beaches, however, are open for daytime hiking, shelling, fishing, and observation of plants and wildlife. Government agencies, private landowners, and conservation organizations have cooperated to preserve the barrier island.

When the state purchased Ossabaw Island in 1978, its Heritage Trust Act was to guide usage and development for natural, scientific, and cultural purposes. Previously, the island's history was like that of other sea islands: Indians used it for hunting and fishing; Spanish friars set up a mission; the English created colonial plantations; and private landowners kept it free of commercial and residential developments. Now, under Heritage Trust guidelines, the island's resources may have limited usage and minimum alterations. Educational and conservation groups can study its natural environment. If you are interested in the island's interior, write to the Department of Natural Resources or the Ossabaw Foundation. (See *Information.*) Access to Ossabaw Island is by boat only; the nearest public launch site is on the Ogeechee River at Fort McAllister. A commercial marina is south of the park on SR 144 (Bryan Neck Road) to a left turn on Kilkenny Road. Go to the dead end at Kilkenny Fish Camp. Boating from here is on Kilkenny Creek to Bear River, the part of the Intracoastal Waterway that separates Ossabaw from the mainland.

Returning to I-95, you will see Exit 13 at US 84/SR 38. Drive east 7.5 miles on old SR 38 and county roads to Sunbury State Historic Site at Medway River. Here you can study a once-thriving seaport that died after the Civil War and plan your boat trip to Saint Catherines Island. At the historic site, at the old Fort Morris fortifications, are a visitor center, exhibits, guided tours, a museum, a picnic area, demonstrations, and interpretive trails. Here and along the nearby rivers William Bartram made many botanical discoveries. Saint Catherines Island is only 10 miles southeast of here, but you will only be able to visit its beaches if you have advance permission to see the interior. In comparison to the other barrier islands, Saint Catherines has an unusual geological history: On its north end, island development during the Pleistocene and the Holocene epochs merge. Before European settlement, the 14,000-acre island was the capital of the Guale Indians. In 1765, pioneer Button Gwinnett, a signer of the Declaration of Independence and governor of Georgia, purchased the island. After the Civil War, General Sherman declared the island, and all other sea islands from Charleston to Jacksonville, property of the freed slaves, except for federal government properties and garrisons. As an independent state, the territory would be governed by Tunis Campbell. Several years later Congress repealed the directive, with some exceptions. Since 1968 the island has played a special role in the study and breeding of endangered wildlife, supervised by the Saint Catherines Island Foundation and the New York Zoological Society. As a result, visitation is limited and requires a reservation from the foundation. Otherwise, there are 12 miles of isolated beaches to explore. The nearest public mainland boat dock is at Sunbury on the Sunbury Channel of the Medway River. Two commercial marinas (with guides) are 8 miles south of Sunbury: Jordan's Halfmoon Marina is off SR 38 on Kings Road at North Newport River, and Yellow Bluff Fishing Camp is at the end of Colonels Island Road at Ashley Creek (see *Information*).

After you return to I-95, go south to Exit 12, take US 17 southeast one mile to South Newport, and go east 7.4 miles on SR 131 to Harris Neck NWR. The refuge does not have any ocean beaches, but its marshes, forests, and estuarine creeks have some of the same appeal as those on the sea islands. Its major distinction from the other Georgia refuges of the Georgia Coastal Complex is that you can drive to it. Formerly a World War II army airfield, the refuge was established in 1962. A public boat launch here at Barbour River Landing accesses Sapelo Sound. You can freely roam throughout its 2,687 acres. Trails are old roads that connect with the abandoned airfield. Deer and songbirds inhabit a forest of large live oak, moss, fern, sweet gum, hickory, holly, yaupon, and pine. A resident flock of Canada geese, and in winter large concentrations of mallards and teals, can be seen in the open marshes. The best time for crabbing is when the tide is going out. Camping is not allowed.

From the refuge, return to South Newport and take US 17 south 1.7 miles to Swinton Road, left. Drive 2.8 miles to Young

Man Road. Left is 3.4 miles to Shellman Bluff at Broad River, and right is 2 miles to Belle Bluff on White Chimney River. At either location you can launch your own boat or, for a reasonable fee, have a licensed charter guide take you to Blackbeard Island NWR. At Shellman Bluff are Kip's Fishing Camp (which does not have camping facilities) and Fisherman's Lodge Marina (which has apartments, cabins, and limited RV facilities). Restaurants are in the village. Ideal for tenting and camping with hookups is the Belle Bluff Island Campground and Marina on White Chimney River. Reach it by returning west to the junction of Swinton Road and Young Man Road; go west on Young Man Road 0.4 mile (past the Welcome Church) and turn left on a secondary road toward Pine Harbor. After 1.5 miles, turn left to Belle Bluff.

Part of the Georgia Coastal Complex, the 5,618-acre island refuge is open for daylight visits only. It has a boat dock, a headquarters office, restrooms, and a picnic area. There are 7 miles of clean beach for swimming, shelling, and watching pelicans, scaups, scooters, and shorebirds. In late spring and summer you may notice the tracks of loggerhead turtles. Twenty miles of old dirt roads provide exciting walks through the forest of slash pine, palmetto, holly, live oak, yaupon, and Southern magnolia. In the winter, waterfowl are prominent at the freshwater ponds, and in the summer, alligators can be seen in the ponds, particularly Flag Pond. Although Blackbeard Island was a haven for pirates who could hide in the rivers behind the tall trees, the only pirates today are the birds and raccoons that will filch your lunch if you leave it unattended. In 1800 the navy acquired the island (which is narrowly separated from Sapelo Island by Blackbeard Creek and small tributaries) as a source of live oak for shipbuilding. From 1830 to 1900 its south tip was the site of a yellow fever quarantine station. It became a refuge in 1940 and in 1975 3,000 acres were designated a wilderness area.

For your trip to Sapelo Island, you can use your own boat, acquire charter service from the marinas, or take the *Sapelo Queen* ferry from Meredian at the Sapelo Island Dock, 1.2

miles east from SR 99. A public dock is also at Ridgeville on SR 99, halfway between Meredian and Darien. When you leave the Belle Bluff Campground, go south 1.1 miles to Pine Harbor, then right 3 miles on Pine Harbor Road to US 17, where you turn left (south) and, after 2.3 miles, which pass through Eulonia, arrive at the junction of SR 99. On SR 99, east, go 9 miles along a country road of pastureland, pine and oak forests, and the villages of Crescent and Valona to Sapelo Island Dock; another 8.7 miles will take you to Darien. (It is 13 miles on I-95 or US 17 from Eulonia to Darien.) The least expensive public transportation to Sapelo Island is by ferry; reservations and tickets are necessary in advance through the Darien Welcome Center. The center, located at the corner of US 17 and Fort King George Drive (north end of the Darien River bridge), is open Monday through Saturday. Ferry schedules are Saturday at 9 A.M. (returns at 1 P.M.), Wednesday at 8:30 A.M. (returns at 12:30 P.M.), and June 1 through Labor Day, Friday at 8:30 A.M. (returns at 12:30 P.M.). For camping in the Darien area, Inland Harbor Campground is on SR 251, on the east side of its juncture with I-95, Exit 10. (For more campgrounds, see *Information*.) Open Gates, an 1878 historic home with high ceilings and antique furnishings, is available for bed and breakfast at Vernon Square in Darien.

Your journey to Sapelo Island will contrast considerably with your visit to Blackbeard Island. Sapelo has permanent residents, and in one community, Hog Hammock, about eighty black families who can trace their heritage to the Gullah culture. With a blend of African and English customs and knowledge, the Gullah developed approximately six thousand words unique to the sea islands of South Carolina and Georgia. Some of the words have been incorporated into standard English usage, including, for example, *goober,* for peanut; *juke,* as in jukebox; and *gumbo,* for okra. On your tour you will see a combination of natural areas: salt marshes, beaches, forests of loblolly and slash pines, compounds of live and laurel oaks, and shrubby interdunes of wax myrtle and yucca. Deer, turkeys, ospreys, snakes, raccoons, wading birds, and shorebirds are among the wildlife. The island tour includes a visit to the Sapelo Island National Estuarine Research Reserve (on the west side of the island); the R. J. Reynolds Wildlife Refuge, and the University of Georgia Marine Institute. If you wish to spend more time than allowed by the ferry, contact the Department of Natural Resources on the island about a full-day visit or primitive camping, or ask the Darien Welcome Center for more information. Room and apartment rentals are available at The Weekender, a quaint facility among the tall pines and ancient oaks at Hog Hammock. Island transportation inland and to the beaches for fishing and seining is furnished by the facility. Pottery shards representing an Indian culture from about 2500 b.c. have been discovered and there is a 200-foot-diameter shell ring on the northern end of the island. From 1760 to 1802 a variety of British and French planters owned the island. In 1802 Thomas Spalding purchased it, dug drainage ditches, and cultivated sugarcane and sea island cotton until 1851. The residents of Hog Hammock claim descendency from the slaves of Spalding's plantation. Howard Coffin purchased the island in 1912 and in 1920 built a freshwater pond to begin a dairy in addition to his commercial fishing operations. Tobacco magnate R. J. Reynolds had the roads paved when he owned the island from 1933 to 1965, though he was never a permanent resident. Reynolds was influential in having the University of Georgia Marine Institute begin a study of the barrier islands and their ecosystems. The state of Georgia purchased about 75 percent of the upper part of the island in 1969 and a chunk of the south end in 1976.

While in Darien, you can visit Fort King George State Historic Site to learn about the history of the town (1736), once the largest commercial port in the state. Before a Spanish mission was established in the mid-sixteenth century, the Guale Indians lived along the Altamaha River in the Darien area. The site of the fort, built in 1721 but no longer in existence, is 1.2 miles east on an SR 25 Spur from the Darien Welcome Center. A museum, exhibits, and trails there are open Tuesday through Sunday. If you are interested in canoeing a 15.5-mile section of the Altamaha River swamp and marsh in the Darien area, put in at Altamaha Park (3 miles north of the town of Everett at US 25/341, on a secondary road that parallels the Seaboard Coast Railroad) and take out on SR 25 Spur from an unpaved road at the Fort King George in Darien. The river features wildlife and scenery through the Lewis Island Natural Area and the Altamaha State Waterfowl Management Area. River hazards are tidal effects, powerboats, lack of rescue accessibility, and potential for getting lost. A USGS quad map or county map is essential if you are unfamiliar with delta passageways. Shuttle miles between the put-in and take-out points are 25.5.

East of Darien is 5,126-acre Wolf Island NWR, which includes Egg Island and 10-acre Little Egg Island in the middle of Altamaha Sound. Established in 1930 as a national wildlife refuge and part of the Georgia Coastal Complex, these islands were designated a national wilderness in 1975. There are not any plans for public-use facilities on the islands, which are principally saltwater marsh, but the narrow beaches can be used in daylight hours for beachcombing, fishing, and bird-watching. Access from marinas at Ridgeville on SR 99, northeast of Darien.

For a different type of adventure, try scuba diving at Gray's Reef, the state's only marine habitat of this type. Located 17.5 nautical miles east of Sapelo Island, the buoy is at 31° 24.00' N, 80° 52.14' W. The reef is within the 17-square-nautical-mile Gray's Reef National Marine Sanctuary, where you can sportfish, spearfish, scuba dive, and take underwater photographs to a depth of about 60 feet. Some of the nearest marinas for the Sapelo Island–Darien area are Kip's Fishing Camp, at the Shellman Bluff on Broad River, and Belle Bluff Island Marina, between Shellman Bluff and Pine Harbor on White Chimney River. Contact the chambers of commerce for other marinas. Among a number of charter services in Brunswick is Golden Isles Dive and Ski. For a more detailed list and a copy of "Recreational Guide to Offshore Georgia," contact the University of Georgia Marine Extension Service in Savannah. (See *Information.*) For safety reasons, if you use your own boat you should have offshore boating experience. Both your boat and the charter boat should be equipped with electronic navigational devices as recommended by the U.S. Coast Guard, the agency responsible for enforcing sanctuary regulations. It is recommended that only experienced divers use the reef because of unusually strong currents and limited visibility; optimum conditions are during neap tide. Snorkeling is hazardous and should not be attempted. The most favorable water and weather conditions and the largest diversity of fish species are during the summer months. Fishing conditions are best at the reef when the waves are 1 to 3 feet high and the wind is less than 10 knots. Trolling, hook-and-line bottom-fishing, and drift fishing are allowed; powerheads for spearfishing are strictly forbidden. Some of the sports fish are mackerel, bonito, barracuda, sea bass, snapper, cobia, grouper, and flounder.

Designated a sanctuary in 1981, the reef is named in honor of Milton B. Gray, for his offshore collections and study of Georgia's benthic coastal communities. The limestone outcrops were formed between 5 and 2 million years ago during the Pliocene epoch. Because of sea-level fluctuations during that time, caverns, troughs, burrows, scarps, ridges, ledges, and slopes have developed. The limestone is hard enough for sponges, hard corals, gorgonions, seaweeds, and bryozoans, but soft enough for burrowing organisms. Called a "live bottom" because of its variety and abundance of marine life, the reef is home to mobile invertebrates such as sea urchins, sea cucumbers, brittle stars, mollusks, shrimps, octopods, and fishes. At least 150 species of fish are here—sharks and rays, eels and morays, groupers and sea basses, jacks and mackerels, snappers and bigeyes, porgy and pinfish, herring and menhaden, blennies, gobies, angelfish and damselfish, filefish, and puffers, to name a few. The secretive gobies and blennies dart from one cave to the next, and schools of less secretive tomtates swim over them. Farther above them are aggregations of spadefish and amberjacks. Loggerhead turtles bask at the surface water or rest under the ledges, and bluefish and barracuda stop by occasionally to feed on the armies of sardines. Dolphin are the most common cetaceans seen here. Colorful tropical reef fish like those at Key Biscayne in Florida—damsels, butterflies, and angels—are seen here mainly during summer months. These fish, with their brilliant hues, lavender and scarlet sponges, and orange sea whips make a colorful sea garden for water photography. Marine scientists have reported seeing the migratory and endangered right whale (*Balaena glacialis*) and calves by the reef.

Continuing on your journey south from Darien, go 5 miles on US 17/SR 25 across the Altamaha River into Glynn County and stop at the Hofwyl-Broadfield Plantation (1.4 miles east of I-95, Exit 9 on SR 99). Here you can sense what life was like in the large rice plantations of coastal Georgia before the Civil War. There are exhibits, trails, and a museum, open every day except Monday. A small fee is charged.

Proceed south to Brunswick (1771) at the Brunswick–Golden Isles Welcome Center, left, near the corner of Torras Causeway to Saint Simons Island. Brunswick, named for the ancestral home of George II, who granted the Charter of Georgia, is the gateway to Saint Simons, Jekyll, and Sea islands. A leading city in shrimp harvesting, Brunswick holds a spring fiesta each Mother's Day weekend to bless the shrimp fleet. The best place from which to view the fleet is the end of Gloucester Street on Brunswick Harbor. Worth a side visit off Gloucester Street is the 13-foot-diameter legendary Lover's Oak at the corner of Albany and Prince streets.

At Torras Causeway cross the marshes to Saint Simons Island. You may first think that the residential resort and commercial development have destroyed all of Saint Simons' natural environment, but a closer look will reveal preserved areas: the forests north of Fort Frederica National Monument, beaches, parks, the Christ Church area, the Epworth-by-the Sea area, and Gascoigne Bluff. After crossing the last bridge of the causeway, turn right on Kings Way and go to Saint

Simons Lighthouse and Museum of Coastal History at 101 Twelfth Street. The lighthouse, built in 1810 and restored in 1872, is maintained by the Coast Guard. You can climb to the top for views of Saint Simons Sound, Jekyll Island, and the Atlantic Ocean. Open every day except Monday and national holidays, it requires a small admission charge. For bird-watching, walk the beach here and also at the north end of Ocean Boulevard. Later follow north on Frederica Road to Fort Frederica National Monument, which is open daily. Established in 1736 by Gen. James Oglethorpe to protect the south flank of colonial Georgia against the Spanish, the fort embraced a community of about five hundred. Near the fort is Christ Church, thought to be the third oldest church in the state, where John and Charles Wesley conducted a service in 1736 under the large oaks. This church and its leaders inspired novelist Eugenia Price to write *The Beloved Invader*, the first book of a trilogy about Saint Simons Island. The area has large gums, maples, and live oaks thickly draped with Spanish moss. A drive or bicycle trip on Sea Island Road to Sea Island will take you past a private luxury resort where native and exotic plants, trees, flowers, and shrubs create exquisite gardens.

Access to Little Saint Simons is by boat or plane. Boat access is at the end of Harrington Road, which goes east from between Sea Island Road and Fort Frederica. The last privately owned barrier island, Little Saint Simons has been open to guests with reservations since 1976. Accommodations are at a rustic lodge for a weekend or a week. The 10,000-acre island once had rice plantations and was owned by Pierce Butler and his English actress-wife Fanny Kemble. She described her day trips to the island in her book *Journal of a Residence on a Georgian Plantation, 1838–1839*. Among the most appealing aspects of the island are its birds and its beaches. Before you leave Saint Simons, stop by the site of the large Hamilton Plantation, now Epworth-by-the-Sea, a Methodist center and museum on Arthur Moore Drive off Sea Island Road, close to the north side causeway entrance to the island. Nearby is the

*Marshes of Glynn, Brunswick.*
PHOTO BY Allen de Hart.

Saint Simons Marina and Gascoigne Bluff, named for Capt. James Gascoigne, who convoyed the ships bringing the first English settlers here in 1736.

To reach Jekyll Island, return to US 17/SR 25 in Brunswick. Turn left (south), and after 0.4 mile turn into the median to see the Lanier Oak. Sidney Lanier (1842–1881) is supposed to have written some of his finest poetry under this tree in the 1870s. Ahead 0.2 mile, left, stop at Overlook Park for an excellent view of the marshes that in 1878 inspired Lanier's "The Marshes of Glynn," of which a few lines follow:

> Vanishing, swerving, evermore curving again into sight,
> Softly the sandbeach wavers away to a dim gray looping of light.
> And what if behind me to westward the wall of the woods stands high?
> The world lies east: how ample, the marsh and the sea and the sky!
> A league and a league of marsh-grass, waist-high, broad in the blade,
> Green, and all of a height, and unflecked with a light or a shade,
> Stretch leisurely off, in a pleasant plain,
> To the terminal blue of the main.
>
> Oh, what is abroad in the marsh and the terminal sea?
> Somehow my soul seems suddenly free
> From the weighing of fate and the sad discussion of sin,
> By the length and the breadth and the sweep of the marshes of Glynn.

After you cross the Brunswick River bridge, turn left on SR 50, Jekyll Island Causeway. En route to the island, stop at the Jekyll Island Welcome Center, left, for information. If you are staying at the Jekyll Island Campground (formerly Cherokee Campground), proceed east on the landscaped Ben Fortson Parkway to Beachview Drive and turn left. The full-service campground is at the north end of the island under Spanish moss–draped live oaks and pines. The island has motels, restaurants, a shopping center, fishing piers, a marina for boating and fishing, picnic areas, recreation parks, an amphitheater, a convention center, and 20 miles of bicycle trails. Bicycles are ideal for getting around the 8-mile-long island to explore beaches and other natural areas and observe wildlife. You can rent a bicycle at the Miniature Golf on North Beachview Drive, north of the shopping center where you turned onto Beachview Drive. Conspicuously different from the other barrier islands you have visited, this state-owned property is supervised and maintained by the Jekyll Island Authority, created to conserve the island's beaches and natural areas while developing it as a year-round vacation resort. The island has a moderate climate, influenced by the sea breezes, and a short winter with occasional freezes; expect to find the weather comfortable during any season.

To encounter a diverse ecology, start from the campground and go north to a picnic area and Driftwood Beach, preferably at low tide. You will notice the wind-sculpted live oaks dramatically exposed by erosive ocean wind and waves. Across the sound is Saint Simons Island, and to the west are grassy sand dunes, intertidal zone, and marshes. To the northwest are grassy low dunes and erosion bluffs, followed by the mouth of Clam Creek, where the beach ends abruptly. Proceeding counterclockwise on the island, cross Clam Creek bridge to the fishing pier for a superb view of the sound. If you are following the bike path in the marsh, pass the Clam Creek picnic area and arrive at Riverview Drive. Along the way you may see deer, otters, herons, kingfishers, and painted buntings. Follow Riverview Drive to the ruins of the Horton House, the du Bignon cemetery, and other historic sites. A picnic area is nearby and a marsh trail, lined with sea oxeye, leads to a tidal creek among red cedars and cabbage palms. When you come to Jennings Road, left, follow it to its end and explore this freshwater lowland among red bays, willows, and buttonbush. Deer and turkeys frequent the area. After you pass Captain Wylly Road you will enter the 240-acre Jekyll

Island Club Historic District, the restored millionaires' village. Next is an excellent bird-watching area between Shell Road and Ben Fortson Parkway.

On the southern half of the island, follow south of Ben Fortson Parkway and 0.2 mile after Summer Wave Water Park look for an oyster-shell footpath at an old gate; the trail extends to a man-made harbor off the west side of South Riverview Drive. Salt cedars and groundsel trees are here, and in the summer you will hear noisy Wilson's plovers trying to deflect your attention from their nests. After you return to South Riverview Drive, go south to the Saint Andrews Picnic Area where you may see painted buntings, turkeys, and meadowlarks. Huge live oaks have a variety of epiphytes. As you go east around the island's tip and toward Saint Andrews Beach you will see pelicans, black skimmers, turnstones, curlews, oystercatchers, willits, godwits, terns, and other bird species. To return on the bicycle route, follow the live oak forest on South Beachview Drive to the Recreation Center and then change to the beachfront route.

The human history of the island began with the Indians, who favored it for hunting and fishing. In 1562 a group of French Huguenots settled, followed by mission-minded Spanish Jesuit friars in 1566. General James Oglethorpe sent Capt. William Horton to establish a land claim on which a tabby house was built in 1742 for a southern British outpost. Oglethorpe named the island for his friend Sir Joseph Jekyll, who assisted the Georgia colony financially. A Frenchman who had fought in the Revolution, Christopher du Bignon, purchased the island after the war. His family sold it in 1886 for $125,000 to the Jekyll Island Club, a group of American millionaires such as the Rockefeller, Gould, Pulitzer, Crane, and Morgan families. At the time it was said that the club members owned 17 percent of the world's personal wealth. But the exclusive winter resort began to decline with the Great Depression; by World War II the island was almost deserted. In 1947 the club was sold to the state of Georgia for $675,000, an incredible bargain. In 1975, a bridge was constructed across Jekyll River for easy passage to the island.

To complete your adventure of the sea islands, return to US 17/SR 25 and go left 5.3 miles to I-95, Exit 6. Go south on I-95 25.7 miles to Exit 2, toward Saint Marys. Take SR 40 east 2.4 miles to Kings Bay Road, left, toward the U.S. Navy Submarine Base for 2.9 miles to SR 40 Spur. Turn left, and after 3 miles you will reach Crooked River State Park, right. This secluded 500-acre park has a full-service campground, cottages, a swimming pool, winterized picnic shelters, a boat dock, and a 1.5-mile hiking trail from the swimming pool to the cottages. Located on the south bank of Crooked River, the park is bordered by large areas of salt marsh. It is not unusual to see ospreys, foxes, feral hogs, or deer within the park. The campground is shaded by tall longleaf pines, live oaks, and Southern magnolias. Saw palmetto is thick in the adjoining forests. All of the eleven cottages are completely furnished, including linen; they can be reserved 11 months in advance. The park is convenient for your journey to Cumberland Island National Seashore, particularly when preplanning is necessary. Motels, restaurants, and shopping centers are in Saint Marys, 7 miles south of the campground.

To prepare for your visit to the 36,544-acre island, make ferry reservations in advance by contacting the park headquarters office in Saint Marys. Mainland departures from downtown Saint Marys at the Saint Marys River are at 9 A.M. and 11:45 A.M. daily except Tuesday and Wednesday (during peak season it may be every day). If you go only for a day, take a day pack with food, a canteen of water, suntan lotion, sunglasses, insect repellent, and rain gear. If you plan to camp overnight (for a maximum of 7 days), take a backpack with all of the above, plus a tent, a sleeping bag, food, clothes, toiletries, a first-aid kit, a portable stove and fuel, a flashlight and batteries, rope ( to tie food out of reach of raccoons), and carry-out trash bags. There are no stores or supplies on the island, and the park service does not allow resupply trips. Pets and bicycles cannot be transported to the island. One of the five campsites, Sea Camp Beach, has water and restrooms; it is 0.5 mile from Sea Camp Dock, the debarkation point for all campers. Four other campsites, three of which are in the wilderness area, are on the northern half of the island. From Sea Camp Dock, Stafford Beach is 3.5 miles; Hickory Hill is 5.5 miles; Yankee Paradise is 7.4 miles; and Brickhill Bluff is 10 miles. Fires are not allowed at any wilderness campsite. Roads and trails intersect and connect between the camping locations, and a dirt road called Main Road (Grand Avenue during the Gilded Age) stretches the island's 16-mile length. A park ranger on the island will assign you a campsite and instruct you on emergency procedures. Take precautions in areas inhabited by diamondback rattlers and do not venture into crumbling ruins or get too close to the wild horses, which will bite and kick.

Cumberland Island is Georgia's largest sea island, with a moderate climate and mild, short winters. Expect sultry summers and thunderstorms with temperatures in the upper 80s and 90s. The island has sections of live oak, salt marshes, freshwater ponds and lakes, short creeks, interdunes, interdune meadows, and wide beaches. In the interior, which is about 3 miles at its widest, spreading low-limbed live oaks are hosts to mosses and ferns. They and other hardwoods, pines (slash, pond, longleaf, and loblolly), and thick wax myrtle support squirrels, deer, raccoons, armadillos, and feral hogs. Ponds throughout the island support otters, alligators, and many species of frogs. Flying over and in the forest and at the beaches and ponds are more than 320 species of birds, most of them winter residents. Do not be surprised to see deer, turkeys, or raccoons ahead of you on the trails, or to hear the plaintive call of a screech owl or the resonant series of hoots by the great horned owl at nighttime. Sea turtles are prominent. The park and the Georgia Marine Turtle Co-operative jointly conduct a Caretta Research Project for loggerhead turtles. For it, the beach is divided into thirty-two units, some part of a study area and others patrolled every 50 minutes or three times each night during the nesting season. Usually about one hundred females nest each year at nighttime between mid-May and mid-August. Project researchers record the turtles' activities and tag them for future identification.

The River Trail and the Dungeness Trail, closest to the Sea Camp Dock, are more frequently hiked than any of the other ten trails. Begin the 4.5-mile combined trail on the 0.8-mile River Trail from Sea Camp Dock. It parallels Cumberland Sound to Dungeness Dock and Visitor Center. At the center are exhibits that explain the history of the island, specifically Dungeness, an early area hunting camp named by the British. The first building at Dungeness was the magnificent four-story tabby mansion of Revolutionary War leader Gen. Nathanael Greene and his heirs. Ten years after General Greene's death in 1786, his wife, Catherine, and her new husband, Phineas Miller, completed the mansion. It was destroyed by fire in 1862 when Union troops evacuated slaves to Amelia Island, and during the 1880s the Thomas Carnegie family built a second Dungeness. The use of that Dungeness declined after the 1920s, and for unknown reasons the house burned in 1959.

Today you will see only parts of the walls and chimneys of the second Dungeness, and a large lawn frequented by wild turkeys and wild horses. As you stand near the ruins, imagine those days in the late 1880s of the Gilded Age when Thomas and Lucy Carnegie built this palace for themselves and their children. Thomas, younger brother of financier Andrew Carnegie, died before the home was finished, but his wife had it completed and later built four other mansions on the island for the children. (One is Plum Orchard, where the park service provides a tour each Sunday from April 1 through September 30 and the first Sunday of each month from October through March.) Eventually Lucy Carnegie owned 90 percent of the island and had two hundred servants maintain her properties. With imagination you can see the children playing on the lawn among exotic plants and flowers and hear the music of the many social occasions in the palatial parlors. Along the trail is part of an elaborate recreational building once used by the Carnegies and their guests. A large white building, now private property, was the home of estate manager William Page. A stucco building, once the carriage house, is now used by the park service.

Follow the trail east to the Greene-Miller family cemetery where "Lighthouse Harry" Lee, Revolutionary War general and father of Robert E. Lee, was first buried. As you approach the interdune meadows you may see nesting terns dive toward you in an effort to protect their eggs which lie flat on the sand. After you pass over foredunes of sea oats and croton you will arrive at a wide beach. (To the right it is 2 miles south on the beach to Pelican Banks and another 2 miles on the South Point Trail to Cumberland Sound, where the trail dead-ends. From here you can see Amelia Island in Florida.) The Dungeness Trail turns north from the beach, and after 1.5 miles you will reach Sea Camp Beach Campground. A west turn for 0.5 mile on a road will complete the loop to Sea Camp Dock.

To truly experience the remoteness and tranquility of the wilderness area on the north half of the island you will need nearly a week to camp and hike all or parts of the 25 miles of trails. Begin by backpacking from Sea Camp Dock 5.5 miles north on the Main Road to Willow Pond Trail, right, which leads to Hickory Hill Camp (no water here). From the camp, north, it is 1.2 miles on Yankee Paradise Trail to Yankee Paradise Camp on Duck House Road. Along the trail is a well with a sulfuric taste. (Boiling and exposing the water by letting it sit in an open container will help to dissipate the taste.) To reach the next campsite, go north 1.5 miles on Tar Kiln Trail and join the Main Road for 2.5 miles to Brickhill Bluff Camp, left, which has a freshwater well. From this camp you can make a full-day 7-mile loop to the Atlantic beach. To extend your enjoyment, plan for a 3-mile spur north on the beach at low tide. Your rewards will be easy fishing on Christmas Creek for large flounder; shelling; and observing waterfowl on sandy Long Point. Although you are not likely to see sharks, they do use the inlet near Little Cumberland Island for a breeding ground. They and the capricious ocean currents are reasons to keep out of the water at Long Point. Your loop route from Brickhill Bluff Camp is north and east 0.7 mile on Brickhill Trail and then on part of Bunkley Trail north to North Cut Road. Turn right (east), and after 1.9 miles you will reach the beach. Turn left (north) to Long Point. On the return, follow the Roller Coaster Trail that begins on the North Cut Road at the beach. The trail parallels the beach and passes Whitney Lake, the island's largest, by an interdune. After 1.7 miles to South Cut Road, turn right (west) 1.5 miles to the Main Road, where you return, right, to complete your 13-mile loop (including the 6 miles to Long Point and back). Another loop of 6.5 miles is north on the 1.7-mile Terrapin Point Trail to salt marshes and then clockwise on roads and the Bunkley Trail.

Human history on the island goes back to at least 2000 B.C., but the first written history is from the mid-1560s when a Spanish mission, San Pedro, was established to convert the Timucuan Indians, the same tribe that the Spanish met across Cumberland Sound on Amelia Island in Florida. Not until 1736 did the English, under the leadership of General Oglethorpe, build forts at each end of the island to lay claim for the Georgia colony. In 1783 Gen. Nathanael Greene purchased a large area for timber harvesting and agricultural production of sea island cotton, corn, and fruits. His mansion burned in 1862 and was replaced by the second Dungeness of the Thomas Carnegie family. After fire destroyed that mansion in 1959, no effort was made to restore it. But with the financial help of the Carnegie heirs, the Mellon Foundation, and conservation groups, the island became a national seashore under the National Park Service in October 1972.

### Information

Counties: Chatham, Bryan, Liberty, McIntosh, Glynn, Camden

Average Temperatures: January, 40°F (low), 62°F (high); August, 71.5°F (low), 90°F (high)

National Properties: Cumberland Island National Seashore, P.O. Box 806, Saint Marys, GA 31558, (912) 882-4335; Fort Frederica National Monument, Rte. 4, Box 286–C, Saint Simons Island, GA 31522, (912) 638-3639; Fort Pulaski National Monument, P.O. Box 98, Tybee Island, GA 31328, (912) 786-5787; Georgia Coastal Refuge Complex (Blackbeard Island NWR, Harris Neck NWR, Savannah NWR, Wassaw Island NWR, Wolf Island NWR), P.O. Box 8487, Savannah, GA 31412, (912) 944-4415

State Properties: Altamaha River Waterfowl Area, DNR (or Dept. of Natural Resources), P.O. Box 19, Sapelo Island, GA 31327, (912) 485-2251; Crooked Creek State Park, 3092 Spur 40, Saint Marys, GA 31558, (912) 882-5256; Fort King George Historic Site, P.O. Box 711, Darien, GA 31305, (912) 437-4770; Fort McAllister Historic Park, Rte. 2, Box 394–A, Richmond Hill, GA 31324, (912) 727-2339; Hofwyl-Broadfield Plantation, 5556 US Hwy. 17 N, Brunswick, GA 31525, (912) 264-9263; Jekyll Island Authority, 375 Riverview Dr., Jekyll Island, GA 31520, (800) 342-1042 in Georgia, or (800) 841-6586 outside Georgia; Jekyll Island Museum, 375 Riverview Dr., Jekyll Island, GA 31520, (912) 635-2236; Ossabaw Island, DNR, P.O. Box 14565, Savannah, GA 31416, (912) 262-3173; Overlook Park, DNR, 1200 Glynn Ave., Brunswick, GA 31523, (912) 264-7330; Sapelo Island, (group camping), DNR, P.O. Box 19, Sapelo Island, GA 31327, (912) 485-2251; Skidaway Island State Park, 52 Diamond Causeway, Savannah, GA 31411, (912) 598-2300; Sunbury Historic Site, Rte. 1, Box 236, Midway, GA 31320, (912) 884-5999; University of Georgia Extension Service, P.O. Box 13687, Savannah, GA 31416, (912) 356-2496; Wormsloe Historic Site, 7601 Skidaway Rd., Savannah, GA 31406, (912) 353-3023

City and County Properties: Oatland Island Education Center, 711 Sandtown Rd., Savannah, GA 31410, (912) 897-3773; Savannah Science Museum, 4405 Paulsen St., Savannah, GA 31405, (912) 355-6705

Government Agencies: U.S. Fish and Wildlife Service, 75 Spring St., SW, 12th Floor, Russell Bldg., Atlanta, GA 30303, (404) 331-6343; Georgia Department of Natural Resources,

205 Butler St., SE, Atlanta, GA 30334, (Fisheries Mgt., [404] 656-3524), (Game Mgt., [404] 656-4994), (State Parks, [404] 656-2770); Georgia Department of Transportation (maps and road conditions), #2 Capitol Square, Atlanta, GA 30334, (404) 656-5336; Georgia Tourist Division, Department of Industry and Trade, P.O. Box 1776, Atlanta, GA 30301, (404) 651-9461

Organizations and Foundations: Bartram Trail Society, 508 E. 57th St., Savannah, GA 31405, and Bartram Trail Conference, 3815 Interstate Court, Montgomery, AL 36109, (205) 277-7050; Coastal Georgia Historical Society, 610 Beachview Dr., Saint Simons Island, GA 31522, (912) 638-4666; Epworth-by-the-Sea Methodist Center, P.O. Box 407, Saint Simons Island, GA 31522, (912) 638-4050; The Georgia Conservancy, 711 Sandtown Rd., Savannah, GA 31410, (912) 897-6462; Georgia Historical Society, Whitaker and Gaston Sts., Savannah, GA 31401, (912) 944-2128; Ossabaw Foundation, Ossabaw Island, P.O. Box 13397, Savannah, GA 31416, (912) 727-3131; Saint Catherines Island Foundation, Rte. 1, Box 207Z, Midway, GA 31320; Skidaway Marine Science Foundation, P.O. Box 13687, Savannah, GA 31416

Chambers of Commerce, Information and Welcome Centers: Brunswick–Golden Isles Tourist and Convention Bureau, 4 Glynn Ave., Brunswick, GA 31520, (912) 264-0202; Darien Welcome Center, P.O. Box 1497, Darien, GA 31305, (912) 437-6684/4192; Georgia Visitor Information Center (I-95) (north), P.O. Box 7208, Garden City, GA 31418, (912) 964-5094, and (south) Rte. 1, Box 363–A, Kingsland, GA 31548, (912) 729-3253; Jekyll Island Convention and Visitor Bureau, P.O. Box 3186, Jekyll Island, GA 31520, (800) 342-1042 in Georgia, (800) 841-6586 outside Georgia; Jekyll Island Information Center, 901 Jekyll Causeway, Jekyll Island, GA 31520, (912) 635-3636; Little Saint Simons Island Information, P.O. Box 1078H, Saint Simons Island, GA 31522, (912) 638-7472; McIntosh County CC, P.O. Box 1497, Darien, GA 31305, (912) 437-4192/6684; Saint Marys Tourism Council, P.O. Box 1291, Saint Marys, GA 31588, (912) 882-4000; Saint Simons Island CC, Neptune Park, Saint Simons Island, GA 31522, (912) 638-

9014; Savannah Visitor Center, 301 Martin Luther King Blvd., Savannah, GA 31499, (912) 944-0456/0444, 238-1779; Tybee Island CC, 209 Butler Ave., Tybee Island, GA 31328, (912) 786-5444

Services and Amenities: *Bed and Breakfast and Special Lodging:* Eliza Thompson House, 5 W. Jones St., Savannah, GA 31401, (800) 845-7638; Gaubert House, 521 Oglethorpe Alley, Saint Simons Island, GA 31522, (912) 638-9424; Open Gates, Vernon Square, Darien, GA 31305, (912) 437-6985; The Weekender, Hog Hammock, Sapelo Island, GA 31327, (912) 485-2277; *Commercial Campgrounds:* Bellaire Woods Campground, I-95 Exit 16 and SR 204, Savannah, GA 31401, (912) 748-4000; Hilton's Sunshine Lake Campground, I-95 Exit 13 and US 84, Midway, GA 31320, (912) 884-2744; Jekyll Island Campground, N. Beachview Dr., Jekyll Island, GA 31520, (912) 635-3021; KOA Savannah South, I-95 Exit 14 and US 17, Richmond Hill, GA 31324, (912) 756-3396; McIntosh Lake Campground, I-95 Exit 11, Townsend, GA 31331, (912) 832-6215; Ocean Breeze Campground, Dover Bluff Rd., Brunswick, GA 31521, (912) 264-6692; South Newport Campground (on US 17), Rte. 2, Box 2071, Townsend, GA 31331, (912) 832-5459; Stoney Crest Plantation Campground, Rte. 1, Box 36, Bluffton, SC 29910, (803) 757-3249; *Motels, Hotels, and Restaurants:* Call or write the chambers of commerce or tourist centers, above

*Adventure Guides:* Coastal Excursions (to sea islands), 534 Jackson Blvd., Savannah 31405, (912) 355-5282; Golden Isles Dive and Ski (scuba diving and other sports), 5701 Altama Ave., Brunswick, GA 31520, (912) 264-1411, and 108 Marina Dr., Saint Simons Island, GA 31522, (912) 638-6627; Wilderness Southeast (overnight canoeing and camping in the Okefenokee Swamp, sea-island kayaking, and backpack and camping on the Cumberland Island National Seashore), 711–VC Sandtown Rd., Savannah, GA 31410, (912) 897-5108; *Bicycle Rentals:* Miniature Golf, Jekyll Island, GA 31520, (912) 635-2648; *Boat Services and Marinas:* Belle Bluff Island Marina, Rte. 2, Box 204B, Townsend, GA 31331, (912) 832-5323;

Fishermen's Lodge (provides daily boat trips to Blackbeard Island), Rte. 2, Box 2436, Townsend, GA 31331, (912) 832-5162; Fort McAllister Supply Center, Spur 144, Richmond Hill, GA 31324, (912) 727-2632; Jordan's Halfmoon Marina, Rte. 1, Box 207–H, Midway, GA 31320, (912) 884-5819; Isle of Hope Marina, 50 Bluff Dr., Savannah, GA 31406, (912) 355-2310; Jekyll Island Marina, 1 Pier Rd., Jekyll Island, GA 31520, (912) 635-2891; Kilkenny Fish Camp, Rte. 2, Box 216, Richmond Hill, GA 31324, (912) 227-2215; Kip's Fishing Camp, Rte. 2, Shellman Bluff, GA 31331, (912) 832-5161; Sapelo Charters, Rte. 1, Box SG-22, Townsend, GA 31331, (912) 832-6122; Saint Simons Marina, 1000 Arthur Moore Dr., Saint Simons Island, GA 31522, (912) 638-9146; The Landings Harbor Marina, Skidaway Island, P.O. Box 13727, Savannah, GA 31416, (912) 598-1902; Yellow Bluff Fishing Camp, Rte. 1, Box 215, Midway, GA 31320, (912) 884-5448; Coastal Resources Division (request a list of boat ramps, marinas, and charter services), Georgia DNR, 1200 Glynn Ave., Brunswick, GA 31523, (912) 264-7218; *Canoeing:* Coastal Canoe Outpost, Rte. 4, Box 451–B, Savannah, GA 31406, (912) 748-7634; Canoe Excursions (Altamaha River day trip, Darien; Redbird Creek and Richmond Hill overnight trip, Canoochee River day trip, Richmond Hill), Georgia Dept. of Natural Resources, (800) 3GA-PARK in Georgia, or (800) 5GA-PARK outside Georgia; *Fishing and Marinas:* Georgia Dept. of Natural Resources (call for a copy of "Coastal Georgia Fishing," with information on seasons, county marinas and boat ramps, charter services, and fishing access), (912) 264-7363/7218; *Scuba Training:* Island Dive Center, 1610 Frederica Rd., Saint Simons Island, GA 31522, (912) 638-6590

## OKEFENOKEE SWAMP

About 1 million years ago the Okefenokee Swamp was a large interdune lake and sandbars formed by the Atlantic Ocean. Had humans seen it then there would be no mystery about what lived in the clear open water above its sandy bottom. But beginning with the American Indians, there has always been an enigmatical and mythical curiosity about this watery wilderness. Without a counterpart, the swamp is nearly 600 square miles in southeast Georgia, bordered on the north by Dixon State Forest and on the south by Baker County, Florida. It is a world of trembling, quaking, floating islands, glassy lakes, misty mornings, acres of lily pads, layers of peat, and tall hammocks of cypress. It is a place of bellowing alligators whose eyes glow red in the moonlight, where snipes cry and bobcats scream in the night, and where jackfish jump into your canoe. It is a place of history and mystery, an inviolate sanctuary of wildlife in a wilderness area. Indians left mounds on the dry piney islands and early white settlers waded in the unknown muck to hunt bear and trap mink, and lived to tell about it. Those who have lived near the swamp have special feelings about the refuge, like the city of Folkston's beloved schoolteacher, poet Mayme Askew Harris (1901–1989). In her "Ode to the Okefenokee" she wrote:

> Beautiful art thou in the silent awesomeness!
> Here the birds, even the eagles, herons and
>   egrets, build their nests in safety.
> Here the bears, unmolested, use their strength
>   for gathering food.
> Here the alligators swim, dive, and lie peacefully
>   in the sunshine without fear.
> Here the deer may live their days in peace which
>   they represent.
> And here man may come to view the unsurpassed
>   spectacle of nature in her various moods.
> Okefenokee, most prominent of America's
>   swamps, your dark waters reflect living images
>   of cypress, pines, oaks, magnolias and palmettos,
>   which grow along your waterways.
> Your islands keep their secrets of former inhabit-
>   ants—the Timucans—who called you their
>   home.
> Only ten burial mounds are left to attest to their
>   former presence.
> Only the soughing of the pines remind us of the

living, breathing human beings who first knew
you.
Their secrets are locked in your vastnesses—
keep them in your bosom forever.
Man, in your humanity, keep forever in peace
this symbol of greatness of God who created
this wonder for your enjoyment.

*What to See and Do:* You have three major options for
experiencing the Okefenokee National Wildlife Refuge. First,
you can stay on dry land and boardwalks and at observation
towers to view the wildlife, exhibits, films, and museums at
the swamp's edge. Or you can take a daytime tour in a sight-
seeing powerboat. Finally, you can canoe on the water trails.
The most exhilarating and adventuresome is to canoe deep
into the swamp and camp overnight.

*Where to Begin:* The swamp has four entrances:
Okefenokee Swamp Park is 8 miles south of Waycross, off US
1/23, on SR 177 for 5 miles; Stephen C. Foster State Park is 17
miles on SR 177 from Fargo and US 441; Suwannee Canal
Recreation Area is 8 miles southeast of Folkston, off SR 121
and 4 miles on the entrance parkway; and Kingfisher Landing
is 11.8 miles north of Folkston (22 miles south of Waycross)
off US 1/23, west 1.5 miles on a dirt road. All but the Okefenokee Swamp Park have connecting canoe routes. From I-95,
Exit 2, on SR 40, it is 22 miles to Folkston. If you arrive at the
Jacksonville International Airport, take SR 115 north to Callahan
and US 301/23/1 north to Folkston, 45 miles from the airport
to the Okefenokee at Suwannee Canal Recreation Area.

*About the Adventures:* If you choose to see the periphery
of the swamp, begin at the Okefenokee Swamp Park, a nongovernmental day-use attraction since 1945 with a lease
agreement by the U.S. Fish and Wildlife Service. The park
acquaints you with the swamp's historical and environmental
background and its plant and animal life. Considered a full-day
"show window" to the swamp, it has interpretive exhibits,
lectures and demonstrations, paved and boardwalk trails, boat
tours, an observation tower, a museum, a serpentarium and

wildlife observatory, and a gift shop. An admission fee is charged. The nearest campground is the Laura S. Walker State Park, 4 miles east on SR 177 from the US 1/23 junction with Okefenokee Swamp Park. The northeast access is 9 miles east of Waycross off US 82 for 2 miles on SR 177. A full-service campground facility, it has access for waterskiing, fishing, and swimming. Its 1.2-mile Big Creek Nature Trail runs among long leaf pines, cabbage palms, and yellow jessamine (jasmine). If you are interested in forestry, visit the Southern Forest World on North Augusta Avenue, 2 miles west of downtown Waycross (1818). Exhibits and trails detail the history of forestry in the South's forests. Next door is the Okefenokee Heritage Center with exhibits and a restored 1840 pioneer house. Both centers are open daily, except Mondays. (See *Information.*)

At the east entrance to the refuge, the U.S. Fish and Wildlife Service manages the recreational facilities of Suwannee Canal Recreation Area. A concessionaire rents canoes, boats, bicycles, and camping and fishing equipment, and carries a limited supply of food. There are guided one-hour and 2-hour group boat tours. The Swamp Edge Visitor Center and refuge headquarters here have films, displays, and exhibits. Two short land trails introduce you to the canal that was built by the Suwannee Canal Company in the 1890s. From the visitor center you can drive a 4.5-mile observation road to Chesson Island Homestead and Wildlife Trail. Deerstand Trail leads to an observation tower for views of the Chesson Prairie. Nearby is a 1.5-mile round-trip Boardwalk Trail to an observation tower overlooking Seagrove Lake. The nearest campground to the Suwannee Canal entrance is Traders Hill Recreation Area, which has hook-ups and hot showers. It is on SR 121, 4.5 miles south of Folkston.

At the west entrance is the 82-acre Stephen C. Foster State Park. Here are a dock for boat and canoe rentals, boating, fishing, and full-service camping. On the Trembling Earth Nature Trail, close to the dock, are oaks, pines, cypress, and hurrah bushes. From the dock you can take a boat to Billy's Island, Floyd's Island, Minnie's Lake, and

*Cedar Hammock Trail, Okefenokee National Wildlife Refuge.*
PHOTO BY Georgia Department of Industry and Trade.

Big Water Lake, and to the Suwannee River sill, all in a short day trip.

The Kingfisher Landing on the northeast edge of the refuge has only a boat dock for fishing and canoeing. But from here, as from the Stephen C. Foster State Park and Suwannee Canal Recreation Area, you can begin your canoe trip to cross the length or width of the swamp, staying on platform campsites each night.

Preplan any overnight canoe excursion on the 107 miles of canoe trails. First, request a color-coded map of the seven trails and regulations from refuge headquarters. After choosing a trail and a date, telephone the refuge for reservations within 2 months of your desired trip. The most popular times are in March and April; you may have problems getting your telephone call through immediately and getting your choice of trails during these months. Although fall and winter are least colorful in the swamp, the temperature during those seasons is generally comfortable compared to the heat and humidity of the summer. You can camp only one night at each rest stop, but your party may include up to ten canoes and twenty people. After you have your permit, plan your food and equipment needs. For convenience, you may wish to rent most everything from the concessionaire. (If you wish to have someone else make your arrangements, contact Wilderness Southeast in Savannah. The guides choose high-quality equipment for you, arrange an itinerary, provide ample meals, and explain the natural environment. See *Information.*) You must begin canoeing before 10 A.M. in order to reach your campsite before dark.

A typical overnight trip follows the 16-mile round-trip Cedar Hammock Trail. Leave from the Suwannee Canal Recreation Area and paddle west 2 miles on the Suwannee Canal to a sign, right. Along the way the canal is wide and free of grass and lilies, but on the sides you will notice a few low spots where alligators sun or nest. To the south, at Cooter Lake, you may hear the rough grunts and bellows of mating alligators. Once you leave the canal, the swamp changes dramatically. Only a narrow and sometimes faint channel among water lilies and golden club is visible in the Mizell Prairie and Double-O Bay. Surrounding you are white ibis, egrets, anhingas, ospreys, blue herons, and northern harriers (marsh hawks). Alligators lie silently on peat banks or bedded grass and sedges, close to the canoe. Near them are bladderwort and exceptionally large clusters of pitcher plant. Near the hammock borders you may first hear and then see 5-foot-tall sandhill cranes, watchmen of the swamp. If a crane is frightened, it will rise from the grass with a cry of alarm that signals a flock of twenty-five or more cranes, and other birds, to flee in a crescendo of flapping wings. Permanent residents of the swamp, the gray brown sandhill cranes are long legged but elegant, wise, and wary; they mate for life. After milepost 6 you will enter a channel wide enough for one canoe. Dense red chokeberry and titi form an arbor, and you begin to hear the noises of wildlife in the thickets. The old way through the swamp, before canoes were used there, was "to wade and carry upon your back the bacon and potatoes," wrote Hank Mizell, author of *History of Okefenokee Swamp*. "The bog in places was so deep that it was often necessary for [father] to throw out his arms and to catch his weight on the water moss, and then he would wallow out to a better footing."

A sudden bend to the left is your route to the campsite, a wooden platform that has a dock, shelter, and chemical toilet. By nightfall there begins a cacophony of frogs and insects, and not long after dark you will hear raccoons prowling around your tent. Because some have learned to unzip a backpack, you should hang your food by a rope from the shelter rafters. On your way back the next day you will likely meet the next campers; the raccoons will be waiting for their new guests. Cedar Hammock Trail is one of two that dead-ends. All other trails connect in a network of short and long loops. Occasionally you may have to get out of your canoe to push it through shallow water or peat bogs that have exploded from marsh gas.

The Okefenokee is an enormous bog filled with dark, tannin-colored, fresh water. Nearly 60 miles long and 30 miles at its widest, the swamp is about 438,000 acres, 396,000 of which are in the refuge. Hundreds of small streams feed into the swamp, thus creating the famous Suwannee River head-waters. Like its most isolated interior, the swamp's name has had a share of mystery. Some historians claim the Choctaw or Timucuan Indians named it *Okefenokee*, meaning trembling earth, with more resonant syllables than the Creek's *Efinocau* from *Ecunnau* (earth) and *finocau* (quiver). Old maps from 1790 show it as *Ekanfinaka*, and in 1818 it was *Oquafanaoka*. William Bartram spelled it *Ouaquaphenogaw* in his *Travels* of the 1770s. From 1776 to 1921, it had at least seventy-five different spellings.

Formed in the early Pleistocene epoch, the Georgia coastline was once about 75 miles farther inland than it is now. In time a long sandbar, now called Trail Ridge, separated the lake from the slowly receding ocean. The water changed from salty to fresh, and plant life developed on the island sandbars. Peat bogs developed from decaying vegetation, and marsh gas pushed them to water level. On the peat began new plant life, floating islands. Eventually large plants and trees grew, and roots took hold on the sandy bottom of the suspended island. The Indians found that these developing pieces of peat quivered and trembled when they set foot on them. These original sandbars and developing islands now number an estimated seventy-five stable, dry islands, the majority of them named. There are two principal outlying islands: the largest, on the north edge, is fertile 9-mile-long Cowhouse Island, named by early white pioneers who drove their cattle on the island in the winter months. The other large island, Chesser (on the east edge) was named for W. T. Chesser, a pioneer who moved to the island in 1858. One of the most historic interior islands is Billy's Island, the last holdout for Seminole Indian Chief Koniphatco (Billy Bowlegs) in the 1830s. Another large inner island, and the highest in the marsh, is Floyd's, named for Gen. Charles Floyd, who led a detachment to rouse the Seminoles. Other islands are Honey, Bugaboo, Strange, Blackjack, Pine, and Soldier's Camp. The latter was named for Civil War deserters who fled here and for soldiers who camped here while hunting the deserters. Whether large or small, all the islands have a common characteristic: Swamp water and dense vegetation surround them.

As the large lake became more infused with vegetation, hundreds of smaller lakes developed. Today they range in size from the alligator holes to the largest, Billy's Lake, 3 miles long and 250 yards wide, near Stephen C. Foster State Park. This lake is among about sixty currently scattered throughout the swamp, ranging from 2 to 40 feet deep. Stories have circulated that saurian beasts live in undiscovered bottomless lakes. North of Billy's Lake, on the main channel, are smaller Minnie's Lake and Big Water Lake. Passageway between them is a crooked, narrow route through huge cypress. Gannet Lake, which covers about 15 acres, is considered one of the swamp's most beautiful. It is located in the Grand Prairie, near the swamp's east edge, and is named for the black-winged cormorant, which early explorers called the gannet. Suwannee Lake, about one mile long, near the north edge, is reputed to be an angler's paradise. Other lake names imply a chief characteristic of wildlife or design: Buzzard's Roost, Sometime Hole, Half Moon, Buck, Trout, Duck, Double, Blackjack, and Alligator.

Often called flooded marshes, the wet prairies give the swamp an open, incredible landscape. Depending on seasonal rains, the prairies rise and fall as much as 2 feet. On the 60,000 acres or more of scattered prairies there is an abundance of waterfowl and brightly colored plants, saw grass, and maiden cane. Two of the larger prairies are Grand and Chase, both near the eastern side of the swamp. Grand Prairie, about 5 by 3 miles, received its name first, before Chase was discovered. Chase was named for hunters who chased deer and bear across its open space.

A fourth and largest category of swamp topography includes the hammocks and bays where forests of cypress, gums, tupelos, bays, maples, pines, and palmettoes grow. Within these clusters, sometimes on dry islands, there are

tangles of bamboo, wax myrtle, red chockberry, and titi.
Pioneers called some of the pockets or clusters of thick
vegetation, a protective forest for wildlife, "houses." Mixon's
Hammock, named for Joshua Mixon, who settled on the island
in the 1850s, is one of the better known. Others are Craven's
(discovered by John Craven), Cedar, and Maul. Timber has
been harvested on all the major hammocks.

Cypress overshadows all other plant life in the swamp.
Buttressed, soft barked, and cathedral high, it is the grandsire
of tree majesty. Hanging from its outstretched limbs is gray
Spanish moss, sometimes as still as the water beneath it and
sometimes waving like silk in the wind. Needleless in the
winter, its gray silhouette exposes other trees, such as the
evergreen cedar, magnolia, loblolly, pine, bay, heath, and
holly. Longleaf and slash pines, oaks, maples, and other
hardwoods thrive on the dry islands. The swamp has varied
species of blue and black huckleberries, loved by the bears
and birds. One of the most unusual, the "wooly coat"
blueberry, has a fuzzy skin. All the berries ripen in June and
July. Gallberries, thick throughout the swamp, are bitter to
humans but tasty to wildlife. In the spring and summer the
swamp has a bright floral display of purple pickerelweed;
pipewort; neverwet; ferns; red, pink, and orange orchids; and
the ever-present fragrant white water lily (*Castalia odorata*),
which closes its petals at night and on cloudy days. Carnivorous trumpets, hooded pitcher plants, yellow bladderworts,
and red sundews, all plentiful on the prairies, trap insects,
small worms, and nematodes for nitrogenous food.

Immediately after you enter the swamp, you see and hear
animal life. King of the Okefenokee is the American alligator.
(See *Wildlife*, Chapter 1.) An extremely fast reptile in the
water, it lies lazily on logs and grassy banks. Almost extinct in
the 1950s and shown in fearsome roles by Hollywood's *Lure
of the Wilderness, Land of the Trembling Earth, Untamed Fury*,
and other films, the alligator has made a comeback and is now
hunted only under strict restrictions. Although it is shy away
from people, you should keep your distance and avoid

agitating or molesting it. About sixty-five other reptiles, including thirty-seven snakes, also inhabit the swamp. Poisonous snakes are the eastern coral, eastern diamondback rattlesnake, canebrake rattlesnake, dusky pigmy rattlesnake, and quick-striking cottonmouth. The snakes, like the alligators, do not stalk you in the swamp, but you must stay aware of your surroundings. There are twenty-two species of frogs and forty species of fish. Tales of successful fishing do not need exaggeration with the generous supply of pickerel, bass, perch, sunfish, bluegill, warmouth, black crappie, and others. The most prominent mammals among about fifty species are the white-tailed deer, raccoon, river otter, squirrel, cottontail, evening bat, round-tailed muskrat, fox, bobcat, and rat. Feral hogs have been on a few islands since the 1850s, and since the armadillo was first seen in 1963 it has become more numerous. Black bear, though rarely seen, wander throughout the refuge.

No families of wildlife are more obvious or vocal than the two hundred species of birds that are resident or migratory. Common in at least two of the seasons are the pied-billed grebe, anhinga, red-shouldered hawk, wood stork, kestrel, owl, shrike, ring-necked duck, vulture, black duck, mallard, green-winged teal, sandpiper, ibis, egret, heron, woodpecker, snipe, kildeer, and, of course, the wildlife watchman, the sandhill crane. Warblers and sparrows make up the largest group of resident or migratory species. If you are in the refuge in March or April, expect to see many wading birds, tree swallows, ducks, phoebes, and waxwings. In March the sandhill cranes perform a nesting dance, and in April their chicks hatch. Also in April you will see ospreys feeding their young.

The first known Indians in the swamp, hunters and fishermen of the Deptford, Swift Creek, and Weeden Island cultures, lived there about 2500 B.C. The Weeden Island group had elaborate tribal ceremonies and created beautiful art designs. Sometime about A.D. 1200 the tall aborigines disappeared. When they went, they left behind mounds on the larger islands, most of which have not been disturbed. The Hebard Cypress Company rail tram cut through one on Floyd's Island, however, revealing a large human skeleton 4 feet below the mound's surface, as well as pottery fragments. When the Spanish explored the swamp's fringe in the sixteenth century they met Timucuan Indians in the south and Apalachee in the west. Most widely known is the Seminole, an independent branch of the Creek nation. Newcomers to the swamp, they were driven out by Gen. Charles Floyd in 1831. Except for a light skirmish, Chief Billy Bowlegs and his followers had already deserted the swamp and fled to Florida.

Pioneer white settlers moved to the edges of the swamp and the islands in the 1820s. One of the earliest was Israel Barber, whose son, Obediah (born in 1825), became a famous bear hunter and earned the title "King of the Okefenokee." Josiah Mixon settled with his family in the 1850s on a hammock that now bears his name, and about 1853 James Lee made a claim on what is now Billy's Island. He sold it to Dan Lee, who took his bride to the isolated island, where the couple raised fourteen healthy children, taught them to read and write, and raised crops and livestock to sustain them. By the time the lumber company arrived with train and tram in the early twentieth century, the Lee descendants worked in an island community that had grown to six hundred inhabitants. Now all you will see are a few scattered bricks, an old car frame, locomotive parts, and raccoons that sometimes meet you at the dock. Other early settlers were Josiah Mizell, who came before the Civil War, and J. D. Hendrix, who came after the Civil War. At the turn of the twentieth century Will Cox became known as the best guide of the Okefenokee. Perhaps the most remarkable character was Lydia A. Stone. Six feet tall, tough, and self-educated, she became "the Queen of Cowhouse Island." The hard-working Stone "could make five dollars out of every dollar." She acquired 30,000 acres and became the wealthiest of the pioneers; her second marriage, at the age of sixty-three, was to 21-year-old J. Milton Crews, whom she called "Baby Doll."

In 1891 the Suwannee Canal Company purchased 238,120 acres for $62,101 from the state of Georgia, which had earlier declared the swamp useless and public property. Under the leadership of Capt. Harvey Jackson, the company completed only 12 channel miles and 8 branch miles for drainage. After the company's bankruptcy and receivership, the swamp was sold to the Hebard Cypress Company in 1889. That company cut the best and largest stands of cypress and pine, nearly half a billion board feet. Logging continued until 1927, 9 years after J. L. Sweat, a state legislator from Ware County, had the Georgia legislature adopt a resolution to make the Okefenokee Swamp "a National Park Reservation." In 1937 the swamp became a national wildlife refuge, and in 1974 353,981 acres of the swamp's natural grandeur and unique ecosystem were protected as a national wilderness area.

## *Information*

Counties: Ware, Charlton, Clinch; Baker, Florida

Average Temperatures: January, 44.2°F (low), 66.1°F (high); August, 74°F (low), 90.1°F (high)

National Properties: Okefenokee National Wildlife Refuge, Rte. 2, Box 338, Folkston, GA 31537, (912) 496-3331/7836

State Properties: Stephen C. Foster State Park, Rte. 1, Box 131, Fargo, GA 31631, (912) 637-5274; Laura S. Walker State Park, 5653 Laura Walker Rd., Waycross, GA 31501, (912) 287-4900; (See Government Agencies under Georgia Sea Islands this Chapter)

County Properties: Traders Hill Recreation Area (administered by Charlton County), County Board of Commissioners, Court House, Folkston, GA 31537, (912) 496-3392/7660

Museums and Commercial Parks: Okefenokee Heritage Center, Rte. 5, Box 406B, Waycross, GA 31501, (912) 285-4260; Okefenokee Swamp Park, Waycross, GA 31501, (912) 283-0583; Southern Forest World, Rte. 5, Box 406A, Waycross, GA 31501, (912) 285-4056

Chambers of Commerce: Folkston CC, P.O. Box 756 (202 W. Main St.), Folkston, GA 31537, (912) 496-2536; Waycross–

Ware County CC, P.O. Box 137 (200 Lee Ave.), Waycross, GA 31502, (912) 283-3742

Services and Amenities: *Bed and Breakfast:* Blueberry Hill Restaurant, Rte. 1, Box 243, Hoboken, GA 31542, (912) 458-2605; *Campgrounds:* See State Properties, above

*Camping Rentals* (tent, sleeping bag, cookwear, poncho, stove, foam pads, tarp, lantern, portable toilet, and other supplies): See Suwannee Canal Recreation Area, below; *Canoe and Boat Rentals:* Suwannee Canal Recreation Area, Rte. 2, Box 336, Folkston, GA 31537, (912) 496-7156; *Canoe Tours and Guides:* Wilderness Southeast, 711 Sandtown Rd., Savannah, GA 31410, (912) 897-5108; *Outdoor Sports Supplies* (fishing, hunting, camping): Okefenokee Sportsman, 411 N. 2nd St., Folkston, GA 31537, (912) 496-7286

# APPENDIX A
## Florida and Georgia Lists of Endangered and Threatened Animals and Plants

### FLORIDA: ANIMALS

#### E: Endangered Species T: Threatened Species

**INVERTEBRATES**

*Corals*
Pillar coral (*Dendrogyra cylindrus*)   E
*Insects*
Butterfly, Schaus' swallowtail (*Heraclides aristodemus ponceanus*)   E
*Molluscs*
Snail, Stock Island tree (*Orthalicus reses*)   E

**VERTEBRATES**

*Amphibians and Reptiles*
Crocodile, American (*Crocodylus acutus*)   E
Skink, blue-tailed mole (*Eumeces egregius lividus*)   T
Skink, sand (*Neoseps reynoldsi*)   T
Snake, Atlantic salt marsh water (*Nerodia fasciata taeniata*)   T
Snake, Big Pine Key ringneck (*Diadophia punctatus acricus*)   T
Snake, eastern indigo (*Drymarchon corais couperi*)   T
Snake, Florida brown (*Storeria dekayi victa*)   T
Snake, Florida ribbon (*Thamnophis sauritus sackeni*)   T
Snake, Miami black-headed (*Tantilla oolitica*)   T
Snake, short-tailed (*Stilosoma extenuatum*)   T
Turtle, Atlantic green sea (*Chelonia mydas mydas*)   E
Turtle, Atlantic hawksbill sea (*Eretmochelys imbricata imbricata*)   E
Turtle, Atlantic ridley sea (*Lepidochelys kempi*)   E
Turtle, leatherback sea (*Dermochelys coriacea*)   E
Turtle, loggerhead (*Caretta caretta caretta*)   T
Turtle, striped mud (*Kinosternon bauri*)   E

*Birds*
Caracara, Audubon's crested (*Plyborus plancus audubonii*)   T
Crane, Florida sandhill (*Grus canadensis pratensis*)   T
Eagle, bald (*Haliaeetus leucocephalus*)   T
Falcon, peregrine (*Falco peregrinus tundrius*)   E
Jay, Florida scrub (*Aphelocoma coerulescens coerulescens*)   T
Kestrel, southeastern (*Falco sparverius paulus*)   T
Kite, Everglade snail (*Rostrhamus sociabilis*)   T
Pigeon, white-crowned (*Columba leucocephala*)   T
Plover, Cuban snowy (*Charadrius alexandrinus tenuirostris*)   T
Plover, piping (*Charadrius melodus*)   T
Sparrow, Cape Sable seaside (*Ammodramus maritimus mirabilis*)   E
Sparrow, dusky seaside (*Ammodramus maritimus nigrescens*)   E

Sparrow, Florida grasshopper (*Ammodramus savannarum floridanus*)　E
Stork, wood (*Mycteria americana*)　E
Tern, least (*Sterna antillarum*)　T
Tern, roseate (*Sterna dougallii*)　T
Warbler, Bachman's (*Vermivora bachmanii*)　E
Warbler, Kirtland's (*Dedroica kirtlandii*)　T
Woodpecker, ivory-billed (*Campephilus principalis*)　E
Woodpecker, red-cockaded (*Picoides borealis*)　T

### Fishes

Darter, crystal (*Ammocrypta asprella*)　T
Darter, Okaloosa (*Etheostoma okaloosae*)　E
Shiner, blackmouth (*Notropis* sp.)　E
Silverside, Key (*Menidia conchorum*)　E
Sturgeon, shortnose (*Acipenser brevirostrum*)　E

### Mammals

Bat, gray (*Myotis grisescens*)　E
Bat, Indiana (*Myotis sodalis*)　E
Deer, Key (*Odocoileus virginianus clavium*)　T
Gopher, Goff's pocket (*Geomys pinetis goffi*)　E
Manatee, West Indian (*Trichechus manatus latirostris*)　E
Mink, Everglades (*Mustala vison evergladensis*)　T
Mouse, Chadwick beach cotton (*Peromyscus gossypinus restrictus*)　E
Mouse, Choctawatchee beach (*Peromyscus polionotus allophrys*)　T
Mouse, Key Largo cotton (*Peromyscus gossypinus allapaticola*)　E
Mouse, pallid beach (*Peromyscus polionotus decoloratus*)　E
Mouse, Perdido Key beach (*Peromyscus polionotus trissyllepsis*)　E
Panther, Florida (*Felis concolor coryi*)　E
Rat, silver rice (*Oryzomys argentatus*)　E
Squirrel, Big Cypress fox (*Sciurus niger avicennia*)　T
Whale, finback (*Balaenoptera physalus*)　E
Whale, humpback (*Megaptera novaeangliae*)　E
Whale, right (*Balaena glacialis*)　E
Whale, sea (*Balaenoptera borealis*)　E
Whale, sperm (*Physeter catodon*)　E
Wood rat, Key Largo (*Neotoma floridana smalli*)　E

## FLORIDA: ENDANGERED PLANTS

Air plant, fuzzy-wuzzy (*Tillandsia pruinosa*)
Arbutus, trailing (*Epigaea repens*)
Aster, Cruise's golden (*Chrysopsis cruiseana*)
Aster, Florida golden (*Chrysopsis floridana*)
Aster, panhandle golden (*Pityopsis flexuosa*)
Autumngrass, riparium (*Schizachyrium niveum*)

Azalea, Alabama (*Rhododendron alabamense*)
Azalea, orange (*Rhododendron austrinum*)
Balm, long-spurred (*Dicerandra cornutissima*)
Balm, scrub (*Dicerandra frutescens*)
Balm, spotless-petaled (*Dicerandra immaculata*)
Balsam apple (*Clusia rosea*)
Beach star (*Remirea maritima*)
Bear grass, Florida (*Nolina atopocarpa*)
Bellflower, Robins' (*Campanula robinsiae*)
Birds-in-a-nest, white (*Macbridea alba*)
Blazing star, Godfrey's (*Liatris provincialis*)
Bonamia, Florida (*Bonamia grandiflora*)
Bromeliad, Fuch's (*Guzmania monostachia*)
Burmannia, Fakahatchee (*Burmannia flava*)
Butterfly-pea, pigeon-wing (*Clitoria fragrans*)
Cactus, mistletoe (*Rhipsalis baccifera*)
Cactus, tree (*Cereus robinii*)
Cactus, West Coast prickly apple (*Cereus gracilis*)
Catopsis, nodding (*Catopsis nutans*)
Cedar, bay (*Suriana maritima*)
Cereus, fragrant wool-bearing (*Cereus eriophorus*)
Clustervine, beach (*Jacquemontia reclinata*)
Clustervine, pineland (*Jacquemontia curtissii*)
Cotton, wild (*Gossypium hirsutum*)
Croomia, few-flowered (*Croomia pauciflora*)
Cupania (*Cupania glabra*)
Dropwort, giant water (*Oxypolis greenmanii*)
Epidendrum, Acuna's (*Epidendrum acunae*)
Epidendrum, dwarf (*Encyclia pygmaea*)
Fern, cuplet (*Dennstaedtia bipinnata*)
Fern, hand adder's tongue (*Ophioglossum palmatum*)
Fern, Hattie Bauer halberd (*Tectaria coriandrifolia*)
Fern, narrow strap (*Campyloneurum angustifolium*)
Fern, tropical curly grass (*Schizaea germanii*)
Flax, sand (*Linum arenicola*)
Four-o'clock, burrowing (*Okenia hypogaea*)
Fringetree, pigmy (*Chionanthus pygmaeus*)
Gayflower, Florida (*Liatris ohlingerae*)
Geiger-tree (*Cordia sebestena*)
Gentian, wire grass (*Gentiana pennelliana*)
Gooseberry, Miccosukee (*Ribes echinellum*)
Gourd, Okeechobee (*Cucribita okeechobeensis*)
Grass, karst pond yellow-eyed (*Xyris longisepala*)
Grass of parnassus (*Parnassia grandifolia*)
Hackberry, iguana (*Celtis iguanaea*)
Hackberry, spiny (*Celtis pallida*)

Harper's beauty (*Harperocallis flava*)
Hellebore, Woods false (*Veratrum woodii*)
Ladies' tresses, Florida Keys (*Spiranthes polyantha*)
Lavender, sea (*Mallontonia gnaphalodes*)
Licaria (*Licaria triandra*)
Lignum vitae tree (*Guaiacum sanctum*)
Lilly-thorn, small-flowered (*Catesbaea parviflora*)
Lily, celestial (*Nemasylis floridana*)
Lily, panhandle (*Lilium iridollae*)
Lily, Simpson zephyr (*Zephyranthes simpsonii*)
Liverleaf (*Hepatica americana*)
Magnolia, Ashe's (*Magnolia ashei*)
Meadowbeauty, small-flowered (*Rhexia parviflora*)
Milkweed, Alabama (*Matela alabamensis*)
Milkweed, Florida (*Matela floridana*)
Milkwort, scrub (*Polygala lewtonii*)
Milkwort, tiny (*Polygala smallii*)
Mistletoe, mahogany (*Phoradendron rubrum*)
Moss, hanging club (*Lycopodium dichotomum*)
Mustard, Carter's (*Warea carteri*)
Neottia, spurred (*Centrogenium cetaceum*)
Orchid, cowhorn (*Cyrtopodium punctatum*)
Orchid, dancing-lady (*Oncidium variegatum*)
Orchid, dollar (*Encyclia boothiana*)
Orchid, ghost (*Polyrrhiza lindenii*)
Orchid, Harris' tiny (*Lepanthopsis melanantha*)
Orchid, hidden (*Maxillaria crassifolia*)
Orchid, leafless (*Campylocentrum pachyrrhizum*)
Orchid, rattail (*Bulbophyllum pachyrrhachis*)
Orchid, snake (*Restrepiella ophiocephala*)
Orchid, violet (*Ionopsis utricularioides*)
Orchid, worm-vine (*Vanilla barbellata*)
Orchid, young-palm (*Tropidia polystachya*)
Palm, buccaneer (*Pseudophoenix sargentii*)
Palm, Florida royal (*Roystonea elata*)
Pea, Big Pine partridge (*Cassia keyensis*)
Pennyroyal, mock (*Hedeoma graveolens*)
Peperomia, cypress (*Peperomia glabella*)
Peperomia, Everglades (*Peperomia floridana*)
Peperomia, Florida (*Peperomia obtusifolia*)
Peperomia, pale-green (*Peperomia simplex*)
Peperomia, spatulate (*Peperomia spathulifolia*)
Pepper (*Peperomia humilis*)
Pigmy-pipes (*Monotropsis reynoldsiae*)
Pinkroot, Florida (*Spigelia loganioides*)
Pinkroot, gentian (*Spigelia gentianoides*)

Pitcher plant, red-flowered (*Sarracenia rubra*)
Pitcher plant, white-top (*Sarracenia leucophylla*)
Red stopper (*Eugenia rhombea*)
Rhododendron, Chapman's (*Rhododendron chapmanii*)
Sachsia, Bahama (*Sachsia bahamensis*)
Saint-John's-Susan (*Rudbeckia nitida*)
Saint-John's-wort, smooth-barked (*Hypericum lissophloeus*)
Satinleaf (*Chrysophyllum olivaeforme*)
Spurge, Allegheny (*Pachysandra procumbens*)
Spurge, Garber's (*Euphorbia garberi*)
Squirrel-banana, white (*Deeringothamnus pulchellus*)
Squirrel-banana, yellow (*Deeringothamnus rugelii*)
Torreya, Florida (*Torreya taxifolia*)
Vetch, Ocala (*Vicia ocalensis*)
Violet, halberd-leaved yellow (*Viola hastata*)
Wake-robin, lance-leaved (*Trillium lancifolium*)
Warea, clasping (*Warea amplexifolia*)
Willow, Cooley's water (*Justicia cooleyii*)
Yellowheart (*Zanthoxylum flavum*)
Yew, Florida (*Taxus floridana*)

## GEORGIA: ANIMALS

### E: Endangered Species   T: Threatened Species

#### VERTEBRATES

##### *Amphibians and Reptiles*
Snake, eastern indigo (*Drymarchon corais couperi*)   T
Turtle, Atlantic hawksbill sea (*Eretmochelys imbricata imbricata*)   E
Turtle, Atlantic ridley sea (*Lepidochelys kempi*)   E
Turtle, leatherback sea (*Dermochelys coriacea*)   E

##### *Birds*
Eagle, bald (*Haliaeetus leucocephalus*)   E
Falcon, peregrine (*Falco peregrinus anatum*)   E
Pelican, eastern brown (*Pelecanus occidentalis*)   E
Warbler, Bachman's (*Vermivora bachmanii*)   E
Warbler, Kirtland's (*Dendroica kirtlandii*)   E
Woodpecker, ivory-billed (*Campephilus principalis*)   E
Woodpecker, red-cockaded (*Picoides borealis*)   E

##### *Fishes*
Cavefish, southern (*Typhlichthys subterraneus*)   E
Sturgeon, shortnose (*Acipenser brevirostrum*)   E

##### *Mammals*
Bat, gray (*Myotis grisescens*)   E
Bat, Indiana (*Myotis sodalis*)   E
Cougar, eastern (*Felis concolor cougar*)   E

Gopher, Sherman's pocket (*Geomys pinetis fontenalus*)   E
Manatee, West Indian (*Trichechus manatus latirostris*)   E
Whale, humpback (*Megaptera novaeangliae*)   E
Whale, right (*Balaena glacialis*)   E

## GEORGIA: ENDANGERED PLANTS

Arrowwood (*Viburnum bracteatum*)
Bells, Oconee (*Shortia galacifolia*)
Buckthorn (*Bumelia thornei*)
Campion, fringed (*Silene polypetala*)
Cinquefoil, three-tooth (*Potentilla tridentata*)
Fimbristylis, Harper (*Fimbristylis perpusilla*)
Goldenseal (*Hydrastis canadensis*)
Grass, Hirst panic (*Panicum hirstii*)
Grass, open-ground whitlow- (*Draba aprica*)
Hellebore, Woods false (*Veratrum woodii*)
Lily, shoals spiderlily (*Hymenocallis coronaria*)
Loosestrife, Curtiss (*Lythrum curtissii*)
Pimpernel, false (*Lindernia saxicola*)
Pitcher plant, northern (*Sarracenia purpurea*)
Pitcher plant, sweet (*Sarracenia rubra*)
Plume, Georgia (*Elliottia racemosa*)
Pool sprite (*Amphianthus pusillus*)
Rattleweed, hairy (*Baptisia arachnifera*)
Starflower (*Trientalis borealis*)
Torreya, Florida (*Torreya taxifolia*)
Trillium, persistent (*Trillium persistens*)
Twinleaf (*Jeffersonia diphylla*)
Willow, Florida (*Salix floridana*)

# APPENDIX B
## Florida Lakes and Forests

Florida has more than 7,700 lakes larger than 10 acres each, the largest of which is 448,000-acre Lake Okeechobee. Below is a list of lakes with 1,000 acres or more, the counties in which they are located, and their types: type 1 has only streams flowing in; type 2 has only streams flowing out; type 3 has streams flowing in and out; and type 4 is landlocked.

### LAKES

| NAME | SURFACE AREA (ACRES) | TYPE OF LAKE | COUNTY |
|---|---|---|---|
| Alligator Lake | 3,406 | 3 | Osceola |
| Ariana Lake | 1,026 | 3 | Polk |
| Bay Lake | 1,060 | 3 | Orange |
| Big Sand Lake | 1,110 | 4 | Orange |
| Blue Cypress Lake | 6,555 | 3 | Indian River |
| Cat Lake | 2,080 | 3 | Osceola |
| Conservation Area 1 Lake | 141,440 | | Palm Beach |
| Conservation Area 2 Lake | 134,400 | | Broward |
| Conservation Area 3 Lake | 585,280 | | Broward |
| Crescent Lake | 15,960 | 3 | Putnam |
| Crooked Lake | 5,538 | 3 | Polk |
| Cypress Lake | 4,097 | 3 | Osceola |
| Dead Lake | 3,655 | 3 | Gulf |
| Deadening Lakes, The | 2,538 | 3 | Washington |
| Deerpoint Lake | 5,000 | 3 | Bay |
| Doctors Lake | 3,397 | 3 | Clay |
| East Lake Tohopekeliga | 11,968 | 3 | Osceola |
| Econlockhatchee River Swamp | 4,108 | 3 | Osceola |
| Gopher Slough | 1,088 | 3 | Volusia |
| Hixtown Swamp | 9,776 | 1 | Madison |
| Jim Woodruff Reservoir | 37,500 | 3 | Jackson |
| Johns Lake | 2,417 | 3 | Orange |
| Kingsley Lake | 1,652 | 3 | Clay |
| Lake Apopka | 30,671 | 3 | Orange |
| Lake Arbuckle | 3,828 | 3 | Polk |
| Lake Ashby | 1,030 | 3 | Volusia |
| Lake Beauclair | 1,111 | 3 | Lake |
| Lake Buffum | 1,543 | 1 | Polk |
| Lake Butler | 1,665 | 3 | Orange |
| Lake Clinch | 1,207 | 4 | Polk |
| Lake Conlin | 6,281 | 3 | Osceola |
| Lake Conway | 1,075 | 3 | Orange |
| Lake Dexter | 1,902 | 3 | Volusia |
| Lake Disston | 1,844 | 3 | Flagler |
| Lake Dora | 4,475 | 3 | Lake |
| Lake Dorr | 1,533 | 3 | Lake |
| Lake Eloise | 1,160 | 3 | Polk |
| Lake Eustis | 7,806 | 3 | Lake |
| Lake Geneva | 1,630 | 3 | Clay |
| Lake Gentry | 1,791 | 3 | Osceola |
| Lake George | 46,000 | 3 | Volusia |
| Lake Griffin | 16,505 | 3 | Lake |
| Lake Hamilton | 2,162 | 3 | Polk |
| Lake Hancock | 4,519 | 3 | Polk |
| Lake Harris | 13,788 | 3 | Lake |
| Lake Harney | 6,058 | 3 | Volusia |
| Lake Hart | 1,850 | 3 | Orange |
| Lake Hatchineha | 6,665 | 3 | Osceola |
| Lake Iamonia | 5,757 | 1 | Leon |
| Lake Istokpoga | 27,692 | 3 | Highlands |
| Lake Jackson | 3,412 | 2 | Highlands |
| Lake Jackson | 4,004 | 1 | Leon |
| Lake Jackson | 1,020 | 3 | Osceola |
| Lake Jessup | 10,011 | 3 | Seminole |
| Lake Josephine | 1,236 | 3 | Highlands |
| Lake June in Winter | 3,504 | 2 | Highlands |
| Lake Kerr | 2,830 | 1 | Marion |
| Lake Kissimmee | 34,948 | 3 | Osceola |
| Lake Livingston | 1,203 | 2 | Polk |
| Lake Louisa | 3,634 | 3 | Lake |
| Lake Marian | 5,739 | 3 | Osceola |
| Lake Marion | 2,990 | 3 | Polk |
| Lake Mary Jane | 1,158 | 3 | Orange |
| Lake Mattie | 1,078 | 4 | Polk |
| Lake Miccosukee | 6,226 | 3 | Jefferson |
| Lake Minnehaha | 2,261 | 3 | Lake |
| Lake Minneola | 1,888 | 3 | Lake |
| Lake Monroe | 9,406 | 3 | Volusia |
| Lake Newnan | 7,427 | 3 | Alachua |
| Lake Norris | 1,131 | 3 | Lake |
| Lake Okeechobee | 448,000 | 3 | Palm Beach |
| Lake Panasoffkee | 4,460 | 3 | Sumter |
| Lake Parker | 2,272 | 3 | Polk |
| Lake Pierce | 3,729 | 1 | Polk |
| Lake Placid | 3,320 | 3 | Highlands |
| Lake Poinsett | 4,334 | 3 | Brevard |
| Lake Rosalie | 4,597 | 3 | Polk |
| Lake Rousseau | 3,657 | 3 | Levy |
| Lake Sampson | 2,042 | 3 | Bradford |
| Lake Talquin | 8,850 | 3 | Gadsen |
| Lake Tarpon | 2,534 | 3 | Pinellas |
| Lake Tibet | 1,198 | 3 | Orange |
| Lake Tohopekaliga | 18,810 | 3 | Osceola |
| Lake Trafford | 1,494 | 3 | Collier |
| Lake Washington | 4,362 | 3 | Brevard |
| Lake Weir | 5,685 | 3 | Marion |
| Lake Weohyakapka | 7,532 | 3 | Polk |
| Lake Wimico | 4,055 | 3 | Gulf |

| NAME | SURFACE AREA (ACRES) | TYPE OF LAKE | COUNTY |
|------|------|------|--------|
| Lake Winder | 1,496 | 3 | Brevard |
| Lake Woodruff | 2,200 | 3 | Volusia |
| Lake Yale | 4,042 | 3 | Lake |
| Ledwith Lake | 1,785 | 3 | Alachua |
| Levy Lake | 4,556 | 3 | Alachua |
| Levys Prairie | 1,938 | 3 | Putnam |
| Little Lake George | 1,416 | 3 | Putnam |
| Little Lake Harris | 2,739 | 3 | Lake |
| Little Lochloosa Lake | 2,642 | 3 | Alachua |
| Little Sante Fe Lake | 1,135 | 3 | Bradford |
| Lochloosa Lake | 5,705 | 3 | Alachua |
| Ocean Pond | 1,774 | 4 | Baker |
| Ocheesee Pond | 2,225 | 3 | Jackson |
| Okahumpka Swamp | 3,226 | 3 | Lake |

| NAME | SURFACE AREA (ACRES) | TYPE OF LAKE | COUNTY |
|------|------|------|--------|
| Orange Lake | 12,706 | 3 | Alachua |
| Pate Pond | 1,045 | 3 | Washington |
| Paynes Prairie Lake | 4,292 | 3 | Alachua |
| Pine Log Swamp Pond | 1,056 | 3 | Washington |
| Puzzle Lake | 1,300 | 3 | Seminole |
| Reedy Lake | 3,486 | 3 | Polk |
| Sand Hill Lake | 1,263 | 3 | Clay |
| Sante Fe Lake | 4,721 | 3 | Bradford |
| Sellers Lake | 1,050 | 3 | Marion |
| South Lake | 1,101 | 3 | Brevard |
| Tiger Lake | 2,200 | 3 | Polk |
| Tsala Apopka Lake | 19,111 | 3 | Citrus |
| Unnamed Lake | 3,778 | 3 | Osceola |

## FORESTS

In 1990 Florida forests covered nearly 50 percent of the state, a declining percentage because of increases in development to accommodate people. In the list below All Land excludes inland waters, and Total Forest includes commercial and noncommercial forest.

| COUNTY | ALL LAND (ACRES) | TOTAL FOREST (ACRES) |
|--------|------|------|
| Alachua | 592,947 | 320,684 |
| Baker | 373,733 | 331,860 |
| Bay | 493,392 | 423,722 |
| Bradford | 186,561 | 136,299 |
| Brevard | 658,846 | 128,103 |
| Broward | 777,502 | 32,473 |
| Calhoun | 363,441 | 301,612 |
| Charlotte | 458,729 | 111,561 |
| Citrus | 390,791 | 236,798 |
| Clay | 388,548 | 316,483 |
| Collier | 1,297,035 | 743,661 |
| Columbia | 511,587 | 371,622 |
| Dade | 1,250,756 | 209,959 |
| De Soto | 405,498 | 51,980 |
| Dixie | 453,981 | 395,155 |
| Duval | 496,061 | 279,380 |
| Escambia | 424,754 | 275,494 |
| Flagler | 315,108 | 253,582 |
| Franklin | 350,738 | 316,998 |
| Gadsden | 330,251 | 229,213 |
| Gilchrist | 224,901 | 141,989 |
| Glades | 570,440 | 99,717 |
| Gulf | 361,423 | 281,739 |
| Hamilton | 332,069 | 242,683 |
| Hardee | 408,445 | 86,999 |
| Hendry | 745,872 | 120,181 |
| Hernando | 313,240 | 179,228 |
| Highlands | 661,215 | 101,984 |
| Hillsborough | 670,891 | 145,958 |
| Holmes | 307,994 | 188,003 |
| Indian River | 320,367 | 44,071 |
| Jackson | 596,396 | 300,884 |
| Jefferson | 388,361 | 279,130 |
| Lafayette | 351,465 | 285,418 |
| Lake | 640,554 | 269,376 |

| COUNTY | ALL LAND (ACRES) | TOTAL FOREST (ACRES) |
|--------|------|------|
| Lee | 569,547 | 171,039 |
| Leon | 436,954 | 292,968 |
| Levy | 721,776 | 480,089 |
| Liberty | 536,385 | 516,581 |
| Madison | 457,788 | 297,382 |
| Manatee | 479,858 | 66,378 |
| Marion | 1,035,667 | 633,423 |
| Martin | 349,153 | 54,645 |
| Monroe | 645,715 | 372,589 |
| Nassau | 415,037 | 338,634 |
| Okaloosa | 598,961 | 471,489 |
| Okeechobee | 495,998 | 42,120 |
| Orange | 584,937 | 203,638 |
| Osceola | 867,706 | 202,656 |
| Palm Beach | 1,254,622 | 131,765 |
| Pasco | 483,683 | 163,832 |
| Pinellas | 180,310 | 32,054 |
| Polk | 1,191,263 | 271,189 |
| Putnam | 469,696 | 363,307 |
| Saint Johns | 396,909 | 292,696 |
| Saint Lucie | 368,443 | 53,325 |
| Santa Rosa | 653,397 | 500,681 |
| Sarasota | 369,620 | 65,159 |
| Seminole | 199,572 | 90,968 |
| Sumter | 364,897 | 170,486 |
| Suwannee | 440,943 | 202,759 |
| Taylor | 668,092 | 595,277 |
| Union | 158,611 | 118,107 |
| Volusia | 726,145 | 517,786 |
| Wakulla | 395,507 | 340,201 |
| Walton | 683,559 | 544,768 |
| Washington | 387,383 | 301,899 |
| TOTAL | 35,002,026 | 17,133,889 |

# APPENDIX C
## Marine and Scuba Diving Information

### NAVIGATIONAL CHARTS

The following coastal navigational charts are useful for approaching the coastline from the open ocean, inside offshore reefs and shoals, offshore sailing between coastal ports, entering large bays and harbors, and for navigating entry to some inland waterways. The charts are listed from Doboy Sound (between Sapelo and Wolf islands in Georgia) south along the east coast, and north and west on the west coast.

| CHART NO. | AREA |
|---|---|
| 11502 | Doboy Sound to Fernandina |
| 11488 | Amelia Island to Saint Augustine |
| 11486 | Saint Augustine to Ponce de Leon Inlet |
| 11484 | Ponce de Leon Inlet to Cape Canaveral |
| 11476 | Cape Canaveral to Bethel Shoal |
| 11474 | Bethel Shoal to Jupiter Inlet |
| 11466 | Jupiter Inlet to Fowey Rocks at Palm Beach Channel |
| 11462 | Fowey Rocks to Alligator Reef |
| 11452 | Alligator Reef to Sombrero Key |
| 11442 | Sombrero Key to Sand Key |
| 11439 | Sand Key to Rebecca Shoal |
| 11431 | East Cape to Mormon Key |
| 11429 | Chatham River to Clam Pass (Naples Bay and Everglades Harbor) |
| 11426 | Estro Bay (near Fort Myers) to Lemon Bay (including Charlotte Harbor and Peace River entrance) |
| 11424 | Lemon Bay to Passsage Key Inlet |
| 11412 | Tampa Bay and Saint Joseph Sound |
| 11409 | Anclote Keys to Crystal River |
| 11408 | Crystal River to Horseshoe Point (to include Waccasassa Bay, Cedar Keys, and Suwannee River entrance) |
| 11407 | Horseshoe Point to Rocks Islands |
| 11405 | Apalachee Bay |
| 11401 | Apalachicola Bay to Cape San Blas (at Saint Joseph Peninsula) |
| 11389 | Saint Joseph and Saint Andrew bays |
| 11388 | Choctawhatchee Bay |
| 11382 | Pensacola Bay and Perdido Key |

The following navigational charts are useful for harbors, small waterways, canals, intracoastal waterways, and more inland waterways. The charts are listed from Saint Simons Sound (in Georgia) south along the east coast, the Florida Keys, and north and west on the west coast to Dauphin Island (in Alabama).

| CHART NO. | AREA |
|---|---|
| 11489 | Saint Simons Sound (in Georgia) to Tolomato River (south of Ponte Verda Beach) |
| 11503 | Fernandina Harbor and Kings Bay (Georgia/Florida state boundary) |

| | |
|---|---|
| 11490 | Approaches to Saint Johns River and river entrance |
| 11491 | Saint Johns River (Atlantic Ocean to Jacksonville) |
| 11492 | Jacksonville to Racy Point and Crescent Lake (on the Saint Johns River) |
| 11495 | Dunns Creek (near Palatka) to Lake Dexter and Lake Harney |
| 11485 | Tolomato River to Palm Shores (north of Malbourne) |
| 11478 | Port Canaveral (Canaveral Barge Canal from Atantic Ocean to Indian River) |
| 11475 | Fort Pierce Harbor |
| 11428 | Okeechobee Waterway (Saint Lucie Inlet to Lake Okeechobee and to Fort Myers) |
| 11472 | Palm Shores to West Palm Beach (Loxahatchee River) |
| 11467 | West Palm Beach to Miami |
| 11470 | Port Everglades (south of Fort Lauderdale) |
| 11468 | Miami Harbor |
| 11465 | Miami to Elliot Key |
| 11463 | Ellliot Key to Tarpon Basin and to Matecumbe |
| 11451 | Miami to Marathon and Florida Bay |
| 11449 | Matecumbe to Grassy Key and to Bahia Honda Key |
| 11448 | Big Spanish Channel to Johnson Keys |
| 11445 | Bahia Honda Key to Sugarloaf Key and to Key West |
| 11447 | Key West Harbor |
| 11438 | Dry Tortugas (and harbor) |
| 11433 | Whitewater Bay (Everglades National Park) (ENP) |
| 11432 | Shark River to Lostmans River (ENP) |
| 11430 | Lostmans River to Wiggins Pass (north of Naples) |
| 11427 | Fort Myers to Charlotte Harbor |
| 11425 | Charlotte Harbor to Tampa Bay |
| 11414 | Tampa Bay (south) |
| 11413 | Tampa Bay (north to include Saint Petersburg) |
| 11410 | Tampa to Anclote Anchorage |
| 11406 | Saint Marks River (and approaches) |
| 11404 | Carabelle to Apalachicola Bay |
| 11402 | Apalachicola Bay to Lake Wimico |
| 11393 | Lake Wimico to East Bay |
| 11391 | Saint Andrew Bay |
| 11390 | East Bay to West Bay |
| 11385 | West Bay to Santa Rosa Sound |
| 11376 | Santa Rosa Sound to Dauphin Island (in Alabama) |
| 11384 | Pensacola Bay entrance |
| 11383 | Pensacola Bay |

Navigational charts can be purchased from the Distribution Division, National Oceanic and Atmospheric Administration, C44, National Ocean Survey, Riverdale, MD 20840, (301) 443-8910, or from local Florida marinas.

## SCUBA DIVING AREAS

The most desirable months for diving on the coastline are May through September. Winter months are better inland because the water is clearer.

**Northwest Coast (Pensacola to Cedar Key)**
Temperature: Winter, 60° F; spring and fall, mid-70°s; summer, 75°
Visiblity: Fall and winter, 25 to 30 feet; spring, 25 feet; summer, 75 feet
Centers: Destin, Fort Walton Beach, Panama City, Pensacola, Perry, Tallahassee, Valparaiso

**West Coast (Cedar Key to the Everglades)**
Temperature: Winter, low 60°s F; spring and fall, mid-70°s; summer, 85°
Visibilty: 5 to 50 feet
Centers: Clearwater, Crystal River, Saint Petersburg, Saint Petersburg Beach, Sarasota, Tampa, Venice

**Upper East Coast (Fernandina Beach to Vero Beach)**
Temperature: Winter, mid-50°s F; spring and fall, high 60°s; summer, 80°
Visibility: Winter, 5 to 10 feet; remainder of year, 15 to 30 feet
Centers: Daytona Beach, Merritt Island, Jacksonville area

**Lower East Coast (Vero Beach to the Keys)**
Temperature: Winter, 68° to 70° F; spring and fall, mid-70°s; summer, 85°
Visibility: 4 to 100 feet
Centers: Dania, Fort Lauderdale, Hialeah, Hollywood, Miami, North Miami Beach, Pompano Beach, Riviera Beach, West Palm Beach

**Florida Keys**
Temperature: Winter, 70° F; spring and fall, low 80°s; summer, high 80°s
Visibility: Winter, variable; remainder of year, 50 to 100 feet
Centers: Islamorada, Key Largo, Key West, Marathon

**Lakes and Rivers**
Temperature: 75° to 83° F
Visibility: 5 to 25 feet

**Springs, Caves, and Runs**
Temperature: All seasons, 68° to 72° F
Visibilty: 100 feet or more

# APPENDIX D
## Government Agencies and Citizens' Groups

### FLORIDA

#### Government Agencies

**Division of Tourism, Visitor Inquiry**
126 W. Van Buren St.
Tallahassee, FL 32399 (904) 487-1462

**Historical Sites, Department of State**
500 S. Bronough St.
Tallahassee, FL 32399 (904) 487-2333

**National Forests, USFS**
227 N. Bronough St. Suite 4061
Tallahassee, FL 32301 (904) 681-7265

**State Forests, Division of Forestry**
3125 Conner Blvd.
Tallahassee, FL 32399 (904) 488-6611

**State Parks, Office of Recreation and Parks**
3900 Commonwealth Blvd.
Tallahassee, FL 32399

**Florida Wildlife (Game and Fresh Water Fish Commission)**
620 S. Meridian St.
Tallahassee, FL 32399 (904) 488-1960 or -2975

**Watersports (Department of Environmental Protection)**
3900 Commonwealth Blvd. (Mail Station #660)
Tallahassee, FL 32399 (904) 488-1195

**Department of Environmental Regulation**
2600 Blair Stone Rd., Tallahassee, 32399, (904) 488-4805

**Department of Natural Resources**
Marjory Stoneman Douglas Bldg., 3900 Commonwealth Blvd.,
Tallahassee, 32399, (904) 488-1554
    **Division of Marine Resources:** (904) 488-6058
    **Division of Beaches and Shores:** (904) 487-4469
    **Division of State Lands:** (904) 488-2725
    **Division of Recreation and Parks:** (904) 488-6131

**Florida Cooperative Fish and Wildlife Research Unit, USDI**
117 Newins-Ziegler Hall, University of Florida, Gainesville, 32611,
(904) 392-1861

**Marine Laboratory, Florida State University**
Rt. 1, Box 219A, Sopchoppy, 32358, (904) 644-4740

**Water Management Districts**
    *Northwest:* Rt. 1, Box 3100, Havana, 32333, (904) 539-5999
    *Saint Johns:* P.O. Box 1429, Palatka, 32178, (904) 328-8321/
    (800) 451-7106 in FL

*South Florida:* P.O. Box 24680, West Palm Beach, 33416,
(407) 686-8800/(800) 432-2045 in FL
*Southwest:* 2379 Broad St., Brooksville, 34609, (904) 796-7211/
(800) 423-1476 in FL
*Suwannee:* Rt. 3, Box 64, Live Oak, 32060, (904) 362-1001

## Citizens' Groups

**Environmental Information Center, Florida Conservation Foundation, Inc.**
1191 Orange Ave., Winter Park, 32789, (407) 644-5377

**Florida Audubon Society**
1101 Audubon Way, Maitland, 32751, (407) 647-2615

**Florida Bass Chapter Federation**
P.O. Box 52, Lake Hamilton, 33851, (813) 439-2156

**Florida Defenders of the Environment, Inc.**
1523 N.W. 4th St., Gainesville, 32601, (904) 372-6965

**Florida Forestry Association**
P.O. Box 1696, Tallahassee, 32302, (904) 222-5646

**Florida Trail Association**
P.O. Box 13708, Gainesville, 32604, (800) 343-1882

**Florida Wildlife Federation**
P.O. Box 6870, Tallahassee, 32314, (904) 656-7113

**Florida Wildlife Sanctuary**
2600 Otter Creek Ln., Melbourne, 32935, (305) 254-8843

**Sanibel-Captiva Conservation Foundation, Inc.**
P.O. Box S (3333 Sanibel-Captiva Rd.), Sanibel, 33957, (813) 472-2329

**Save the Manatee Club**
500 N. Maitland Ave., Maitland, 32751, (407) 539-0990

**Sierra Club (Florida Chapter)**
P.O. Box 1692, Maitland, 32751, (407) 699-9819/875-5032

**The Conservancy**
1450 Merrihue Dr., Naples, 33942, (813) 262-0304

**The Nature Conservancy**
2699 Lee Rd., #500, Winter Park, 32789, (407) 628-5887

**Wildlife Society (Florida Chapter)**
3991 S.E. 27th Ct., Okeechobee, 34974, (813) 763-7469/452-4119

## GEORGIA

### *Government Agencies*

**Department of Industry and Trade**
Tourist Division, 230 Peachtree St., Suite 605, Atlanta, 30303, (404) 656-3545

**Department of Natural Resources**
270 Washington St., S.W., Atlanta, 30334, (404) 656-3500
    **Game and Fish Division:** (404) 656-2523
    **Parks, Recreation and Historic Sites:** (404) 856-2770

**Forestry Commission**
Box 819, Macon, 31298, (912) 744-3211

**Georgia Cooperative Fish and Wildlife Research Unit**
School of Forest Resources, University of Georgia, Athens, 30602, (404) 546-2234

**Institute of Natural Resources**
University of Georgia, Room 13, Ecology Bldg., Athens, 30602, (404) 542-1555

### *Citizens' Groups*

**Georgia Audubon Society**
(Call national office for chapter information: (212) 832-3200)

**Georgia Bass Chapter Federation**
11575 Northgate Trail, Roswell, 30075, (404) 993-6597/526-6385

**Georgia Environmental Council**
P.O. Box 2388, Decatur, 30031, (404) 352-3679

**Georgia Forestry Association, Inc.**
40 Marietta St., N.W., Suite 1020, Atlanta, 30303, (404) 522-0951

**Georgia Wildlife Federation**
1930 Iris Dr., Conyers, 30207, (404) 929-3350

**Sierra Club (Georgia Chapter)**
1841 Montreal #215, Tucker, 30080, (404) 491-7689

**The Georgia Conservancy, Inc.**
8615 Barnwell Rd., Alpharetta, 30201, (404) 642-4000

**The Nature Conservancy**
1401 Peachtree St., N.E., Atlanta, 30309, (404) 873-6946

**Wildlife Society (Georgia Chapter)**
DNR, Game and Fish Dept., 2150 Dawsonville Hwy., Gainesville, GA 30501, (404) 535-5700

# APPENDIX E
## Foreign Consular Offices

Antigua and Barbuda: Miami
Argentina: Miami
Austria: Miami
Bahamas: Miami
Barbados: Miami
Belgium: Miami; Tampa
Belize: Miami
Bolivia: Miami
Brazil: Miami
Canada: Orlando
Chile: Miami
Colombia: Coral Gables; Fort Lauderdale; Miami; Miami Beach; Tampa
Costa Rica: Miami
Denmark: Jacksonville; Miami; Tampa
Dominican Republic: Jacksonville; MacClenny; Miami; Miami Beach
Ecuador: Coral Gables; Fort Lauderdale; Miami
El Salvador: Miami; North Palm Beach; Tampa
Finland: Coral Gables; Jacksonville; Lake Worth; Tampa
France: Jacksonville; Miami; Orlando
Germany: Jacksonville; Miami; Saint Petersburg
Great Britain: Miami
Guatemala: Coral Gables; Fort Lauderdale; Miami

Haiti: Miami
Honduras: Miami; Tampa
Iceland: Hollywood; Tallahassee
Israel: Miami
Italy: Jacksonville; Miami; Tampa
Jamaica: Miami
Japan: Coral Gables
Jordan: Palm Beach
Korea: Miami
Luxembourg: Miami
Mexico: Miami; Tampa
Monaco: Delray Beach
Netherlands: Jacksonville; Miami; Tampa
Norway: Jacksonville; Miami; Pensacola; Tampa
Paraguay: Coral Gables
Portugal: Miami
Senegal: Miami
Spain: Coral Gables; Palm Beach; Jacksonville
Surinam: Miami
Sweden: Clearwater; Fort Lauderdale; Jacksonville
Thailand: Coral Gables
Togo: Miami
Tunisia: Miami
Turkey: Miami
Uruguay: Miami
Venezuela: Coral Gables
Yugoslavia: Jacksonville

**Air plant**—See *Epiphyte* and *Bromeliad*

**Algal blooms**—Excessive algae growth caused by nutrient enrichment, in lakes and other freshwater bodies

**Alluvial**—Refers to silt or other loose materials deposited by running water

**Aquifer**—A geologic formation, group of formations, or part of a formation that contains sufficient saturated and permeable material to yield significant quantities of water to wells and springs

**Blackwater**—A river or stream dyed rusty red by tannic acid from trees

**Brackish water**—Mixed fresh and salt water of varying salinity

**Bromeliad**—A plant in the pineapple family; many are air plants that grow on tree trunks but are not parasitic

**Channelization**—Digging a channel down the center of a stream to expedite removal of flood waters

**Chickee (Chikee)**—A stilt house open on all sides (with a thatched roof) made by the Seminole Indians or an open platform campsite over water (with a wood or metal roof) made by the U.S. National Park Service

**Cracker**—A white pioneer from Georgia or Alabama; there are two theories of origin—"corn cracker" for a farmer and "whip cracker" for a cattle driver with a bullwhip

**Deciduous tree**—A tree that sheds its leaves annually

**Discharge (water)**—The volume of water that passes a given point within a specific period of time

**Ecology**—The study of the relationship of living things to one another and to their physical environments

**Ecosystem**—A functional system that includes the organisms and their environment

**Eddy**—The water behind an obstruction in a current or behind a river bend

**Effluent**—The outflow of water, as from a lake or a channel

**Endangered**—A species of plant or animal that, throughout all or part of a significant range, is in danger of extinction

**Epiphyte**—A plant that derives its moisture and nutrients from the air and rain and that usually grows on another plant

**Estivation**—A prolonged dormant or sleeplike state that enables an animal to survive the summer in a hot climate

**Estuary**—A semi-enclosed coastal body of water connected to the open sea and affected by the rise and fall of the tide

**Eutrophication**—The process that leads to a higher concentration of dissolved nutrients in a body of water

**Exotic**—A plant or animal that has been introduced, intentionally or by accident, into a new area

**First-magnitude spring**—A spring having an average discharge of 64.6 million gallons or more per day

**Floodplain**—A relatively level valley floor built on material transported by a stream and deposited beyond the stream channel during floods

**Fluvial**—Pertaining to or produced by the action of a stream; or existing, growing, or living in or near a stream

**Food chain**—A series of plants and animals linked by their food relationships, beginning with a green plant and ending with a predator

**Gauging station**—An installation for measuring the discharge of a stream

**Groundwater**—Subsurface water

**Habitat**—The immediate surroundings, living and unliving, of an organism

**Hammock**—A dense growth of broad-leaved trees on a slightly elevated area, not wet enough to be a swamp

**Hardwood trees**—Trees with broad leaves, usually deciduous but may retain all or some of the leaves throughout the year

**Hazardous wastes**—Substances that present a hazard to human health or safety or to the environment unless properly stored, transported, treated, or disposed of

**Headwaters**—The source and upstream waters of a stream

**Hurricane**—A powerful storm with winds of 74 or more miles per hour

**Hydrology**—A science concerned with the occurrence, circulation, distribution, and properties of the earth's waters

**Karst**—An irregular area underlain by limestone, dolomite, or gypsum and marked by sinkholes and underground drainages

**Key**—A reef or low-lying island in a body of water or a hammock raised above the surrounding wetlands

**Left bank**—The left bank of a river when facing downstream

**Limestone**—A sedimentary rock formed from the shells and skeletons of animals deposited in seas and consisting mostly of calcium carbonate

**Mangrove**—Any of a group of tropical or subtropical trees growing in estuaries and other low-lying coastal areas and usually forming a dense growth

**Marl**—A loose or crumbling earthy deposit of mixed limestone, sand, silt, or clay

**Marsh**—A wetland of either salt or fresh water, where few if any trees and shrubs grow but where there are usually grasses, sedges, and cattails

**Muck**—Dark, finely divided, well-decomposed organic matter intermixed with mineral matter, usually silt, which forms soil

**Oxbow lake**—A crescent-shaped lake in a floodplain caused by the former stream cutting through the neck of a bend in the stream

**Riparian**—The banks of a stream or lake, or the shore of a sea

**Saltwater intrusion**—Salt water that moves laterally or vertically to replace fresh water

**Sinkhole**—A depression in the land surface formed either by the collapse of the roof of an underground cavern or channel or by solution of near-surface limestone or similar rocks

**Slough**—A channel of slow-moving water in a coastal marshland

**Swamp**—A wetland characterized by shrubs or trees such as maples, gums, bald cypresses, and mangroves

**Threatened**—A species still present in its range but in such reduced numbers that, without significant changes in condition, it may become endangered

**Tropical storm**—A storm with a maximum wind speed of 39 to 73 miles per hour

**Watershed**—An area in which surface runoff collects and from which it is carried by a stream and its tributaries

# APPENDIX G
## Bibliography

### FLORIDA

#### Government Publications: Federal

*Canoe Trail Guides of Eglin Air Force Base.* Eglin Air Force Base, FL: AD/ DEMN, 1982.

*De Soto Trail: National Historic Trail Study (Draft Report).* Atlanta: U.S. Department of the Interior, National Park Service, Southeast Regional Office, 1989.

*Environmental Impact Statement* (National Forests of Florida). Atlanta: U.S. Department of Agriculture, Forest Service, Southern Region, 1986.

*Florida National Scenic Trail (Comprehensive Plan).* Tallahassee: U.S. Department of Agriculture, Forest Service, Southern Region, 1986.

*Florida National Scenic Trail Certification Plan.* Tallahassee: U.S. Department of Agriculture, Forest Service, Apalachicola National Forest.

*Lakeside Recreation in the Southeast.* Jacksonville: U.S. Army Corps of Engineers, District 2.

*Land Resource Management Plan* (National Forests of Florida). Atlanta: U.S. Department of Agriculture, Forest Service, Southern Region, 1986.

*National Forest in Florida: Recreation Area Directory.* Tallahassee: U.S. Department of Agriculture, Forest Service, Southern Region.

*National Wildlife Refuges System.* Atlanta: U.S. Department of the Interior, Region IV, Fish and Wildlife Service.

*The Impacts of Rail-Trails.* Washington: U.S. Department of the Interior, National Park Service, 1992.

#### Government Publications: State

*Aquatice Preserves.* Tallahassee: Department of Natural Resources, Division of Recreation and Parks, and Bureau of Land and Aquatic Resource Management.

*Cabbage Palm—Our State Tree, The.* A. S. Jensen. Gainesville: University of Florida, School of Forest Resources and Conservation.

*Everglades Forever Act,* Tallahassee: Florida Senate Bill 1350, May 3, 1994.

*Facts for Florida Vessel Owners.* Tallahassee: Department of Natural Resources.

*Florida Bicycle Laws; Florida Bicycle Trails;* and *Information for Bicycle Tourists.* Tallahassee: Dept. of Transportation, Florida Bicycle Program.

*Florida County Atlas, and Municipal Fact Book.* Tallahassee: Institute of Science and Public Affairs, Florida State University.

*Florida County Comparisons.* Tallahassee: Florida Department of Commerce, Division of Economic Development.

*Florida Freshwater Sport Fishing Guide and Regulations Summary.* Tallahassee: Florida Game and Fresh Water Fish Commission, annual.

*Florida Geological Survey List of Publications.* Tallahassee: Department of Natural Resources, 1990.

*Florida Panther.* Tallahassee: Florida Game and Fresh Water Fish Commission.

*Florida Panther Reintroduction*. Tallahassee: Florida Game and Wild Fish Commission.

*Florida Visitor Study, 1990, Executive Summary*. Tallahassee: Department of Commerce, Division of Tourism.

*Hunter Education Is for Everyone*. Tallahassee: Florida Game and Fresh Water Fish Commission.

*Land Acquisition and Management Plan, 1988–1989*. Live Oak, FL: Suwannee River Water Management District.

*Legal Protection for Florida's Endangered Species, Threatened Species and Species of Special Concern*. Tallahassee: Florida Game and Fresh Water Fish Commission, 1990.

*Outdoor Recreation in Florida*. Tallahassee: Department of Natural Resources, Division of Recreation and Parks, 1989.

*Poisonous Snakes of Florida*. A. S. Jensen. Gainesville: University of Florida, Cooperative Extension Service.

*Publications of the Florida Department of Natural Resources*. Tallahassee: Department of Natural Resources (Bureau of Education and Information: backpacking, boating, camping, canoeing, diving, estuarine sanctuaries, fishing, hiking, historic information, horse trails, manatee material, marine topics, natural resources, recreation services, state park information and brochures, wildlife), 1990.

*Save Our Everglades: A Status Report*. Tallahassee: Office of Governor Lawton Chiles, January and April 1992; October, 1993; March and August, 1994.

*Suwannee River Floods: Florida and Georgia*. Jacksonville: U.S. Army Corps of Engineers, 1974.

*Waste Utilization on Forest Lands in Florida*. H. Riekerk. Gainesville: Institute of Food and Agriculture Sciences.

*Wildlife Management Area Regulations Summary and Area Map*. Tallahassee: Florida Game and Fresh Water Fish Commission, annual.

### Books, Magazines, and Newspapers

Addison, David. *Boardwalk Guide to Briggs Memorial Nature Center*. Naples, FL: The Conservancy.

Akerman, Joe A., Jr. *Florida Cowman: A History of Florida Cattle Raising*. Kissimmee, FL: Florida Cattleman's Association, 1976.

Anderson, Robert. *Guide to Florida Vanishing Wildlife*. Altamonte Springs, FL: Winner Enterprises, 1988.

*Archbold Biological Station*, 5th ed. Lake Placid, FL: Archbold Expeditions, 1986.

Ashton, Ray E., Jr., and Patricia Sawyer Ashton. *The Snakes: Handbook of Reptiles and Amphibians of Florida*. Miami: Windward Publishing, 1981.

*Bantam's Florida, 1991*. New York: Bantam Books, 1990.

Bartram, William. *Travels*. (Reprint). New Haven, CT: Yale Univ. Press, 1958.

Belden, Robert C. *The Florida Panther*. New York: National Audubon Society, 1989.

Bell, C. Ritchie, and Bryan J. Taylor. *Florida Wild Flowers and Roadside Plants*. Chapel Hill, NC: Laurel Hill Press, 1982.

Beresky, Andrew E. *Fodor's 90 Florida.* New York: Fodor's, 1990.

Bethel, Rodman. *A Slumbering Giant of the Past: Fort Jefferson, U.S.A., on the Dry Tortugas.* Hialeah, FL: W. L. Litho, 1979.

Blake, Nelson M. *Land into Water—Water into Land; A History of Water Management in Florida.* Tallahassee: University Presses of Florida, 1980.

Bloodworth, Bertha E., and Alton C. Morris. *Place in the Sun: The History and Romance of Florida Place Names.* Gainesville: University Presses of Florida, 1978.

Brookfield, Charles M., and Olliver Griswold. *They All Called It Tropical.* Miami: Historical Association of Southern Florida, 1985.

Bunnelle, Hasse, and Shirley Sarvis. *Cooking for Camp and Trail.* San Francisco: Sierra Club Books, 1972.

Burnett, Gene M. *Florida's Past.* Vol. 1. Sarasota, FL: Pineapple Press, 1986.

Burt, Al. *Becalmed in the Mullet Latitudes: Al Burt's Florida.* Port Salerno, FL: Florida Classics, 1983.

Carr, Archie F., and C. J. Goin. *Guide to the Reptiles, Amphibians and Fresh Water Fishes in Florida.* Gainesville: University of Florida Press, 1990.

Carter, Elizabeth F. *A Hiking Guide to Trails in Florida.* Birmingham: Menasha Ridge Press, 1987.

Carter, Elizabeth F., and John L. Pearce. *A Canoeing and Kayaking Guide to the Streams of Florida (North Central Peninsula and Panhandle).* Birmingham: Menasha Ridge Press, 1985.

Cavanaugh, Peggy, and Margaret Spontak. *Protecting Paradise.* Fairfield, FL: Phoenix, 1992.

Clary, Mike. "Everglades on the Brink of 'Ecosystem Collapse.'" *Los Angeles Times,* November 12, 1989.

Cline, Howard F. *Florida Indians.* Vol. 2. New York: Garland Publishing Company, 1974.

*Corkscrew Swamp Sanctuary.* New York: National Audubon Society, 1981.

Council, Clyde C. *Suwannee Country.* Sarasota, FL: J & G Publishers, 1988.

Curtis, Sam. *Harsh Weather Camping.* Birmingham: Menasha Ridge Press, 1986.

De Golia, Jack. *Everglades: The Story behind the Scenery.* Las Vegas, NV: KC Publications, 1986.

Doran, Barbara. "Tallahassee Volunteers Blaze a Trail Across the Panhandle." *Tallahassee Magazine* (Spring 1989): 55–58.

Douglas, Marjory Stoneman. *The Everglades: River of Grass,* rev. ed. Saint Petersburg, FL: Pineapple Press, 1988.

———. *Florida: The Long Frontier.* New York: Harper & Row, 1967.

———. *Voice of the River.* (An Autobiography.) Saint Petersburg, FL: Pineapple Press, 1987.

Elsken, Katrina. *La Belle, Our Home.* La Belle, FL: La Belle Leader, Publishers, 1985.

Fairbanks, Charles. *Florida Indians.* Vol. 3. New York: Garland Publishing Company, 1974.

Fernald, Edward A., Ed. *Atlas of Florida.* Tallahassee: Florida State University Foundation, 1981.

Fischer, David, Ed. *Florida's Sandy Beaches.* (An Access Guide.) Gainesville: University Presses of Florida, 1985.

Fitzpatrick, James J. "We're Giving Federal Resources Away." *Universal Press Syndicate,* March 4, 1989.

Fitzpatrick, John W., and Glen E. Woolfenden. "The Helpful Shall Inherit the Scrub." *Natural History* (1984): 55–63.

*Florida Camping Directory.* Tallahassee: Florida Campground Association, annual.

*Florida Fish Finder* (monthly magazine). Orlando, FL: Fish Finders Industries.

*Florida Outdoor Guide.* Miami: The Miami Herald and Surfside Publishing, 1991.

Frisbee, Louise. *Peace River Pioneers.* Miami: E. A. Seemann Publishing Company, 1974.

Gillford, Bill, et al. "Inside the Environmental Groups." O*utside* (September 1990): 69–84.

Glaros, Lou, and Doug Sphar. *A Canoeing and Kayaking Guide to the Streams of Florida.* Vol. 2: *Central and South Florida.* Birmingham: Menasha Ridge Press, 1987.

Greenberg, Jerry and Idaz. *The Living Reef.* Miami: Seehawk Press, 1985.

Griswold, Oliver. *The Florida Keys and the Coral Reef.* Miami: Graywood Press, 1965.

Grow, Gerald. *Florida Parks: A Guide to Camping in Nature.* Tallahassee: Longleaf Publications, 1987.

Hall, F. W. *Birds of Florida.* Saint Petersburg, FL: Great Outdoors Publishing Company, 1979.

Hanna, Alfred J., and Kathryn A. Hanna. *Lake Okeechobee: Wellspring of the Everglades.* Indianapolis: Bobbs-Merrill, 1948.

Harris, Larry D. "Enhanced Linkages," in *Conservation in the 21st Century.* London: Oxford University Press, 1988.

Harrison, Hal H. *The World of the Snake.* New York: J. B. Lippincott Company, 1971.

Hays, Holly M. "From Pensacola to Key West." *Lake Wales Daily Highlander,* November 1, 1983.

Hendricks, L. M. "Juniper Springs." *Florida Living* (March 1988): 38–39.

Hiendlmayr, Jackalene Crow. *The Florida Bicycle Book.* Sarasota, FL: Pineapple Press, 1990.

Hiller, Herbert. *Guide to the Small and Historic Lodgings of Florida.* Sarasota, FL: Pineapple Press, 1988.

Hirth, Diane. "Martinez Wants Stronger Florida Coastal Protection." *Fort Lauderdale News Sentinel,* January 8, 1989.

Hudson, Charles M., Ed. *Four Centuries of Southern Indians.* Athens: University of Georgia Press, 1975.

Huffstadt, Jim. "Gator Hunters Renew a Florida Tradition." *Florida Wildlife* (November-December 1988): 17–19.

Hughes, Lacy J. "Florida's Buccaneer Trail." *Vista USA* (Spring 1989): 38.

Jahoda, Gloria. *Florida, A Bicentennial History.* New York: W. W. Norton & Company, 1976.

———. *The Other Florida.* New York: Charles Scribner's Sons, 1967.

Kale, Herbert W., and David S. Maehr. *Florida's Birds.* Sarasota, FL: Pineapple Press, 1989.

Kalma, Dennis. *Boat and Canoe Camping in the Everglades Backcountry.* (And Ten Thousand Islands Region.) Miami: Florida Flair Books, 1988.

Kals, W. S. *Land Navigation Handbook.* San Francisco: Sierra Club, 1983.

Keller, John M., and Ernest A. Baldini. *Walking the Florida Trail.* Gainesville: Florida Trail Association, 1988.

Kerr, James. "Pensacola: Florida's Western Anchor." *Vista USA* (Winter 1988–89): 40–43.

Lancaster, John. "Everglades Engineers Hope to Restore What They've Wrecked." *The Washington Post,* April 22, 1990.

Lane, James A. *A Birder's Guide to Florida.* Denver: I. & P Press, 1981. Revised 1984 by Harold D. Holt.

Lanier, Sidney. *Florida: Its Scenery, Climate and History.* (Reprint of 1875 ed.) Gainesville: University Presses of Florida, 1973.

Lea, Douglass. "Partial Pathways." *Wilderness* (Summer 1988): 25–26.

Lendt, David L. *Ding: The Life of Jay Norwood Darling.* Monticello, IA: Julin Printing Company, 1984.

Lewis, Gordon. *The Book of Florida Fishing.* Saint Petersburg, FL: Great Outdoors Publishing Company, 1957.

Lockey, Richard F., and Lewis Maxwell. *Florida's Poisonous Plants, Snakes, Insects.* Tampa: Maxwell Publishers, 1986.

Logan, William B., and Vance Muse. *The Smithsonian Guide to Historic America. The Deep South.* New York: Stewart, Tabori and Chang, 1989.

Mahon, John K. *The Second Seminole War.* Gainesville: University of Florida Press, 1968.

Martell, Scott. *Island Journeys.* Sanibel, FL: Island Graphics, 1986.

Marth, Del and Marty, Eds. *The Rivers of Florida.* Sarasota, FL: Pineapple Press, 1990.

McCoy, Randolph E. "What's Killing the Palm Trees?" *National Geographic* (January 1988): 120–30.

McGowan, Elizabeth. "A Winter's Trail." *Backpacker* (January 1986): 29–30.

Milanich, Jerald T., and Charles Fairbanks. *Florida Archaeology.* New York: Academic Press, 1980.

Minno, Marc C. *Insects of the Archbold Biological Station.* Gainesville: University of Florida, Department of Zoology, 1987.

*Mobile Travel Guide.* Englewood Cliffs, NJ: Prentice-Hall, annual.

Mott, Michael. "On the Florida Trail." *Brown's Guide to Georgia* (Jan./Feb. 1976): 58–61.

Murraine, St. Clair. "Tallahassee's Sheridan Is First to Complete Trek of Florida Trail." *Tallahassee Democrat,* April 12, 1989.

Myers, Ronald L., and John J. Ewel, *Ecosystems of Florida.* Orlando, FL: University of Central Florida Press, 1991.

Myers, Ronald L. *Plants of Archbold Biological Station.* Lake Placid, FL: Archbold Biological Station, 1984.

Neill, Wilfred T. *Florida's Seminole Indian.* Saint Petersburg, FL: Great Outdoors Publishing Company, 1956.

Nordheimer, Jon. "Extravaganza in the Everglades." *The New York Times,* May 14, 1989.

Ogburn, Charlton. "Island, Prairie, Marsh, and Shore." *National Geographic* (March 1979): 350–61.

Olsen, Chris M. *Wildlife Drive Guide, Darling NWR.* Sanibel, FL: Press Printing Company, n.d.

Oppel, Frank, and Tony Meisel, Eds. *Tales of Old Florida.* Secaucus, NJ: Castle Book Sales, 1987.

O'Reilly, John. "South Florida's Amazing Everglades." *National Geographic* (January 1940): 115–42.

Orr, Katherine. *The Wonderous World of the Mangrove Swamps of the Everglades and Florida Keys.* Miami: Florida Flair Books, 1989.

Parks, Arva Moore. *The Forgotten Frontier.* Miami: Banyon Books, 1977.

Parks, Pat. *The Railroad that Died at Sea.* Key West, FL: Langley Press, 1986.

Peters, William L., and Jerome Jones. "Historical and Biological Aspects of the Blackwater River in Northwestern Florida." Tallahassee: Proceedings of the First International Conference on Ephemeroptera, 1970. Offprint.

Pierce, Charles. *Pioneer Life in Southeast Florida.* Miami: University of Miami Press, 1970.

Pilkey, Orrin, et al. *Living with the East Florida Shore.* Durham, NC: Duke University Press, 1984.

Pope, Patricia E. *Seashore and Wading Birds of Florida.* Saint Petersburg, FL: Great Outdoors Publishing Company, 1974.

Purdum, Elizabeth D., and James R. Anderson, Jr., Eds. *Florida County Atlas and Municipal Fact Book.* Tallahassee: Florida State University Press, 1988.

Ravo, Nick. "Cedar Key Is What Key West Once Was." *The New York Times,* June 4, 1989.

Roberts, Harry. "Canoe-Camping at Its Best." *Backpacker* (March 1984): 50–57.

Rowan, Thomas. *Newcomer's Guide to Florida.* Saint Petersburg, FL: Great Outdoors Publishing Company, 1986.

Rudloe, Jack and Anne. "The Suwannee." *National Geographic* (July 1977): 20–29.

Schueler, Donald G. *Adventuring along the Gulf of Mexico.* San Francisco: Sierra Club Books, 1986.

Sebring, Tom. "The Canoe Test." *Backpacker* (August 1990): 34–41.

Smith, Harriet. *The Naturalist's Guide to Cedar Key, Florida.* Levy County, FL: Rife's Printing, 1987.

Spears, Gregory. "Seminole War Chief Sought to Erase White Culture." *Knight-Ridder News Service,* January 31, 1988.

Springer, Marylyn, and Donald A. Schultz. *Frommer's Dollarwise Guide to Florida.* Englewood Cliffs, NJ: Prentice-Hall, biannual.

Sprunt, Alexander. *Florida Bird Life.* New York: Coward-McCann and the National Audubon Society, 1963.

Stachowicz, Jim. *Diver's Guide to Florida and the Florida Keys.* Miami: Windward Publishing, 1985.

Stevenson, George B. *Trees of the Everglades National Park and the Florida Keys.* Miami: Banyan Books, 1986.

Stringer, Margaret. *Watch Wauchula Win.* N.p., 1979.

Tebeau, Charlton W. *A History of Florida.* Coral Gables, FL: University of Miami Press, 1987.

———. *Man in the Everglades.* Coral Gables, FL: University of Miami Press, 1968.

———. *The Story of the Chokoloskee Bay Country.* Miami: Banyan Books, 1986.

Timms, Ed. "Florida Gives a Tamed River Back to Nature." *The Dallas Morning News,* February 11, 1990.

Toops, Connie. *The Alligator. Monarch of the Marsh.* Homestead, FL: Florida National Parks and Monuments Association, 1988.

Truesdell, William G. *A Guide to the Wilderness Waterway of the Everglades National Park.* Coral Gables, FL: University of Miami Press, 1985.

Tucker, James A. *Florida Birds.* Tampa: Maxwell Publishers, 1986.

Unterbrink, Mary. *Manatees: Gentle Giants in Peril.* Saint Petersburg, FL: Great Outdoors Publishing Company, 1984.

Van Meter, Victoria Brook. *The Florida Panther.* Miami: Florida Power & Light Company, 1988.

———. *The West Indian Manatee in Florida.* Miami: Florida Power & Light Company, 1985.

Wallace, David Rains. *Bulow Hammock.* San Francisco: Sierra Club Books, 1988.

Weber, Jeff. *Everglades.* Miami: Florida Flair Books, 1986.

West, Don. "Cracker Boy," in *In a Land of Plenty.* Minneapolis: West End Press, 1982.

White, Jesse R. "Man Can Save the Manatee." *National Geographic* (September 1984): 414–18.

Will, Lawrence E. *A Cracker History of Okeechobee.* Belle Glade, FL: Glades Historical Society, 1977.

Williams, Joy. *The Florida Keys.* New York: Random House, 1987.

Wolf, John B. *The Battle at the Loxahatchee River: The Seminole War.* Jupiter, FL: Loxahatchee Historical Society, 1990.

*Woodall's Eastern Campground Directory.* Bannockburn, IL: Woodall Publishing Company, annual.

Woodman, Jim. *Key Biscayne, Romance of Cape Florida.* Miami: Hurricane House Press, 1961.

## GEORGIA

### *Government Publications: Federal*

*Fishes of Gray's Reef National Marine Sanctuary.* Washington, DC: U.S. National Oceanic and Atmospheric Administration, Marine and Estuarine Management Division, 1989.

*National Wildlife Refugees of the Georgia Coastal Complex.* Washington, DC: U.S. Department of the Interior, Fish and Wildlife Service, 1983.

*Okefenokee National Wildlife Refuge.* Washington, DC: U.S. Department of the Interior, Fish and Wildlife Service, 1987.

## Government Publications: State

*Coastal Georgia Fishing.* Atlanta: Department of Natural Resources, 1988.
*Georgia Coastal Charisma.* Atlanta: Department of Natural Resources, 1990.
*Georgia State Parks and Historic Sites.* Atlanta: Department of Natural Resources, 1990.
*Jekyll Island.* Jekyll Island, GA: Jekyll Island Convention and Visitors Bureau, 1990.

## Books, Magazines, and Newspapers

Blockson, Charles L. "Nowhere to Lay Down Weary Head." *National Geographic* (December 1987): 735–63.
Coleman, Kenneth, Ed. *The Colonial Records of the State of Georgia,* Vols. 20, 30, 31, and 32. Athens: University of Georgia Press, 1985.
———. *A History of Georgia.* Athens: University of Georgia Press, 1977.
Floyd, Charlotte V. "Sapelo Island." *Seabreeze* (Nov./Dec. 1986): 42–43.
Gibson, Dot Rees. *Okefenokee.* Waycross, GA: Gibson Publications, 1987.
Hanie, Robert. *Guale, The Golden Coast of Georgia.* San Francisco: Seabury Press, 1974.
Harris, Ron. "Sea Island Blacks Leave or Labor on Plantations." *Los Angeles Times,* October 2, 1988.
Herndon, Nancy. "Sea Islanders Fight Tourism's March." *Christian Science Monitor,* July 10, 1988.
*Historic Savannah Visitors' Guide.* Savannah: Savannah Publishing Company, 1990.
Hodler, Thomas W., and Howard A. Schretter. *The Atlas of Georgia.* Athens: University of Georgia, Institute of Community and Area Development, 1986.
Kemble, Frances A. *Journal of a Residence on a Georgia Plantation in 1838–1839.* (Reprint.) Arlington Heights, IL: Metro Books, 1969.
Logan, William B., and Vance Muse. *The Smithsonian Guide to Historic (Deep South) America.* New York: Stewart, Tabori and Chang, 1989.
Mayo, Lois B. *Settlers of the Okefenokee.* Folkston, GA: Okefenokee Press, 1975.
McKee, Gwen, Ed. *A Guide to the Georgia Coast.* Savannah: The Georgia Conservancy, 1985.
McQueen, A. S., and Hamp Mizell. *History of Okefenokee Swamp.* (Reprint.) Folkston, GA: Charlton County Historical Society, 1984.
Pendleton, Louis. *In the Okefenokee: A Story of War Time and the Great Georgia Swamp.* (Reprint of 1895 ed.) Salem, NH: Ayer Company Publisher.
Pennington, John. "Cumberland, My Island for a While." *National Geographic* (November 1977): 648–61.
Rogers, George A., and Frank R. Saunders. *Swamp Water and Wiregrass, Historical Sketches of Coastal Georgia.* Macon, GA: Mercer University Press, 1984.
Russel, Francis. *The Okefenokee Swamp.* New York: Time-Life Books, 1973.

Schoettle, H. E. Taylor. *A Field Guide to Jekyll Island.* Athens: University of Georgia, Marine Extension Service, 1983.

Scruggs, C. P. *Georgia Historical Markers*, rev. ed. Valdosta, GA: Bay Tree Grove Publisher, 1984.

Sehlinger, Bob, and Don Otey. *Southern Georgia Canoeing.* Birmingham: Menasha Ridge Press, 1980.

Temple, Sarah B., and Kenneth Coleman. *Georgia Journeys.* Athens: University of Georgia Press, 1961.

Trowell, C.T. *The Suwannee Canal Company of the Okefenokee Swamp.* Douglas, GA: South Georgia College, 1984.

Vanstory, Burnette. *Georgia's Land of the Golden Isles.* Athens: University of Georgia Press, 1981.

# INDEX